INSIGHT GUIDES
VANCOUVER

APA PUBLICATIONS L
Part of the Langenscheidt Publishing Group

HOW TO USE THIS BOOK

This book is carefully structured both to convey an understanding of the city and its culture and to guide readers through its attractions and activities:

◆ The Best Of section at the front of the book helps you to prioritize. The first spread contains all the Top Sights, while the Editor's Choice details unique experiences, the best buys or other recommendations.

◆ To understand Vancouver, you need to know something of its past. The city's history and culture are described in authoritative essays written by specialists in their fields who have lived in and documented the city for many years.

◆ The Places section details all the attractions worth seeing. The main places of interest are coordinated by number with the maps.

◆ Each chapter includes lists of recommended shops, restaurants, bars and cafés.

◆ Photographs throughout the book are chosen not only to illustrate geography and buildings, but also to convey the moods of the city and the life of its people.

◆ The Travel Tips section includes all the practical information you will need, divided into four key sections: transport, accommodation, activities (including nightlife, events, tours and sports) and an A–Z of practical tips. Information may be located quickly by using the index on the back cover flap of the book.

◆ A detailed street atlas is included at the back of the book, with all restaurants, bars, cafés and hotels plotted for your convenience.

PLACES AND SIGHTS

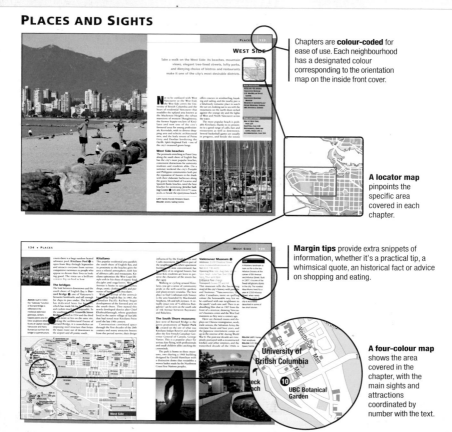

Chapters are **colour-coded** for ease of use. Each neighbourhood has a designated colour corresponding to the orientation map on the inside front cover.

A locator map pinpoints the specific area covered in each chapter.

Margin tips provide extra snippets of information, whether it's a practical tip, a whimsical quote, an historical fact or advice on shopping and eating.

A four-colour map shows the area covered in the chapter, with the main sights and attractions coordinated by number with the text.

PHOTO FEATURES

Photo features offer visual coverage of various aspects of the city, from winter sports to maritime history and innovative architecture.

SHOPPING AND RESTAURANT LISTINGS

Shopping listings provide details of the best shops in each area. **Restaurant listings** give the establishment's contact details, opening times and price category, followed by a useful review. Bars and cafés are also covered here. The coloured dot and grid reference refers to the atlas section at the back of the book.

International

Pacific Institute of Culinary Arts
1505 West Second Ave.
Tel: 604 734 4488. www.bistro101.com Open: L & D
Mon–Fri. $ 44 p275, C4

TRAVEL TIPS

Public Transport – TransLink

Public transport in Vancouver is the responsibility of **TransLink** (tel: 604 953 3333; www.translink.ca), which also looks after the network and facilities for...

Travel Tips provide all the practical knowledge you'll need before and during your trip: how to get there, getting around, where to stay and what to do. The A–Z section is a handy summary of practical information, arranged alphabetically.

Contents

LEFT: view of
Burrard Inlet.

Maps

Travel Tips

Inside front cover:
Vancouver Orientation Map.
Inside back cover:
Around Vancouver

THE BEST OF VANCOUVER: TOP SIGHTS

At a glance, the attractions in and around Vancouver that you can't afford to miss, from iconic buildings and picturesque beaches to quaint fishing villages and magnificent mountains.

△ **Grouse Mountain**. The view comes first, but take the time to explore the other activities available, which are both fun and educational. *See pages 178–9.*

△ **Granville Island Food Market**. From the chilli-flavoured chocolate ganache to seven different kinds of salt and twenty types of pâté, the stunning displays make everything irresistible and showcase how Vancouverites like to live. *See page 126.*

▷ **Stanley Park**. Jog along the seawall, take a peaceful walk through the forest to Beaver Lake, marvel at the totem poles or commune with the orca whales at the aquarium – truly something for everyone. *See pages 115–21.*

▽ **Canada Place and the Convention Centre**. Canada Place, jutting out into the water, looks renewed beside its new neighbours, the expansion to the Convention Centre and the 2010 Winter Olympics cauldron. *See page 82.*

▽ **Museum of Anthropology.** An exceptional collection of Pacific Northwest art is housed in an architectural beauty set on the tip of the world, overlooking the spectacular Pacific Ocean and Coastal Range mountains. *See pages 137–8.*

△ **Lynn Canyon Park.** It's a beautiful way to explore the temperate rainforest on a walk or hike to suit every level. There's even a suspension bridge over the canyon – and it's all free. *See pages 174–5.*

▷ **The water.** Get out on the water any way you can. Take a ride on the SeaBus or a jaunt on the little ferries that shuttle people around False Creek. *See page 246.*

▽ **Steveston.** The fishing boats are manned by two types of people: those who catch the fish and those who sell it. A great place to see the ocean's bounty and people-watch. *See page 165.*

▷ **Kitsilano Beach.** A leisurely stroll from Kits Pool to Vanier Park will allow you to soak up Vancouver's outdoor culture and appreciate its beautiful setting. *See pages 133–4.*

THE BEST OF VANCOUVER: EDITOR'S CHOICE

Setting priorities, saving money, unique attractions...
here, at a glance, are our recommendations, plus some
tips and tricks even the locals won't always know.

ONLY IN VANCOUVER

- **Sunbathe and ski** on the same day. Sandy beaches and world-class ski slopes are within easy reach of the city. *See page 55.*
- **Capilano Suspension Bridge** Wobble across the deep Capilano gorge on a historic bridge above the trees. *See page 173.*
- **The Aquarium** Watch beluga whales and sea otters swimming. *See page 121.*
- **Carol Ship Parade of Lights** The spirit of Christmas in a dazzling display on water. *See page 259.*

- **Cycle round Stanley Park** Or jog, or rollerblade... or watch a game of cricket and have tea. *See pages 115–21.*
- **Flight in a seaplane** Experience the West Coast's common form of transport – fly to Victoria Island, or take a scenic flight at Tofino. *See pages 204 and 244.*
- **Whale-watching** See whales at their most impressive. *See page 263.*
- **Bears** Orphaned bears in safe captivity on Grouse Mountain. *See pages 178.*

BEST VIEWS OF THE CITY

- **Sunset over English Bay** Head to Second Beach and savour the magnitude of Stanley Park behind you and the Pacific Ocean ahead. *See page 120.*
- **Harbour Centre Tower – Vancouver Lookout** The best orientation viewpoint in the city. *See page 99.*
- **Grouse Mountain** The lights of the city

spread out below one of its three ski hills. *See page 178.*
- **Queen Elizabeth Park** The finest views over the mountains of North Vancouver. *See page 149.*
- **Burrard and Granville bridges** From here you can look down on English Bay and Vanier Park or the busy scene of False Creek. *See page 134.*

ABOVE: English Bay from Burrard Bridge.
RIGHT: the spectacular view from Grouse Mountain.

BEST MUSEUMS

● **Vancouver Art Gallery**
Important collection of modern art and photographs, as well as temporary exhibitions. *See page 86.*

● **Vancouver Museum**
Lively introduction to the city's history and development. *See page 135.*

● **Vancouver Maritime Museum**
Worth a visit just to see the *St Roch* schooner and hear the story of its epic voyage. *See page 136.*

● **Museum of Anthropology**
A museum of international renown for its building and contents. *See page 137.*

● **Royal BC Museum, Victoria**
Internationally acclaimed museum with terrific First Nations exhibits. *See page 194.*

● **Fort Langley National Historical Site**
The best way to gain an insight into the lives of the early pioneers. *See pages 227–8.*

BEST BOAT TRIPS

● **Ferry around False Creek**
For a different perspective, hop on one of the tiny ferries at Granville Island and enjoy the view of the city from the water. *See page 246.*

● **Sunset dinner cruise around the harbour**
A romantic way to watch the sun go down and enjoy Vancouver's incomparable setting. *See page 247.*

● **Whale-watching**
Any boat trip along the West Coast of Vancouver Island is a scenic delight, whales or not. *See page 263.*

● **Kayaking in English Bay, False Creek or the Burrard Inlet**
Sheltered and beautiful waters for paddling. *See page 263.*

● **Ferry from Tsawwassen to Swartz Bay**
Weave through the Gulf Islands. *See page 247.*

BEST SHOPPING

● **Granville Island Market**
Fantastic produce, plus a host of craft shops and galleries nearby. *See page 126.*

● **Robson Street**
The place to go for clothes and fashion. *See page 91.*

● **Main Street**
Full of quirky little

shops selling things you'll never see anywhere else, with great prices to boot. *See page 102.*

● **West 4th Avenue, Kitsilano**
The perfect neighbourhood shopping area, with good places to eat or have coffee. *See page 134.*

ABOVE TOP: carved boat in the Museum of Anthropology.
ABOVE TOP RIGHT: rowing in the harbour. **ABOVE:** totem poles at the Royal BC Museum in Victoria. **RIGHT:** window-shopping on Robson Street and in Gastown.

BEST RESTAURANTS

- **Bishop's**
Outstanding meals brought to you by Vancouver's ultimate host, John Bishop.
See page 140.
- **Le Crocodile**
Alsatian food that is perfect in every way.
See page 92.
- **Il Giardino di Umberto**
Fantastic courtyard and wonderfully authentic Italian cuisine.
See page 93.
- **Lumière**
Serious gastronomy for a special occasion.
See page 140.
- **Le Pied-à-Terre**
A small room that is so reminiscent of Paris that you'll be wondering which Metro stop to head for after your meal. *See page 151.*
- **Raincity Grill**
Casual feel but great attention is paid to food sourcing; makes the most of what the West Coast offers.
See page 93.
- **Tojo's Restaurant**
The ultimate experience in sushi and sashimi; put yourself in the hands of the master. *See page 151.*

ABOVE: behind the scenes at the Lumière restaurant. **LEFT:** the Vancouver Hotel, a city landmark. **BELOW:** befriending a goat at Maplewood Farm, North Vancouver.

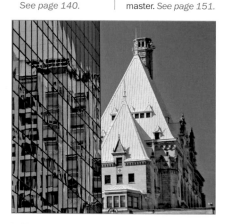

BEST BUILDINGS

- **Marine Building**
Iconic Art Deco building with exceptionally fine detailing. *See page 83.*
- **Museum of Anthropology**
A classic Arthur Erickson design out at the University campus.
See page 137.
- **Hotel Vancouver**
The grande dame of Vancouver's hotels retains the unique ambience and style of the Canadian Pacific Railway's legendary hotels. *See page 85.*
- **Canada Place**
The perfect match of form and function; includes the world's greenest convention centre. *See page 82.*
- **Fairacres – Burnaby Art Gallery**
Arts and Crafts house in a lovely garden setting. *See page 158.*

BEST FOR CHILDREN

- **La Casa Gelato**
With 218 flavours of ice cream on offer.
See page 113.
- **The Waterpark**
Near the Kids' Market; a great place to let off steam. *See page 130.*
- **Sutcliffe Park**
Adventure playground next to Waterpark.
See page 130.
- **H.R. MacMillan Space Centre**
Fun and education combine in this colourful attraction.
See page 136.
- **Science World**
An object lesson in how to keep children amused for hours, while teaching them useful skills and information. *See page 109.*
- **Maplewood Farm**
Meet farm animals in a pretty setting.
See page 177.
- **Kitsilano Pool**
Huge heated saltwater swimming pool beside the sea.
See page 134.
- **The Aquarium**
Sea otter feeding time is hugely popular with children.
See page 121.

BEST GARDENS

- **Stanley Park**
Rose garden and colourful mass planting in large beds in amongst giant cedar trees. See pages 115–21.
- **Van Dusen Botanical Garden**
An outstanding collection of plants and trees in beautifully designed and individual settings. See

page 147.
- **Dr Sun Yat-Sen Chinese Garden**
Classic garden with series of rooms and spaces. See pages 104–5.
- **UBC Botanical Garden**
A plantsman's garden. See page 139.
- **Queen Elizabeth Park**
Large expanse of gardens and parkland with spectacular effects in two quarries. See page 149.
- **Butchart Gardens on Vancouver Island**
A magnificent garden in an old quarry with dazzling displays. See pages 200–1.

ABOVE TOP: jogging and cycling in Stanley Park. **ABOVE:** the Van Dusen Botanical Garden.

BEST WALKS

- **The Stanley Park seawall**
The one walk everyone should do. See page 115.
- **Lynn Canyon.**
A good place to get a feel for BC's forests and have a pleasant walk. See pages 174–5.
- **Grouse Grind**
Not so much a walk as a test of endurance. Great views, with a cable car for the descent. See page 178.
- **Lighthouse Park**
Lovely ocean views and rainforest. See page 182.
- **Baden Powell Trail**
Serious walking for the experienced and fit. See page 182.

BEST FESTIVALS

- **Bard on the Beach**
Four Shakespeare plays in Vanier Park. See page 259.
- **HSBC Celebration of Light**
Two-week international firework competition lights up summer evenings. See page 259.
- **International Jazz Festival**
Ten days of jazz in venues around the city. See page 259.
- **Folk Music Festival**
International performers on seven different stages set out in the park beside Jericho Beach. See page 259.
- **International Film Festival**
Close to 400 films from 75 countries. See page 259.
- **PuSh International Performing Arts Festival**
Showcases new and challenging works to sold-out crowds. See page 258.
- **Vancouver Playhouse International Wine Festival**
Well over 120 wineries gather to pour their best. See page 258.

MONEY-SAVING TIPS

The **Smartvisit Card** (tel: 604 295 1157 or 1 877 295 1157; www.see vancouvercard.com) offers unlimited entry to more than 50 attractions, tours and outdoor adventures in Vancouver and outlying areas. The pass is valid for two, three or five days – a two-day pass is $119 for adults and $79 for children aged 4–15.

Playhouse Theatre has a pay-what-you-can option at the first Saturday matinee of every production ($10 dona-

tion recommended). It's a low-risk way to see what local theatre is offering.

On Tuesday evenings, many **museums** offer discounts. From 5.30–9pm, admission to the Vancouver Art Gallery is by donation and the Museum of Anthropology has a flat rate of $7 (instead of $14) per person.

Transportation can really add up, so it's worth investing in a **Translink day pass** ($9). It costs less than a return "3-zone" regular fare, and you

can take as many trips as you like on buses, SkyTrain and SeaBus.

A day up at **Lynn Canyon Park**, a 35-minute drive from the centre of town, offers a great suspension bridge and walking or hiking in the rainforest. It's all free, so pack a picnic and you can have the perfect West Coast experience. If you are craving the sunshine, head to **Jericho Beach** instead. You can splurge on the fish and chips at the concession stand and still feel like you have had a bargain day.

CITY OF GLASS

Back in 1939, King George VI took his leave of the young city with the comment: "I think Vancouver is the place to live." He would say the same today: thoroughly modern Vancouver is one of Canada's most vibrant cities.

O nce you've been to Vancouver it comes as no surprise to read of the city's constant ranking as a top place in the world to visit or live in, from *Condé Nast Traveler* magazine to the Mercer Quality of Life index. Broaden the tourist criteria of ambience, friendliness, culture and sights, restaurants, accommodation, environment and shopping to include issues of importance to residents, and it's ranked the world's most liveable city by the Economist Intelligence Unit.

Vancouver is a place where you can ski in the morning, sunbathe by the sea in the afternoon and eat at a world-class restaurant in the evening. Even on rainy days, life in Vancouver is lived out of doors – beaches, parks and the scenic seawall are thronged with walkers, cyclists and rollerbladers.

Take away the sea and the mountains and much of Vancouver's superficial appeal would disappear. Only on closer acquaintance would the city's other virtues become apparent. Foremost would be the fantastic restaurants, bars and cafés, which make the place a gastronomic joy

– not only for the inventiveness and competence of chefs, but also the quality of ingredients, with a growing emphasis on organic origin and healthy combinations. Twenty years ago, the wines of British Columbia were barely drinkable; today there's no need to drink anything else. The friendliness of Vancouverites is another big plus. Pull out a map on a street corner and chances are someone will stop to help you on your way.

Vancouver is a cosmopolitan city, and its multiculturalism lends it added vitality. There are vibrant theatres and dance companies, plenty of great venues for jazz and other music, and festivals galore. But it is also a city without pretension, with a relaxed and casual approach to life that delights its more than 20 million annual visitors. ❑

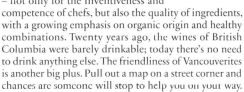

PRECEDING PAGES: moorings off Stanley Park; Georgina Point lighthouse, Mayne Island. **LEFT:** a cruise ship sails out to sea. **ABOVE LEFT:** Downtown Vancouver. **ABOVE RIGHT:** Canada Place.

LIVING IN VANCOUVER

Blessed with an equable climate, a stunning location and an enviably laid-back lifestyle, it's no wonder that the city is regularly voted one of the world's most desirable places to live.

Vancouver is unlike any other North American city. Superficially it may resemble others with its high-rise downtown, busy streets, sprawling suburbs and overdependence on the car, but the lifestyle of most Vancouverites makes the city an object of desire for many urban Canadians and those of other nationalities.

It's a young city and a city of the young – in spirit if not in age. Chat with docents in museums who will tell you of their youth here 75 years ago – as if it were last month. Walk or cycle the seawall around Stanley Park and you'll see retired people as fit and vigorous as most people 20 years younger. Vancouverites live so much of life outdoors: sailing, canoeing, windsurfing, walking, cycling, swimming, tennis, golf, playing beach volleyball, kite flying in Vanier Park, eating alfresco. Even in winter, when it can rain for days on end, it's never too cold to go walking, jogging or even to the golf course or tennis courts.

Perhaps because of the outdoor nature of society, Vancouver is a casual city. It's not a place to make a living out of selling ties and briefcases, and many businessmen look as though it was dress-down Friday every day. While casual attire is complemented by a relaxed, easy-going manner, it's certainly not at the expense of common courtesy, and many visitors from other cities are struck by the warm politeness that seems a hallmark of social intercourse.

Outward-looking

Right from the beginning, resource-rich Vancouver has been cosmopolitan, always looking overseas for trading opportunities and labour. Its first shipload of lumber was exported to Australia in 1864, and the first ship to dock at its new deep-water port in 1887 came from across the Pacific carrying tea and silk and 80 Chinese "visitors".

It hasn't all been plain sailing, and Vancouver has seen its racial tensions explode into violence, but since World War II the city has developed an ingrained liberalism that overlooks differences. It's clear that for all the vicissitudes of the past, the South Asians have embraced Vancouver as their home, investing in both high-rise apartments around False Creek and large homes around the city.

Counterculture

At the last count, 68 ethnicities were represented in the city, as well as members of scores of the 197 British Columbia First Nations bands, who play an important and growing role in the economic, social and artistic life in the province. As the founding artistic director of the Vancouver Opera, Irving Guttman, was quoted as saying, "I get the impression that people of the West Coast, regardless of ethnic origins, are able freely to be themselves." This liberalism is reflected in the counterculture of the arts, the fertile ground for cooperative housing schemes, a strong concern for the environment, and in a diverse population. Vancouver has one of the largest per capita gay and lesbian communities in North America.

The greening of a city

Concern for the environment, too, goes back a long way. Even though the decision of the city fathers to protect Stanley Park has been disparaged as a ploy to protect their existing

landholdings and rents, it shows an early awareness of the need for green space. More than 10 percent of the city area is parkland, dominated by the large Pacific Spirit Regional Park on the University Endowment Lands and Stanley Park. Beyond the city centre are vast protected areas along the mountains of the north shore.

Much of Vancouver is easy on the eye, helped by over 130,000 street trees (including more than 17,000 Japanese flowering cherries),

DISTINCTIVE DISTRICTS

Despite the sprawl of its suburbs, Vancouver is not like other North American cities in having little or no sense of neighbourhood. The city's districts retain an individual character and clusters of independent retailers that are very different from the anodyne malls that are often the only option elsewhere.

Take the shopping area of Dunbar at the southern end of the eponymous street as an example: it has an excellent supermarket that has been in the same family for generations, an independent bakery redolent of the 1950s, a bike shop, second-hand bookshop, independent DVD rental shop and a cinema.

LEFT: rollerblading in Stanley Park. **ABOVE TOP:** in a Chinatown grocery. **ABOVE BOTTOM:** cyclists in Gastown. **ABOVE RIGHT:** on Kitsilano Beach.

though the typical North American feature of electricity poles and cables is an undeniable eyesore. The enormous asset of the sea is exploited by the creation of public space along more than half the city's waterfront, with the longest stretch of 23km (14 miles) between Crab Park and Kitsilano Beach Park. New developments often incorporate imaginative landscaping and sometimes water features which help to soften the city and provide a pleasing sound amid the hubbub of traffic.

Recycling figures large in the city's policies, with colour-coded bins for household collections. In an effort to minimise their footprint, many of the leading hotels go beyond the self-serving offer to leave your towels for another day. Leading restaurants have signed up to Vancouver Aquarium's "Ocean Wise" kitemark to help diners make sustainable choices when choosing their fish. Green Table goes a step beyond, focusing on everything that can make a restaurant more sustainable, from composting organic waste to reducing water and electrical use.

Revitalising the centre

It has been Vancouver's proud boast that it offers the world a "model for sustainable living", and it likes to think of itself as an environmentally responsible city. Certainly it has nurtured some notable environmentalists, including some of the founders of Greenpeace and Dr David T. Suzuki, the award-winning scientist and environmentalist who was a professor at UBC. But the success of the regeneration of the downtown area as a place where people would choose to live – in marked contrast to many other North American cities – came about in good measure because of an initial failure of the re-zoning of downtown south, from commercial to mixed use. It was the danger of this developing into a kind of developmental anarchy that provoked a reaction by concerned residents. A forum organised by the Community Arts Council convinced the City

of the need for the more structured and properly planned approach with which the city's then co-director of planning, Larry Beasley, became associated.

In many ways, Vancouver has become a showcase for the virtues of high-density living as the redevelopment of the Expo '86 site directly contributed to halting and even reversing the flight from the centre to the suburbs. The philosophy of creating areas with high-density, mixed-income housing with plenty of parks and facilities for families has been a spectacular success, so much so that Beasley left city hall and now advises other cities all over the world. The concept taps into all the requirements of sustainability and concern with climate change to minimise the footprint of housing and transport. Simply put, density is more efficient than sprawl.

Vancouver may be a successful model for a new kind of urbanism in North America, but the high demand for housing has had some

curious effects. Because of the high turnover of land and quick obsolescence of buildings, one sees jarring juxtapositions of a swanky new apartment building standing cheek-by-jowl with a run-down hotel whose status is obvious from its unsavoury substitutes for curtains. It has also led to a sharp decline in affordable rental accommodation, as a result of which

> With a vibrant and dense central core, two-thirds of journeys downtown forsake the car in favour of walking, cycling or public transport. With more people on the streets, everyone is safer.

there are noticeably more people living rough on the streets and begging (euphemistically called "panhandling" in Canada) than even five years ago.

The increase cannot simply be attributed to the preference of the homeless for the mild climate of Vancouver rather than the searing temperatures or bitter cold of the central and eastern provinces. Many social experts see a

FAR LEFT: Edwardian façades. **LEFT:** cycle-friendly city. **ABOVE TOP:** brand-new waterfront condos. **ABOVE BOTTOM:** the tranquil Dr Sun Yat-sen Chinese Garden. **ABOVE RIGHT:** the old reflected in the new.

direct link between the growing homeless problem and a series of provincial government changes, from changing the level of services provided to the mentally ill to making it much more difficult to qualify for social assistance (welfare). While both local and provincial governments acknowledge there is a serious problem, the proposed solutions are often short-term, failing to address the underlying issues of poverty, mental illness and drug addiction.

Sustainable transport

SkyTrain has been a success, with the new Canada line to the airport and Richmond exceeding ridership projections almost as soon as it opened in 2009, and a fleet of new electric trolley-buses and new lines has improved the transportation grid. Nonetheless, a consequence of discarding in the 1950s the electric trams that carried 100,000 people a day in 1912 is that a quarter of the land area of Vancouver is now given over to roads or parking, and 300,000 cars a day enter and leave the downtown core.

The creation of dedicated bicycle lanes on Burrard Street has encouraged many more people to shift to a two-wheeled commute down-

town. There is a continuous conflict with other jurisdictions as additional road capacity leading into the city is a priority for suburban dwellers, something that seems to threaten Vancouver's credentials as a model of sustainable development. The city is opposed to this expansion of suburban road capacity, which will increase downtown congestion and pollution. It is clear that additional public transit, including a light-rail system, is the logical way forward, beginning with the long-proposed extension of the heritage line from Granville Island through Waterfront to Stanley Park. However, finding the capital funding for this project is extremely challenging.

Economic growth

Like all major cities, the economic meltdown of 2008 had a huge impact on disposable income and on government funding of projects to support growth. Fortunately for Vancouver, at the time when other cities were frozen by financial collapse, the construction contracts for the 2010 Winter Olympics were under way and the success of the Games was linked to completing everything from the new Canada line to the Olympic athletes' village and assorted venues for both sporting and cultural events. It may be that Vancouver has weathered the economic downturn better than most, but whether the

A growing number of restaurants use as much local and organic produce as possible, with chefs focused on delivering meals that have been sourced from within a 160km (100-mile) radius.

Olympics will translate into additional jobs and more prosperity for Vancouverites remains to be seen.

The area in which Vancouver has seen a growth in employment is overwhelmingly in service-related industries – finance, insurance, retail, hi-tech and education – though mining and forestry remain cornerstones. Vancouver is Canada's largest port, generating employment in shipping and connecting transport by the two transcontinental railway lines. Tourism has boomed, not only in Vancouver itself but as a gateway to BC and a point of call for the cruise ships heading for Alaska. It's a popular city for conferences and for film-makers – it's common to encounter a crew and their pantechnicons of equipment commandeering a section of street.

Pressure for jobs and growth in BC's traditional industries inevitably arouses controversy and sometimes conflict. Long-standing battles with lumber companies over the felling of old-growth forest are ongoing, and offshore oil and gas exploration plans meet with serious concerns about disrupting the fragile marine ecosystem.

The Olympic legacy

The legacy of Expo '86 was the revitalisation of the central core of the city. The hopes for the 2010 Winter Olympics are similar: that the redevelopment of False Creek through the construction of the Olympic Village will bring even more people into an area that is vibrant and liveable. Much of this success is assured, as the lifestyle this area affords is one to which so many people aspire. The challenge will be the same as all international cities, that of the conflict between affluence and poverty, so apparent in the inner city. The drug problem that continues to afflict the east side of the downtown area will not magically disappear and the spotlight of international media is unlikely to unearth a new viable solution to one of Vancouver's greatest challenges. ❑

Far Left: SeaBuses ply the waters between the Waterfront and North Vancouver. **Left:** the famous SkyTrain passing over the Fraser River and through Burnaby. **Above:** British Columbia's economy is centred on the timber industry. **Right:** Olympic Village accommodation.

Gay Vancouver

While it lacks the nightlife of some Canadian cities, Vancouver's relaxed attitude and vibrant LGBT scene are a big draw for gay and lesbian travellers.

When Vancouver hosted the 2010 Winter Olympics, it was the first host city in history to provide a gay venue for athletes, workers and visitors, Pride House.

"Canada's San Francisco" has emerged as a leading international tourist destination for gay and lesbian travellers. Americans in particular appreciate its relaxed, live-and-let-live attitude and highly visible gay presence. Vancouver's LGBT (Lesbian, Gay, Bisexual and Transgender) community is strongly represented in municipal government, and has played a pivotal role in the city's high quality of life and growing cosmopolitanism.

That said, Vancouver does not offer the range of exciting nightlife found in Canada's bigger gay travel destinations, Montreal and Toronto. Instead, visitors enjoy a range of recreational activities afforded by the city's natural surroundings and numerous gay-friendly options, amenities and accommodations.

Gay neighbourhoods

The downtown **West End** neighbourhood is home to the city's gay village. Gay bars, restaurants and shops stretch west of Burrard Street along Davie Street. Hot pink bus shelters and litter bins and streetlamps festooned with rainbow flags and banners by LGBT artists line several blocks. A number of gay establishments continue north along Denman Street, which intersects with Davie by the beach at English Bay.

Among the favourite hangouts in this neighbourhood are:
1181 (1181 Davie Street; tel: 604 687 3991; www.tightlounge.com), a slick, trendy gay cocktail lounge that appeals to an upmarket crowd.

Delilah's (1789 Comox Street at Denman; tel: 604 687 3424; www.delilahs.ca), with its fabulous postmodern rococo decor, is a local tradition, and with good reason. The upscale restaurant regularly receives rave reviews for its fabulous food, famous Martinis and friendly staff.

The Fountainhead Pub (1025 Davie Street), where the reasonably priced drinks and pub food, jovial staff, smoking patio and relaxed ambience attract a diverse, all-ages crowd of men and women.

Junction Public House (1138 Davie Street; tel: 604 669 2013; www.pulsenightclub.com) also appeals to a diverse clientele, offering dance nights, televised sports events, games and cabaret.

Melriches Café (1244 Davie Street; tel: 604 689 5282; www.melriches.com) is a favourite hangout with the java and laptop crowd, and a good place to strike up conversations with strangers. Wireless internet connection is pay-per-use by credit card. **Delaney's Coffee House** (1105 Denman Street; tel: 604 662 3344) is the same deal, but without wireless.

Oasis (1240 Thurlow Street at Davie; tel: 604 685 1724; www.oasis-nightclub.com) is a casually sophisticated, New York-style lounge featuring live entertainment most nights, along with a tasty menu, a huge Martini list and a pleasant smoking patio.

Pumpjack Pub (1167 Davie Street; tel: 604 685 3417; www.pumpjackpub.com), a down-to-earth bar, attracts an older, mainly male denim-and-leather crowd.

Score (1262 Davie Street; tel: 604 632 1646; www.scoreondavie.com) is a popular gay sports bar with a sizeable food and drink menu, as is **Speakeasy Bar and Grill** (1239 Davie Street; tel: 604 685 5761; www.thespeakeasy.ca).

A few kilometres from downtown, bohemian and multicultural **Commercial Drive** on the city's east side stretches north of Broadway to Hastings Street. The area is home to a large lesbian and transgendered community. Lined with funky shops, cafés, bars and restaurants, "The Drive" is a favourite hangout for artists and writers. The American magazine *UTNE Reader* lists The Drive as one of North America's "hippest neighbourhoods".

Located across English Bay from the West End, and anchored by 4th Avenue, the hilly, beachside **Kitsilano** neighbourhood was home to a growing counterculture of gays and lesbians during the burgeoning years of Gay Liberation in the late 1960s and early '70s. Kitsilano was then Vancouver's version of San Francisco's Haight Ashbury, and its ambience was captured in the 1977 novel *The Young in One Another's Arms* by Jane Rule. Today, most of the original woodframe Edwardian houses have been renovated or razed, replaced by million-dollar-plus homes and luxury condos. Kitsilano remains a gay-friendly neighbourhood and home to a large number of affluent gay and lesbian couples.

Western Canada's largest Pride parade

Once a year, Vancouver holds an impressive Pride parade. Drawing crowds of more than half a million, it is the city's largest annual event. The parade caps a week of related celebrations. The Greater Vancouver Regional District also hosts two other Pride celebrations: East Side Pride in mid-June, and Surrey Pride, which takes place in a satellite city in mid-July (tel: 604 687 0955; www.vancouverpride.ca).

LEFT AND RIGHT: the city's popular Gay Pride parade takes place every August.

Gay weddings

Canada is one of a handful of countries where same-sex couples may legally marry, and Vancouver has become a popular wedding and honeymoon location for a growing number of gay people. To date, more gay Americans have been married in Vancouver than gay Canadians. Same-sex wedding planners **Two Dears and a Queer** (tel: 604 306 1340; www.twodearsandaqueer.com) and **Experiential Weddings** (toll free: 1 866 921 9801; www.experientialweddings.ca) can plan and arrange every detail in advance for visitors wishing to marry here.

Sources of information

Xtra West (www.xtra.ca) is Vancouver's biweekly gay and lesbian newspaper, distributed for free in establishments and newspaper boxes across the city centre.

Gayvancouver.net (www.gayvancouver.net) offers comprehensive information on all aspects of gay life in Vancouver.

Gayvan.com (www.gayvan.com) caters for gay and lesbian visitors to Vancouver, with information on hotels, bars and gay-friendly businesses.

LOV (Living Out Vancouver; www.lovmag.com) is a glossy lifestyle magazine aimed at gay men.

For gay and lesbian nightlife, accommodation and other listings, see the Travel Tips section at the back of the book. ❑

DECISIVE DATES

is founded in Montreal.

1791
Spanish navigator José Maria Narváez explores the Strait of Georgia and sails into what became Burrard Inlet.

1791–5
George Vancouver's exploration of the West Coast.

1808
Simon Fraser arrives down the river that took his name.

1827
Original Hudson's Bay Company Fort Langley founded on Fraser River.

1836
SS *Beaver* arrives from England after a six-month voyage, making her the first steamship to reach the Pacific Ocean.

1843
Fort Victoria founded on Vancouver Island.

1670
Hudson's Bay Company founded in London to wrest the lucrative beaver-pelt trade from the French.

1757
George Vancouver is born in England (in King's Lynn, Norfolk).

1779
Captain James Cook explores the west coast of Vancouver Island.

1783
The North West Company

1858
Discovery of gold on Fraser River attracts over 25,000 prospectors. British Columbia declared an official crown colony.

1861
First newspaper established, New Westminster's *British Columbian*.

1865
First telegraph message from abroad, announcing assassination of President Lincoln.

1866
Crown colonies of Vancouver Island and British Columbia united.

1867
First stagecoach service, between New Westminster and Burrard Inlet, established. Confederation of Canada created, incorporating New Brunswick, Nova Scotia, Ontario and Quebec. Gastown springs up around sawmill and Jack Deighton's saloon.

1868
Canada's capital is moved from New Westminster to Victoria.

1869
Hudson's Bay Company surrenders Rupert's Land, part of Canada, to the Crown.

1870
Gastown is incorporated as Granville, taking its name

from the British colonial secretary, Earl Granville.

1871
British Columbia joins the Confederation of Canada following the promise of a transcontinental railway by the prime minister John A. MacDonald.

1883
First local telephone call, from Port Moody to New Westminster.

1885
Last spike ceremony at Craigellachie on 7 November marks the completion of the transcontinental railway. Land Commissioner Lauchlan Hamilton starts laying out township of Vancouver.

1886
The name Granville is

LEFT TOP: Royal Navy officer and explorer George Vancouver. LEFT: Captain Cook's ship, the HMS *Resolution*, moored off Vancouver Island, c.1777. ABOVE: 19th-century lumber wharf on the North Pacific coast.

changed to Vancouver, and city status is conferred by royal assent on 6 April.

1886
Fire destroys all but a few of Vancouver's buildings on 13 June. The first transcontinental passenger train arrives at Port Moody on 4 July.

1887
First passenger train arrives in Vancouver on 23 May. First imported cargo arrives in harbour, of tea and silk from China. First use of electricity in the city.

1888
Stanley Park formally opened and named.

1889
First Capilano suspension bridge opened. First Granville Street Bridge opened; its successors opened in 1909 and 1954.

1890
Tramcar service begins on

a rectangular route along Main, Cordova, Granville and Pender streets on 28 June.

1891
Sarah Bernhardt performs at Opera House. First interurban line opens, between Vancouver and New Westminster.

1900
Vancouver exceeds Victoria in size.

c.1907
First petrol station opens in Canada, at the foot of Cambie Street, near Smithe.

1908
University of British Columbia (UBC) inaugurated.

1909
First export shipment of grain from Vancouver. The first skyscraper, the Dominion Trust Building at Hastings and Cambie, opens. Regular ferry service across Burrard Inlet

begins. City of New York presents poisoned chalice gift of eight pairs of grey squirrels.

1911
The world's largest indoor ice rink opens, at 1805 West Georgia, on corner of Denman.

1913
Sam Kee building erected.

1914
Canadian Pacific Railway station on Cordova Street opened.

1915
University of British Columbia (UBC) receives its first students.

1920
First Polar Bear Swim.

1922
Driving switches from left to right side of street from 1 January.

1925
The first Second Narrows Bridge links the city with North Vancouver.

1928
First traffic light comes into use.

1929
Wall Street Crash. Marine Building is completed.

1932
Burrard Street Bridge is opened.

1936
New City Hall is dedicated at 12th and Cambie.

1938
Lions Gate Bridge opens.

1939
The third Hotel Vancouver is opened.

1942
More than 8,500 people of Japanese origin are removed from the BC coast and interned inland by order of the federal government. Alaska Highway built.

1949
The second Hotel Vancouver is demolished.

1954
British Empire and Commonwealth Games are held in Vancouver. Current Granville Bridge opened.

1956
Re-zoning of West End to allow higher density and high-rise developments.

1959
George Massey Tunnel under Fraser River completed, joining Delta to Richmond.

1960
Second Narrows Bridge opened (later renamed Ironworkers' Memorial Bridge).

1965
Simon Fraser University (SFU) established.

1971
Environmental organisation Greenpeace is formed in a Dunbar living room, developed from the Don't Make a Wave Committee. Metropolitan population tops 1 million.

1974
Royal Hudson begins regular steam-hauled trains to Squamish.

1975
The refurbished Orpheum Theatre reopens.

1977
SeaBus services across Burrard Inlet begin. Vancouver Lookout opened.

1979
Arthur Erikson's Courthouse and Robson Square complex completed. Granville Island Market opens.

1983
BC Place Stadium, the largest air-supported dome stadium in the world, inflates and is opened to the public.

1985
SkyTrain between Vancouver and New Westminster opens.

1986
Expo '86 marks Vancouver's centenary.

1988
First Gay Pride Festival held, now an annual week-long event.

1993
Closure of the landmark Woodward's department store, following bankruptcy.

1995
New public library and the Centre for the Performing Arts open.

1997
The Chan Centre for the Performing Arts opens at UBC.

2001
Millennium line of SkyTrain opens.

2003
Vancouver is chosen to host the 2010 Winter Olympics and Paralympics.

2006
A winter wind storm devastates Stanley Park, ripping out thousands of trees and changing the landscape overnight.

2010
The 2010 Winter Olympics and Paralympics place the world's attention on Vancouver and Whistler. Canada wins a record-breaking 14 gold medals. The legacies of the games include affordable housing and new winter sports facilities.

LEFT TOP: 1930s luggage label for the landmark Hotel Vancouver. **LEFT:** the 1954 British Empire and Commonwealth Games mile race, won by Roger Bannister. **RIGHT:** Canadian Mounties lower the flag at the closing ceremony of the 2010 Winter Olympics.

THE MAKING OF VANCOUVER

**Vancouver's history began long before the arrival
of intrepid mariners, fur trappers and gold prospectors.
The land that now supports a diverse population
of more than 2 million was settled by First Nations
tribes 10,000 years ago.**

The story of the European settlement of Vancouver occupies a tiny fraction of the human history of the area. Over 3,000 years ago, and probably much longer, First Nations people from the ancient Musqueam ("people of the grass") and Squamish ("strong winds") cultures lived in communities all across the Fraser River delta in what is now the metropolis of Vancouver. As recently as the 1930s, there were still elderly First Nations people who could remember the location of villages and houses they had known as children.

First Nations

The first inhabitants of the region are thought to have been ancient Mongolian tribes who came across the Bering Strait about 10,000 years ago. Their descendants formed the West Coast tribes

Legislation in 1885 provided that anyone "celebrating the Indian festival known as the 'Potlatch'…shall be liable to imprisonment for a term not more than six nor less than two months in a jail…".

which based their livelihoods on the abundant salmon migrations and the cedar tree from which they built large plank houses along the shores of Burrard Inlet, each housing up to 60 people.

Left: mother carrying her baby in a papoose.
Right: woodcut illustrating the traditional houses and dress of Vancouver's First Nations people c.1890.

The fecundity of the region and the harmonious balance the First Nations people maintained with nature and the environment are reflected in the thousands of years they lived in this way.

The artistic traditions of these West Coast natives found expression in their prominent totem poles, elaborate masks, decorated boxes, longboats and other wooden artefacts. Some artwork was created to proclaim and record family clan rights which would be asserted through the unique ceremony of the potlatch. These were elaborate and costly events, and an important elder would host only two or three in his lifetime. During the two-week ceremony,

trials or marriages might be conducted, property rights granted, feuds settled and noble births proclaimed.

In a society without written records, the potlatch served as a means of impressing these transactions and occasions on the collective memory. This was formalised by certain people being asked to bear future witness to them, should the need arise. In return, they were given gifts such as longboats and intricately carved chests, as well as being royally entertained. The Canadian government, encouraged by the missionaries focused on conversion of the native population to Christianity, banned potlatches between 1885 and 1952, even imprisoning elders and confiscating their regalia, arguing that they were wasteful and worse, though it is also argued that this was merely a pretext in the pursuit of compulsory assimilation.

Before Europeans arrived in BC, at least 80,000 native people lived in the region; by 1885 their population had been decimated by disease and alcohol. Smallpox was the worst killer, since the First Nations people had no immunity; for example, it killed a third of the native population of Victoria.

Venture capitalists

Long before the first European came to the West Coast of Canada, a company was founded in London that would have a profound effect on the development of Canada and the settlement of the West Coast. The Hudson's Bay Company (HBC) is the oldest incorporated joint-stock merchandising company in the English-speaking world, and it was given its royal charter by Charles II on 2 May 1670. To his cousin Prince Rupert and his associates, Charles granted 3.9 million sq km (1½ million sq miles) of land in western and northern Canada, to be known as "Rupert's Land". Charles believed it was his to give away because no other Christian monarch had claimed it.

The company's primary objective was to make money by wresting control of the fur trade from the French, who had enjoyed a monopoly over it during the 17th century.

The HBC's success was unchallenged for more than a century, until the North West Company in Montreal was established in 1783, with the explicit intention of breaking the HBC's stranglehold on the fur trade. It looked to develop trade in areas not covered by the HBC's charter, dispatching expeditions led by Alexander Mac-

kenzie, Simon Fraser and David Thompson to explore and map the western territories.

British hegemony over the West Coast was no foregone conclusion. Spanish and British mapping expeditions had both cordial and hostile meetings along Vancouver Island. The Spanish are thought to have reached as far inland as the Okanagan, where the last of their depleted band were killed.

Voyages of discovery

Part of the impetus for naval exploration of the region was the search for the elusive Northwest Passage to link the Atlantic and Pacific oceans, long the dream of navigators. Parliament had offered a reward of £20,000 to anyone discovering such a passage, and its western exit was the purpose of James Cook's third and final voyage.

Cook left England in the summer of 1776, and in March 1778 he put into Nootka Sound on Vancouver Island for repairs. With him were William Bligh as master of the *Resolution*

(and later of the infamous *Bounty*) and midshipman George Vancouver. When Cook's ships reached China on the return voyage, the 1,500 beaver and otter pelts they had acquired at Nootka Sound in exchange for trifles fetched upwards of $100 each – equal to two years' pay for an ordinary seaman. As a plaque in Vancouver's Christ Church Cathedral says, it was Cook's expedition that revealed the wealth of the region. It also led later to the hunting of otters to near extinction. It was on the way home on 14 February 1779 that Cook was killed by natives on the Sandwich Islands (now Hawaii).

Fourteen years later, George Vancouver was sent by the Admiralty in two ships, the *Discovery* and the *Chatham*, to receive the formal surrender from Spain of land the Spanish had seized around Nootka Sound on Vancouver Island. He sailed from Falmouth on 1 April 1791 and, travelling by way of the Cape of Good Hope, Australia and Hawaii, first sighted the northwest coast of America on 17 April 1792. It was on this voyage that Vancouver explored what would be named Burrard Inlet, writing that it "requires only to be enriched by the industry of man with villages, mansions, cottages, and other

LEFT: HMS *Discovery* and HMS *Chatham* exploring the shores of Burrard Inlet in 1792. **ABOVE:** scene in a Hudson Bay trading store.

George Vancouver

George Vancouver was born in 1757, the son of a customs officer at the thriving port of King's Lynn on England's east coast. He had the sea in his blood, being descended on his mother's side from the Elizabethan seafarer Sir Richard Grenville, whose death on the *Revenge* was one of the most heroic actions in British naval history.

Through his maritime connections, George's father secured his son a place on Cook's second voyage (1772–5), which gave him an unparalleled training in seamanship, navigation and surveying. After serving on Cook's third voyage (1776–80), Vancouver was appointed lieutenant and served in the West Indies. In 1790 he commanded

an expedition making a detailed survey of the northwest coast of America from California to Alaska. To try to ascertain once and for all whether an entry to a Northwest Passage existed, Vancouver spent three years surveying the coast, during which time he named over 400 topographical features, most of which remain in use, and concluded that a Northwest Passage did not exist.

Vancouver returned to England in 1795, having sailed about 105,000km (65,600 miles) with the loss of only five of the 180 crew during the four years, a quite exceptional achievement for the time which reflects his care for his men. He died in 1798, aged just 40.

buildings to render it the most lovely country that can be imagined…"

Approaches from the east

While Vancouver was mapping the West Coast, emissaries of the North West Company were exploring the river systems that they knew must flow west to the Pacific, with a view to assessing their trading potential. In 1792–5 Alexander Mackenzie (1764–1820) made a trip from the North West Company's fort at Fort Chipewyan

on Lake Athabasca to the Pacific, using a 7.5-metre (25ft) birch-bark canoe of exceptional strength. He crossed the Great Divide and came down a tributary of the Fraser, eventually completing his journey to the Pacific on foot, reaching the coast on 20 July 1793 by the Bella Coola River. He then returned to the fort by the Peace River.

Another Scotsman in the employment of the North West Company, Simon Fraser (1776–1862), led a party of 24 in four canoes from Fort

George (now the city of Prince George, in central BC) in May 1808, quickly discovering that the warnings given by the native inhabitants about the river were all too justified. Hauling the canoes around the rapids was extremely difficult too, leading the party to abandon them above present-day Lillooet after just 13 days' slog through several mountain ranges. They reached the coast on foot, occasionally borrowing canoes from local tribes with whom Fraser established good relationships.

When Fraser's party arrived at the lower reaches of the river, near today's Vancouver, the Musqueam people gave chase, denying Fraser more than a glimpse of the Strait of Georgia. By this point, however, he had realised that the river he had been following was not the Columbia but an entirely different river. His attempt to find a river link between Fort George and the fur-trading posts of the lower Columbia River had failed, but Fraser became the first-known European to travel the river that would subsequently take his name to its mouth.

The squabbles and skirmishes between the two fur-trading companies came to an end in 1821 with the forced merger of the North West and Hudson's Bay companies.

Just before Christmas 1824 a party of 40 men led by a Hudson's Bay Company Chief Factor, James McMillan, explored the lower reaches of the Nicomekl, Salmon and Fraser rivers, McMillan marking a tree at what is now Langley. Over two years later, on 27 July 1827, he was back at the tree with orders to build a fort. Within five years, Fort Langley was shipping out over 2,000 beaver pelts a year, trapped by the local Kwantlen people.

Salted salmon soon became another major industry, with much of it going to the Sandwich Islands (now Hawaii). In 1839 the fort was abandoned and moved to its present site (*see page 227*).

Gold fever

Vancouver Island had been declared a crown colony in 1849, but the future governance of the region was transformed by an event in 1858, when gold was discovered along the banks of the Fraser River. Not everyone was thrilled. The idea of prospectors invading the fur-trading grounds aroused the proprietorial instincts

LEFT: Fort Langley, where many an unsuccessful gold miner ended up. **ABOVE:** an outfitter's store for gold diggers.

of HBC officials, and the Chief Factor, James Douglas, wrote to Sir Edward Bulwer-Lytton at the Colonial Office in London, even requesting a single company of infantry. The response was the dispatch of four vessels carrying a corps of Royal Engineers (the Columbia Detachment) under the command of Col. Richard Moody. A further response was a parliamentary Act creating the new mainland colony of British Columbia, and Douglas was offered the governorship providing he severed his links with the fur trade. That agreed, he was inaugurated as governor at Fort Langley.

Col. Moody, his wife and four children travelled via Panama, crossed the isthmus over land (the Canal was not opened until 1914), and arrived in Victoria after a two-month journey. Moody and his sappers (a word derived from the spade Royal Engineers used to dig trenches) accomplished an astonishing amount of work during their four years based at the site he chose for the new capital of New Westminster.

Within a year he had built a road through the forest linking New Westminster with Port Moody on ice-free Burrard Inlet, ensuring that the capital would not be cut off during a severe winter. He surveyed suitable sites for settlement, including a good part of what became downtown Vancouver, and built the Cariboo and Hope–Similkameen roads.

Douglas's fears about the impact of the gold rush were justified. By July 1858 there were about 30,000 miners in the colony, most of them "the worst of the population of San Francisco – the very dregs in fact of society" as Douglas put it. The first ship to carry prospectors was the *Surprise*, a sternwheeler from California which entered the Fraser River on 5 June 1858 and reached Fort Hope the next day. The rapids claimed many lives before roads were built, but that first summer of 1858 saw claims on every creek and sandbar from Hope to Lytton.

History repeated itself three years later when reports leaked of Ned Campbell finding 900 ounces of gold in a day, this time in Cariboo country around Barkerville. Both gold rushes encouraged the establishment of farms around today's Burnaby and Delta and further north in Cariboo country to provide milk and meat for the hungry miners.

ABOVE: Spences Bridge, one of the settlements on the gold rush trail. **RIGHT:** first Vancouver City Council meeting after the fire, 1886.

THE PEOPLE BEHIND THE PLACE NAMES

Many of Vancouver's landmarks carry the names of the explorers and pioneers who opened the region up to Europe. Naming the young town after George Vancouver *(see page 34)* was the idea of the Canadian Pacific Railway's president, who maintained that Vancouver was more famous for his exploits in the region than Granville, after whom the city was originally named.

Simon Fraser began exploring the country west of the Rockies in the early 19th century, establishing trading posts and trade routes. In 1808 he travelled down the river that now bears his name with a view to taking possession of that country and setting up forts along the way.

In 1788, Scotsman Alexander Mackenzie founded Fort Chipewyan, the first settlement in Alberta. Information about local waterways gleaned from First Nations people encouraged Mackenzie to follow the river that was later to bear his name, only to discover that it did not flow into Cook Inlet in Alaska as he had hoped, but to the Arctic Ocean.

In 1858 Col. Richard Moody of the Royal Engineers was appointed Chief Commissioner of Lands and Works and Lieutenant Governor of the new colony of BC. Moody's name was given to the port on Burrard Inlet which was chosen as the original western terminus of the Canadian Pacific Railway.

Real estate

While many disappointed miners moved on to the next report of gold, others stayed to form the nucleus of many a settlement and business, none more famously than a Yorkshire potter named John Morton and two fellow countrymen, Sam Brighouse and William Hailstone. In 1862 they pooled their resources to buy 225 hectares (550 acres) of what became the West End of Vancouver, with a view to making bricks on the site. Neither this nor any of their other money-making ideas came to much, but they still owned the land when the Canadian Pacific Railway (CPR) directors decided to extend the transcontinental line beyond the original terminus of Port Moody to Burrard Inlet, transforming the value of their land. The water at Port Moody was too shallow for ever-larger ocean-going ships.

Another Yorkshireman, Jack Deighton *(see page 101)* started the fledgling community's first bar and hotel in 1867, the same year that nearby

Hastings Mill began processing timber and the year that three eastern British colonies formed the Confederation of Canada. The boundaries of districts such as Langley, Maple Ridge, Surrey, Delta and Richmond were laid out during the 1870s. But even by the beginning of the 1880s, the population of Granville (later renamed Vancouver – *see panel, page 37*) was still in the low hundreds. Electric light arrived first on the north shore in 1882 in the village of Moodyville that grew up around a mill owned by an Amer-

ican, Sewell Moody (no relation to the Royal Engineer). A prescient writer for the Portland-based *West Shore Magazine* advised "those who have money to investigate the merits of Vancouver…before making other investments" because "it is only once in a lifetime that the public have such a chance as the present."

Support for the colony of British Columbia joining Canada was orchestrated by the Confederation League. Fear of annexation by the United States was a significant factor in its arguments, as was the debt burden created by developing the infrastructure needed to cope with the rapid population increase. Moreover, the economy needed to be placed on a firmer footing than the fly-by-night enterprises engendered by the gold rush; its end had been followed by an inevitable depression.

Vancouver's future was secured when the Prime Minister, Sir John A. Macdonald, promised that a transcontinental railway line would

RUDYARD KIPLING'S VIEW

When the writer Rudyard Kipling first came to Vancouver in 1889, he was 23 and his well-known short story *The Man Who Would Be King* had just been published. He wrote about his visit to the young city in *From Sea to Sea*:

"Vancouver three years ago was swept off by fire in sixteen minutes, and only one house was left standing. Today it has a population of fourteen thousand people, and builds its houses out of brick with dressed granite fronts. But a great sleepiness lies on Vancouver as compared with an American town: men don't fly up and down the street telling lies, and the spittoons in the delightfully comfortable hotel are unused; the baths are free and their doors are

unlocked… An American bade me notice the absence of bustle, and was alarmed when in a loud and audible voice I thanked God for it…

"Vancouver possesses an almost perfect harbour. The town is built all round and about the harbour, and young as it is, its streets are better than those of western America. Moreover, the old flag waves over some of the buildings, and this is cheering to the soul. The place is full of Englishmen who speak the English tongue correctly and with clearness, avoiding more blasphemy than is necessary, and taking a respectable length of time to getting outside their drinks."

be built if British Columbia joined the Confederation. The pledge and an agreement to take over its debt won the colony over, and on 20 July 1871 British Columbia became the sixth province of the Confederation (though the boundaries were not finalised until 1903).

The Great Fire

Vancouver became a city by royal assent on 6 April 1886, and within three months 500 buildings had been erected. The sounds of two-man saws and axes could be heard around the city's edges as the hemlocks and firs were felled, but the frenetic pace of forest clearance brought a nemesis: on 13 June a fire to burn brushwood went out of control and in 45 minutes destroyed almost everything that had been built, though sparing Hastings Mill.

City Hall was relegated to a tent where the city was replanned, using stone and brick rather than wood. Six months later, the city boasted 23 hotels, 51 stores, a church, a school, hospital,

livery stable, opera house, bank and new City Hall. The population was over 8,000.

The railway arrives

It is a measure of the financial and engineering difficulties in fulfilling Macdonald's commitment that 16 years would pass before the first passenger train from Montreal came to a hissing stand beside Burrard Inlet, on 23 May 1887; it had completed what was then the world's longest continuous train journey at 4,655km (2,909 miles).

Being Queen Victoria's Golden Jubilee year, it carried a large picture of the queen on the front and was festooned with garlands. Port Moody had had its "15 minutes of fame" as the temporary terminus for 10 months.

For speculators, there was a pot of gold at the end of the steel rainbow: land prices more than tripled in just over two months in anticipation of the effect the railway would have in spurring the city's growth. For the CPR it was a bonanza, having been given 3,750 hectares (6,000 acres) of land in and around the city as reward for the huge sums it had spent in construction. The CPR has remained a major property player for decades, from the early days when it spent $2 million

FAR LEFT: interior of a Canadian Pacific Railway sleeping car, 1888. ABOVE LEFT: driving in the last spike of the Canadian Pacific Railway. ABOVE: Canadian Pacific Railway steam train.

laying out leafy Shaughnessy before a single house was built to today's interests in waterfront development and the Arbutus right of way through its real-estate arm, Marathon Realty.

The economy of BC has always been based on the extraction of resources from lumber to mining, so completion of the railway was as much of a boost to the broader economy as property: the mining, forestry, agriculture and fishing industries were able to send their products east as well as to the port at Vancouver for shipment. Given the heavy nature of the mining and forestry industries and the perishable products of agriculture and fishing, they could achieve little without the railway. Cattle ranching in the Cariboo and Chilcotin, and fruit growing in the Okanagan became major industries to support the growing population.

Early immigrants

The reasons for Vancouver's early success are easy to see: its natural deep-water harbour encouraged its choice as terminus of the first trans-Canada railway line; wood, salmon and other plentiful natural resources in the region added to its exports; and its glorious location and equable climate made it an attractive place to live and visit.

The largest group of early "visitors" was Chinese, many of them contracted to help complete the railway on little better than slave wages, but once that task was complete, they were in competition with European immigrants for each job. Their willingness to work for 75 cents a day when white labourers expected $1.25–$2 led to the first outbreak of job-market-induced violence in 1887 when a Chinese camp at False Creek was attacked.

Measures were taken to limit or stop the immigration of Chinese, but as early as 1907 the *Illustrated London News* was describing Vancouver as "probably the most cosmopolitan city in the world". Many poor Chinese from Hong Kong and Canton saw working in BC as a temporary measure that would allow them to go back home with enough money to buy land. Many never returned to China, choosing instead to send for their families.

Saloons to opera

The few decades before World War I saw the city in that transitional state between raw

frontier town and a city adopting the more sophisticated and cultured mores of the well-to-do. At the same time as Sarah Bernhardt was treading the boards at the CPR's newly built Opera House, Vancouver was topping the league for alcohol consumption in Canada. This wasn't helped by yet another influx of miners, this time on their way to the Yukon gold rush of 1898. Tramcars rattled along the streets among the horse dung, and the first petrol arrived in barrels to fuel the mixed blessing of the motor car.

A second transcontinental railway line, the Grand Trunk Pacific (GTP) through the Yellow-head Pass and Prince George, opened to the coast at Prince Rupert in 1914, and the Canadian Northern (later Canadian National) arrived in Vancouver in 1916, using the lines of the Great Northern from the Fraser River bridge, creating a rival to the CPR for east–west traffic. The financial distress of both the GTP and Canadian Northern prompted the creation of Canadian National in 1922 to take over their operations.

War and Prohibition

The city's population roughly tripled between 1900 and 1910, helping to make the city's four newspapers immensely profitable as new arrivals scanned the columns for jobs and property. The opening of the Panama Canal a few weeks after war was declared in 1914 dramatically shortened the sea journey between BC and Europe, stimulating trade and particularly shipments of grain that arrived by rail from the Prairie provinces.

The supply of professional soldiers from local regiments as well as volunteers was complemented by fundraising and a greater role for women in replacing men who had left for Europe. It was the newly empowered women who voted in Prohibition during the war to counter the city's reputation for heavy drinking, but it didn't last long as BC was the first English-speaking province to repeal Prohibition, paving the way for a new business for local entrepreneurs.

A quick post-war way to riches, providing you weren't caught, was rum-running to the US during the Prohibition era from 1920 to 1933. This illicit trade put serious money into the Vancouver economy. One of the vessels at the Britannia Heritage Shipyard at Steveston (*see page 165*), MV *Fleetwood*, was built specifically for contraband trade, with a diesel engine and two 450hp aircraft engines that would enable her to outrun government patrol ships.

HARD TIMES

Although shipbuilding in North Vancouver had grown during World War I, the yards experienced a downturn long before the Wall Street Crash heralded the Great Depression. For other industries the 1920s were buoyant, though contemporary accounts speak of heavily polluted air from the mills, food-processing plants, shoe and clothing factories and breweries. Despite the modest prosperity, many returning soldiers found jobs occupied by immigrants from Europe. Fringe political parties sprang up to articulate their grievances; some later became part of the left-of-centre Co-operative Commonwealth and the right-of-centre Social Credit parties.

FAR LEFT: Hastings Street, 1939. **LEFT TOP:** relocating a Japanese Canadian. **LEFT BOTTOM:** Chinese "visitors" in front of a post office. **ABOVE:** Roger Bannister breaks the four-minute mile record in 1954.

The Great Depression

With the crash of 1929, Vancouver's streets filled with the unemployed from shut-down factories, mines, lumber camps and canneries. It was preferable to be destitute in Vancouver's mild climate than in the towns of the interior where it was freezing in winter and too hot in summer, so hard-up unemployed men headed west along the tracks of the CPR and Canadian National Railway, earning the city the reputation of being the "hobo capital of Canada". Hobo shanties around the False Creek and Burrard Inlet rail yards became home to thousands. By 1931 Vancouver's unemployment levels were the highest in Canada at 28 percent. Schoolteachers even agreed to work the month of December 1933 without pay to prevent the near-bankrupt authorities closing the schools. Industrial unrest boiled over in April 1935 when 2,000 men marched on City Hall demanding work and wages.

Much more serious was the 1938 occupation of the main post office, Hotel Georgia and the Art Gallery by 1,500 demonstrators demanding a works programme on the lines of Edgar Hoover's in the US. It was a month before batons and tear gas were used to evict the occupiers, but not before some most un-Canadian scenes of looting and violence. The docks at Vancouver were effectively under martial law for almost three years. Some public works to reduce unemployment were instigated, such as Kitsilano swimming pool and the Burrard Bridge.

World War II brought an end to the Depression, as Vancouver geared up for the requirements of conflict and women returned to the workplace in greater numbers than ever.

Preliminary siting of gun batteries and the creation of recruitment centres were overshadowed by the attack on Pearl Harbor, prompting nightly blackouts and the uprooting and internment of Japanese Canadians far from the coast in rudimentary camps. Despite their contribution in the previous world war, their property was seized and liquidated, and little of it was ever returned, though token compensation was eventually paid.

Post-war boom

With the return of peace, many veterans who had trained in BC returned to settle, and immigration resumed in 1947. The Social Credit premier W.A.C. Bennett dominated BC politics for two decades, riding the wave of post-war baby-

boomer prosperity with policies that reflected the "frontier ethic of limitless resources". Much of the growth was fuelled by the port, which had its facilities and channels enlarged for bigger ships. The 1954 British Empire and Commonwealth Games in Vancouver made world headlines when Roger Bannister broke the four-minute mile record. Traffic congestion became a chronic problem, compounded by lack of investment in a transit system that was allowed to contract; as a consequence transit use halved between 1946 and 1964, despite the population doubling to 800,000.

The 1960s saw the beginnings of Whistler as a ski resort and construction of the Grouse Mountain Skyride, but Vancouver's future appeal as a tourist destination is thanks in large part to the students and hippies who protested against plans to put a highway through Chinatown and around Coal Harbour to English Bay, pressing instead for more pedestrian-friendly streets. In 1971 this concern for the environment was translated into the formation of Greenpeace, when 12 activists sailed to protest against US atomic testing off Alaska.

The long period of Social Credit (Socreds) provincial government under W.A.C. Bennett came to a brief end in 1972 before his son was elected as premier in 1975. This was a period of phenomenal growth in the suburbs at the expense of the central areas, a trend that the city has tried to counter by imaginative regeneration over the last two decades. It was Expo '86, celebrating Vancouver's centenary, that marked the turning point in the development of the city. Notionally it had a transportation theme: Skytrain and the Coquihalla Highway between Hope and Merritt were rushed to completion just in time, and the exhibition was a huge success, attracting over 21 million visitors. But it was decisions about the use of the exhibition-site land that were to transform the city.

LEFT: Greenpeace activists. **ABOVE TOP:** Hungarian refugees boarding the Air Bridge to Canada. **ABOVE BOTTOM:** World War II recruitment poster.

The legacy of Expo '86

In 1989 the great uncertainty over the future of Hong Kong led to a huge influx of capital and residents, pushing up real-estate prices. Asian money financed the majority of new development projects in downtown Vancouver, seen as a prudent investment. Because of the constraints on expansion imposed by Vancouver's topography, land is often more valuable than the property on it, leading to frequent demolition of older buildings and

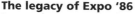

ENVIRONMENTAL CONCERNS

The green movement has targeted the logging of old-growth forest and particularly the destructive clear-cut method of laying waste entire swaths of forest. But raw materials remain a cornerstone of the BC economy, including the mining industry with gross revenues of $4 billion a year and accounting for 56 percent of all railway revenues and 69 percent of port revenues. BC is the fifth-largest silver producer in the world. Some of the surviving older mines have become fascinating tourist attractions, though many regret that the huge Sullivan mine at Kimberley was not saved. It closed in 2001 after almost a century of activity.

constant efforts to build taller buildings.

In 1997 a "Skyline Study" was commissioned which concluded that the city's skyline would benefit from a few buildings exceeding the current limits. Under the General Policy on Higher Buildings, five suitable downtown sites were identified where heights up to 137 metres (450ft) would be acceptable and two where 122 metres (400ft) would be considered. Five of the sites have been or are being developed, the tallest being the Shangri-La Hotel and residential tower, which sold out within minutes of the units being put up for sale, long before construction began.

Population shifts

With the rapid expansion of high-rise apartment buildings in central Vancouver, the decline in the proportion of population in the downtown core compared to the metropolitan area had been arrested. Between 1981 and 1995, the population of the central area increased by 107,000. The desirability of living near work and entertainment has led younger people to sacrifice square footage for the convenience of the central core. The suburbs remain somewhat affordable for young families, where North

American values still dictate that a detached home with a yard is important for children.

The 2010 Olympics

Vancouver's success in securing the 2010 Winter Olympics brought with the construction of the Olympic Village the final significant urban redevelopment of the land around False Creek. Though Whistler was the site of the main skiing and sledding events, the existing arenas in Vancouver were the logical locations for hockey and figure-skating events. New speed-skating facilities in Richmond and a new Hillcrest/Nat Bailey Stadium Park facility (near Queen Elizabeth Park) are some of the legacies, the latter resulting in a new ice-hockey rink and eight sheets of curling ice.

While the long-term benefits of the Olympics are impossible to predict, there is no question that upgrading the road to Whistler and the expansion of SkyTrain service to Richmond and the airport will benefit both those who live in Vancouver and those who visit. ❑

Since 1986 the shift in population, primarily due to immigration from Asian countries, has given the city an international flavour, where more than 40 percent now have a mother tongue other than English.

FAR LEFT AND ABOVE LEFT TOP: water playground and SkyTrain at Expo '86. **ABOVE LEFT BOTTOM:** Grouse Mountain Skyride. **ABOVE:** the bright lights of Downtown Vancouver. **RIGHT:** Olympic Village development, False Creek.

THE PERFORMING ARTS

Vancouver's multicultural heritage has produced a thriving arts scene that's dynamic, diverse and unafraid to experiment. The theatre and dance scenes are particularly active, and there are many great venues for live music. Summer in the city is celebrated with a series of lively festivals.

Vancouver exhibited a strong interest in culture and live entertainment at a very young age. Its first theatre, Blair's Hall, was built in the year of the city's incorporation, 1886. This was followed by the Imperial Opera House, and then the de luxe Vancouver Opera House in 1891. The city's population was 8,000 and the theatre was designed to seat 2,000. It was filled to the rafters when the premiere performance of Wagner's *Lohengrin* was given and was again packed when Sarah Bernhardt performed.

A theatre district sprang up in Gastown. The heart of Vancouver from the late 19th century to the early 1900s, this area saw the construc-

tion of numerous vaudeville theatres, owned and operated by theatrical entrepreneur Alexander "something for everyone" Pantages. Among them was the Empress Theatre, where Anna Pavlova performed in 1910. Sadly, Vancouver's oldest surviving theatre, the 1907 purpose-built vaudeville Pantages theatre on East Hastings Street, fell into serious disrepair before it could be renovated and is now beyond repair.

Showing an ankle

As Vancouver was on the touring minstrel-show circuit, many variety acts came to town, with great vaudeville names like Charlie Chaplin, Stan Laurel and English Music Hall Queen Marie Lloyd creating quite a stir.

Lloyd, who was known for her somewhat risqué humour, was asked to discontinue performing one of her more colourful numbers, "The Ankle Watch", during which she lifted her skirts to reveal her ankle. The outraged city's licence inspector declared: "It might go all right in London but Vancouver will not stand for it."

Principal venues

Vancouver's love of the arts has grown with the city. Today's audiences can enjoy performances in many languages, with many different aesthetics and from a wide variety of performing traditions and styles. Commercial Drive, South Granville, Old Strathcona/Gastown and Granville Island are hubs of activity, with galleries, theatres, clubs and cafés. Even the suburban areas of Greater Vancouver have numerous performing and visual arts centres.

The city's largest performance venues are

concentrated in downtown Vancouver: the opulent Orpheum Theatre, home to the Vancouver Symphony Orchestra, and the Commodore Ballroom, with one of the best dance floors in the city. The Centre for the Performing Arts, designed by Moshe Safdie as a companion piece to the Public Library, was originally used for Broadway musicals, but in recent years has become known for producing large-scale musicals, often based on Asian stories and themes.

Across the street from the library, the Queen Elizabeth Theatre and Playhouse host touring musical theatre productions as well as serving as performance venues for the Vancouver Opera, Ballet BC and the Playhouse Theatre Company. Right next door, General Motors Place sports arena serves as a venue for big-name acts like The Rolling Stones, Van Morrison and The Dixie Chicks.

The Vancouver East Cultural Centre, locally referred to as the "Cultch", is one of a number of small but funky cultural venues dotted around the city. In a converted church with great acoustics, it offers an eclectic programme of contemporary dance, theatre and music from around the world. Set in a converted railway depot in Yaletown is the splendid Roundhouse Community Centre. Among its many facilities is a performance centre used for theatre and dance, and an exhibition hall.

> Popular artists such as Bryan Adams, Diana Krall, Nelly Furtado, Sarah McLachlan and Michael Bublé all built their careers in and around Vancouver.

Housed in a 100-year-old fire station in the Old Strathcona/Gastown area, the Firehall Arts Centre produces and presents dance, theatre and interdisciplinary work by some of the city's most exciting new artists.

Granville Island has a number of performance spaces used by many of the city's independent theatre and dance companies,

including Performance Works, Festival House and the Waterfront Theatre, as well as outdoor stages where in the summer months dance, theatre and music groups entertain.

The summer months see outdoor performances in many of the city's parks, offering audiences the opportunity to enjoy Vancouver's beautiful surroundings to the sound of music.

Music

Vancouver's live music scene ranges from classical concerts by the Vancouver Symphony Orchestra to a wide range of rock, pop, folk, jazz and blues bands who perform at festivals, pubs and clubs like the Railway, the Commodore Ball Room, the Yale and Rossini's. For those who like their music loud, live and with an edge, Vancouver's underground music scene is alive and kicking (see www.livemusicvancouver.com for band listings).

The beautiful Chan Centre, in the grounds of the University of British Columbia, has the best acoustics in the city and stages everything from classical and choral music to folk and world music. Vancouver Opera provides a challenging mix of traditional and contemporary interpretations of classics such as their recent

PRECEDING PAGES: the Duane Andrews quartet perform at the annual Vancouver Jazz Festival. LEFT: home-grown singer-songwriter Nelly Furtado. ABOVE: outside the Queen Elizabeth Theatre.

aboriginally-themed production of *The Magic Flute*. Look out also for performances by Vancouver-based Japanese drummers Uzume Taiko and SWARM, the extreme percussion orchestra.

Comedy

Vancouver's comedy scene is going from strength to strength, and there are numerous venues dedicated to stand-up and improv. Comedy clubs such as LaffLines, Yuk Yuks and Vancouver Theatresports League launched the careers of Ryan Stiles (*The Drew Carey Show*, *Whose Line Is It Any-*

way?), Colin Mochrie (*This Hour has 22 Minutes*) and Brent Butt (*Corner Gas*).

Theatre

With more than 60 professional theatre companies, Vancouver's theatre scene is very active. The largest of these, the Arts Club Theatre, operates year-round producing a mix of contemporary and classic Canadian, British and American plays along with Broadway musicals at its flagship theatre, the Stanley, and at the Granville Island Stage. The Vancouver Playhouse, the oldest professional theatre company in the city, performs at the Queen Elizabeth Theatre complex in an eight-month season.

Smaller companies such as the Firehall Arts Centre theatre company have led the way in producing theatre that reflects the city's pluralism, bringing many First Nations and culturally diverse voices to the stage.

Vancouver is recognised for its physical theatre work, and Axis Theatre's *The No. 14* has been touring internationally since its

conception in the early 1990s. Other international hits by Vancouver playwrights include *Billy Bishop Goes to War*, *The Overcoat*, *Vigil* and *Mum's The Word*.

Each summer Vanier Park is taken over by Bard on the Beach, a very successful festival of Shakespearean work that is performed nightly in tents with the cityscape as its backdrop. The company presents four plays every season, not only the favourites like *Comedy of Errors* and *Othello*, but also more obscure works of the bard, such as *Titus Andronicus* and *Troilus and Cressida*. Further east in the inner city, Leaky Heaven Circus puts together a lively carnival, complete with trapeze artists, clowns and performing dogs.

Dance

Vancouver's flourishing contemporary dance scene grew out of the work of choreographers Anna Wyman, Judith Marcuse and Paula Ross. The 1980s saw a huge period of growth with the establishment of the EDAM (Experimental Dance and Music), Mascall Dance and Kokoro companies.

Holy Body Tattoo, formed in the early 1990s, continues to create new works that have been performed all over Asia, Europe and the United States. Vancouver choreographer Crystal Pite's company, Kidd Pivot, is kicking up a storm internationally, while graduates of the Simon Fraser University contemporary dance programme flow into the milieu, mixing contact improvisation, West Coast, Asian and modern aesthetics to create unique dance works.

Ballet BC has been known for breaking new ground in creating original contemporary ballets while also performing in repertoire works of William Forsythe, Twyla Tharpe and James

Kadelka. By 2008, it had incurred substantial debt and hovered on the brink of bankruptcy, but has been able to recover, with a 2010 relaunch of the company.

Places to catch dance include the Scotiabank Dance Centre, the Vancouver East Cultural Centre, the Firehall Arts Centre and the Queen Elizabeth Theatre. Each July, the annual Dancing on the Edge Festival of Contemporary Dance brings together choreographers and dance companies from across Canada and beyond for 10 energetic days of dance. ❏

FAR LEFT: the renowned Vancouver International Jazz Festival. **LEFT:** flower ladies at the annual Gay Pride parade. **ABOVE:** Tall Ships Festival, Victoria. **ABOVE RIGHT:** the Vancouver Playhouse production of Stephan Sachs' *Miss Julie: Freedom Summer*.

LISTINGS AND TICKETS

The most useful guide for just about everything is the free weekly publication, the *Georgia Straight*. For live music listings, www.livemusicvancouver.com is also a good source. Advance tickets for major events and performances can be bought through Ticket Master (tel: 604 280 3311; www.ticketmaster.ca) or on the same day from the Tickets Tonight booth in the tourist information centre near Canada Place (Plaza level, 200 Burrard Street; tel: 604 231 7535; www.ticketstonight.ca).

• *For further information and useful websites, see the Activities section, pages 258–64.*

THE GREAT OUTDOORS

With mountains, beaches, rivers, lakes and ocean all on their doorstep, it's no surprise Vancouverites are passionate about their outdoor pursuits. The possibilities for recreation and adventure are endless.

The south coast of British Columbia is a kaleidoscope of eye-popping geography, with the snowcapped Coast Mountain Range, powerful Fraser River, freshwater lakes and towering forests, edged by the sparkling Pacific. Its setting in the midst of all this majestic nature is the single best reason for visiting Vancouver – that and the limitless opportunities for outdoor recreation.

For outdoor enthusiasts, the crowning glory is the weather. The fact that you can ski and sail on the same day is something Vancouverites rub in the noses of less climatically blessed Canadians. A temperate coastal climate brings a winter requiring little more than a warm jacket and an umbrella. Cold enough, however, to deposit ski-worthy snow on the local North Shore peaks and deliver world-class skiing at Whistler.

Mixing pleasures

Spring comes early and softly, with a February average temperature of 7°C (44°F). Summer follows quickly, stretching the sunny weather well into October, with longer days that are perfect for outdoor pursuits. Vancouverites think nothing of making a beeline from their hiking, biking or golf activity to attend a symphony concert at the Orpheum Theatre, a grande dame among the city's entertainment venues. Jeans and fleece jackets are at home beside gowns and tuxes.

Whether you're in the mood for a leisurely sunset stroll along one of the city's 11 beaches or an adrenalin-pumping challenge such as zip-trekking down the narrow valley between Whistler and Blackcomb mountains, Vancouver and its environs offer plenty of opportunities for activity. From the gentle to the extreme, the choices are endless: within minutes of the downtown core, cycling along the city's extensive bike routes, in-line skating along English Bay, kayaking off Jericho Beach or ocean swimming at Kitsilano Beach.

Further afield, you can go hiking in Mount Seymour Provincial Park, salmon fishing in Horseshoe Bay, mountain biking in a dozen communities including Burnaby, North Van-

LEFT: bungee jumping near Whistler. **RIGHT:** cycling along one of the many cycle paths in and around Vancouver.

couver and Whistler, river rafting on the mighty Thompson River or smaller but equally exciting Chilliwack River. The area also has dozens of golf courses.

Protected parkland

You don't have to venture far to immerse yourself in nature. In the heart of the city, Stanley Park's marked inner trails lead through a dense forest to Beaver Lake, where sightings of raccoon, rabbit and coyote are common. Huge

Pacific Spirit Regional Park adjacent to the University of British Columbia campus offers more rugged but well-marked trails through diverse terrain, with western red cedar, Douglas fir, Sitka spruce and western hemlock towering over a carpet of lush ferns and moss that cover the forest floor.

On the North Shore, Lighthouse Park in West Vancouver is home to the last old-growth forest in the area: the giant stands of Douglas fir are scattered with red-barked arbutus trees,

---

WINTER SPORTS

The peaks of Grouse Mountain, Mount Seymour and Cypress Bowl are lined up on the North Shore across Burrard Inlet. They are all well equipped for winter sports and easily accessible, and each has its own specialities.

Grouse, with 26 runs for skiers and boarders, is easy to reach by car or bus across the Lions Gate Bridge. It offers ski and boarding lessons and stupendous views from the summit. Sleigh rides and ice-skating are alternative attractions.

Cypress is a magnet for cross-country skiers as well as boasting the largest vertical downhill drop of the three peaks. As the home of the 2010 Olympic Winter Games' snowboarding and freestyle skiing events, Cypress has

benefited from both upgraded facilities and a much higher profile. For beginners, the ski lessons, snowshoe trails and snow-tubing thrills of Mount Seymour are a great draw.

North America's top ski resort, **Whistler**, is 120km (75 miles) away, and its ski season is a long one, running from late November to the end of April and beyond, with glacier skiing in summer for passionate skiers.

Aside from skiing, other winter sports enjoyed in and around Vancouver include snowboarding, ice-skating, curling, tubing and snowshoeing. In Whistler, add dog-sledding, snowmobiling, snowcat tours and sleigh rides to the list *(for more information, see pages 184–5).*

a tree unique to British Columbia. In North Vancouver, Lynn Canyon Park is a wilderness close to civilisation, with an informative ecology centre and a suspension bridge that swings between the giant firs.

Outside the city, there are many areas of protected wilderness to explore – some of these provincial parks offer the bare minimum in the way of amenities, others have fully equipped campsites which can accommodate everything from tents to huge recreational vehicles.

Just beyond Vancouver's urban boundaries is the Cypress Provincial Park, a 3,012-hectare (7,443-acre) protected area with many well-marked trails which make it a popular spot for

> *Scuba divers need to remember that the water in these parts is cold and currents can be strong; make sure your wet suit is thick enough, or consider renting one* (see page 262).

day-trippers from the city. The further north you go, the more rugged the terrain in this park gets.

Just off Highway 99, between Squamish and Whistler, the Garibaldi Provincial Park has been a favourite since it was established in 1920. An area of close to 195,000 hectares (480,000 acres), it is a stunning wilderness of mountains, glaciers, forests, lakes and rivers. It also includes the Garibaldi Volcanic Belt, part of the Pacific Ring of Fire. The last eruption, more than 11,000 years ago, left some remarkable landmarks, such as the Barrier, a 300-metre (980-ft) high cliff created by a meeting of molten rock and glacier ice. Cinder Cone also resulted from volcanic fires, this time beneath glacial ice. The effect acted like a jelly mould, leaving the amazingly flat-topped, steep-sided cone. The park has an extensive network of clearly signed trails, with numerous campsites and recreation sites. It is also popular with mountaineers and cross-country skiers, and

Whistler and Blackcomb Ski Mountains are not far away.

From small parks with swimming lakes such as Alice Lake Provincial Park near Squamish to Golden Ears Provincial Park, at 62,540 hectares (almost 155,000 acres), one of the largest parks in BC, activities in all these well-cared-for environs include exceptional (and inexpensive) camping, fishing, swimming, hiking, birdwatching, canoeing, kayaking and other pursuits. For a full list of parks in the Vancouver area, their facilities and how to reach them, visit www. metrovancouver.org.

Sea kayaking and whitewater rafting

Centuries ago, First Nations of the Pacific Northwest paddled the ocean in impressive dugout canoes made of red cedar. Sitting low on the water, kayaks offer a similar experience and the chance to see seals and water birds up close. It is not difficult to master the manoeuvring of these stable craft. The best place to learn is the more urban setting of False Creek, where waters are generally calmer. On the North Shore, flanked by mountains, the finger-shaped fjord known as Indian Arm is an idyllic setting for kayaking. At the top of the inlet and just a 30-minute bus ride from downtown, both kayak and canoe rentals and lessons are available in Deep Cove.

FAR LEFT: skiing is one of British Columbia's main attractions. **ABOVE LEFT TOP:** extreme skiing at Whistler. **ABOVE LEFT BOTTOM:** kayaking off Granville Island. **RIGHT:** volleyball at sunset on Kitsilano Beach.

Whitewater river rafting is offered at various locations on the Fraser, Nahatlatch, Thompson, Green, Elaho, Birkenhead and Lillooet rivers. Strict safety regulations apply, which is reassuring in the face of such notorious rapids as the Chilliwack River's Darth Vader, Gun Barrel and Pinball *(see page 264 for operators)*.

Fishing

Most people come to Vancouver expecting to eat fish. For those who want to catch their own,

---

WHALE-WATCHING

The best place to embark on a whale-watching expedition is from Tofino on the west coast of Vancouver Island. In March and April thousands of grey whales swim past en route from the calving lagoons of Baja California to Alaska, returning south from October to December. Sightings of these and other whales including orca (also known as killer whales) are common in this area.

If you haven't time to get to Tofino, tours leave from Steveston village in Richmond *(see page 166 for transport details)*. While not guaranteed, sightings of some combination of orca, seals and Dall's porpoises are likely *(for more information, see page 263)*.

Vancouver is the jumping-off point for some of the world's finest fishing. Whether you want to fish from a boat offshore for salmon and halibut, wade wilderness streams for trout, or experience one of the province's 24,000 lakes, BC has it all. From world-class resorts offering complete packages, to rustic Forestry campsites for your tent and canoe, there are opportunities for any budget.

For the best saltwater fishing, most will head to Vancouver Island, or further north to River's Inlet or the Queen Charlotte Islands (now known as Haida Gwaii). But you can still hire a boat at False Creek or Horseshoe Bay in Vancouver and find fish while enjoying the local scenery. Trout and steelhead fishermen will head to the Chilcotin/Cariboo or the Kamloops area, but can find closer water too, heading up to Whistler or out to the Fraser Valley.

Finally, for those who want the scenery but don't care so much for the fishing, many resorts offer ecotours with the opportunity to see bears,

ABOVE: whitewater rafting near Whistler. **RIGHT TOP:** diving off Vancouver Island. **RIGHT BOTTOM:** fishing on the Fraser River. **FAR RIGHT:** there are several swimming pools in Vancouver, including the Granville Island aqua park.

eagles or killer whales – all the things wild BC has to offer.

Swimming

With so many beaches on their doorstep, sunbathing, swimming and people-watching are favourite pastimes among locals. After a vigorous hike, bike or in-line skate around the 10km (7-mile) Stanley Park seawall, head to the outdoor pool at Second Beach, overlooking English Bay.

It's an easy bus ride from downtown to Kitsilano Beach on the opposite shore of English Bay. It is a hedonistic setting, complete with adjacent, 137-metre (450ft) Kitsilano Pool overlooking the sandy beach. At almost three times the length of an Olympic pool, this is the longest pool in Canada and Vancouver's only heated outdoor saltwater pool. Following the shoreline west is a series of attractive beaches, including Jericho Beach and Spanish Banks (both on the bus route).

Further west below the cliffs of the University of British Columbia is Wreck Beach, Vancouver's notorious nude beach (where ogling clothed visitors are most unwelcome). *For more on Vancouver's beaches see pages 142–3.*

Diving and windsurfing

Scuba divers come to this world-class coastline to explore more outstanding natural beauty beneath the ocean's surface. Close to Vancouver, Cates Park in Deep Cove, Whytecliff Park near Horseshoe Bay and Porteau Cove Marine Park on Howe Sound are all recommended sites. Further afield, Vancouver Island offers even more spectacular diving. In many of these sites underwater playgrounds have been lovingly created with artificial reefs that have formed on specially sunken ships and, near Chemainus, a Boeing 737.

Back above water, windsurfing is also popular. Jericho Beach and English Bay are good for the less experienced, and there are opportunities here to rent windsurfers and wet suits and take lessons *(see page 264)*. The real pros head for the town of Squamish, 64km (40 miles) north of Vancouver, which offers some of the world's best windsurfing conditions. Cold air funnels down the Cheakamus and Squamish valleys over Howe Sound, averaging 40 knots on the water with gusts as powerful as 70 knots.

Birdwatching

Along the Fraser River, casual birders can be found strolling along the level dyke system that begins in Steveston, a village now incor-

Golf

The natural setting of Vancouver's golf courses, with a backdrop of mountains, sky and water, is hard to beat.

Closest to downtown are the University Golf Club, Langara, McCleery and Fraserview courses, which are all open to non-members and are very affordable. There are also pitch-and-putt courses at Stanley Park and Queen Elizabeth Park.

En route to Whistler, nestling on the mountainside overlooking Howe Sound, the Furry Creek course is the most scenic. In Whistler itself, three 18-hole courses are joined by an additional course in Pemberton to the north *(see page 263)*.

porated into the City of Richmond. Keen birdwatchers should head for the Reifel bird sanctuary in the heart of the Fraser River estuary, with 300 hectares (850 acres) of protected wetland. More than 280 species of birds frequent the area, including great blue herons, eagles, hawks, ducks, swans and owls. A real highlight is the snow geese that number in the tens of thousands, stopping here during the autumn migration.

Mountain trekking and climbing

At night, the lights of the three local slopes of Grouse Mountain, Cypress Bowl and Mount Seymour form a twinkling backdrop to the city. Each peak is only 30 minutes away by car. In winter they are transformed into playgrounds for a wide variety of snow sports *(see page 54)*. In summer you can hike on these same three peaks that are full of trails, some of which are wheelchair- and stroller-accessible.

For those up to a challenge, the 30km (18-mile) Howe Sound Crest Trail is the way to go. Tackling the Grouse Grind, a 2.9km (1.8-mile) hike almost straight up the gnarly face of Grouse Mountain, is a badge of courage for many Vancouverites, but don't attempt the Grind unless you are fit and prepared.

Further afield, the Highway 99 corridor from Vancouver to Whistler passes through the logging town of Squamish, "the outdoor recreation capital of Canada". Aside from being the country's windsurfing capital, and offering great hiking, mountain biking, fishing and kayaking, Squamish is also one of Canada's top rock-climbing destinations, thanks to the granite monolith known as the Stawamus Chief. Climbers from around the world flock here to tackle one of the 1,000 routes along the 652-metre (2,139ft) face of one of the world's largest free-standing rocks.

Adrenalin sports

New adrenalin sports appear with regularity on the West Coast. One of the latest is surf skiing, a more extreme version of kayaking. The sport began with the invention of special sleek kayaks used by lifeguards to break through surf. Manoeuvring the delicately balanced vessels straight into the waves is part

of the rush. The vessels are available for hire from the Deep Cove Canoe and Kayak Centre (*see page 263*).

Heli-skiing, a once-in-a-lifetime dream experience for many advanced skiers, was invented by

> *You don't have to be young and athletic to enjoy zip-trekking at Whistler. You only need to be able to walk through the forest, climb some stairs and step off into thin air above a mountain canyon.*

a British Columbian. Hans Gmoser hailed from Brunau, Austria, arriving in BC in the early 1950s. A daring mountain climber, Gmoser founded the Association of Canadian Mountain Guides in 1963, and introduced the first heli-ski tours in 1965. The audacious sport is now an international phenomenon. Established operators use Bell 212 twin-engine helicopters with skiing

from 1,371 to 1,838 metres (4,500 to 6,000ft).

Soaring and skydiving are spring-to-early-autumn activities. Soaring operates in the Fraser Valley from Hope Airport (150km/93 miles from Vancouver), which has the longest turf airfield in Canada, and from the Pemberton Soaring Centre, located north of Whistler.

Skydivers leave from the Pitt Meadows Airport (40km/25 miles from Vancouver) to float above spacious meadows with a view of Vancouver Island and the towering white-capped peak of Mount Baker in Washington State to the south. Paragliding is closer to home at Grouse Mountain, where two-person paraglides catch the high currents.

Zip-trekking is a Whistler-area sport that makes the most of the forest setting. Participants wear custom harnesses to launch themselves along a cable from a tree-top deck on Blackcomb Mountain. After soaring 610 metres (2,000ft), they land on Whistler Mountain. Passing below spectacularly at a speed of 80kmh (50mph) are the steep Whistler Valley and the white waters of Fitzsimmons Creek.

Bungee jumping is offered year-round above the Cheakamus River near Whistler, as well as near Nanaimo on Vancouver Island. ❑

FAR LEFT: the Okanagan has some wonderful horse-riding trails. **LEFT:** exploring Deep Cove by kayak. **ABOVE:** zip-trekking in Whistler.

FLORA AND FAUNA

Remarkably close to the skyscrapers and busy boulevards of the city is a vast wilderness of coastal rainforest, Alpine meadows and glacial mountains. Beneath towering canopies of red cedars and Douglas firs, black bears, coyotes and cougars roam.

orests cover almost two-thirds of the province of British Columbia, and what a vast area of trees and mountains that is – and more than 5.7 million hectares (about 14 million acres) of these forests are protected. Much of the Coast Forest Region, which runs from just south of Vancouver up to the Alaska panhandle, is uninhabited wilderness. In fact, most of BC's four million residents are concentrated in and around the cities of Vancouver and Victoria, in the province's southwestern corner. Barren mountain peaks, vast forests, mighty rivers and fertile valleys cover just about all the rest.

British Columbia has been dubbed the "Wet Coast". Annual precipitation in the Coast Mountains averages 2 metres (6½ft), as storm winds filled with moisture roll in from the Pacific, hit the mountains, rise, cool and condense into rain or snow. The resulting rainforests are lush nurs-

Native to Chile and Argentina, the monkey puzzle tree (Araucaria araucana) thrives in Vancouver – several magnificent examples dating from the 1920s provide imposing structure to older neighbourhoods.

eries for Douglas fir, western hemlock, western red cedar and Sitka spruce.

Arbutus trees, the only broadleafed evergreen trees in Canada, grow on stony ridges along the

water's edge. The red-brown, papery peeling bark of the arbutus makes it one of the easiest coastal trees to identify. Lighthouse Park in West Vancouver is one of the best places to encounter a variety of these magnificent coastal trees. The park's old-growth forest includes giant Douglas firs, western red cedar, contorted shore pines, hemlocks and arbutus *(for more about provincial parks, see pages 54–5).*

Gold rushes

Two major gold rushes in the mid-19th century brought thousands to British Columbia seeking their fortunes. But it was the primeval forests of the coast that drew settlers, who honed their

LEFT: British Columbia's spectacular landscape.
RIGHT: old-growth forest, Vancouver Island.

years later Stanley Park was a reality, located on a peninsula jutting out into Burrard Inlet. Until then, Musqueam and Squamish aboriginal people had lived there in the village of Khwaykhway. Park development effectively put an end to their habitation. The park had already been logged, but a few old-growth trees remained. The Hollow Tree, a huge western red cedar tree trunk with a girth of 18 metres (60ft), is a remnant of its massive rainforest ancestors. Other old-growth trees, including Douglas firs, hug Beaver Lake in the interior of the 405-hectare (1,000-acre) enclave.

Garden city

It's ironic that two of Vancouver's most popular public gardens were built with donations from powerful lumber barons. Queen Elizabeth Park's Bloedel Floral Conservatory was financed by lumber magnate Prentice Bloedel, who had a passion for gardening. The Van Dusen Botanical Garden was funded by Whitford Julian Van Dusen, another lumber tycoon and philanthropist.

Queen Elizabeth Park, built on Little Mountain, the highest point in Vancouver at 167 metres (505ft) above sea level, offers splendid panoramic views. The basalt hill began life as a quarry for Vancouver's growing road system. In 1929, the Vancouver Park Board began work on the abandoned 52-hectare (130-acre) site. Over the years, it has been transformed into a lovely sloping park dotted with examples of every native Canadian tree and many international ones. Trails weave through the old quarries past waterfalls and grottoes filled with blooms. At the top of the hill stands the Bloedel Floral Conservatory, opened in 1969. Inside the climate-controlled triodetic glass dome are over 500 varieties of exotic plants and tropical flowers and more than 100 free-flying birds.

axes and ran their steam donkeys to pull the massive old-growth forest logs to the ocean for transport to all corners of the globe.

Vancouver's founders recognised the area's unique natural beauty even as they exploited its bountiful forests. On 13 June 1886, the fledgling city burnt down in what is known as the "Great Fire". Given the rare opportunity to start over, land surveyor and alderman Lauchlan Alexander Hamilton suggested the creation of a large park on the outskirts of the city. Three

THE MIGHTY CEDAR

The cedar, both western red and yellow varieties, is the traditional wood of choice for coastal First Nations people. This giant tree was originally used to build huge longhouses for communal families. It was shaped into canoes for whale hunting, travelling and raiding. Everyday objects such as storage boxes were made from cedar, then painted with curved forms to become objects of beauty and refinement. Cedar is also the preferred material for totem poles and masks. Some carved poles tell family history, others commemorate respected individuals. A collection of old and new poles is proudly displayed at Stanley Park's Brockton Oval.

The Van Dusen Botanical Garden is located on a former golf course built over an early city water reservoir. After the golf course closed in the 1960s and the reservoir was abandoned and sealed in the 1970s, the site was transformed into a world-renowned botanical garden. Its 22 hectares (54 acres) are planted with more than 7,500 varieties of flowers, shrubs and trees. Spring's blossoming trees and flowers include camellias, rhododendrons, magnolias, Pacific dogwood and glorious Japanese cherries (more than 17,000 such trees have been planted throughout the city). Seasonal displays continue through to winter's bursts of shiny green holly dotted with red berries.

Further afield but easily accessible via the limited-stop No. 99 city bus, the University of British Columbia (UBC) on Point Grey comprises a wealth of parks and gardens. British Columbia's oldest university, established in 1915, takes pride in having one of the most beautiful campuses in Canada. The dense forests of UBC's Pacific Spirit Regional Park are crisscrossed with trails that transport you back to a time when forests dominated the West Coast. The park even includes a bog with its own world of wetland wonders such as frogs and bog cranberries.

Many gardens dot the UBC landscape. Overlooking the Pacific Ocean, the picturesque Rose Garden features some 300 varieties. Nearby is the Nitobe Memorial Garden, designed by outstanding Japanese landscape architect Kannosouke Mori to feature native trees and shrubs. Another prominent area is the UBC Botanical Garden and Centre for Plant Research. This 28-hectare (70-acre) site is home to rare and unusual plants and includes a stunning rhododendron grove.

FAR LEFT: giant red cedar tree, Stanley Park. **LEFT:** Van Dusen Botanical Garden has plant species from all over the world. **ABOVE:** the beautifully landscaped Queen Elizabeth Park. **RIGHT:** Stanley Park contains an estimated half a million trees.

canneries. Salmon was so plentiful that it was unimaginable that they would ever disappear. Yet they almost did. Coastal salmon are now struggling to recover from the past's greedy harvesting.

Nevertheless, the Fraser's estuary and delta are marvellous resources that continue to nourish the countless animals and plants thriving where fresh water meets salt water. Trails along the river in Vancouver, Richmond and further inland provide opportunities to see beaver, muskrat, river otter, deer, black bear, mink, red fox, skunk, coyote, raccoon, opossum and squirrels. More than 1 million migratory birds stop over here along the Pacific flyway, resulting in the largest concentration of wintering waterfowl and shorebirds in Canada. Geese, ducks, shorebirds and songbirds nest in the tidal flats, marshes and forests along the river banks. Overhead, bald eagles, marsh hawks and other raptors circle their prey.

The river feeds into the Pacific which counts chum, chinook and coho salmon, orca (killer) whales, grey whales, octopus, seals and sea lions among its treasures. ❑

The Fraser River

The great Fraser River is the backbone of British Columbia. Originating in Mount Robson Provincial Park, the river meets the sea after a journey of 1,375km (854 miles) at its estuary in Vancouver, where it merges with the Pacific Ocean among vast wetlands. The Fraser is the largest salmon river in the world, notable for its sockeye runs. In the late 19th century, Steveston, the town at the mouth of the river *(see page 165)*, was awash with thriving salmon

---

FESTIVAL OF EAGLES

Bald eagles are revered by First Nations people, who admire their skills of sight and flight. Nearly half of the world's bald eagles make their home in British Columbia. Few sights are as powerful as these huge birds of prey nesting, roosting or diving for salmon along the Squamish River near Brackendale, 10km (6 miles) north of Squamish. Bald eagles boast a wingspan that can exceed 2 metres (6½ft). Their size and distinctive white head and tail feathers make them easy to spot.

Since 1985, volunteers have gathered in Brackendale every January to count the feathered multitudes. The Brackendale Winter Eagle Festival and Count attracts

devotees from around the world armed with binoculars and cameras. Hundreds of birds roost in eyries in the cottonwood trees along the river. Snowcapped Mount Garibaldi, at 2,678 metres (8,786ft), acts as a backdrop, adding to the grandeur of the scene.

Eagle numbers are highest during January and February, but they can be seen in smaller numbers year-round. Guided walks and kayak tours in the Squamish area are a great way to learn about eagles and other flora and fauna. River kayaking reveals seals, herons, cormorants and trumpeter swans. Golden eagles are sometimes seen among the bald eagle congregation.

Whistler's Wild Animals

One of the great attractions of Vancouver is that you don't have to travel far from the city to find all kinds of wildlife.

Forty years ago the Whistler Valley consisted of a few fly-fishing lodges and isolated homesteads with an unpaved highway cutting beneath the high, glaciated mountains. Today Whistler is a four-season resort with cobbled streets, shops, restaurants and countless hotels, lodges and condominiums.

The vast wilderness in which this top resort is set, however, has remained relatively unchanged. Coastal hemlock and cedar forests share the rugged mountains with Alpine meadows – this is the typical habitat of the black bear. Some 50 bears make their home in the old-growth forests of Whistler and Blackcomb mountains. Between May and July, they are often seen on the slopes, feeding on the grass growing on the open ski runs. They also wander through high-elevation timber-shrub forests foraging for huckleberries, red raspberries and insect larvae. From August to October, bears eat voraciously, fattening up for winter hibernation.

Whistler campaigns to limit bear and human interaction and locals understand that "a fed bear is a dead bear". Simple initiatives like introducing bear-proof garbage bins have greatly reduced the number of bears that must be destroyed.

Year-round residents

Bears are not alone in the Whistler area. They have a profusion of other birds and animals for company. In April, trumpeter swans stop over on their migration north, resting on Green Lake, while hummingbirds return from wintering in South America. Snows melt in May, and mountain goats can be seen on the south face of

Wedge Mountain in the Black Tusk Nature Conservancy. In northern areas, moose graze along shorelines.

Birdwatchers are likely to see eagles, hawks, warblers, woodpeckers, osprey and great blue herons. Grebes, geese and beaver can be spotted along the romantically named River of Golden Dreams.

In the summer months, deer, coyote and cougar roam the area. Smaller mammals include minks, weasels, squirrels, pikas and marmots. On the Gates and Birkenhead rivers north of Whistler, red Pacific sockeye salmon make their way upriver to spawn. In September, the salmon runs are at their peak. By late Novem-

ber, bald eagles return to Brackendale (*see box on opposite page*), south of Whistler, to feast on chum salmon.

Protecting nature is important to the region. Environmental and conservation groups play a vital role in managing growth and sustainable development along the Sea to Sky Highway 99 corridor to Whistler and beyond. ❑

FAR LEFT: a bald eagle catches a fish. **LEFT:** coyote pups. **RIGHT:** black bear.

FOOD AND WINE

Vancouver is heaven for food-lovers. A happy combination of circumstances makes it home to a tremendous variety of superb cuisine at relatively affordable prices.

people here have embraced what is good from everywhere else, improving it with local ingredients and often imparting a West Coast imprint on the recipes. Vancouver is about variety – even in shopping malls, fast-food choices are far more extensive and exotic than the usual hamburger stall or sandwich place.

British settlers set the tone, bringing their recipes along. But since the first settlers made Vancouver their home almost 125 years ago, countless waves of newcomers have overwritten the food template, easing their own recipes and approaches to food into the mainstream. Italian and Chinese restaurants that first opened to serve homesick immigrants are now so much a part of the culture that the food is a real fusion of their original "home cooking" and the Canadian palate. Spaghetti Bolognese and chop suey are more Canadian than anything else, but some hint of the old country still shines through.

Food as lifestyle

The success of these "new immigrant" restaurants has led to a second eruption of eateries, looking to emulate the best of what is being done today in the old country, while taking advantage of the fresh produce British Columbia has to offer – all this, while aiming to please a discerning public.

Vancouverites are very demanding when it comes to eating. Food is lifestyle, and the West Coast lifestyle translates into time to sit and have coffee with friends *(see panel, page 69)*, time to devote a day to cooking a meal. The Canadian organic food movement is deeply rooted in this province; food stores with a

Some people visit Vancouver on the strength of the food alone. Ethnic diversity has spawned a cosmopolitan city where there is room for pretty much every kind of food, and the quality is exceptionally high. During a typical week of eating in Vancouver, it would be easy to travel around the world with tuna tataki (Japan), fettucine alle vongole (Italy), prawn vindaloo (Indian), dim sum (Chinese), lamb souvlaki (Greek), pho (Vietnamese) and *coq au vin* (French). For the less adventurous, keen on having something "Canadian", salmon, halibut and even buffalo burgers are almost as common as the regular kind.

There is no standard Canadian food, so

In addition to participating in the "Ocean Wise" sustainable seafood programme, many restaurants belong to "Green Table", committing to "innovative solutions that measurably reduce the impact we have on our world."

focus on organic and "green" are a huge success here, with Choices, Capers and Whole Foods all competing for consumer dollars. Mainstream supermarkets have followed suit, understanding that people here want to know where their food comes from, and many are willing to pay a significant premium for that knowledge.

Although there are very few French-speaking inhabitants in Vancouver, it's one nationality that is over-represented in the restaurant industry. Tradition is important, and restaurant names like Le Crocodile and Le Gavroche may seem familiar to those who follow Michelin stars. From the first, expect excellent Alsatian fare; from the latter, enjoy one of the continent's best wine cellars, with a selection that includes everything from vintage Bordeaux to New World cult wines, and a lot of good drinking in between. The array of French restaurants (including Le Pied à Terre, Le Mistral, Pastis and La Régalade) will satisfy any cravings for traditional as well as innovative French cuisine.

The fine distinction between French, continental and contemporary cuisine is navigated quite comfortably by a number of outstanding upper-end restaurants, with proprietors who focus on the ingredients to produce beautiful and tasty, if sometimes small, plates. While the food may be world-class, the prices aren't – coming from New York or Paris, the value here is undeniable. Whether it is John Bishop's eponymous restaurant along an unprepossessing section of West 4th Avenue in Kitsilano, Market in the new Shangri-La Hotel downtown, or Fraiche in West Vancouver, the obsession with quality is apparent. Getting a reservation may be a challenge – if a phone call brings a "sorry, no room", it may be worth using the services of the hotel concierge. They often have access to the few tables kept free for emergencies.

LEFT: fresh ocean fish, like this pan-roasted wild BC halibut, is the highlight of many a menu. **ABOVE:** the busy kitchen of Yaletown's popular Blue Water Café.

Asian food

It's a phrase that conjures up countless images – in Vancouver, they are jumbled and confusing, as there are so many good choices. Different provinces of China have completely different styles of food (hot and spicy, more or less meat, exquisite use of tofu to create amazing vegetarian dishes), and restaurants range from the ultra-formal Imperial (in a beautiful Art Deco building) to the quick and simple in strip malls all over the city. Other Asian cuisines include Thai, Japanese,

Vietnamese, Korean, Malaysian and Philippine.

Chinese dim sum is a bit like tapas – a chance to try many dishes without investing too much in the mysterious. A safe strategy is to choose a restaurant that still brings the food around on trolleys to patrons. That way, even though you don't know what something is called, if it looks appetising, you can give it a try. On this occasion, there is a definite advantage to sitting near the kitchen – you can grab the most appealing baskets while they are still piping hot.

Fish and seafood

Salmon and other West Coast seafood is the type of food most sought out by tourists. If British Columbia has a speciality, then it is ultra-fresh wild salmon. It can be sublime when properly prepared, and disappointing if overcooked.

This is one type of meal where choosing the restaurant carefully is worthwhile, as it is so easy

to produce mediocre salmon. Seek out a restaurant known for its seafood, and confirm that the salmon is wild, not farmed. Don't ignore some of the other fabulous offerings from the Pacific Ocean, including halibut, as well as oysters and crab. Many restaurants participate in "Ocean Wise", an initiative started in 2004 by the Vancouver Aquarium to encourage restaurants and food stores to shift to more sustainable seafood.

For the vegetarian, many restaurants automatically ensure they have three or four meat-free selections. Allergies? Mainstream restaurants and holes-in-the-wall alike are comfortable with enquiries about wheat, dairy, egg, nuts and other common allergens. Of course, not every restaurant is compliant, but having special dietary requirements is rarely a problem.

Neighbourhoods and streets

Wonderful neighbourhoods that are well suited to wandering, shopping and eating are easily accessible by public transport. There are many, but these four offer a good sampling.

Both sides of Denman Street, in the West End, are jammed with restaurants, from casual places to pick up a bite to take to the beach at nearby English Bay, to more formal places for a full meal. Most stay open late along this strip.

To understand the obsession with fresh and local, a visit to Granville Island and its wonderful market will bring it into focus. The speciality stalls offer an amazing selection of foodstuffs – at Oyama Sausage, organic bison carpaccio sits beside pâtés of every description, while across the way, Duso's has over a dozen types of fresh pasta.

Along Main Street from Broadway south past King Edward, a full day can be devoted to wandering in and out of vintage clothing stores and antique shops, stopping along the way for coffee, then for a Jamaican lunch at The Reef, and finally at The Main for a Greek dinner and live music.

Yaletown is where the cool people hang out. The concentration of excellent restaurants in this hip district will make choosing a place difficult. Most have good websites, so planning in advance is not a problem. ❑

COFFEE CULTURE

Like its American cousin Seattle, Vancouver has embraced coffee in all its forms. The cafés along Commercial Drive still cater to the Italian immigrants who arrived 40 years ago, and similar spots on West Broadway serve as meeting places for their Greek counterparts. But the real eye-opener is the number of coffee shops here. The ubiquitous Starbucks will feed a habit, but seek out the smaller chains and the independents – Parallel 49, Wicked Café, Agro Café and the Elysian Room are a few. Free wireless is pretty much *de rigueur* in Vancouver, so you won't have any trouble staying connected, but may have to fight with the budding novelists for power outlets.

FAR LEFT: Blasted Church vineyard. **LEFT:** succulent beef and BC prawns. **ABOVE AND RIGHT:** Granville Market.

PLACES

A detailed guide to Vancouver and its surroundings,
with the principal sites numbered and clearly
cross-referenced to the maps.

The heart of Vancouver is the peninsula between Stanley Park and the
eastern end of False Creek. It encompasses the site of the city's first muddy
streets in Gastown and areas of surprisingly different character: the downtown shopping streets of Robson, Howe and Granville, the trendily revived
warehouse district of Yaletown, the quiet residential
streets of West End, the clusters of tower blocks overlooking the water at both Coal Harbour and False Creek, and
the commercial buildings northwest of Georgia.

Because the grid-pattern streets are so long, their character can change dramatically: Nelson Street, for example,
starts off as a quiet, tree-lined street and morphs into a hive
of retail commerce. Equally their length makes it necessary to know at which point along the street you are, or
want to be: the best way to make it obvious you're not
from Vancouver is to use "Street" when you're asking for
directions; locals simply refer to Robson, or 21st and Dunbar, which means 21st Avenue off Dunbar Street.

Many of Vancouver's districts still have a strong neighbourhood feel, with
residents' and business associations working to foster a sense of community
and improve amenities. Some areas owe their origins to waves of immigration, most obviously Chinatown, but also the district now known as Commercial Drive ("the Drive"), still referred to as Little Italy. Today it is more
cosmopolitan, with Portuguese, Spanish and Latin American shops and restaurants. More recently, the name Punjabi Market has been given to an area
populated by a community that has its origins in the Punjab.

Many visitors never venture much beyond the downtown core and Kitsilano. It would be absurd to suggest that you would miss the best of Vancouver by not exploring further afield, but there are some jewels that it would
be a shame to miss: Steveston for anyone with a love of the sea and boats;
New Westminster (briefly BC's capital), Burnaby and Fort Langley for those
interested in architecture and social history; North and West Vancouver's
mountain trails for walkers and winter sports aficionados; Delta and Burns
Bog for natural historians.   ❑

PRECEDING PAGES: the Vancouver Convention and Exhibition Centre and downtown
Vancouver by night; Queen Elizabeth Park. **LEFT:** totem poles in Stanley Park.
RIGHT: flower stall on Robson Street, Vancouver's most famous shopping street.

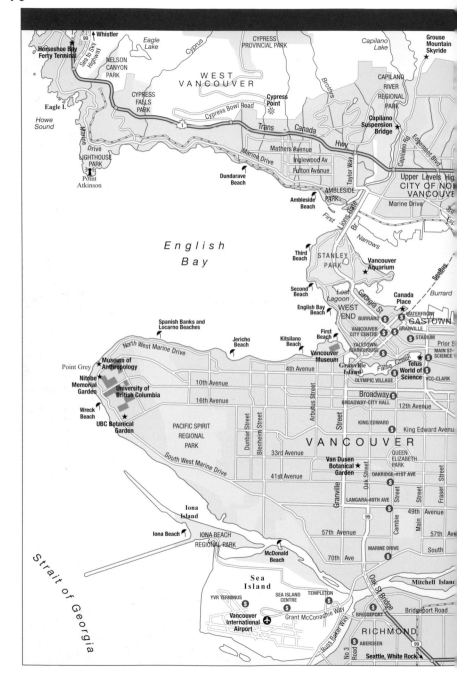

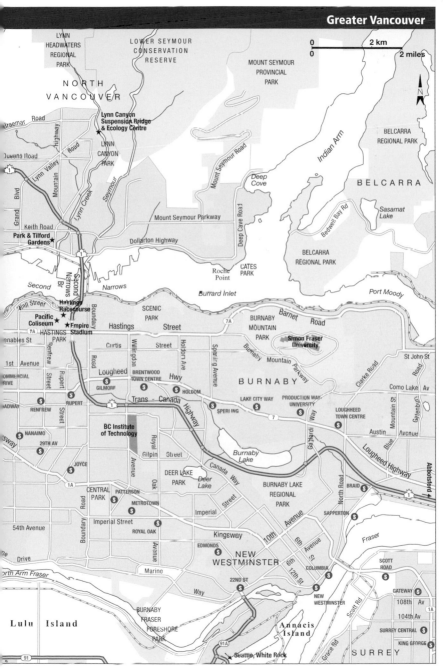

LYNN HEADWATERS REGIONAL PARK

LOWER SEYMOUR CONSERVATION RESERVE

MOUNT SEYMOUR PROVINCIAL PARK

NORTH VANCOUVER

BELCARRA REGIONAL PARK

Braemar Road

Lynn Canyon Suspension Bridge & Ecology Centre

Indian Arm

BELCARRA

Queens Road

LYNN CANYON PARK

Lynn Valley

Mountain Highway

Road

Lynn Creek

Seymour

Mount Seymour Road

Deep Cove

Sasamat Lake

Bedwell Bay Rd

Grand Blvd

Keith Road

Mount Seymour Parkway

Deep Cove Road

Park & Tilford Gardens

Dollarton Highway

Roche Point

CATES PARK

BELCARRA REGIONAL PARK

Second Narrows Br

Second

Narrows

Burrard Inlet

Port Moody

Hall Street

Hastings Racecourse

SCENIC PARK

Barnet Road

Pacific Coliseum

Empire Stadium

Boundary

Hastings Street

7A

BURNABY MOUNTAIN PARK

Simon Fraser University

Venables St

HASTINGS PARK

TA

Curtis Street

Willingdon

Holdom Ave

Sperling Avenue

Burnaby Mountain Parkway

St John St

1st Avenue

COMMERCIAL DRIVE

Renfrew Street

Road

Lougheed Hwy

BRENTWOOD TOWN CENTRE

HOLDOM

BURNABY

Clarke Road

Como Lake Av

Rupert Street

GILMORE

Trans - Canada Highway

LAKE CITY WAY

PRODUCTION WAY-UNIVERSITY

LOUGHEED TOWN CENTRE

Mountain St

Gaglardi

BROADWAY

RENFREW

RUPERT

SPERLING

7

Way

Austin Avenue

NANAIMO

29TH AV

BC Institute of Technology

Royal

Gilpin Street

Canada Way

Burnaby Lake

Blue Mountain St

Lougheed Highway

Gatensbury

Abbotsford

JOYCE

Oak

Avenue

DEER LAKE PARK

Deer Lake

BURNABY LAKE REGIONAL PARK

North Road

BRAID

1

1A

CENTRAL PARK

PATTERSON

METROTOWN

Imperial

SAPPERTON

54th Avenue

Boundary Road

Imperial Street

ROYAL OAK

Kingsway

10th Avenue

6th Avenue

Fraser

SCOTT ROAD

North Arm Fraser

Avenue

EDMONDS

NEW WESTMINSTER

6th Ave

12th St

COLUMBIA

GATEWAY

Marine

22ND ST

NEW WESTMINSTER

Scott Rd

108th Av

104th Av

1A

Drive

Way

BURNABY FRASER FORESHORE PARK

SURREY CENTRAL

Lulu Island

Annacis Island

Grace Rd

KING GEORGE

91

91A

Seattle, White Rock

SURREY

0 2 km
0 2 miles

N

MIDTOWN AND WEST END

Many of Vancouver's main sights are concentrated
in this area, and all are within walking distance
of each other: from the harbour's epicentre,
Canada Place, via the city's premier art gallery,
to the appealing West End neighbourhood
and the city's busiest shopping street.

Main Attractions

CANADA PLACE AND
    CONVENTION CENTRE
VANCOUVER ART GALLERY
ROEDDE HOUSE
ROBSON STREET SHOPPING

Maps and Listings

MAP OF MIDTOWN AND
    WEST END, PAGE 80
SHOPPING, PAGE 90
RESTAURANTS, BARS AND
    CAFÉS, PAGES 92–3
ACCOMMODATION, PAGES
    250–2

The sea and residential density
are the two qualities that distinguish Vancouver from Canada's
other cities. Nowhere in downtown
Vancouver is very far from the shoreline, and the gentle hill on which it is
built means that water is often part of
the view. The conscious policy to foster a much higher density of population close to the central business
district has helped to make Vancouver one of the most attractive and
liveable cities in the world.

The centre does not become a
ghost town once the office and service industry workers have gone home,
because home for at least some of
them is within walking or cycling
distance of work. They live in everything from tiny bachelor apartments
to luxurious penthouses, enjoying
the lifestyle of living and working
in the centre of the action, avoiding
the painful commutes of their col-
leagues who must make the trek over
the Port Mann or Lions Gate Bridge
every day.

This vibrancy is certainly helped
by the location of so many hotels in
the downtown area, which fosters the
city's exceptional restaurant scene.
Burgeoning demand for city-centre
property and the regeneration policies

of the city have combined to enlarge
the downtown area into Yaletown and
even Gastown (see pages 97–109). But
the office district remains largely west
of Granville, with a forest of glass-clad
towers where firs and cedars once
grew. It's hard to credit that it is less
than 150 years since the land herea-
bouts was going for $1–2 an acre.

Pacific gateway

In 1862 three Englishmen bought a
chunk of land corresponding roughly
to today's West End. One of them, a

LEFT: cruise ship docked at Canada Place.
RIGHT: a bustling corner of Denman Street.

Midtown and West End

N

500 m
500 yds
0
0

SeaBus Route

Burrard Inlet

Deadman's Island

Coal Harbour

1 Harbour

STANLEY PARK

North Vancouver, West Vancouver, Whistler

Lost Lagoon Drive

Park Lane

English Bay Beach

Sylvia Hotel 15

Beach Avenue

Inukshuk Statue

First Beach (Sunset Beach)

VANIER PARK

Vancouver Museum & H R MacMillan Space Centre

Vancouver Aquatic Centre 17

Gabriola Mansion

14

Denman Place Mall

Fire Hall No. 6 West End

West End Community Centre

NELSON PARK

Lane Cottage

Roedde House Museum 16

Robson Public Market

WEST END

Watson House

St Paul's Hospital 11

Pendrell St

Barclay St

Haro Street

Robson Street

Comox Street

Nelson Street

Pendrell Street

Davie Street

Burnaby Street

Harwood Street

Pacific Street

Beach Avenue

Thurlow Street

Bute Street

Jervis Street

Broughton Street

Nicola Street

Cardero Street

Bidwell Street

Chilco Street

Gilford Street

Denman Street

Westin Bayshore Hotel

MARINA SQUARE

Bayshore

CARDERO PARK

Georgia Street

Alberni Street

Robson Street 19

Haro Park Centre

Pacific Palisades Hotel

Manhattan Apartments

Winchester

Blue Horizon Hotel

Abbott House 18

St Andrew's-Wesley Church 13

Sutton Place Hotel

Sheraton Vancouver Wall Centre Hotel 12

Law Courts 8

Wedgewood Hotel 6

Vancouver Art Gallery 9

Hotel Georgia 7

Christ Church Cathedral

Fairmont Hotel Vancouver

Hyatt Regency Hotel

Robson Square

Commodore Ballroom

Orpheum Theatre

Vogue Cinema

Pacific Centre

Hudson's Bay Company Department Store 10

Centre for Performing Arts

Public Library

Library Square

Queen Elizabeth Theatre

Post Office

Georgian Court Hotel

former Bank of Nova Scotia

YALETOWN

Richmond

Richards on Richards

Helmcken St

Nelson Street

Smithe Street

Richards Street

Homer Street

Mainland St

Hamilton St

Cambie Street

Beatty Street

BC Place Stadium

BC Sports Hall of Fame & Museum

Expo Boulevard

Pacific Boulevard

ANDY LIVINGSTON PARK

General Motors Place Stadium

STADIUM

Regiment Square

Drill Hall and Armoury

Dunsmuir St

Victoria Square

Vancouver Community College

Sun Tower Building

London Building

Beaux Arts Building

Rogers Building

Royal Bank's HQ

St Regis Hotel

Granville

Seymour

Pender

Dominion Trust Building

Edgett Building

Steam Clock

GASTOWN

Water St

Cordova St

Abbott St

Cambie St

Hudson House

The Landing

Waterfront Station

Waterfront Centre Hotel

The Vancouver Lookout

Harbour Centre

Sinclair Centre 3

Pan Pacific Vancouver Hotel

World Trade Centre

Canada Place

Vancouver Convention & Exhibition Centre 2

IMAX Cinema

SeaBus Terminal

Waterfront Road West

HARBOUR GREEN PARK

Harbor Air Seaplane Terminal

Marina

Vancouver Convention and Exhibition Centre Extension

Marine Building 5

Vancouver Club

Canada Place Way

Hastings Street

Pender Street

Cordova Street

Howe St

Hornby St

Burrard Street

Thurlow Street

Bute Street

Melville

Alberni St

Evanleigh St

DOWNTOWN

Hastings Street West

Pender Street West

Dunsmuir Street

potter called John Morton from York-shire, tried his hand at making bricks but found he was too distant from the only good market at New West-minster to make a profit. The "three greenhorns", as they were dubbed, talked of creating a city comparable to Liverpool, but for two decades that looked a forlorn hope.

All that changed with the arrival of the Canadian Pacific Railway at Port Moody in 1886, a momentous year in which Vancouver was both incorporated and consumed by fire *(see page 39)*. The CPR's first land commissioner, Lauchlan Hamilton, had the task of laying out the streets in the downtown peninsula, which had been granted to the company in exchange for building the transcon-tinental railway. The railway opened its terminus on the waterfront at the end of Howe Street on 23 May 1887, and within a week a ship sailed in laden with silks and teas bound for London, heralding Vancouver's role as a gateway to Pacific trade.

Coal Harbour

Looking at the affluent surroundings of **Coal Harbour ❶** today, with its yacht and rowing clubs and multi-million-dollar apartments, it is a world away from the image conjured by its name, bestowed simply because a thin seam of coal was found here, the site of Vancouver's first pier. Its later suitability as a landing place for seaplanes was anticipated in March 1919 when the first international air mail service in North America took off for Seattle. Its pilot was one Wil-liam E. Boeing, president of the epon-ymous aircraft company based in neighbouring Washington State. The sight of seaplanes gliding gracefully in and out of the harbour, against a backdrop of shimmering glass towers on one side and mountains and pines on the other, captures the essence of Vancouver's character.

The marina at Coal Harbour ech-oes False Creek *(see pages 124–30)* as a favoured mooring for yachts and cabin cruisers, as well as offering a

ABOVE: a floatplane coming in to land at Coal Harbour.
BELOW: children playing in a newly laid-out park, part of the Coal Harbour district redevelopment.

variety of day cruises. As part of the area's redevelopment along Burrard Inlet as far as Canada Place, a linear park includes segregated cycle and footpaths through landscaped areas with numerous places to sit and watch the constant activity on the water.

Canada Place and Waterfront

Built out into Burrard Inlet, Canada Place stands on the site of Pier B-C, which opened in 1927 as the terminal for Canadian Pacific's rapidly growing trade with the Orient. Here millions of dollars of teas, spices and silks were unloaded and transferred to waiting trains *(see panel, below)*.

The present pier was built for the **Vancouver Convention and Exhibition Centre ❷**, which opened in 1986 as a showcase pavilion for Expo '86. Because the building was also designed to become a cruise-ship terminal, it was given a strongly nautical feel with its five brilliant white sails made of Teflon-coated fibreglass and the sense as you walk around it of promenading the deck of a liner. It's a good vantage point from which to watch the busy

ABOVE: seaplanes are common here, but for most visitors, a flight in one of these tiny, noisy craft will be a new experience. **BELOW:** freight trains at Waterfront Station.

water- and air-borne traffic. The 2009 convention centre expansion was constructed to LEED (Leadership in Energy and Environmental Design) gold standards and features a living roof, seawater heating and cooling, on-site water treatment and a fish habitat built into the foundation.

Cruise ships dock on the eastern flank, and just beyond, backing on to the main station, is the busy SeaBus terminal, where ferries connecting downtown and North Vancouver dock *(see page 246 for details of ferry services)*. The western flank of Canada Place is taken up by the seaplane terminal *(see page 244)*.

As well as the convention centre, the Canada Place complex contains the **World Trade Centre** and, rising above it all, the impressive **Pan Pacific Vancouver Hotel** – one of the city's most luxurious (and expensive) hotels, with panoramic views from its rooms.

Other than a yard full of freight trains, the only reminder of the once dominant presence of the railway along the shoreline is **Waterfront Station ❸**, which has become the

The Silk Train

No regular train on the Canadian Pacific Railway had higher priority than the famous silk trains that whistled their way across Canada with only guarded stops for locomotive changes and to take on water. Even express passenger trains were held to allow unimpeded passage for these prestigious trains. At the time accounting for 40 percent of Japan's exports, silk was a perishable commodity subject to fluctuating prices, so attention was focused on getting it off the boat and to its destination, usually the National Silk Exchange in New York. The apogee of the silk trains was the 1920s, with the opening of a shorter route via the Niagara Falls Bridge.

principal interchange between all SkyTrain lines, the West Coast Express (a commuter train to cities east of Vancouver) and the SeaBus. Inside the classical Beaux Arts-style CPR station, which was built in 1914, part of the public area is decorated with 16 paintings of landscapes that can be seen from a transcontinental train journey through the Rockies.

Almost opposite Waterfront Station at 750 Cordova Street is the **Sinclair Centre ❹**, an imaginative amalgam of four period buildings into a single retail and office centre. On the southeast corner is the former Beaux Arts post office and clock tower of 1905–10 which was the main post office until 1958. On display in the public area is the bronze bell which used to be on the roof, and the mechanism of the clock – both manufactured in England.

In the southwest corner is the 1908–11 building named after R.V. Winch, who made a fortune in the salmon-canning industry. The **Cus-toms and Excise Building** (1911–13) occupies the northwest corner, and the **Federal Building** (1937) – one of the city's few surviving Art Deco buildings – the northeast corner.

Established in 1889, the elite **Vancouver Club** (tel: 604 685 9321; www.vancouverclub.ca) occupies an elegant 1913 building at 915 West Hastings Street. Its lovely entrance facade is frequently used as a film location.

Art Deco treasure

Still in the vicinity of Canada Place, the **Marine Building ❺** (355 Burrard Street on Hastings) is an outstanding example of Art Deco and one of Vancouver's treasures. Sir John Betjeman, acclaimed British commentator on architecture, even thought it the best Art Deco office building in the world. Panelled terracotta vignettes of transport – ships, trains and airships – form a band around the building. Step through the seashell-encrusted brass surround of the revolving doors into the entrance lobby and admire

ABOVE: Canada Place.
BELOW: outside the World Trade Centre.

ABOVE AND BELOW: the splendid entranceway of the Marine Building. At 25 storeys and 97.8 metres (321ft), it was the tallest building in the British Empire when it opened in 1930, and had the fastest elevators outside New York.

the ships' prows forming lights above the lifts, the marble floor incorporating the 12 signs of the zodiac and the mosaic surrounds to the five lifts.

The building was designed to put Vancouver on the map and exploit its growing importance as a port following the opening of the Panama Canal in 1914. Construction began on 14 March 1929, and it was formally opened just 19 months later, on 7 October 1930, by which time the world was in recession and only four floors were let. In 1933 it was bought by the Guinness family for $900,000; it had cost $2.3 million. A.J. Taylor was put in charge of the building, and he and his wife lived in the two-storey, three-level penthouse. Unfortunately his wife was afraid of heights and he had to abandon his eyrie, which was subsequently let to a woman who kept a Shetland pony on the balcony.

West Georgia

One of the grandest and best-loved buildings in the city is **Fairmont**

Hotel Vancouver ⑥ (900 West Georgia Street, at Burrard Street). Construction began in 1928, to replace the Canadian Pacific's second Hotel Vancouver, which it had built in 1916 with several ballrooms and a glassed roof garden. The new hotel was to be 17 storeys high at 111 metres (364ft). However, construction was suspended when the Depression affected trade and only resumed in expectation of the royal visit of King George VI and Queen Elizabeth in 1939. In common with CPR's other grand hotels across the country, it was a distinctive pastiche of French and Scottish castles with a steeply pitched copper roof and gabled dormers.

The rush to complete the hotel for the royal visit was needless, as the royal couple did not stay the night, arriving at the CPR station in the morning and embarking for Victoria the same afternoon. Grand as the Royal Suite was with its 90-sq-metre (972-sq-ft) reception room (since divided), perhaps even more remarkable is the Lieutenant-Governor's Suite; its Art Deco interiors have remained unchanged since 1939. It was Vancouver's tallest building until 1957.

Opposite the hotel is **Christ Church Cathedral** ❼ (tel: 604 682 3848; www.cathedral.vancouver.bc.ca), the oldest church building in Vancouver. This Gothic Revival sandstone building with narrow arched windows and hammerbeam truss roof was built in 1889–95. It became a cathedral in 1929 as the seat of the Anglican diocese of New Westminster. Its atmospheric interior has been greatly enhanced by restoration schemes in which the cedar ceiling and Douglas fir floor were renovated. Additional lighting supplements the striking 1930s lanterns installed along the nave and choir.

Among the many stained-glass windows is a depiction of Captain James Cook in remembrance of his role in opening up the West Coast, and there is a wall plaque to Henry John Cambie (1836–1928), who was born in Tipperary and died in Vancouver. A founder of Christ Church,

he is remembered as an explorer, surveyor and engineer and "the last and one of the greatest of the pathfinders of the CPR". Cambie Street was named after him. The church hosts frequent concerts.

Hornby and Howe

The main feature of these streets is the complex formed by the Law Courts and the Vancouver Art Gallery, with Robson Square sandwiched between them. These three city blocks are bounded by Hornby Street to the north and Howe Street to the south.

The seven-storey **Law Courts** ❽ (1979) were designed by award-winning architect Arthur Erickson, the creative force behind many of the city's landmark buildings, who is famous for his love of concrete. The building is distinguished by its vast sloping glass roof, which shelters 35 court rooms. Outside, copious amounts of greenery and waterfalls soften the concrete. Government and university offices also occupy some buildings, and the stepped lower sections are a favourite place for alfresco picnic lunches on weekdays and

ABOVE: the Law Court building accommodates 35 courtrooms, including two that were specially designed for complex commercial cases.
BELOW: the Fairmont Hotel Vancouver.

Hotel Vancouver

When the CPR built its first hotel immediately after the Great Fire of 1886, it chose the highest spot at 43 metres (140ft) above sea level, thereby helping to move the embryonic city's centre inland. Even there, "on quiet nights, the creak of ships at anchor can be heard". There have been three Hotel Vancouvers, the current one taking eleven years to complete, as construction was suspended during the great Depression, finally opening in time for the royal visit of King George VI and Queen Elizabeth in 1939. Since then, its guests have included all sorts of notables, from Bing Crosby to Indira Gandhi. Its rooms have been carefully refurbished to retain the hotel's hallmark elegance.

For a quiet place to sit and rest, off Hornby between Robson and Georgia is an oasis of green between Christ Church Cathedral and the Chief Dan George Centre for Advanced Education, part of Simon Fraser University. This attractively landscaped area is easily missed by visitors.

summertime concerts. Under a domed section of the lower level near the Art Gallery is a recessed floor providing a skating rink in winter. Having been closed for almost a decade, the rink reopened to coincide with the 2010 Winter Olympics.

Vancouver Art Gallery ⑨

Address: 750 Hornby Street, www.vanartgallery.bc.ca
Tel: 604 662 4722
Opening Hrs: Wed–Mon 10am–5pm, Tue 10am–9pm
Entrance Fee: charge, Tue eve by donation
Transport: buses 5, 10 and 22

The **Vancouver Art Gallery** occupies what was originally the Provincial Courthouse, designed in 1905 by Francis Mawson Rattenbury, and a west wing added in 1912 by Thomas Hooper. The neoclassical building with massive Ionic columns, a central dome and ornately carved stonework has been turned round so that the purpose of the original entrance front, flanked by lions (modelled on those of the New York Public Library), has been lost. It was converted into an art

gallery in 1983 by Arthur Erickson.

Founded in 1931, the Art Gallery owns about 9,000 works; they include some 170 paintings by the Canadian Group of Seven, who emulated the Impressionists in preferring to work outside from life, but its most famous collection is its 200 works by Emily Carr, British Columbia's best-known painter. She is said to capture the haunting mysticism of the region's First Nations, particularly the Haida.

The gallery specialises in buying contemporary art as well as hosting changing exhibitions of both historical and contemporary art.

Granville Street

One of the principal entertainment and shopping streets, Granville had a period of transition during the excavation work on SkyTrain's Canada Line and the concurrent reconstruction of part of the Pacific Centre in 2007–09. The building-site atmosphere and felling of trees has not done any favours for those blocks. But the arts scene remains vibrant, and elsewhere are some of the best historic corporate buildings.

BELOW: outside the Vancouver Art Gallery.

On the corner of Hastings and Granville is the **Royal Bank**'s imposing BC headquarters (1931), built of Haddington Island sandstone with Romanesque decorations. Its interior layout mimics the nave and aisles of a church, with a magnificent roof created by Italian craftsmen hung with huge brass chandeliers. Square marble columns are matched by counters of Belgian black and gold and Travertine marbles.

Between Pender and Hastings on the east side is the white-glaze-tiled 11-storey **Rogers Building** (1911), designed by Seattle architect Carl F. Gould. The building takes its name from Jonathan Rogers, who was born near Llangollen in north Wales and arrived in Vancouver on the first transcontinental train, fortified by an aunt's legacy. He used this to buy four plots of forest now in the heart of the downtown area, becoming a builder and developer.

On the west side approaching Georgia is the cream terracotta pile of the **Hudson's Bay Company Department Store** ❿ (commonly referred to as just "The Bay"), which dates from 1914. The company's first Vancouver store opened on Cordova Street in Gastown in 1887. Granville Street SkyTrain station can be accessed from the store's lower two floors.

The Bay is one of the cornerstones of the **Pacific Centre Mall**, the massive downtown shopping centre. With Vancouver's weather, shopping here is preferable to getting wet along Robson and the selection of stores offers virtually everything a shopper could want. There are a lot of the American chains, but also Canada's upscale Holt Renfrew, where you can find the ultimate in designer clothing and accessories – it's a beautiful store, worth looking at, even if your budget doesn't stretch to $500 jeans. Although the mall has been around for decades, it has had numerous renovations and expansions, in part to

accommodate access to the SkyTrain.

Heading south down Granville Street is the red-brick, Art Deco-influenced **Commodore Ballroom**, with curious tiled panels beneath the windows that resemble mosaics and Venetian windows.

On the south corner of Granville and Smithe is the **Vogue Cinema**, built in 1941, and another great product of Art Deco. It has a V-shaped front surmounted by the winged golden figure of the goddess Diana. Built to accommodate both movies and live shows with curved walls and a tiered ceiling, it has superb acoustics and dramatic lighting. It has gone through many threats of redevelopment, despite being A-listed on the Vancouver Heritage Register list (a symbolic status, offering no legal protection). Doubtless its survival will depend on whether it can book enough acts to generate the income to justify its continuation as a theatre.

On the northeast corner of Granville with Davie is the former Bank

ABOVE: Hudson's Bay Company Department Store. **BELOW:** in its heyday, the Vogue Theatre, renowned for its state-of-the-art acoustics and elegant decor, played host to some of the biggest names in showbiz.

of Nova Scotia (1929), its facade all that's left to front a glass confection dumped on top of and behind it. The building is now the **Scotiabank Dance Centre**, producing and presenting everything from ballet and contemporary to flamenco and classical East Indian and Chinese, to salsa and tap.

Burrard Street

Three blocks north of Granville, linking Canada Place and Burrard Bridge, Burrard Street is another of the main downtown thoroughfares lined with hotels, shops and office blocks. The first landmark if you're heading to Canada Place from the Burrard Bridge end is the **St Paul's Hospital** ⓫ (1913). This fine red-brick building with decorative bands of beige brick and stone cornicing was built in the shape of a cross to a design by German-born Robert F. Tegen. It was sympathetically extended with two flanking wings in 1931–6.

Opposite Century Plaza and fronted by a pleasant green space is **Sheraton Vancouver Wall Centre Hotel ⓬**. Behind the striking design

and coloured-glass facade lies a turbulent story, for the building wasn't supposed to look like this. Its developer, Peter Wall, chose a dark silver-blue colour for the glass, but when it began to be installed the city planning authorities got cold feet and insisted a lighter colour had been chosen. Writs flew until a compromise was reached, whereby the dark glass was retained for the lower 30 floors that form the Sheraton Hotel and lighter glass was installed for the luxury condominiums above.

A little to the northeast, on the corner with Nelson Street stands the Gothic Revival-style church of **St Andrew's-Wesley** ⓭ (tel: 604 683 4574), opened in 1933. Its congregation is a model of ecumenicalism since the United Church of Canada is the outcome of a merger between four Protestant denominations. It has many stained-glass windows, mostly made in England by Morris and Co., and the organ was donated in memory of Mrs Thomas Bingham "who pioneered Scottish country dancing in Vancouver". Jazz Vespers are held every Sunday at 4pm.

The West End

Northwest of Burrard Street was, and remains, a largely residential district, though condominiums have replaced many a mansion, and it took years for the western side to be developed – as late as 1900 you could pick blackberries near the junction of Thurlow and Davie streets, and there was nothing but tree stumps and scrub as far as Denman Street. Only then did development get under way, with sites close to English Bay used for grander Edwardian mansions prior to the area's gradual eclipse by Shaughnessy (*see pages 145–6*) as the most desirable residential district from 1909.

Until re-zoning in the 1950s, the area remained a genteel and relatively cheap place to live with nothing higher than the eight-storey

BELOW: car-free zone.

Sylvia Hotel *(see below)*. Then over a decade of crass redevelopment saw most of the two-storey houses swept away in favour of over 220 high-rise blocks, many so badly configured and designed that most residents had no views of sea or mountains.

That said, there is something very appealing about this inner-city district. Quiet as it seems, it is in fact one of the city's most densely populated neighbourhoods and home to a vibrant gay community. Its leafy streets, its close proximity to Stanley Park, friendly atmosphere and relatively reasonable rents are what make it so liveable.

Almost the only surviving indication of what the West End once looked like is the **Gabriola Mansion** ⓮ at the western end of Davie Street. This elegant Queen Anne-style house was built in 1900–1 for B.T. Rogers, founder of the BC Sugar Refining Company. It took its name from the Gulf island that provided the sandstone with which it is faced. It has lived a life or two as a restaurant, and a local restaurateur is working on plans to restore it to its former elegance.

Another West End landmark is the **Sylvia Hotel** ⓯ overlooking English Bay Beach on the corner of Morton Avenue and Gilford Street. Opened as the Sylvia Court Apartments in 1912, the eight-storey brick and terracotta building was converted into a hotel in 1936. It even had a roof garden and an eighth-floor restaurant that advertised "dining in the sky". Sylvia Ablowitz, after whom the hotel was named (by her father who built it), died in 2002 at the age of 102. This is the hotel that locals always suggest to friends on a budget coming to town – its location simply can't be beaten.

Thurlow, Bute and Jervis

These streets embrace an area with the finest collection of heritage houses in the downtown area.

Roedde House ⓰

Address: 1415 Barclay Street, www.roeddehouse.org
Tel: 604 684 7040
Opening Hrs: Tue–Fri noon–4pm, 2–4pm tea and tour on Sun
Entrance Fee: charge
Transport: bus 5

DRINK

Downtown Vancouver is stuffed with bars and cafés. Just follow your nose or ask any Vancouverite where they go. People here take their coffee-drinking very seriously, and there is a strong trend towards organic, fair-trade coffee. Most coffee places will also sell snacks and light lunches, and some have downright adventurous menus. For recommendations, see page 93.

BELOW LEFT: one of the West End's leafy streets.
BELOW: one man and his dog.

TIP

The stretch of Davie Street west of Burrard Street and the northern end of Denman Street, near the beach at English Bay, form the hub of the West End's gay community. Both streets are interspersed with gay bars, restaurants and shops, and dotted with decorated bus shelters and bus stops (see pages 24–5).

Within Barclay Heritage Square is Vancouver's only house museum. Built in 1893 in the Queen Anne Revival style, it was almost certainly designed by Francis Rattenbury, who was a friend of Gustav Roedde, the first bookbinder in Vancouver, who had learned his trade at home in Leipzig. Guided tours take you round the furnished rooms with entertaining anecdotes about the family and their life in the house. The walls of the drawing room are panelled with cedar, and the deep cornice is also of wood. Some ceilings have a special wallpaper to reflect the light from oil lamps, and the main bedroom is downstairs to take advantage of heat from the kitchen stove. There is a delightful small room on the first floor, which must have had lovely views when the house was built; it was used by Matilda Roedde for sewing and reading.

The other nine houses on **Barclay Square** are of a piece with Roedde House and make an attractive ensemble, with landscaped grounds and places to sit beside the footpaths.

Nearby, on Nicola Street, is **Fire Hall No. 6 West End** in beige brick with red-brick trimmings and banding and an Italianate tower. Built in 1907, it was claimed to be the first firehall in North America built to accommodate motor vehicles. A little to the south, at 962 Jervis Street on the corner with Barclay, is **Winchester**, a classic four-storey apartment building with the typical Vancouver sash-windows of glazing bars on the upper sash and none on the lower.

On the corner of Thurlow with Robson is the West End's first apartment block, the **Manhattan Apartments** (1908). Between Bute and Thurlow in the block between Comox and Pendrell streets is another collection of wooden clapboard heritage houses with verandas and decorative bargeboards, but some of these are not on their original site. The **Watson House** (1897) was the home of Rev. Cloverdale Watson, minister of the Homer Street Methodist Church; it was donated to the city in 1986 and

SHOPPING

Pacific Centre (see page 87) is considered the main shopping mall in the city, both because of its downtown location and its department store anchor tenants, The Bay (see page 87) and Sears. But it is Robson Street that has the sex appeal of a true shopping street. Go there just for the atmosphere and you are bound to find something to covet.

Harry Rosen
700 West Georgia (Pacific Centre). Tel: 604 683 6861.

www.harryrosen.com p276, A2
This elegant menswear shop has top-name brands and, more important, top-quality service.

Plenty
1107 Robson St. Tel: 604 689 4478. www.getplenty.com Off map
An independent clothing store that focuses equally on local and international designers; lots of denim. Other locations in Kitsilano, Metrotown and Richmond.

Robson Optical
1132 Robson St. Tel: 604 689 8813. www.robsonoptical. com Off map

In the optical world, it's all about who has the best selection of the latest styles. Robson Optical aims to have the best selection in Canada – and when the sun comes out in this city, everyone brings out their best shades.

Roots
1001 Robson St. Tel: 604 683 4305. www.roots.com p276, A1
The Canadian clothing success story, with the "Canada" line the most popular. Stocks accessories, including leather bags decorated with national flags.

Birk's
698 West Hastings St.
Tel: 604 669 3333.
www.birks.com p276, A1
A Canadian institution, in business since 1879, Birk's is best known for jewellery, but also carries silver and china, and vintage jewellery.

Palladio
855 West Hastings St. Tel: 604 685 3885. www.palladio canada.com p276, A1
Custom jewellery for the well-heeled, it's great just to do a bit of window-shopping here.

moved here in 1989. Once the home of a Yaletown plasterer, nearby **Lane Cottage** dates from 1901. An attractive footpath links the two streets.

Near the western end of Thurlow Street off Beach Avenue is the **Vancouver Aquatic Centre** , a 50-metre (164ft) pool and one of the very few public heated saltwater pools in the world. There's also a diving tank, whirlpool, sauna and fitness centre.

Georgia and Alberni

By far the most important northwest/southeast street in the downtown area, Georgia Street was developed from 1888 as part of the Canadian Pacific's landholdings. The expensive houses it sold to the fledgling city's affluent gave the section of Georgia Street and adjacent Hastings Street the nickname of "Blueblood Alley". But even during the first decade of the 20th century, apartment buildings were starting to replace the city's first family mansions. Just one remains, the **Abbott House**  at 720 Jervis Street between Alberni and Georgia. This red-painted house clad in wood lap siding and cedar shingles was built by Harry Abbott, who was the first superintendent of the Pacific Division of the Canadian Pacific Railway and a prominent figure in the city's development. When built in 1900, the house had a great view over Stanley Park and the mountains.

Robson Street

Last but not least, **Robson Street** . Vancouver's most famous shopping street used to be known as Robsonstrasse, but it has been decades since its German heritage was palpable. Schnitzel and schnapps have become croissants and cappuccino. Shoppers should head for the three-block section between Hornby and Bute where many of the best-known brand names of fashion are to be found, such as Ferragamo, Armani Exchange, Club Monaco, Guess, BoysCo, BeBe, Zara, Laura Ashley, Banana Republic, Nike, Levi's and Gap. The Virgin Megastore occupies the former library building.

It's also easy to find good restaurants all along Robson Street, many of them on the second floor, so don't forget to look up (*see pages 92-3*). ❑

ABOVE: Nelson Park, after-work meeting place for dogs and their owners.
BELOW: Vancouver Aquatic Centre.

BEST RESTAURANTS, BARS AND CAFÉS

Restaurants

Chinese

Kirin Mandarin
1166 Alberni St. Tel: 604
682 8833. www.kirin
restaurant.com Open: L & D
daily. **$$** ❶ p275, D1
Awarding-winning restaurant that specialises in
northern Chinese cuisine,
particularly in live seafood prepared in both
traditional and exotic
styles. Dim sum, freshly
prepared, is a daily feature and has many fans.

Fish and Seafood

**Burrard Bridge Marine
Bar and Grill**
1–1012 Beach Ave. Tel: 604
676 2337. www.burrardbridge.
com Open: L, D daily. **$$**
❷ p275, D3
Great location for watching False Creek marine
traffic, with a patio for the
sunny days. Enjoy generous portions of mussels
served several ways, fish
and chips (go for the halibut) or classic pub fare.
The intelligent wine list is
appealing, but so is the
selection of rums – close
to 20 at the last count.

"C" Restaurant
2–1600 Howe St. Tel: 604
681 1164. www.crestaurant.
com Open: L Mon–Fri, D
daily. **$$$$** ❸ p275, D3
"C" is all about fish and
fireworks. Finesse and
presentation are high on
chef-of-the-year Robert
Clark's agenda. Menu
items change with sea-

sons and availability, with
sustainability Clark's
mantra. Crispy trout with
Dungeness crab couscous, watermelon radish
and fennel is an example
of a lunch entrée. The
large patio overlooking
False Creek is lovely in
the early evening.

O'Doul's
1300 Robson St. Tel: 604
661 1400. www.odouls
restaurant.com Open: B, L & D
daily. **$$** ❹ p275, D1
Set in the Listel Hotel,
O'Doul's is not only a
great place to eat, it also
has live jazz every night.
Eclectic, fresh and reasonably priced, the food
ranges over a number of
cultures – try their West
Coast interpretation of
seafood bouillabaisse
made with Dungeness
crab, Qualicum Bay scallops, Arctic char and BC
Spot prawns.

French

Bacchus
845 Hornby St. Tel: 604 608
5319. www.wedgewoodhotel.
com Open: B, L & D daily.
$$$ ❺ p275, E2
Set within the award-winning Wedgewood
boutique hotel, this dining room oozes Old World
charm – dark wood,
comfy soft furnishings
and an open fire. The
food is modern French
with lighter saucing and
makes great use of local
ingredients. The bar is the
perfect place to meet at

the end of the day or
before a concert or the
theatre.

Le Crocodile
100–909 Burrard St.
Tel: 604 669 4298.
www.lecrocodilerestaurant.com
Open: L Mon–Fri, D Mon–
Sat. **$$$$** ❻ p275, E2
Elegance is the catchword in this lovely Alsatian restaurant. From the
lobster salad with potatoes, radish, shallots and
basil to the double-cut
veal chop on the bone,
everything is prepared
with painstaking attention
to detail – and the flavours consistently reward
Michel Jacob's loyal
patrons.

Le Gavroche
1616 Alberni St. Tel: 604
685 3924. www.legavroche.ca
Open: L Mon–Fri, D daily.
$$$ ❼ p273, C4
Set in a pretty Victorian
house, Le Gavroche has
been serving French cuisine with West Coast
flair since 1979. The
extensive wine list ranges from 1945 Mouton
Rothschild to the most
exclusive garage wines
from California. A strong
commitment to the best
BC wine ensures something for everyone and
every budget.

Hotdogs

JapaDog
530 Robson St, and street
locations on Burrard St.
Open: 11am–late daily. **$**
❽ p275, E2

It's a bit of a fad, but
worth a try – some people are addicted to the
odd combinations of
bratwurst with plum
sauce and turkey sausage with teriyaki sauce
and Japanese mayonnaise, but don't knock
'em til you've tried 'em.

International

Market by Jean-Georges
1128 West Georgia St. Tel:
604 689 1120. www.shangri-
la.com Open: B, L & D daily.
$$$$ ❾ p275, E1
The restaurant that was
anticipated for years does
not disappoint. Jean-
Georges Vongerichten
offers four distinct spaces
in a single restaurant.
Those in for the splurge
will definitely choose the
fine-dining room with its
seven-course tasting
menu. The experience will
be leisurely and delightful, and only outrageous
if you let the wines get
out of control. For the
more cost-conscious, the
lunch special does not
disappoint.

Italian

**CinCin Ristorante
and Bar**
1154 Robson St. Tel: 604
688 7338. www.cincin.net
Open: D daily. **$$$**
❿ p275, D1
A lovely room overlooking
the street, with tables
outside in fine weather.
Modern Italian food using
local produce is the

focus, and the menu changes with the seasons and market availability. Try the slow-cooked "kobe"-style beef short ribs braised in Barolo with polenta, wilted rapini and lemon. The pastas are all house-made, and the wine list formidable.

Il Giardino di Umberto
1382 Hornby St. Tel: 604 669 2422. www.umberto.com Open: L Mon–Fri, D daily. **$$$$** ⓫ p275, D3
This Italian restaurant is a Vancouver institution, boasting the best courtyard in the city. The combination of decor, exceptional food and attentive service makes it easy to forget you are in Canada and think you are somewhere in Tuscany. The proprietor, Umberto Menghi, is somewhat of a legend in Vancouver and each of his four restaurants – two in Vancouver,

Prices for a three-course dinner per person with a half-bottle of house wine:
$ = under C$30
$$ = C$30–50
$$$ = C$50–80
$$$$ = over C$80

two in Whistler *(see page 225)* – are worth a visit.

Japanese

Hapa Izakaya
1479 Robson St. Tel: 604 689 4272. www.hapaizakaya. com Open: D daily. **$$** ⓬ p275, D1
A loud and lively Japanese restaurant where orders are shouted across the room in traditional style. Beautifully presented sushi and Korean hot stone dishes are wonderful. Kick off with a cocktail from the imaginative list. Draws a young crowd. There are two other branches in Kitsilano and Yaletown.

Organic

Raincity Grill
1193 Denman St. Tel: 604 685 7337. www.raincitygrill. com Open: L Sat & Sun, D daily. **$$–$$$** ⓭ p275, C1
Award-winning Raincity Grill has a sublime 100-mile tasting menu – all ingredients are organic and come from within 100 miles of Vancouver. Each

ABOVE: teriyaki dishes are one of the delights of Japanese cuisine.

Bars and Cafés

There are several downtown branches of **Caffè Artigiano** (1101 West Pender Street ❶ p275, E1; also 763 Hornby St. and 740 West Hastings St.), a small chain offering superior coffee, brunch, salads and panini. It's worth stopping in for a drink at the **Granville Room** (957 Granville St. ❷ p275, E2), in part to look at the people, in part to enjoy the breadth of the cocktail selection. For great coffee, but even better drinking chocolate, head to **Mink** (863 West Hastings St. ❸ p275, E1), where the staff are passionate and the chocolate worth a detour. The 50g bars make perfect gifts – try the Taj Masala or the Key Lime.

Sciué (110–800 Pender St. ❹ p276, A1) provides great soups and paninis at good prices – you'll see a lot of the working crowd race in for takeaway. **Trees Organic Coffee Co.** (450 Granville St. ❺ p276, A1) prides itself on selling 100 percent organic fair-trade coffee, roasted on the premises in small batches. Fresh pastries, cheesecakes and sandwiches are also served. **Shore Club** (688 Dunsmuir St. ❻ p275, E2) has a lounge and a bar, with live music six days a week. **Smiley's** (911 West Pender Street ❼ p275, E1) is a typical Irish pub, with a large selection of whiskeys and beers, and live music some evenings.

of the courses is paired with a superb local wine. Both the people in the kitchen and the front-of-house staff are passionate about food and sustainability – this was one of the first "Green Table" restaurants in the city.

Steakhouse

Hy's Steakhouse
637 Hornby St. Tel: 604 683 7671. www.hyssteakhouse.com Open: L Mon–Fri, D daily. **$$$** ⓮ p275, E1
Wood panelling, red velvet seating and prints of Old Masters give this dependable place for carnivores a club like atmosphere. The cheese toast is a must, before any one of the perfectly aged steaks that you can order

according to appetite, from the smallest filet mignon to the 22oz-porterhouse.

Tapas

Bin 941 Tapas Parlour
941 Davie St. Tel: 604 683 1246. www.bin941.com Open: D daily. **$$** ⓯ p275, D2
This small, lively space has a tapas-only menu, but what tapas! Try to get a seat at the bar overlooking the kitchen so you can watch the cooks prepare a host of fabulous dishes, such as crabcakes with burnt orange chipotle sauce and lamb confit. Offers a good wine list. No reservations. The sister spot, Bin 942 on Broadway, works the same magic.

MARITIME VANCOUVER

Vancouver's history and identity have been forged by its relationship with the sea.

The coastline of British Columbia is so indented that it measures 27,200km (17,000 miles), and its topography has inevitably made for a very close relationship with sea. In the early 19th century, the sailing ships that had explored the coast on behalf of Spain and Britain started to give way to steamships. Commerce with the Orient began in the late 1860s. As volumes grew, the Canadian Pacific Railway built some outstandingly elegant clipper-bowed liners for trade with Japan and China. The first, *Empress of India*, arrived in Vancouver on 28 April 1891, followed by *Empress of Japan* and *Empress of China*. Besides passengers, they carried valuable cargoes such as silk and tea, which were unloaded at Pier B-C. Canada Place now stands on the site of this terminal, where millions of dollars of teas, spices and silks were unloaded and transferred to special trains.

Passenger ships no longer ply the Pacific on scheduled services, but Vancouver remains a major commercial and cruise-ship port.

BELOW: the AquaBus ferries that dart around False Creek add colour and atmosphere to the inlet, as well as saving long walks across the bridges to Granville

ABOVE: the golden age of travel: two little girls salute the captain of the Canadian Pacific liner *Duchess of Bedford*, 1931.
LEFT: Hong Kong-bound Canadian Pacific liner, *Empress of France*, 1928.

LEFT: the maritime lifeblood of BC is the BC Ferries system. Thirty-six ships serve 47 ports of call, carrying more than 21 million passengers annually. The BC Ferries fleet includes the largest double-ended ferries in the world, each capable of carrying 370 vehicles and 1,650 passengers. The ferry pictured here is the service from Horseshoe Bay, West Vancouver, to Nanaimo on Vancouver Island.

BURRARD INLET

Ferries have been running across Burrard Inlet since May 1900, but today's frequent SeaBus catamarans have transformed the short journey between downtown and North Vancouver. For most of the 20th century, the northern shoreline of Burrard Inlet was home to busy shipbuilding yards. Efforts to convert some of the surviving slipways and buildings near Lonsdale Quay into a new maritime centre have fallen foul of budget cutbacks, leaving North Vancouver with the challenge of upgrading the area with a less costly plan. The inlet remains a busy waterway, dominated by commercial traffic carrying mineral and timber cargoes delivered to Vancouver by rail from Prince George.

In summer and at weekends, the inlet to the west of Lions Gate Bridge shares the sea with up to 30,000 pleasure craft – yachts, cabin cruisers and kayaks off the beaches around English Bay. The spectacle of huge white cruise liners passing under the Lions Gate Bridge and easing round the corner to berth at Canada Place is worth seeing, if you can time your walk or cycle round the seawall to coincide.

ABOVE: container and bulk cargo ships with coal, sulphur, grain, timber and petroleum from the resource-rich western provinces sail mainly to Australia, Japan, the US, Brazil, Korea, China and Taiwan, while the cruise ships sail principally up the Inside Passage to Alaska.

BELOW: the province's many maritime museums trace the story of man's use of the sea, from fishing by the First Nations to today's busy trading links of the West Coast ports and the intensive pleasure use off the spectacular coastline. Below is the modified cedarwood canoe *Tilikum* in which Captain John Voss circumnavigated the world from Victoria to Margate in Kent in 1901–4. The vessel was exhibited at Earl's Court in 1905 and then sold. She was discovered in 1929, returned to Victoria and is now in the Maritime Museum of BC.

BELOW: salmon remains a major export from BC, though the vast majority is now farmed. New conservation measures have been agreed between the US and Canada to try to avoid a repetition of the destruction of the Newfoundland cod-fishing industry, but 2008 results suggest the fishery is still in serious jeopardy.

GASTOWN, CHINATOWN AND YALETOWN

Wander the cobbled streets where it all began, meditate in a Chinese garden, admire Vancouver's first tall buildings, browse the designer shops in uptown Yaletown, then hop on a ferry and take in the cityscape from the water.

The eastern side of downtown Vancouver contains far more contrasts than the West End and midtown. Some areas have been totally transformed – someone who knew False Creek at the end of World War II, for example, would barely recognise the place today, with multi-million dollar yachts moored in front of luxury condominiums. At the opposite end of the spectrum, inner-city grit in the extreme bleeds into touristy Gastown. This is where the fledgling city was established, taking its name from the loquaciousness of its first bartender.

In the saloons of early pioneers like Gassy Jack (*see panel, page 101*), prospectors talked up the probability of a quick path to riches in the goldfields of the Kootenays and the Cariboo. In the stores they gathered supplies for the long journey to the goldfields, while traders built warehouses close to the quays of Burrard Inlet. For decades Gastown retained this function, as housing, hotels and offices migrated to surrounding, more fashionable, districts.

What all the areas covered by this chapter have in common is a greater wealth of historic buildings than the western downtown areas. This is evident in the number of walking tours on offer. You can go with a guide or pick up one of the widely available leaflets for self-guided exploration.

GASTOWN

For tourists interested in Vancouver's early days, Gastown is a good place to start. At the point where Alexander and Powell streets merge to become Water Street, there is something unusual in downtown Vancouver: a space approaching a small square. It can also claim to be the centre of old Gas-

LEFT: gateway to Chinatown.
RIGHT: café on Water Street.

town. On the south corner is a **statue of Gassy Jack ❶**, erected on the site of a maple tree to which was pinned the notice of the first civic election in Vancouver, in November 1886. On the corner of Water and Carrall streets is the 1886–7 **Byrnes Building ❷**, built on the site of Gassy Jack Deighton's second hotel, which then offered a great view of the harbour. The Byrnes Building has been described as the symbol of Gastown. Decorated with pediments and pilasters, this commercial block was built shortly after the Great Fire of 1886. One of the city's first brick buildings,

it was built by Victoria developer George Byrnes and housed the relatively opulent Alhambra Hotel, one of the few in town then charging more than a dollar a night. It became one of the first buildings in Gastown to be rehabilitated in the late 1960s, in one of the first attempts to revive the district.

In the apex of Alexander and Powell streets is Vancouver's flatiron building, the **Hotel Europe ❸**, which was designed by Parr and Fee in 1908–9 using their trademark glazed brick. Clad in beige brick above marble facing, it was Vancouver's first

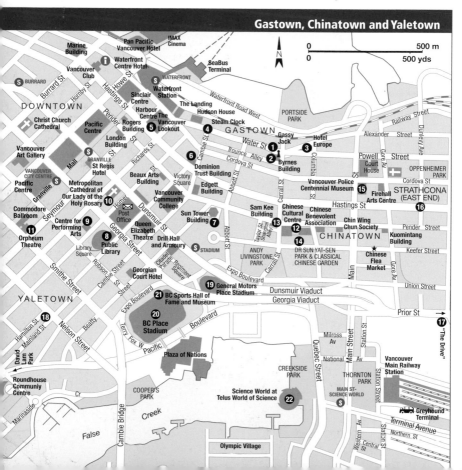

Gastown, Chinatown and Yaletown

continued to spruce up the neighbourhood. It still attracts clusters of tourists waiting for the quarter-hour hissing and whistling.

Near the Water Street junction with Cordova is **Hudson House**, the Hudson's Bay Company's original warehouse for fur and liquor; built in 1895 and used until the 1960s, it was converted into offices in 1977.

DOWNTOWN
The Vancouver Lookout ❺
Address: 555 West Hastings Street, www.vancouverlookout.com
Tel: 604 689 0421
Opening Hrs: May–mid-Oct daily 8.30am–10.30pm, mid-Oct–Apr daily 9am–9pm
Entrance Fee: charge; tickets valid all day, with multiple visits possible
Transport: SkyTrain Waterfront
On the 50th storey of the Harbour Centre Tower, this 150-metre (500ft) -high viewing gallery provides a 360-degree view of the city. It is reached by glass-walled lifts on the outside of the building, giving a spectacular, almost too rapid, 50-second ride. The glass of the gallery is sharply angled to deflect

reinforced-concrete building and has a fine glazed-brick and tiled entrance hall. It is not open to the public, as it has been converted into subsidised housing. It was built for the Italian-Canadian hotelier Angelo Colari to be the best hotel in Vancouver, with a "sitting parlour" on every floor.

For those with a strong interest in architecture, there are several buildings constructed of stone or red brick between the 1890s and 1920s and often in an Italianate style. However, the sections of Cordova and Hastings between Abbott Street and Chinatown form a shabby, drug-infested enclave which is best avoided.

Water Street
The hotels along Water Street were built on the south side, as the north side of the street was often under water until the Canadian Pacific Railway fully reclaimed it in the 1890s. By 1900 Gastown was the headquarters of the city's food and dry goods wholesalers, a role it retained until the 1940s.

At the crossroads with Cambie is the type of tourist attraction that makes locals shudder. The **steam clock** ❹ is generally believed to be a slice of Gastown history, but it's actually powered by electricity and dates back to the 1970s, when efforts

ABOVE: almost everyone stops to watch the famous steam clock, which hisses and whistles every 15 minutes. **LEFT:** Water Street. **BELOW:** Hotel Europe, the city's flat-iron building.

ABOVE: view from the Vancouver Lookout Harbour Centre Tower (**BELOW**). **ABOVE RIGHT**: Sun Tower Building.

the sun's rays and to allow visitors to look vertically down. On a clear day, you can see Mount Baker in the US, 145km (90 miles) to the south, and the most northerly of 11 volcanoes in the Cascade Mountain Range.

West Hastings and Pender

During the first half of the 20th century, the area around Hastings and Pender at the northeastern end of Cambie Street was the heart of Vancouver's financial district. It was distinguished by a series of tall buildings that laid successive claims to be the tallest in the British Empire. Most were built between 1907 and 1913, the "golden years" of Vancouver's growth. The first was the idiosyncratic 13-storey **Dominion Trust Building** ❻ (1908–10) at Hastings and Cambie. Its distinctive bands of tan terracotta and brick rise to 53 metres (175ft) and are surmounted by a three-storey mansard roof reminiscent of late 19th-century Parisian town houses. Its architect, J.S. Helyer,

died after falling from a staircase in the building.

This was followed by one of the city's most striking buildings, the six-sided, 17-storey **Sun Tower Building** ❼ on the corner of Pender and Beatty. When completed in 1912 to a design by W.T. Whiteway, the Beaux Arts-style building was known as the World Building and was the tallest in the British Empire at 83 metres (272ft), but only for two years. It was built by Vancouver's longest-serving mayor, Louis D. Taylor, who had bought *The World* newspaper in 1905 when advertising revenues were booming. His tower was to be a new home for the paper, but the 7,560 sq metres (84,000 sq ft) of office accommodation were too much for the recession of 1913, and in 1915 he lost the paper and the building.

Steel for the tower's frame was taken from dismantled ships. The lower part of the building is adorned with terracotta panels, arched windows and classical details, but it is the supports to the cornice halfway up the walls that arrest everyone's attention – a row of nine bare-breasted maidens in sensuous poses, executed by the sculptor Charles Marega *(see opposite)*. When unveiled, these sculptures scandalised many of Vancouver's more prudish citizens. An excuse to ogle the maidens was provided in 1918 when Harry Gardiner, the "Human Fly", climbed the building, and again in 1920 when Houdini suspended himself from the top. The dome on the top looks like weathered copper but is in fact painted. The building was bought in 1937 by the *Vancouver Sun*, which was published there until 1965.

On the east corner of the intersection of Pender and Cambie overlooking Victory Square is the **Edgett Building** (1911). This newspaper building originally housed what was claimed to be the "largest, best and most complete grocery store in the Dominion of Canada". It is now home to the Architectural Institute of BC, which organises six architectural walking tours of the city between early July and the end of August *(see page 262)*.

Beatty Street

The fortress-like building on Beatty Street between Georgia and Dunsmuir is the **Drill Hall and Armoury** of the British Columbia Regiment

(Duke of Connaught's Own). Flanking the two central towers are a Sherman tank which fought in a 14-hour tank battle north of Falaise and a Ram Mk II tank of which 1,949 were built by the Montreal Locomotive Works in Quebec. The building has served as the regimental headquarters since its opening in 1901 by HRH the Duke of Cornwall and York, and its 90cm (3ft) -thick walls were built of brick and Gabriola Island sandstone.

Georgia Street

On the corner of West Georgia and Homer opposite the main post office is Library Square and the Colosseum-like **Public Library ❽**, clad in pre-cast concrete the colour of rich African soil. Designed by Moshe Safdie and Associates and opened in 1995, it has a spectacular atrium entrance to the seven levels of stacks housing 1.2 million books as well as shops and government offices. Across the street is the **Centre for Performing Arts** ❾ (tel: 604 602 0616; www.centreinvancouver.com), also designed by Moshe Safdie in 1995, which has a spiral glass cone to its curvilinear marble staircase

No sculptor has left a greater mark on the city than Charles Marega (1871–1939), who emigrated to Vancouver from Italy in 1909. He produced a wide range of civic works including the statue of George Vancouver in front of City Hall, the lions that flank Lions Gate Bridge, the busts of Vancouver and Burrard on Burrard Bridge, motifs on the Marine Building, and the 14 statues of figures from BC's past on Victoria's Parliament Building.

BELOW: statue of Gassy Jack.

Six Acres

John "Gassy Jack" Deighton

It is said that John Deighton was Vancouver's first settler, in 1867. He quit New Westminster and his work as a Fraser River pilot to become a saloonkeeper by – legend has it – offering to reward anyone who would help build the bar with all he could drink once it was up. The makeshift pub was in business within a day, and with it was born a reputation for its owner's garrulousness. Gastown was a world away from the Hull in Yorkshire where Jack was born in 1830: he later wrote that the Globe Saloon was "a lonesome place when I came here first, surrounded by Indians. I cared not to look outdoors after dark. There was a friend of mine about a mile distant found with his head cut in two." He had the eye of a sailor when he presciently forecast that Burrard Inlet's suitability as a harbour would one day make it a great port. By 1870 the tiny settlement of 2.4 hectares (6 acres) around the saloon had been named Granville after the British colonial secretary, Earl Granville. Jack built a better, two-storey establishment on Water Street called the Deighton Hotel, with a veranda shaded by a maple tree where his statue now stands. Jack died in 1875 aged 44, 11 years before his hotel was consumed in the conflagration that destroyed the city.

ABOVE: inside the Moshe Safdie-designed Public Library.

TIP

Catch a performance at the dynamic Firehall Arts Centre (www. firehallartscentre.ca), which offers a varied programme of avant-garde theatre and contemporary dance, often used to showcase new or emerging talents. The theatre is set in a converted fire station at 280 East Cordova, not far from Chinatown, and has a cosy lounge bar and outdoor courtyard stage for fair-weather performances.

and an auditorium with 1,800 purple velvet seats and impeccable acoustics.

Dunsmuir Street

You won't miss the **Metropolitan Cathedral of Our Lady of the Holy Rosary** ❿ on the corner of Dunsmuir and Richards if you're near it on Sunday morning, when the eight large bells in its 66-metre (217ft) east tower ring long and loud. The Gothic Revival church with steeply pitched roof and pointed windows and doorways was built in 1899, becoming a cathedral in 1916.

At 602 Dunsmuir, the Edwardian-style **St Regis** (1913) is the last of the pre-World War I hotels to survive as a hotel. It was completely renovated in 2009 and, other than the exterior, little of the original building remains.

Seymour Street

The best-known building on Seymour Street is the **Orpheum** ⓫ on the corner of Smithe. The fine heritage theatre is home to the Vancouver Symphony

Orchestra. When it opened in 1927 it was the largest theatre in Canada and the Pacific northwest, with 2,800 seats. It hosted Chicago-based vaudeville shows and still has its original 1927 Wurlitzer 240 organ, believed to be the only vaudeville organ still in operation in its original setting. The theatre's extravagant decor is Spanish Baroque-inspired, the arches and tiered columns decorated with mouldings in marble, travertine and plaster.

CHINATOWN

Vancouver's compact Chinatown, dating from 1885, is the biggest in Canada and the third largest in North America (after San Francisco and New York), having defeated freeway proposals in the 1960s that would have destroyed much of the area. It stretches for several blocks east from **Main Street**, bounded to the north by Hastings Street and the Georgia Street viaduct to the south, and its centre is a ten- to fifteen-minute walk from downtown, or easily reached by SkyTrain or bus.

Chinese Cultural Centre ⑫

Address: 555 Columbia Street,
www.cccvan.com
Tel: 604 658 8850
Opening Hrs: Tue–Sun 9am–5.30pm
Entrance Fee: charge
Transport: SkyTrain Stadium, Keefer
street exit; buses 7 and 16

This small museum provides a good introduction to the role of the Chinese in western Canada's history. The frontispiece of the concrete post-and-beam structure is a traditional gateway, made in China and erected here after having first been installed at Expo '86. The first Chinese immigrants came primarily from Hong Kong and Guangdong Province in south China, leaving in waves both to escape famine and in the hope of quick riches with the discovery of gold. By 1863 there were 4,000 Chinese working on construction of the Cariboo Wagon Road, and in 1881–5 17,000 Chinese labourers were under contract to finish building the western section of the CPR. On the corner of Columbia and Main streets is a statue commemorating the contribution made by the Chinese to the construction of the railways and during World War II.

In 1885, concern over the levels of immigration prompted the government to impose a head tax of $50 on all persons of Chinese origin entering the country, increasing in 1900 to $100 and three years later to $500. With many Chinese taking the low-paid jobs, resentment built up, and anti-Asian riots broke out in 1907. In 1923 the Exclusion Act closed the door to Chinese immigrants. Change was slow: only in 1945 was a bar lifted against the use of the Crystal swimming pool by Chinese, and it was not until 1988 that David Lam became the first Lt Governor of British Columbia of Chinese origin.

Chinatown is a popular tourist destination for its won-ton and dim-sum houses, market stalls and exotic shops selling things you won't find anywhere else in the city. From esoteric Chinese herbs and spices to jade and silks, there are numerous specialist shops along East Pender and Keefer streets to fascinate even the most shopping-averse. The **Chinese flea market** is on Keefer Street between Gore and Main.

ABOVE: Columbia Street, Chinatown.
BELOW: car trolley en route to Chinatown.

ABOVE: Chinatown grocery store.

Chinatown buildings

Because of its appearance in the *Guinness Book of Records* as the narrowest building in the world, the **Sam Kee Building ⑬** at 8 West Pender Street on Carrall is on many a visitor's itinerary. This curiosity came about when the city expropriated land without compensation on either side of the street to widen it. This left Chang Toy with a property just 1.5 metres (4ft 11in) deep. Rather than sell cheaply to his neighbour, Chang Toy defiantly commissioned a two-storey building with protruding bay windows on the first floor and a cellar under the pavement lit by glass blocks. The latter accommodated a bathhouse used as an escape route from opium dens in nearby Shanghai Alley by means of a connecting tunnel. The building is made entirely of riveted steel.

Further along Pender at No. 108 is the **Chinese Benevolent Association Building** (1909). The CBA had been formed in 1895 to help destitute railway workers after completion of the CPR. This fine example of southern Chinese architectural style with recessed balconies, decorative tiles and ornate ironwork housed its offices and meeting rooms. The fusion of Chinese and Western elements can be seen in the pedimented building of the **Chin Wing Chun Society** at 160 East Pender.

Of historical rather than architectural interest is the Kuomintang Building at 296 East Pender Street. This was the western headquarters of the Kuomintang, founded in 1912 by Dr Sun Yat-sen to overthrow the Manchu dynasty.

Dr Sun Yat-sen Park and Classical Chinese Garden ⑭

Address: 578 Carrall Street, www.vancouverchinesegarden.com
Tel: 604 662 3207
Opening Hrs: May–mid-June daily 10am–6pm, mid-June–Aug daily 9.30am–7pm, Sept daily 10am–6pm, Oct–Apr daily 10am–4.30pm, Nov–Apr closed Mon

After the bustle and noise of commerce in Chinatown, this garden fulfils the original purpose of providing a sanctuary of nature within a bustling city. Built in 1985–6 by 52 artisans who came over from China with all the materials and tools they required, the garden claims to be the first full-scale classical Chinese garden built outside China. Its design is based on elements from private Ming-dynasty gardens of the 14th century and relies more on architectural forms than plants for its effect, with courtyards, pavilions, bridges, covered galleries, sculptured rocks and jade-green areas of water, symbolising tranquillity.

Covering 1 hectare (2½ acres), the garden was designed to create a proper yin and yang from the elements and to achieve the harmony between the man-made and natural worlds that lies behind the design of Chinese gardens.

NORTH OF CHINATOWN

Vancouver Police Centennial Museum **15**

Devotees of P.D. James and Colin Dexter will enjoy this museum, located in the former Coroner's Court built in 1932 for the investigation of unusual deaths. The rooms include displays about unsolved murder cases, police firearms, a gruesome collection of confiscated weapons, the history of the city's force which dates from 1858 and the establishment of Fort Langley, early breathalyser devices such as the "Drunkometer" of 1953, fingerprinting, forgery, drugs, gambling, uniforms and hats, police dogs, the marine squad and even cast models of police cars from around the world. The autopsy room with body drawers comes with a health warning for the squeamish about the various specimens on display. Children can play with computers storing fake police records.

EAST OF CHINATOWN

The area between Chinatown and Clark Drive has been called the East End as well as **Strathcona 16**, and has been home to successive waves of

ABOVE: the Vancouver Police Centennial Museum will appeal to those with a taste for the macabre. **LEFT:** statue commemorating the Chinese contribution in World War II. **BELOW:** the famously narrow Sam Kee building.

Dr Sun Yat-sen (1866–1925) has been described as "the father of modern China", but it was his political philosophy rather than his practical contribution to the revolution that was more influential. He was the first provisional president of China when the republic was founded in 1912.

immigrants from Italy, Scandinavia, the Ukraine, Japan and China since its establishment in the 1880s. Its eclectic mix can still be seen in the variety of religious buildings, such as the Korean Foursquare Gospel Church and the Holy Trinity Russian Orthodox Church. It has the city's largest concentration of historic houses built before World War I, but little thought was given to their qualities in the 1950s and '60s when the area was regarded as a ghetto. Freeway proposals that would have swept them away were again defeated, and now the charming wooden Victorian and Edwardian houses are gradually being restored with a strong sense of community and pride.

"The Drive"

If you've more time on your hands another district worth exploring is the bohemian quarter to the east of Gastown. This is where you'll find cosmopolitan Vancouver at its most culturally diverse. The northern end of Commercial Drive between Venables Street and Grandview has become one of the city's trendiest

areas. Today best known as **"The Drive"** ⓱ but also called Little Italy, the character of the area has been shaped by various immigrant groups, starting with Italian, but now including Portuguese and Central American communities. With numerous cafés and restaurants and the sort of eclectic shops that sell things you're unlikely to find in anodyne malls, it's a good area to wander round for an afternoon. Specialist chocolates, coffee, ethnic crafts, music, bookshops, antiques and bric-a-brac and furnishings can all be found here, as well as the wackier end with such items as belly-dancing accoutrements.

YALETOWN

This former warehouse and commercial district has undergone an extraordinary renaissance to become one of the city's liveliest areas, packed with great restaurants, up-market grocery stores, cafés, upscale boutiques and furnishing stores and galleries, serving the scores of new residential high-rise buildings in the area, as well as drawing people from all over the city.

BELOW: the serene Sun Yat-sen Garden.

The area's name was bestowed in the late 19th century when the Canadian Pacific Railway moved its repair facilities from Yale in the Fraser River canyon *(see page 235)*. The only reminder of the era of whistles and clashing boxcars around the north shore of False Creek is the 1888 locomotive roundhouse which today forms the centrepiece of **Roundhouse Park** (daily; admission free). This was restored as a pavilion for Expo '86 and then turned into a community centre. Inside a glass-walled extension is locomotive No. 374, which hauled the first transcontinental train into Vancouver from Montreal on 23 May 1887, carrying 150 passengers. The locomotive is wheeled out onto the turntable on the anniversary for a day of celebration.

Yaletown was a pretty rowdy place in its early years, encouraging the more respectable residents to move to the more salubrious West End. Many of the warehouses built in the early 20th century have survived to become restaurants on the ground floor, with the loading dock as an open-air terrace, and flats or offices above, benefiting from generous areas of glazing.

The main hub of activity is around **Hamilton** and **Mainland streets** ⑱, which have a concentration of trendy interior design stores, "in" restaurants and an up-market supermarket. It's also a focal point for different crowds of people at different times: before hockey or football games, the sports fans congregate on outdoor patios, followed by the fine-dining crowd, with the cocktail crowd moving in much later to finish off the night.

False Creek

Along the north shore of False Creek *(see also pages 124–30)* the CPR was enticed into building its yards and repair facilities by a 20-year exemption from local taxes. These and the workforce that manned them were moved from Yale, with whole buildings being loaded onto flat cars. The extensive yards were cleared for the site of Expo '86. Once the fair was over, it was expected that the land would be developed by a Crown corporation, but the provincial governor of the day had different ideas and sold the entire 84-hectare (208-acre) site to a single top bidder, Hong Kong billionaire Li Ka-shing, who paid $320 million over 15 years. It was not a popular decision: too hasty, too small a sum and not enough transparency were typical accusations. Equally, the high-rise residential towers that have risen along the waterfront are too close to one another for many people's liking, but **David Lam Park** and the seawall path for cyclists and walkers are an unquestionable benefit to the city as a whole.

Near the eastern end of False Creek on the north shore are the city's two principal sporting stadiums: the **General Motors Place Stadium** ⑲ on Griffiths Way, opened in 1995 with seats for 20,000 at the annual 170-odd concerts, shows and sporting events. The ferociously competitive game of

ABOVE: view across False Creek to Yaletown.
BELOW: East Vancouver's bohemian neighbourhood centres on "The Drive".

TIP

To get an idea of how Vancouver's residential streets looked before World War I, take some of the turnings off Commercial Drive, such as Grant Street, Napier Street and Salsbury Drive, where many older houses survive.

ice hockey is Canada's national sport, and this is the place to watch the Vancouver Canucks on their home ice. During the 2010 Olympics, it was the main site for men's hockey and the women's hockey finals (renamed "Canada Hockey Place" for the duration of the games because General Motors was not the official automobile sponsor for the Olympics).

Dwarfing GM Place is the nearby **BC Place Stadium** ⑳, completed in 1983 as the biggest air-supported domed stadium in the world, covering 4 hectares (10 acres) and seating 60,000. The fibreglass and Teflon roof collapsed in early 2007, hastening the decision to replace the inflatable roof with the world's largest retractable roof, due for completion in 2011. The stadium is home to the BC Lions football team as well as providing a large venue for big-name acts such as David Bowie and The Rolling Stones. It also hosted the opening and closing ceremonies of the 2010 Winter Olympics.

BC Sports Hall of Fame and Museum ㉑

Address: Gate A, BC Place Stadium, www.bcsportshalloffame.com
Tel: 604 687 5520
Opening Hrs: daily 10am–5pm
Entrance Fee: charge

SHOPPING

The shopping in these very different neighbourhoods offers one unifying element: the fierce independence of the store owners and the variety of things to buy or to fantasise about owning.

Art

Coastal Peoples Fine Art Gallery
1024 Mainland St. Tel: 604 685 9298 www.coastal peoples.com p275, E3
For everything from intricate sweet-grass baskets and exquisite silver jewellery to massive ceremonial masks and totem poles, this store will impress. There is also a sister store in Gastown (312 Water Street).

Inuit Gallery of Canada
206 Cambie St. Tel: 604 688 7323. www.inuit.com p276, B2
This is a great place to get an introduction to Inuit art, not only the impressive stone sculptures, but also the drawings and prints. The store also boasts a large selection of Pacific Northwest art.

Books

Book Warehouse
1068 Homer St. Tel: 604 681 5711. www.book warehouse.ca p276, A3
This local independent bookseller has all the current releases (at a discount), but also a fascinating selection of more arcane reading, including lots of Canadiana. Several other stores are located in and around Vancouver.

Gifts

Barking Babies
1188 Homer St. Tel: 604 647 2275. www.barking babies.com p275, E3
This is a store devoted to providing "fashionably hip, urban goods that are well designed, functional and fun" – for dogs.

Home

Chintz and Company
950 Homer St. Tel: 604 689 2022. www.chintz.com p275, E2
A huge store with every sort of home accessory, including lovely tablewares. A great place to browse and get ideas.

Marimekko
1233 Hamilton St. Tel: 604 609 2881. www.marimekko. com p275, E3
The only Marimekko concept store in Canada, this storefront has a broad range of the Finnish design company's wares.

Ming Wo
23 East Pender St. Tel: 604 683 7268. www.mingwo. com p276, B2
This Chinatown institution, here for more than 90 years, sells the expected kitchenwares as well as some unexpected treasures, including marvellous meat cleavers, mortars and pestles, and the Japanese equivalent to the French mandolin, generally at more attractive prices than elsewhere. There are several store branches in other neighbourhoods, but this one has the comfortable, cluttered atmosphere of a store that has been around forever.

Shoes

Kalena's Shoes and Accessories
1526 Commercial Drive. Tel: 604 255 3727. www. kalenashoes.com p277, E3
This is the kind of store where you will find either nothing or six pairs. If you find six pairs, buy them and you won't regret it. Kalena's has been around for more than 40 years, with good reason.

Transport: SkyTrain Stadium

Within the enormous structure of the BC Place Stadium the BC Sports Hall of Fame and Museum honours the province's athletes and teams. There are plenty of touch screens in the sections which are each devoted to a decade, with more general displays to evoke the spirit of the times. The museum highlights the contribution made by two sporting heroes in particular, Terry Fox and Rick Hansen (*see panel, below*).

Science World at Telus World of Science ㉒

Address: 1455 Quebec Street, www.scienceworld.ca
Tel: 604 443 7440
Opening Hrs: Mon–Fri 10am–5pm, Sat–Sun 10am–6pm
Entrance Fee: charge
Transport: SkyTrain Main Street-Science World

One of the landmarks on False Creek is the huge shiny golf ball at its eastern end, built as the main entrance and centre of Expo '86 and adapted to become Science World, an interactive heaven for children of all ages,

with two floors of buttons, levers, wheels, joysticks and computer mice to improve their understanding of scientific principles.

There are supervised workshops building something different each day, a host of machines to test such things as your reactions or ability to relax, and entertaining scientific demonstrations on its centre stage. The hands-on electricity exhibit focuses on generating hydroelectric power, but also includes a kinetic wheel, a wind tunnel and solar panels. The 400-seat **OMNIMAX theatre** (separate admission charge) has a domed screen as opposed to the IMAX rectangular screen. The screen is 27 metres (89ft) in diameter and has a six-track sound system to match.

To the east of Science World is Vancouver's **main railway station**, the former Canadian Northern/National terminus on Station Street. Today it is served by VIA and Amtrak trains. The imposing station was opened in 1919 to the design of Ralph Pratt, chief architect of the Canadian Northern. The large neon sign along its two wings dates from the 1930s. ❑

ABOVE: for a swan's-eye view of the glistening glass towers, learn to kayak in False Creek.
BELOW: the shiny dome of Science World dominates the eastern shore of False Creek.

Sporting Heroes

Terry Fox was a university student when he discovered in 1977 that he had bone cancer in his right knee. During his Marathon of Hope across Canada, he hobbled 5,342km (3,339 miles) in 144 days before a recurrence of the cancer cut short his run and his life. He had raised C$24 million for cancer charities. Annual Terry Fox runs across Canada continue to raise huge sums.

A car crash left 15-year-old Rick Hansen a paraplegic, but he went on to win 19 wheelchair marathons and three world championships before embarking on a round-the-world trip in 1985. In two years he wheeled through 34 countries, raising C$24 million for spinal cord research and wheelchair sports.

BEST RESTAURANTS, BARS AND CAFÉS

Restaurants

Belgian

Chambar
562 Beatty St. Tel: 604 879 7119. www.chambar.com Open: D daily. **$$$**
p276, B2

This is the restaurant that started the Belgian beer craze in Vancouver, although now its success is based more on its amazing food. The braised lamb shank tagine with honey, figs, cinnamon and cilantro is a must-try. You'll probably want to make sure someone at the table orders a side of the frites, and, even if you don't really like beer all that much, try one of their unique offerings.

Brew Pubs

Yaletown Brewing Company
1111 Mainland St. Tel: 604 681 2739. http://mark james group.com/yaletown.html Open: L & D daily. **$$**
p276, A3

Soups, pizza, noodles, burgers, sandwiches and salads are served in Vancouver's original brew pub, which is housed in a converted industrial building with wood-beamed ceiling. (A brew pub produces beer on site and only sells it within the pub. It isn't available anywhere else.) Voted Best Brew Pub in Canada on several occasions, the Yaletown is a very popular after-work stop for Vancouverites. Try the Bricks and Beam IPA (India Pale Ale) along with any of the noodle bowls, which effectively represent the flavours of six or seven very different cuisines.

Chinese

Floata
400–182 Keefer St. Tel: 604 602 0368. www.floata.com Open: B, L & D daily. **$**
p276, C2

This gargantuan Chinese restaurant in the heart of Chinatown gives mass-dining a whole new meaning – 1,000 seats make this the largest restaurant in western Canada. It serves largely Cantonese cuisine, but does a good line in local seafood specialities and dim sum. Needless to say, it is a popular spot for big Chinese weddings and celebrations, and anyone after reasonable and very cheap Chinese food.

Szechuan Chongqing
2808 Commercial Drive (East 12th Ave). Tel: 604 254 7434. www.szechuan chongqing.com Open: B, L & D daily. **$** Off map.

This Chinese restaurant, along with its sister on Broadway, has pioneered Szechuan cuisine in Vancouver – the hot and sour soup is exceptionally good, as are Szechuan green beans and beef in black bean sauce. Rated one of the top Chinese restaurants in the city (in spite of the plain decor).

Wild Rice
117 W. Pender St. Tel: 604 642 2882. http://wildrice vancouver.com Open: D daily. **$–$$** p276, B2

An Asian-influenced restaurant that focuses on local ingredients and sustainability, Wild Rice is a member of both Ocean Wise and Green Table programmes. It's been dairy-free since day one, and staff are very helpful with food allergy issues.

Fish and Seafood

Bluewater Café and Raw Bar
1095 Hamilton St. Tel: 604 688 8078. www.bluewater cafe.net Open: D daily. **$$$$**
p276, A3

A Yaletown star specialising in wild seafood of the utmost freshness, the Bluewater is housed in a brick-and-beam warehouse conversion made elegant by the clever use of lights and wood. The kitchen is overseen by chef Frank Pabst, a classically trained European who has helped make this restaurant an international success. You can have meat if you want, but with such sublime fish and seafood on offer, such as Arctic char and Dungeness crab, why would you? The oyster menu is laid out like a wine list – a selection from Washington State

LEFT: Bluewater Café and Raw Bar.

and the East Coast if you must, but the best of all are the BC oysters, 12 types, each one lovingly described. Really well-informed and friendly service and excellent wine list.

Rodney's Oyster Bar
1228 Hamilton St. Tel: 604 609 0080. www.rodneysoysterhouse.com Open: L & D daily, D only Sun. **$**
21 p276, A3
In addition to fabulous oysters, crab cakes, clams and mussels, this informal seafood place also has the best Caesar cocktail in town.

Elixir
322 Davie St. Tel: 604 642 6787. www.elixirvancouver.ca Open: B, L & D daily. **$$**
22 p276, A3
Cleverly designed brasserie-style restaurant with four distinct areas to suit your taste and mood. The French bistro-inspired food produced by chef Don Letendre (who has worked in Tokyo and also in Britain for Raymond Blanc and Bruno Loubet at l'Odeon) sets it apart from the crowd.

Provence Marinaside
1177 Marinaside Crescent. Tel: 604 681 4144. www.provencevancouver.com Open: B, L & D daily. **$$**

Prices for a three-course dinner per person with a half-bottle of house wine:
$ = under C$30
$$ = C$30–50
$$$ = C$50–80
$$$$ = over C$80

23 p276, A3
Another Yaletown stalwart with a Provençal flavour – offering predominantly fish, but with an oyster bar and an antipasti showcase. A pretty patio and a casual atmosphere make it a great spot for lunch and weekend brunch as well as dinner.

Boneta
1 West Cordova St. Tel: 604 684 1844. www.boneta.ca Open: D Mon–Sat. **$$$**
24 p276, B2
A beautiful room serving imaginative food like seared Pacific scallops with lemon and arugula risotto – ask sommelier Neil Ingram to pair your meal with wine and you won't be disappointed.

Chili Winston
3 Alexander St. Tel: 604 288 9575. www.chillwinston.ca Open: L & D daily. **$$**
25 p276, B1
A motto of "Eat, Drink, Chill" says it all about this lounge and restaurant aimed at a hungry, hip crowd that likes meat. Many of the daily dishes focus on beef, but tempura, scallops, organic greens and crab cakes all make a showing. Good wine, good beer, good place to hang out.

Salt Tasting Room
45 Blood Alley. Tel: 604 633 1912. www.salttastingroom.com Open: L & D daily. **$$**
26 p276, B1/2
This tasting room makes things both simple and

complicated: patrons choose from among 10 artisanal cheeses, 10 types of small-batch cured meats and 10 condiments. Then, they choose from the ever-changing choice of wines, beer or sherry. Simple, but complicated, because everything is so good – it's probably best to let your server make some of the choices for you.

Top of Vancouver Revolving Restaurant
555 West Hastings St. Tel: 604 669 2220. www.topofvancouver.com Open: L & D daily. **$$$**
27 p276, B1
A glass elevator whisks you to the top of the downtown Harbour tower to the most spectacular view over the city. The restaurant makes a complete revolution every 60 minutes, so that every diner has a panoramic view. Open for brunch, lunch

and dinner, with a fairly straightforward menu of pasta, seafood and meat dishes; the main attraction here is the view, which, on a clear day, is truly stunning.

Amarcord
104–1168 Hamilton St. (Davie and Helmcken). Tel: 604 681 6500. www.amarcord.ca Open: L Mon–Fri, D daily. **$$**
28 p276, A3
This unpretentious trattoria acts as an antidote to the uber-trendiness of many Yaletown restaurants, serving traditional pastas, fish and meat dishes and risottos from the Emilia-Romagna region. Gnocchi alla reggiana with Italian sausage, fresh tomato and basil is simplicity itself but perfect. The service is super and the welcome genuinely warm.

RIGHT: Chill Winston.

Capone's Restaurant and Live Jazz Club

1141 Hamilton St. Tel: 604 684 7900. www.capones restaurant.net Open: D daily. **$$** ㉙ p276, A3

This restaurant with terrace in an old industrial building was here before all the Yaletown trendies, and continues to attract a real mix of those who have been coming for years and the super-cool who have discovered a good deal and the great music – there is live jazz seven nights a week. For food, the pizzas are the most popular – try the Big Smoke (smoked duck, smoked applewood cheddar, charred cherry tomatoes and crème fraîche.

La Terrazza

1088 Cambie St. Tel: 604 899 4449. www.laterrazza.ca Open: D daily. **$$$$** ㉚ p276, A3

Italian dining with style

and panache, this Yaletown restaurant also boasts an impressive wine list that spans not only the regions of Italy, but also France and California. If there is a winemaker's dinner while you are in town, do your best to snag a couple of tickets.

Latin American

Cobre

52 Powell St. Tel: 604 669 2396. www.cobrerestaurant. com Open: D daily. **$$** ㉛ p276, C2

Self-described as "Nuevo Latino", Cobre offers a wide selection of Caribbean and South American-inspired dishes, including prawns with Honduran coconut ginger mojo and Maple chipotle tamarind glazed wild boar belly.

Havana

1212 Commercial Drive. Tel: 604 253 9119. www. havanarestaurant.ca Open: L &

D daily. **$$** ㉜ p277, E3

Trendy Cuban and Latin American-influenced restaurant/bar with a lively Latin vibe. The patio outside is great for gawping at the local colour on the street; inside it's lined with photographs of old Havana on the distressed walls. Latin American-influenced salads, sandwiches, soups and tapas served all day; burgers are a reliable choice, or any of the brunch items. A 60-seat theatre is one of the city's top spots for poetry, slam and plays, while the art gallery attached to the restaurant showcases local and international artists.

Lebanese

Café Nuba

1206 Seymour St. Tel: 778 371 3266. www.nuba.ca Open: L & D Mon–Sat. **$** ㉝ p275, E3

Nuba offers classic Lebanese food that fills you up without emptying your wallet. There are all the usual mezes, from baba ghanooj and taboulleh for vegetarians to lamb kafta and chicken tawook for the carnivores. There are main plates that come with two or three accompaniments plus pitta bread and rice. The price is impossible to beat, particularly in this neighbourhood. The original restaurant is in Gastown (207B West Hastings St.)

LEFT: the exquisite Glowbal Grill Steaks and Satay.
RIGHT: microbrewery.

and is another great spot to grab a hearty meal.

Steaks and Satay

Glowbal Grill Steaks and Satay

1079 Mainland St. Tel: 604 629 3424. www.glowbalgrill. com Open: L & D daily. **$$$$** ㉞ p276, A3

One of the seen-and-be-seen places, Glowbal has a decade of success on the top street in Yaletown. While it promotes itself as a steak and satay restaurant, feel free to succumb to the temptation of the lobster grilled cheese (with creamed leeks and three kinds of cheese) at lunch.

Tapas

Stella's Tap and Tapas Bar

1185 Commercial Drive. Tel: 604 254 2437. www.stellas beer.com Open: L & D daily. ㉟ p277, E3

While you may be drawn here by the incredible variety of beer, not only Belgian, but also some of the best Canadian brews, it will probably be the atmosphere and the food that you remember. Sitting on the large heated patio with selection of small plates, you'll get a good idea of how people in Vancouver like to live.

Prices for a three-course dinner per person with a half-bottle of house wine:
$ = under C$30
$$ = C$30–50
$$$ = C$50–80
$$$$ = over C$80

Bars and Cafés

At the western end of Gastown, **Brioche Urban Baking** (401 West Cordova ⑧ p276, B1/2) is a popular place for pastries, panini and coffee. The **Irish Heather** (217 Carrall Street ⑨ p276, B2) is a gastropub, but it's much more. Together with **Shebeen** (in a courtyard behind), this is the place to go for that whisky you can't find anywhere else. Whether you want to spend $6 or $60 for a wee dram, you'll find a whisky (or rye or bourbon) to suit. They offer an inspired beer list and compact but quality wine list as well for those odd moments when you don't want a whisky.

The **Pourhouse** (162 Water Street ⑩ p276, B1) a newer establishment, offering peasant food with a flare: try the espresso braised shortrib or the vegetarian option of a Welsh Rarebit with aubergine and tomato ratatouille. At 375 Water St. is the **Steamworks Bar and Restaurant**. (⑪ p276, B1) Canada has been treated to an explosion of small brewing companies, and Vancouver is blessed with several. Steamworks gets its name from the famous Gastown steam line that runs through its premises, which provides the steam to fire its on-site brewing kettles. The food is straightforward pub fare, but good quality and good value. Needless to say, the beer is excellent!

Over in Yaletown, the **Opus Bar** (322 Davie Street ⑫ p276, A3) in the eponymous hotel has a tapas-inspired menu and innovative cocktails. It's definitely the place to be seen. Nearby **Boulangerie la Parisienne** (1076 Mainland Street ⑬ p276, A3), a café and bakery with a pretty all-blue interior, serves the usual pastries and decent coffee and opens up onto the pavement in the summer. On 177 Davie Street is **Urban Fare** (⑭ p276, A3), a huge grocery store that also has a café serving breakfast and light lunches, pasta, salads and the like.

At the edge of downtown and Yaletown sits **Uva** (900 Seymour Street ⑮ p276, A2), which also straddles day and night with ease. It's an espresso bar in the day, with locally roasted 49th Parallel coffee and eat-in or take-out paninis; by night, it's an elegant wine bar with great choices in wine, beer and spirits, with lots of cocktail choices as well.

Waves (492 West Hastings Street ⑯ p276, B1/2), the first in a small Vancouver chain, provides free Wi-fi along with decent coffee and the usual muffin-pastry-cake scenario.

Commercial Drive is heaving with trendy coffee places, ethnic cafés and bars. The section between Broadway and Venables is particularly lively. It is worth a cruise up and down, looking for somewhere that appeals, although you will be spoilt for choice. **Juicy Lucy's Juice Bar and Eatery** (1420 Commercial Drive ⑰ p277, E3) is a good place for freshly squeezed fruit and vegetable juices, or a quick snack of fresh sandwiches and pastries. **La Casa Gelato** (1033 Venables Street ⑱ p277, D2/3) claims to sell the largest selection of ice cream in the world, with 218 flavours on offer from its repertoire of over 500 varieties. There is something for everyone, with non-fat, non-dairy, low-fat and sugar-free ice creams in flavours ranging from the imaginable honeydew melon or chocolate Oreo cookie to off-the-wall ideas such as wild asparagus or pear and gorgonzola.

Prado Café (1938 Commercial Drive at East 4th Ave ⑲ p277, E4) is a minimalist Wi fi café open from 7am serving organic fair-trade coffee, organic juices, smoothies and baked goodies made in-house. **Tony's Deli** (1046 Commercial Drive ⑳ p277, E3) specialises in delicious Italian salads, including sun-dried tomato penne, a dozen different panini, muffins, coffee cakes and rich Italian coffee, all served in a homey, authentic setting.

Uprising Breads Bakery (1697 Venables Street ㉑ p277, E2/3) produces organic and wholegrain breads and sells home-made soup, sandwiches, salads, baked goodies and organic fair-trade coffee. **La Grotta del Formaggio** (1791 Commercial Drive ㉒ p277, E4) is a gourmet deli with a sidewalk patio where you can grab a bite and a coffee. **Latin Quarter** (1305 Commercial Drive ㉓ p277, E3) serves excellent tapas to a local crowd.

STANLEY PARK

This spectacularly located park is Vancouver's playground and exercise yard. Healthy hordes of cyclists, joggers and in-line skaters share the Seawall Promenade with amblers taking in the views at a more leisurely pace.

Main Attractions

SEAWALL PROMENADE
TOTEM POLES
SIWASH ROCK
HOLLOW TREE
VANCOUVER AQUARIUM

Maps and Listings

MAP OF STANLEY PARK,
PAGE 116
RESTAURANTS AND CAFÉS,
PAGE 121

It's hard to imagine Vancouver without Stanley Park. It is one of the attributes that makes it such a spectacular city, and it's all thanks to the threat of US invasion; when the US occupied the San Juan Islands (south of Vancouver) in 1859, concern about maintaining sovereignty arose, and the land was set aside in 1863 as a military reserve. This saved it from development until the need for it had passed and far-sighted advocates for its preservation came forward. In 1887, Stanley Park was designated a recreational reserve.

It was named after Lord Stanley, who was the first Governor-General of Canada to visit Vancouver. As an observer recorded, "Lord Stanley threw his arms to the heavens, as though embracing within them the whole of one thousand acres of primeval forest, and dedicated it 'to the use and enjoyment of peoples of all colours, creeds and customs, for all time.'"

A village in the park was occupied until the late 19th century by the Squamish band of the Coast Salish First Nations, and the army created sports facilities for the soldiers billeted in the eastern side of the park, such as a cricket field, rugby pitch

and tennis courts, but all trace of the original facilities has gone. Scout camps were also held here before World War I, when the company of bears was not unknown.

Seawall Promenade

Today Stanley Park is the green lung of Vancouver and one of the largest parks in any city, covering 405 hectares (1,000 acres). The 9km (5½-mile) **Seawall Promenade** for walkers and cyclists follows the sea around the park and is so heavily

LEFT: cycling along the seawall.
RIGHT: mesmerised by beluga whales in the Aquarium.

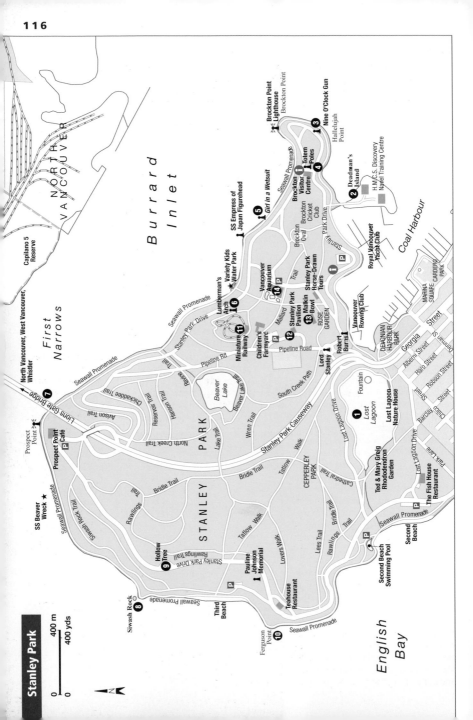

Stanley Park

0 ————— 400 m
0 ————— 400 yds

N

NORTH VANCOUVER

Capilano 5
Reserve

Burrard Inlet

First Narrows

North Vancouver, West Vancouver,
Whistler

Lions Gate Bridge **7**

SS Beaver Wreck ★

Prospect Point ‡
Prospect Point Café **P**

Siwash Rock Trail
Seawall Promenade

Siwash Rock **8**

Seawall Promenade

Third Beach

Teahouse Restaurant

Ferguson Point **10**
Seawall Promenade

English Bay

Hollow Tree **9**

Pauline Johnson Memorial

Lovers Walk

CEPPERLEY PARK

Tatlow Walk

Rawlings

Bridle Trail

Bridle Trail

Lees Trail

Rawlings Trail

Stanley Park Drive

Rawlings Trail

Tatlow Walk

STANLEY PARK

Cathedral Trail

Lees Trail

Second Beach Swimming Pool

Second Beach

P

Ted & Mary Greig Rhododendron Garden

The Fish House Restaurant **P**

Lost Lagoon Drive

Seawall Promenade

Park Lane

Barclay Street

Lost Lagoon Drive

Lord Stanley **i**
Robert Burns **i**

1 *Lost Lagoon*

Lost Lagoon Nature House

Fountain

ROSE GARDEN

Malkin Bowl **13**

Stanley Park Pavilion **12**

Vancouver Rowing Club

Vancouver Yacht Club
Royal Vancouver Yacht Club

DEVONIAN HARBOUR PARK

MARINA SQUARE

CARDERO PARK

Georgia

Alberni Street
Haro Street
Robson Street

Cardero Street
Nicola Street

Coal Harbour

H.M.C.S. Discovery Naval Training Centre

Deadman's Island **2**

Hallelujah Point

Nine O'Clock Gun **3**

Brockton Point ‡
Brockton Point Lighthouse
Brockton Point

Totem Poles **4**
Brockton Visitor Centre **i 1**

Brockton Cricket Club

Brockton Oval

Park Drive

Park Drive

Stanley Park Horse-Drawn Tours **i**

P

Girl in a Wetsuit
SS Empress of Japan Figurehead **5**

Seawall Promenade

Vancouver Aquarium **14**

Lumberman's Arch **i 6**

Variety Kids Water Park

Stanley Park Drive

Seawall Promenade

Children's Farmyard

Miniature Railway **11**

Pipeline Road

Mallard

Pipeline Rd

Beaver Lake

Beaver Lake Trail

Lake Trail

Wren Trail

Reservoir Trail

Ravine Trail

Chickadee Trail

Avison Trail

North Creek Trail

Stanley Park Causeway

South Creek Path

Stanley Park Drive

Seawall Promenade

used that cyclists and in-line skaters are allowed to use it only in an anti-clockwise direction. The seawall took 53 years to build, and for 32 of them a Scottish master stonemason named James Cunningham coordinated its construction; his dedication is commemorated by a plaque opposite Siwash Rock and by the James Cunningham Seawall Race held on the last Sunday of October.

Step inland into the forest onto the extensive network of paths partly made out of old logging roads and within minutes you will find relative solitude, even in high summer. After a walk through the quieter parts of the forest, it comes as no surprise to learn that Stanley Park inspired some of Emily Carr's first landscapes, while she was teaching children's art in Vancouver in 1906.

The best way to explore and appreciate the park properly is by bike if you're short of time, or on foot. In summer there is a steady stream of cyclists crossing Georgia Street to pick up the path – it has become one of the most popular activities for visitors, since the views are enough to convince anyone of Vancouver's claim to be one of the most beautifully situated cities in the world. It's also a great way to see the impressive sight of the cruise ships leaving from Canada Place in the late afternoon, and watch them passing through the First Narrows at close range. Just before Denman Street reaches Georgia Street, there is a cluster of bike rental shops providing all kinds of bikes, child seats and trailers. Go early if you want to have a relatively unobstructed ride or rollerblade around the city.

Another, albeit more limited, way to see the park is to hop on one of the horse-drawn carriages (see Activities, page 262). The roomy carriages are drawn by Grey Shire, Clydesdale, Percheron or Belgian horses, which meander along the roads with a pro-fessional guide to interpret the sites. The hour-long tours leave from a kiosk at Coal Harbour car park adjacent to the information booth.

An anticlockwise tour

The waterfront area between Canada Place and Stanley Park is known as Coal Harbour, after a thin seam of coal first noted by Captain Vancouver. The waters that once teemed with herring and clams are now filled with pleasure craft, behind which soars a glittering row of glass towers. Together they form one of the classic postcard views of the city, seen across the water from Stanley Park. As you enter the park from Georgia Street, the body of water on your left, known as the **Lost Lagoon ❶**, was part of Coal Harbour until the causeway was erected in 1916, turning it into a freshwater lake fed from the city's supply. The rush-fringed lake dotted with small islands is a haven for swans, ducks and Canada geese. Beside the south side of the lake is the **Lost Lagoon Nature House**, operated by the Stanley Park Ecology Society (call or check website

ABOVE: bike hire shop on Denman Street, perfect for excursions around the seawall.
BELOW: horse-drawn carriage in Stanley Park.

ABOVE: an evening stroll along the Seawall Promenade. **BELOW:** the Nine O'Clock Gun.

island has been a regular source of dispute. A 99-year lease of the island by the federal government in 1930 stipulated that it should be used as a park, but it has been a naval reserve, HMCS *Discovery*, since 1944.

Every night at 9 o'clock the boom of a cannon issues from Hallelujah Point, so named because it was the frequent meeting point of a small troop of the Salvation Army. The **Nine O'Clock Gun** ❸ was cast in England in 1816 and has been fired since 1894, initially from a site near the present-day Hudson's Bay Company store. Some say it started as a fishing curfew signal, others that it's just a noisy timepiece. It's fired electronically from the harbourmaster's perch on top of a skyscraper, and is protected by a fence to stop a repetition of its kidnap by UBC students who ransomed the gun for a donation to a children's hospital.

Just off the main path are nine **totem poles** ❹ representing the Kwakwaka'wakw, Haida and Squamish nations, and each is explained by interpretive boards at the nearby **Brockton Visitor Centre** (www.city.vancouver. bc.ca). In 2008, three carved gateways by renowned Coast Salish artist Susan Point were installed nearby. These red cedar portals are constructed to represent the traditional slant-roof style of Coast Salish architecture with carved welcome figures in the doorways. As you round Brockton Point, North Vancouver and the Coast Mountains are spread out in a majestic sweep to the north. The point is marked by a small red-and-white-striped lighthouse built in 1914.

When a licence to install a replica of Copenhagen's famous waterfront statue of the Little Mermaid was refused, a contemporary version was commissioned from Elek Imredy. The *Girl in a Wetsuit* ❺, complete with goggles, was unveiled in 1972.

A slight detour inland, **Lumberman's Arch** ❻ is a replica of the arch

for opening hours, tel: 604 257 6908; www.stanleyparkecology.ca), which offers natural history information and guided walking tours.

Pipeline Road leads to a cluster of visitor attractions. Near the entrance to the park, directly behind the Rowing Club building, is a **statue of the poet Robert Burns** which was unveiled by Ramsay MacDonald on 25 August 1928, a year before he became British Prime Minister for the second time. Near by is a **statue of Lord Stanley** (1960) by English sculptor Sydney Marsh, which captures Stanley's expansive gesture at the ceremony.

Beyond the Royal Vancouver Yacht Club lies **Deadman's Island** ❷, so named because it was once a native burial ground when bodies were ceremoniously placed in bentwood boxes high in the Douglas firs and red cedars. It became an isolation site and burial ground after smallpox epidemics in 1888 and 1892, but the

built over Pender Street in 1912 to welcome Queen Victoria's son, the Duke of Connaught, while he was Governor General of Canada. The arch was built near the site of a Squamish village of four houses and a lodge until the 1860s, where potlatches attended by thousands of native people were held. Tonnes of seashells from the village midden were used to surface the first roads through the forest.

Just after passing underneath the **Lions Gate Bridge ❼** *(see below)* is Prospect Point, site of the most famous wreck in Vancouver history when the first steamship on the West Coast, the *Beaver*, went aground in 1888. She sat on the rocks for four years, being steadily stripped by souvenir hunters, until the wake of a passing ship sent her to the bottom. Many of the salvaged items can be seen in the Vancouver Museum and the Maritime Museum, and she is depicted in a mural in the Marine Building *(see page 83)*.

In December 2006, a storm hit Prospect Point, the gale-force winds ripping downs trees as they whipped through the park. An estimated 10,000 trees were lost – about 10 percent of the total. While devastating at the time, the damage focused efforts on the need to clear up the mess and revitalise the park. The restoration project attracted both public and private funding, financing overdue repairs to badly eroded cliffs and ensuring the park remains safe for the more than 8 million visitors the park attracts annually.

The offshore 15m (49ft) -high column of grey basalt rock is known as **Siwash Rock ❽**, created according to Indian legend when four giants were so impressed by the devotion of a young chief to his newborn son that they turned him to stone, as a monument to probity in fatherhood. This curious notion of a reward was recorded by Pauline Johnson (1861–1913), an Ontario performer and writer of Mohawk descent who spent her last four years in Vancouver chronicling legends and stories of the Squamish Nation as told to her by Chief Joe Capilano. Her grave inland from Ferguson Point is the only marked grave in Stanley Park.

Just beyond the tarmac road inland

ABOVE: look out for the *Girl in a Wetsuit* just after Brockton Point. The unmistakeable bright yellow mounds visible on the north shore beyond are piles of sulphur. **BELOW:** Lions Gate Bridge.

Lions Gate Bridge

For most people, the Lions Gate Bridge is the most striking of Vancouver's many bridges, spanning the waters between the forest of Stanley Park and the steeply rising land of the north shore. Astonishingly it was not a city or federal project but constructed for the Guinness family in Ireland, designed both to enhance the development potential of the 1,620 hectares (4,000 acres) of land they had bought along the north shore of Burrard Inlet but also to provide jobs during the Depression. Construction began in March 1937, and it opened to traffic in November 1938, having cost C$5.8 million. It was formally opened by King George VI and Queen Elizabeth in May 1939 during the first visit of a reigning monarch to Canada.

Officially known as the First Narrows Bridge, the bridge has a total length of 1,820 metres (5,890ft) and a tower height of 111 metres (364ft). The centre of three lanes is reversed according to the direction of commuter traffic, and heavy trucks are banned. The bridge was sold by the Guinness family to the province in 1955 for C$5.9 million, and in 1963 the tolls were abolished. The lighting that makes the bridge look so spectacular at night was given to the city by the Guinness family in 1986.

from Siwash Rock is the **Hollow Tree** , a huge red cedar. The 700-year-old tree began to list dangerously following the 2006 windstorm, but plans to take it down were met by a public outcry. Private donations financed the recent straightening and stabilising of the landmark, just in time for the 2010 Winter Olympics. It is probably Canada's most photographed tree, thanks to an early 20th-century photographer who spent years snapping visitors beside this remnant of old-growth forest.

Past Third Beach is **Ferguson Point** , site of the Teahouse restaurant *(see opposite)*, created out of a tearoom that was opened on the site of a World War II gun battery. Continuing anticlockwise, Second Beach has been a favourite picnic spot since the 1880s. Now, there is a 50-metre (164ft) summer-only freshwater swimming pool overlooking the sea, tennis courts, miniature golf course and even an outdoor dance floor.

The seawall trail ends near the **Ted and Mary Greig Rhododendron Garden**, which is composed of 4,500 plants, along with many interesting

BELOW: the Teahouse at Stanley Park.

trees. The best time of year to walk along the wood-chip path between the massed blooms of pastel-coloured flowers is May.

Park attractions

Accessible from the Plaza off Pipeline Road is a **miniature railway**  winding through the forest, with a diesel-powered replica of steam locomotive No. 374 which pulled the first transcontinental train into Vancouver in 1886. Nearby is a **children's farmyard** (both summer, 11am–4pm) with goats, sheep, cows, ponies and pigs, although funding problems have put the future of the farmyard in question. **Stanley Park Pavilion**  was designed to resemble a Swiss chalet, originally housing the Vancouver Park Board offices and a refreshment area. Constructed of stone and wood in 1911 to the design of Otto Moburg, it was grand enough to host a reception given by the Prince of Wales in 1919 for the families of soldiers killed in World War I. The summer-only café has a terrace overlooking the garden and serves light meals and drinks.

The open-air theatre and concert

Flora and Fauna

Most of Stanley Park's red cedar, hemlock and Douglas fir trees are second- and third-growth forest, since it was logged several times in the second half of the 19th century. One of the park's most famous trees, the old-growth National Geographic Tree (so named because it was featured in a 1978 article in that magazine) fell down in 2007, after surviving an estimated 800–1,000 years. The tree had a diameter of 5 metres (16ft) and was 45 metres (130ft) tall. It had been struck by lightning and damaged over the centuries, but was thought to have weathered the massively destructive storm of December 2006. However, the tree had been in decline and its loss was keenly felt by locals. The park is home to large populations of raccoons, squirrels, skunks and coyotes. The open water of Beaver Lake and Lost Lagoon attract migratory birds, though many Canada geese, swans and ducks have made the park their permanent home. You may also spot a blue heron or a wood duck.

The best way to experience all this wonderful nature and wildlife is to abandon the seawall, and follow one of the many hiking trails through the tranquil woods.

area known as the **Malkin Bowl** ⓭ was built in 1934 by the grocery wholesaler and former mayor W.H. Malkin in memory of his wife. Theatre Under the Stars presents musicals in the crescent-shaped proscenium arch all summer long.

Though the large garden south of the Malkin Bowl is described as a **Rose Garden**, it is actually the thoughtful colour combinations of the massed bedding plants that provide the more impressive displays between April and September. To the east is a memorial to US President Warren Harding, who visited Vancouver in 1923. He was the first US president to visit Canada, and created such a favourable impression that Vancouverites were stunned when he had a heart attack and died in San Francisco seven days after leaving Canada. A competition was held for the design of a monument, won by Charles Marega *(see page 101)*, to be erected on the spot where Harding spoke to the public.

Vancouver Aquarium ⓮
Address: 845 Avison Way, www.vanaqua.org

Tel: 604 659 3474
Opening Hrs: Sept–June daily 9.30am–5pm, July–Aug daily 9.30am–7pm
Entrance Fee: charge
Transport: bus 19

Of the more than 70,000 animals at this popular aquarium, the most popular are the beluga whales, living in massive tanks with underground viewing windows to watch the vast, blubbery creatures in motion. The vibrant colours of the tropical corals are spectacular, and children are fascinated by such weird-looking fish as the box-shaped black porcupine fish. An area devoted to Amazonia has a tank of some extraordinary fish found in the river, such as redtailed catfish, tambaqui and the arapaima, – the world's largest freshwater fish, growing up to 4.5 metres (15ft).

But of all these fascinating sea creatures, those in the outside pools are the biggest crowd-pullers, particularly at feeding times. It's hard not to be mesmerised by the sea otters' balletic performance as they spin around excitedly retrieving the fish, then use their tummies for a dining table. ❏

ABOVE: tanks filled with marine life from a variety of habitats fascinate at the Vancouver Aquarium, but the snowy white beluga whales steal the show.

RESTAURANTS AND CAFÉS

The Fish House
8901 Stanley Park Drive. Tel: 604 681 7275. www.fishhousestanleypark.com
Open: L & D daily, Brunch Sat–Sun. **$$$** ㊱ p272, B4
Award-winning seafood restaurant in a charming 1930s building overlooking English Bay. Karen Barnaby, chef here for more than 15 years, also offers cooking classes so people can create amazing food when they go home. Exquisite afternoon teas with a range of teas,

sandwiches and cakes served daily.

Prospect Point Café and Lions Bar
Prospect Point Lookout, 5601 Stanley Park Drive. Tel: 604 669 2737. www.prospectpoint.ca Open: L & D daily in summer (from Victoria Day), L only in winter. **$$** ㊲ p272, B1
This great viewing point, nestled on the cliffside overlooking Lions Gate Bridge, offers indoor and outdoor seating for up to 200 people. "Ocean-wise" seafood choices

abound, as well as good salad and burger options. The adjacent Prospect Point Café Express is open daily, from 9am–8pm in summer and 9am–5pm in winter. It offers a takeaway service, including fish and chips as well as chicken, salmon and veggie burgers. A step up from the average concession.

Teahouse at Stanley Park
Ferguson Drive, Stanley Park Drive. Tel: 604 669 3281. www.vancouverdine.com
Open: L & D daily, Brunch Sat–Sun. **$$$** ㊳ p272, A3

This is a great place for a leisurely lunch on a sunny day or, even better, a meal while you watch the sun set. The menu is extensive and the wine list offers plenty of choices by the glass. Local seafood is the natural choice, but there are plenty of options for meat lovers, although less for vegetarians.

• • • • • • • • • •

Prices for a three-course dinner per person with a half-bottle of house wine.
$$$$ = over C$80, **$$$** = C$50–80, **$$** = C$30–50, **$** = under C$30.

MODERN ARCHITECTURE

In a generation the skyline of Vancouver has been pierced by a succession of ever taller buildings, reflecting the return of residents to the city centre.

In its short history, Vancouver has developed a reputation for innovative architecture, helped by being the home of some leading 20th-century architects, most famously Arthur Erickson. Like every city, there are plenty of buildings that contribute little or nothing to the city's visual appeal, and equally it would have benefited from a more sparing use of the wrecking ball. But there is much to celebrate from most periods of Vancouver's development.

Until the 1960s the pace of change was slow, and someone who knew the city before World War I would have had no difficulty recognising it half a century later. But since then the appearance of the city has been utterly transformed, giving opportunities for architects to design new, and adapt old, mostly industrial buildings, for residential and office use. Most of the attention goes to the large sites and commissions such as Simon Fraser University and the redevelopments around Coal Harbour and False Creek, but West Vancouver has some exceptional modern houses by such architects as Ron Thom, Peter Thornton and Erickson.

LEFT: the interior of the Museum of Anthropology at UBC was designed in 1976 by Arthur Erickson to house the outstanding collection of ethnographic and archaeological objects. The traditional West Coast post-and-beam structures of First Nations peoples were the inspiration for the design. Glass walls 15 metres (49ft) high light the interior.

ABOVE: the floor-to-ceiling windows in the Convention Centre expansion seduce visitors with spectacular vistas of ocean, mountain and cityscapes.
LEFT: the city's Central Library invites comparison with Rome's Colosseum, though architect Moshe Safdie has denied that it inspired his design.

RIGHT: at the top of the 177-metre (581ft) Harbour Centre Tower is The Lookout! Perched on top of a conventional office building, the pod designed by Eng and Wright in 1977 contains a viewing platform and a revolving restaurant.

SHANGRI-LA AND THE OLYMPIC VILLAGE

In 2009, the Shangri-La Hotel opened at 1128 West Georgia Street, becoming Vancouver's tallest building at 199 metres (652ft). Designed by James K.M. Cheng, the 61-storey triangular building has no levels 4 or 13 in accordance with feng shui principles. With 119 rooms, the hotel occupies the first 15 floors of the building, while floors 16–42 contain 227 condominiums. On floors 43–59, there are "private access residential units", with two penthouses on the top two floors. The upper one has a roof garden and swimming pool.

During the 2010 Winter Olympics, the Olympic Athletes' Village in False Creek accommodated more than 2,200 athletes in purpose-built condominiums. The plan to dismantle the temporary Olympic structures and sell off most of the residential units, while keeping some for social housing, has had its critics, particularly when the City of Vancouver had to find additional funds to cover cost overruns on the project.

Another Olympic venue, the Richmond Oval for speed-skating events, forms the centrepiece of a 13-hectare (32-acre) redevelopment along the banks of the Fraser River with a waterfront plaza and park. The 8,000-seater Oval itself will become a multi-purpose sports and recreation centre.

ABOVE: the overhang at the Pan Pacific Hotel takes advantage of the light while protecting people from rain.

BELOW: the "sails" of Canada Place, overlooking the Inner Harbour, which was designed by Toronto's Zeidler-Roberts Partnership with Downs-Archambault for Expo '86. The building contains a hotel, cruise-ship terminal and conference centre.

BELOW: at the east end of False Creek is the geodesic dome of 766 triangles designed by Bruno Freschi for Expo '86 and adapted by Boak Alexander into the popular attraction of Science World.

GRANVILLE ISLAND AND FALSE CREEK

Once the site of sawmills and heavy industry, this patch of land has been transformed into a model of urban living. At its hub, a thriving farmers' market offers regional produce to a health-obsessed clientele. With museums, theatres, restaurants and artists' studios you have the elements of a perfect day out.

Main Attractions

PUBLIC MARKET
GRANVILLE ISLAND BREWERY
ARTISTS' STUDIOS
FALSE CREEK SEAWALL

If there's one area of Vancouver that almost every visitor goes to, it's Granville Island, lying in the shadow of Granville Bridge on the south shore of False Creek. This model of urban regeneration is packed with theatres, craft workshops and studios, restaurants, cafés, bars and a huge fresh-produce market, making it one of the most vibrant parts of the city. There are still chandlers, boat companies, an engineering workshop and a cement plant to give the area some "grit", and the island is also an appropriate home for the Emily Carr University of Art and Design, which offers degree programmes in both fine and applied arts.

A few people live on the island in attractive houseboats, and there is a hotel, a couple of microbreweries and an artisan sake maker. Two parks and plenty of trees soften the well-adapted industrial buildings, and the views across the water from the perimeter of the island are some of the best in Vancouver. The only blight is the traffic which clogs the narrow streets in the generally vain hope of finding somewhere to park. Savvy locals know to walk or take public transit.

During the 2010 Winter Olympics, a new railway was demonstrated for moving people from the Olympic SkyTrain station to Granville Island, but the long-term future of the line depends on government funding, already stretched to cover the cost of putting on the Games.

The most pleasant way of reaching the island is by the double-ended small ferries operated by AquaBus (which takes bikes) and False Creek Ferries (which does not). *For more information on ferry transport in False Creek see page 246.*

LEFT: False Creek Ferries docked at Granville Island.

Artificial island

Until the arrival of Europeans, False Creek had teemed with fish, and its south shore had been a wintering ground of the Squamish nation. False Creek was so named in 1859 when Captain George Richards found a dead end during Royal Navy survey work instead of the expected link to coal deposits that he had found in Burrard Inlet. Mills were erected around the creek to process the immense stands of Douglas fir in the district that became Shaughnessy, and factories making sash windows and doors grew up alongside the mills.

The decision of the Canadian Pacific Railway (CPR) to terminate its transcontinental line at English Bay rather than Port Moody, coupled with construction of the first of three Granville bridges and settlement of the south shore after the 1886 fire, increased the importance of this once peaceful inlet.

Granville Island was created in 1915 when 760,000 cubic metres of sea mud was sucked from the bed of False Creek and poured into wooden shuttering to form the island. It was part of a much larger scheme to reclaim 25 hectares (61 acres) of land for railway yards, which reduced False Creek to one-fifth of its original size. The island was an immediate success, quickly occupied by a range of companies, from ironworks and shipyards to manufacturers of rope and machinery geared to the needs of the mining and forestry industries. Most occupied corrugated-iron factories, and many had barges on one side and rail lines on the other. False Creek echoed with the constant shunting of boxcars and the noise of heavy machinery.

By the end of World War II, the rail-linked lumber yards, sawmills and greasy rat-infested wharves had degenerated into such a state that studies were made into completing the job of filling in the entire creek. Thankfully the prohibitive cost forced the development of more imaginative solutions. The city and the CPR agreed a land swap, but having gained control of the creek's south side, the city was split over whether it should continue to be used by industry or whether it

BELOW: view across False Creek.

Siegel's Bagels (inside the Public Market) makes authentic Montreal bagels, kettle-boiled and then baked in a 25-ton wood-burning oven, producing a smoky flavour, crunchy on the outside and chewy on the inside.

ABOVE AND RIGHT: fresh produce at Granville Market.

should be turned over to housing. Campaigners for the latter won. The waterfront was cleaned up and walled and the popular neighbourhood of False Creek came into being.

Foodie heaven

In the late 1970s, a serious effort to transform the island took place – the idea of a place where people would choose to come seemed madness, as the island consisted of heavy industry and abandoned buildings. It was, however, a brilliant idea, and today the main **Public Market ❶** is one of the most successful markets in North America. It is actually five buildings brought together to form a covered market. In sheds that once repaired mining equipment and made wire rope is a farmers' market of astonishingly high-quality produce: piles of beautifully arranged fruit and vegetables, great counters of ice-cooled seafood; fresh pasta; well-butchered and trimmed meat;

sausages and pâtés to rival the best Europe has to offer; over 150 different kinds of cheese; herbs, spices and breads to meet the needs of the city's cosmopolitan population; and specialist makers of fudge, chocolate and gourmet ready meals.

In the northern corner is a Food Court where you can buy healthy hot and cold food of a quality that matches the market. There is an area to eat inside, but unless it's raining most people eat outside overlooking

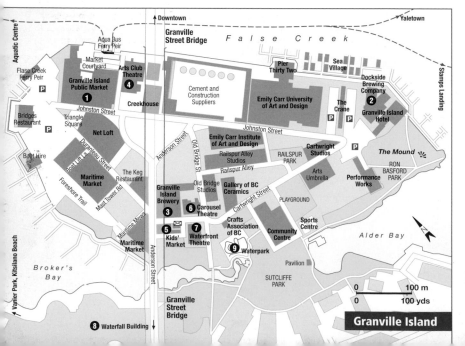

Granville Island

the water and Burrard Bridge and listening to the street musicians or watching mime artists, clowns and comedians.

The small island is home to two microbreweries. **Dockside Brewing Company ❷** at 1253 Johnston Street produces eight beers which can be sampled in the Dockside Lounge of the Granville Island Hotel (which has special offers on beers on Tuesday and Wednesday).

The **Granville Island Brewery ❸** was Canada's first microbrewery, founded in 1984. It produces five staple and additional seasonal brews, which are on offer in the brewery's taproom. It also offers daily tours of the brewery at noon, 2pm and 4pm followed by tastings.

Artists and artisans

Granville Island is home to some 50 studios or workshops of creative people who can be found in a free leaflet, "Artists and Artisans of Granville Island". Many of the studios are shared by three or more artists, so the range of work is astonishing: jewellery, ceramics, slippers, embroideries,

paintings, Shaker oval boxes, paper, silk weaving, letterpress printing, tapestries, baskets, furniture, beadworks, hats, even a designer and maker of handmade eyewear in wood, horn, gold or silver who has made glasses for Elton John.

In addition to individual studios, there are five not-for-profit associations or cooperatives that showcase hundreds of other artists. The Gallery of BC Ceramics on Cartwright Street is a good place to find useful as well as decorative items by a variety of potters. A few doors along, the Crafts Association of BC has crafts ranging from fibre to metal from its 400 members. Circle Craft Cooperative has more than 200 members who showcase their work in the Net Loft and at an extremely popular Christmas Market downtown in the Convention Centre. There are also numerous shops selling artists' supplies, postcards, clothes, stationery and native crafts.

Besides ateliers, the barn doors of the **Arts Club Theatre ❹** are often wide open in summer so that passers-by can watch the scenery makers

ABOVE: view of Burrard Bridge. **BELOW LEFT AND RIGHT:** native crafts in the Raven and the Bear store.

BC Microbrews

British Columbians love a beer as much as the next person and the province's award-winning microbrews offer a superb range of thirst-quenching ales.

You can't go far in British Columbia without coming across a local microbrew – or craft beer, to use the hophead vernacular. The province is home to dozens of brewpubs and independent breweries, so you'd need a mighty thirst to sample all of BC's indigenous suds during your stay, but here are a few lagers and ales worth quaffing.

First, the big craft-beer players: Granville Island Brewery, Canada's first microbrewery, and Okanagan Spring Brewery. They fashion preservative-free beer using just four primary ingredients: barley, hops, yeast and water, producing good-quality products like the GI Cypress Honey Lager and the OK Spring stout-like Old English Porter, a hit at 8.5 percent alcohol. Both breweries have won many international awards and their success has paved the way for the smaller breweries.

For small batch, both Storm Brewing and R&B Brewing have awards from the local chapter of CAMRA, the Campaign for Real Ale. The brewmasters at these outfits are passionate about big, flavourful ales, as Storm's Highland Scottish Ale and R&B's **Hoppelganger IPA** (India Pale Ale) will attest. Also in the Vancouver area, you'll find several top-notch brewpubs, such as Dix BBQ and Brewery, the Steamworks Brewing Company and the Howe Sound BrewPub, located in the mountains near Whistler. For a taste of a uniquely BC sensibility, try the latter's Mettleman Copper Ale, brewed in honour of a nearby mountain-bike race. In keeping with BC's environmental awareness, the Mettleman bottle is re-closable, making it reusable and meeting the company's green packaging objectives.

Ale trails

Vancouver may have its share of craft breweries, but Victoria is a favourite destination for beer lovers. On the self-guided Ale Trail, visit Spinnakers Gastro Brewpub, the country's oldest such establishment, for a sleeve of the clove-scented Hefeweizen, a German-style wheat beer. Close by, Swans Brewpub serves standouts such as the strong Raspberry Ale and the Buckerfield's Bitter. And finally, Phillips Brewing Company's smooth Longboat Double Chocolate Porter definitely lives up to its name.

The wine-producing Okanagan is BC's third microbrew hub. From the Cannery Brewing Company in Penticton there's the punchy Anarchist Amber Ale, whose recipe calls for three kinds of hops. Made in the same town, the Tin Whistle Brewing Company's Killer Bee Dark Honey Ale adds five different barley malts to the mix. Drink it slowly so you don't miss any.

Many of these beers are available for takeaway at their respective breweries and brewpubs, in both bottles and kegs. British Columbia's government liquor stores also carry a wide variety. For prices and availability, see www.bcliquorstores.com or call 1 800 667 9463. ❑

LEFT: Granville Island Brewery's award-winning beers are made from 100 percent natural ingredients.

at work, as are the doors to a company making delicate architectural models.

The Kids' Market ❺ sells clothes, toys, books, CDs, magic and party supplies, and has play areas and cafés with "child-friendly" menus.

To see why the island is such a focus of cultural life and activity, visit www.granvilleisland.com.

Entertainment

Besides the Arts Club, Carousel ❻ and Waterfront ❼ theatres (see page 261), the island is home to a number of smaller venues, including Performance Works at 1218 Cartwright Street,

set up in a 1920s machine shop to provide a rehearsal and performance space which hosts year-round events and productions.

The numerous spaces make it an ideal location for festivals such as the September Fringe Festival (with more than 400 performances in 11 days, the vast majority of them on Granville Island) and the Vancouver International Writers and Readers Festival. During the 2010 Winter Olympics, Granville Island was one of the focal points for parties, when part of the island became know as the French Quarter with free entertainment and

TIP

For sailors, the walk along Duranleau Street and into the Maritime Market can provide hours of entertainment – from clothing to charts to books, there is something for everyone.

SHOPPING

Without question, Granville Island offers the widest collection of small independent shops. The focus of the island is dual: food and artisan workmanship. While the latter can mean anything from violins to furniture, the majority of the shops offer something that can be safely transported home.

Crafts

Circle Craft Co-operative Shop and Gallery
1–1666 Johnston St. (in the Net Loft). Tel: 604 669 8021. p275, D3
More than 200 artists display work in contemporary and traditional craft in clay, glass, fibre, wood, metal and mixed media.

Dundarave Print Workshop
1640 Johnston St. Tel: 604 689 1650. www.dundarave printworkshop.ca p275, D3
This contemporary fine art printmaking studio

has wonderful prints at very attractive prices.

Fibre Art Studio
1610 Johnston St. Tel: 604 688 3047. p275, D3
Everything here, from original handwoven tapestries and needle-felted soft sculptures to hand-dyed mohair, wool, cotton and handspun yarns, is created on the premises.

Gallery of BC Ceramics
1359 Cartwright St. Tel: 604 669 3606. www.bcpotters.com p275, D4
Owned by the Potters Guild of BC, this store sells ceramics from more than 100 potters. Prices are fair and quality outstanding.

Hammered and Pickled
3–1494 Old Bridge St. Tel: 604 689 0615. p275, D4
This store has everything from jewellery to toys. The wallets and tote bags are imaginative, well priced and a useful souvenir.

The Original Paper-Ya Co Ltd.
9–1666 Johnston St. (in the

Net Loft). Tel: 604 684 2531. www.paper-ya.com p275, D3
Beautiful handmade papers and notebooks.

Food

Artesan Sakemaker
1339 Railspur Alley. Tel: 604 685 7253. www.artisansake maker.com p275, D4
Masa Shiroki had a dream: to make small batches of premium sake in Canada. His passion for his craft makes a visit to the studio a treat.

Edible British Columbia
1681 Johnston St. (in the main food market). Tel: 604 812 9660. www.edible-british columbia.com p275, D3
A dedicated and passionate staff makes shopping here a breeze. This is also the place to sign up for foodie walking tours.

Liberty Wine Merchants
1660 Duranleau St. Tel: 604 602 1120. www.libertywine merchants.com p275, D3
One of the original private wine stores, Liberty

stocks wines in every price range; its staff are extremely knowledgeable.

Women's Clothing

Edie's Hats
4–1666 Johnston St. (in the Net Loft). Tel: 604 683 4280. www.ediehats.com p275, D3
A hat store with something for everyone – even more intriguing, the owner is part of Vancouver's flamenco community.

Maiwa Handprints
6–1666 Johnston St. (in the Net Loft). Tel: 604 669 3939. www.maiwa.com p275, D3
Clothing made with natural fabrics and dyes that is elegant, comfortable and great value. Jewellery is unusual and captivating.

Silk Weaving Studio
1531 Johnston St. Tel: 604 687 7455. www.silkweaving studio.com p275, D3
A wide selection of handwoven silk garments, plus yarns and fibres for those who want to create their own wearable art.

ABOVE LEFT: kayaking in False Creek. ABOVE RIGHT: Granville Island Water Park. BELOW: craft-beer from Granville Island's own brewery.

a constant party atmosphere.

The idea of free entertainment is something that fits in with the whole approach on the island, and buskers have their scheduled spots throughout the market, politely packing up their gear when the next artist arrives for his or her shift. It's very civilised and works astonishingly well.

Though just off the island at 1540 West 2nd Avenue, the **Waterfall Building** ❽ housing the Elliott Louis Gallery should not be missed by admirers of Arthur Erickson's work. Built in 1996, the Waterfall Building – actually five buildings designed for commercial and live/work use around an atrium – is approached past a thin curtain of water falling into a rectangular pond.

Activities

Children adore racing through the water jets and fountains in the **waterpark** ❾ (daily 10am–6pm from the third weekend of May to the first weekend of September) at Sutcliffe Park, where there is also a playground.

Cycling the traffic-free path along the seawall is one of the most popular ways of appreciating Vancouver's stunning location, and Granville Island is a good starting place. Heading west, the path winds past the condominiums and houses that line the creek before reaching Vanier Park and Kitsilano Beach.

The Seawall

The majority of the houses and apartments along the south side of False Creek South between the Granville Street and Cambie Street bridges were built in the late 1970s and early 1980s. The development left lots of room for parks and the seawall is a great place for a leisurely walk. The last remnants of the area's industrial past underwent redevelopment with the construction of the Olympic Athletes' Village. The completion of this area has meant that the waterfront almost all the way around False Creek now offers an urban walkway that in some ways mimics the Stanley Park seawall, with water in its centre instead of trees. ❑

BEST RESTAURANTS, BARS AND CAFÉS

Restaurants

European

Dockside Restaurant
1253 Johnston St. Tel: 604 685 7070. www.dockside brewing.com Open: B, L & D daily. **$$** 39 p275, D4
Part of the Granville Island Hotel, the cooking revolves around the wood-fired grill, rotisseries and pizza oven. In summer the patio offers a great view over False Creek. The beer brewed on the premises is refreshing any time of year.

Fish and Seafood

Monk McQueens Fresh Seafood and Oyster Bar
601 Stamps Landing. Tel: 604 877 1351. www.monk mcqueens.com Open: L & D daily. **$$$** 40 p275, E4
A lovely position overlooking False Creek and Yaletown, Monk's has a downstairs bar with huge patio and a more formal restaurant upstairs. Aside from oysters, there are a number of interesting small plates, perfect to have with a glass of wine watching the sunset.

Sandbar Seafood Restaurant
1535 Johnston St. Tel: 604

Prices for a three-course dinner per person with a half-bottle of house wine:
$ = under C$30
$$ = C$30–50
$$$ = C$50–80
$$$$ = over C$80

669 9030. www.vancouver dine.com Open: L & D daily. **$$$** 41 p275, D3
Though specialising in seafood with such signature dishes as Wok Squid (with chillies, garlic and ginger) and Cedar Plank West Coast Salmon, carnivores are also catered for. Great view over False Creek marina. Pre-theatre menu available for those going on to the Arts Club.

Tony's Fish and Oyster Café
1511 Anderson St. Tel: 604 683 7127. www.tonysfish-granvilleisland.com Open: L & D daily. **$** 42 p275, D4
For a quick meal without blowing the budget, the halibut and chips will give you the energy to tackle the market.

French

Bridges Restaurant and Bistro
1696 Duranleau St. Tel: 604 687 4400. www.bridges restaurant.com Open: L & D daily. **$$$** 43 p275, C/D3
The superb location facing the marina, the Durrard Street Bridge and the sunset is the key to this restaurant's success. The bistro menu is sensibly divided into small, medium and large portions, while upstairs the restaurant has a more limited and expensive menu focusing on fish.

RIGHT: the delightful Bridges bistro.

Bars and Cafés

Agro Café (1363 Railspur Alley 24 p275, D4). Organic fair-trade coffee, snacks and lunch. Patronised by people who work on the island. Enough said. The **Arts Club Back Stage Lounge** (1585 Johnston St. 25 p275, D3) has a great selection of beer on tap, as well as an extensive cocktail repertoire – it's a good place to meet for a drink, but also offers light lunches, pizza, smoked salmon and bruschetta in a waterfront setting. **Blue Parrot** (1689 Johnston St. 26 p275, D3) serves great organic coffee, strudels, gooey cinnamon buns and grilled focaccia sandwiches. Hidden on the back side of things at the north end of the Island under the bridge is **GI Gelato and Coffee House** (27 p275, D3), providing a break from the craziness of the market. **Pedro's Coffee House** (1496 Cartwright St 28 p275, D4) sells organic coffee, light meals and refreshments.

International

Pacific Institute of Culinary Arts
1505 West Second Ave. Tel: 604 734 4488. www. bistro101.com Open: L & D Mon–Fri. **$** 44 p275, C4

Culinary students prepare three-course set lunch and dinner menus in the marina-view restaurant. There is also a café and bakery on the premises with really great pastries.

WEST SIDE

Take a walk on the West Side: its beaches, mountain views, elegant tree-lined streets, lofty parks, and dizzying choice of bistros and restaurants make It one of the city's most desirable districts.

Not to be confused with West Vancouver or the West End, the West Side covers the University of British Columbia and the heart of residential Vancouver that straddles the upland area known as the Mackenzie Heights: the sylvan mansions of western Shaughnessy; the former hippie enclave of Kitsilano and now one of the city's favoured areas for young professionals; Kerrisdale, with its diverse shopping area and eclectic architectural mix; and the leafy streets of Point Grey and Dunbar bordering the Pacific Spirit Regional Park – one of the city's treasured green lungs.

West Side beaches

The peninsula stretching to Point Grey along the south shore of English Bay has the city's most popular beaches, convenient distractions for university students and residents alike. On a summer weekend the city's Punjabi and Philippine communities both put the reputation of Aussies in the shade with their elaborate barbecues along the grassy hinterland of Locarno and Spanish Banks beaches, rated the best beaches for swimming. **Jericho Sailing Centre ❶** (tel: 604 224 4177; www.jsca.bc.ca) beside the eponymous beach

offers courses in windsurfing, kayaking and sailing, and the nearby pier is a fabulously romantic place to watch the sun set, looking out to sea with the mountains on the north shore etched against the orange sky and the lights of West and North Vancouver across the water.

The most popular beach is probably Kitsilano, thanks to its proximity to a good range of cafés, bars and restaurants as well as downtown. Several basketball games are usually in progress, and beside the tennis

LEFT: family friendly Kitsilano Beach.
BELOW: Jericho Sailing Centre.

courts there is a huge outdoor heated saltwater pool. **Kitsilano Pool ②** is open from May through September and attracts everyone from serious competitive swimmers to people who appear to devote their lives to looking good. The vistas on a brilliant summer day are hard to beat.

The bridges

The link between downtown and the south shore of English Bay is **Burrard Bridge ❸**, one of Vancouver's favourite landmarks and tall enough for ships to pass under. The bridge has dedicated lanes for bicycles, which has made life for both walkers and cyclists much more enjoyable. To the southeast stands **Granville Street Bridge**, opened in 1954 and the third bridge more or less on the same site. Lacking the architectural finesse of Burrard Bridge, it is nonetheless an imposing steel structure that forms the main route out of downtown to the airport and all points south.

ABOVE: built in 1932, the "Gateway" function of Burrard Bridge is reflected in the medieval-style town gateways, lantern-topped pylons and Art Deco sculptural details. Busts of Captain George Vancouver and Harry Burrard jut out from the bridge's superstructure.

Kitsilano

This popular residential area parallels the south shore of English Bay, and its proximity to the beaches gives the area a relaxed atmosphere, with lots of alfresco cafés and restaurants. Kitsilano epitomises the West Coast lifestyle with its fair share of organic food disciples and yoga-lovers. West 4th Avenue is home to upscale kitchen shops, exotic clothing stores and purveyors of handcrafted chocolates.

With the arrival of the streetcar line along English Bay in 1905, the Canadian Pacific Railway began development of the forested area on the south shore. They named this newly developed district after Chief Khahtsahlanough, whose grandson lived in the native village of Sun'ahk that had stood near Kitsilano Point until the late 19th century.

Construction continued apace through the first decades of the 20th century and many attractive houses from this period survive, their design

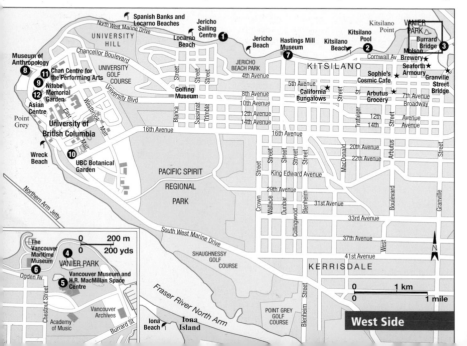

influenced by the English Arts and Crafts movement. The eastern part of the neighbourhood, where apartment buildings are now concentrated, has lost many of its original houses, but most Kits residents are keen to preserve the character of the streets further west.

Walking or cycling around Kitsilano, you get a sense of community pride in the well-cared-for gardens and plant-strewn verandas. The best place to find Craftsman-style houses is the area bounded by Macdonald, Stephens, 5th and 6th avenues. A virtually intact row of "California Bungalows" can be seen on the south side of 5th Avenue between Bayswater and Balaclava.

The South Shore museums

Just west of Burrard Bridge is the green promontory of **Vanier Park** ❹, created on the site of what was Kitsilano Indian Reserve and named after the first French-Canadian Governor General of Canada, George Vanier. This is a popular place for serious kite flying, with professionals and small children alike catching the crosswinds.

The park is home to three museums, two sharing a 1968 building designed by Gerald Hamilton with a distinctive dome that resembles a woven basket made by the Northwest Coast First Nations peoples.

Vancouver Museum ❺

Address: 1100 Chestnut Street, www.museumofvancouver.ca
Tel: 604 736 4431
Opening Hrs: July–Aug daily 10am–5pm, Sept–June Tue–Sun 10am–5pm, Thur until 8pm
Entrance Fee: charge
Transport: buses 22 and 44

This museum tells the fascinating story of the city's history with panache and humour: "Vancouverites, like other Canadians, insist on spelling colour the honourable way, lest we be confused with our neighbours to the south," reads one card. There is an absorbing film shot in 1907 from the front of a streetcar, showing Vancouver's business centre and the West End mansions as they were a century ago.

There are themed rooms and displays on Chinese immigration, work, trade unions, the Salvation Army, the interwar boom and bust years, and the Japanese internment camps set up in the interior of BC during World War II. The post-war decades are evocatively portrayed with a reconstructed kitchen and other interiors, and the watershed decade of the 1960s is

TIP

A Kitsilano landmark to look out for is the tiny Arbutus Grocery at the corner of 6th Avenue and Arbutus Street. Built in 1907, it is one of the finest old grocery stores in the city. The novelist Alice Munro lived for a year at 1316 Arbutus Street, when newly married in 1952. The city is accurately described in some of her short stories.

BELOW LEFT: Vanier Park sculpture.
BELOW: H.R. MacMillan Space Centre.

covered, when protest saved Vancouver from being as severely subordinated to the car as most US cities were. The Vancouver origins of Greenpeace and its early environmental protests are very well documented. The museum also has Pacific Rim and World Heritage collections.

H.R. MacMillan Space Centre ❺

Address: 1100 Chestnut Street, www.hrmacmillanspacecentre.com
Tel: 604 738 7827
Opening Hrs: July–Aug daily 10am–5pm, Sept–June Tue–Sun 10am–5pm
Entrance Fee: charge
Transport: buses 22 and 44

The space centre charts the history of space exploration and looks at celestial subjects that affect us more directly, such as light pollution. The domed theatre offers several different shows throughout the day, designed to educate and entertain children and adults alike. There is also a Disneyland-style ride with changing missions (preventing an asteroid hitting the earth, a rescue mission to Mars in the late 21st century).

ABOVE: totem pole in the Museum of Anthropology at the University of British Columbia (**BELOW**).

The Vancouver Maritime Museum ❻

Address: 1905 Ogden Avenue, www.vancouvermaritimemuseum.com
Tel: 604 257 8300
Opening Hrs: Victoria Day–Labour Day daily 10am–5pm, 1st Mon in Sept–3rd Mon in May Tue–Sat 10am–5pm, Sun noon–5pm
Entrance Fee: charge
Transport: buses 22 and 44

Two minutes' walk away from the Space Centre, the Maritime Museum houses the stout schooner *St Roch*. Built in North Vancouver in 1927 as a supply ship and patrol vessel for the Royal Canadian Mounted Police, it was the first vessel to negotiate the Northwest Passage in both directions and the first to circumnavigate North America using the Panama Canal. After a film about the ship, visitors can go aboard and inspect the cramped cabins and wheelhouse. In a connected building are some superb ship models. Other sections look at pirates, ships named *Vancouver*, the first container ship, lighthouses, shipwrecks, fishing, diving, Canadian Pacific Railway steamers, old Vancouver and native canoes. There are several educational play areas for children with reconstructed ship decks.

Hastings Mill Museum ❼

Address: 1575 Alma Street
Tel: 604 734 1212
Opening Hrs: 15 June–15 Sept Tue–Sun 1–4pm, 16 Sept–14 June Sat–Sun 1–4pm
Entrance Fee: charge
Transport: buses 4 and 44

At the eastern end of the large expanse of Jericho Beach Park is Vancouver's oldest surviving building, though it is not on its original Dunlevy Avenue site. The Hastings Mill Museum occupies the former store that stood beside the Hastings lumber mill on Burrard Inlet; one of less than a dozen buildings to survive the fire of 1886. It was moved to its present site in 1930

and now contains a large collection of Vancouver memorabilia. A cairn on Dunlevy Avenue marks the original site of Hastings Mill and commemorates its first export of lumber, to Australia in July 1867.

The University of British Columbia (UBC)

BC's principal university is much more than a seat of learning for its 50,000 students: it has some of Vancouver's major tourist attractions and some impressive buildings. Easily reached in 30 minutes by the frequent 99 B-Line bus from downtown, UBC enjoys a wonderful location on Point Grey, with ocean on three sides and 763 hectares (1,885 acres) of upland temperate rainforest to the east, designated the **Pacific Spirit Regional Park**. More than 50km (31 miles) of trails are enjoyed by locals out for a stroll, a jog, a mountain bike ride or a jaunt through the woods on horseback.

UBC is home to some of the most important things to see in Vancouver and the attractions have joined together to offer preferential pricing for a "passport ticket".

Hastings Mill

The mill set up in Gastown flourished because of the Canadian Pacific's decision to terminate on the south shore of Burrard Inlet. In an age when wood was the major component of buildings and ships throughout the world, demand was almost insatiable. But at that time it took a whole day to fell an 800-year-old tree – on one side an axeman worked on a "springboard" notched into the trunk a metre or so above the ground, while a two-man saw cut away on the other. Within weeks of the mill starting work, as many as four ships at a time were being loaded. The mill miraculously survived the fire of 1886 and retained a key role in the community until it closed in the 1920s.

Museum of Anthropology ❽

Address: 6393 NW Marine Drive, www.moa.ubc.ca
Tel: 604 827 5932
Opening Hrs: mid-May–Sept daily 10am–5pm, Sept–mid-May Wed–Mon 10am–5pm, Tue until 9pm
Entrance Fee: charge
Transport: buses 4, 44 and 99

The Museum of Anthropology has three main draws: its location, its architecture and its collection. The museum is built on a site sacred to the Coast Salish people, on traditional Musqueam First Nations land, facing out north across the water towards Howe Sound with spectacular views of both the ocean and the mountains. The building was designed in the mid-1970s by Arthur Erickson (*see page 122*) and uses a repeated motif of concrete arches to echo the wooden gateways and post-and-beam style of many Pacific cultures. Since initial construction, it has been renovated extensively and expanded to accommodate its growing collection.

ABOVE: Hastings Mill Museum occupies Vancouver's oldest building. **BELOW:** the False Creek ferry stops right outside the Maritime Museum, housed in a distinctive A-frame building.

In terms of the collection, more than 36,000 ethnological objects and 535,000 archaeological objects are curated by a staff with a teaching focus – this is Canada's largest teaching museum. More than 10,000 picces arc on display at any one time, everything from massive totem poles and house posts to exquisite silver, gold and argillite carvings. The huge walls of glass maximise the view of the mountains and sea and are perfectly appropriate for the museum's exceptional collection of Northwest Coast totem poles. In the smaller and more intimate spaces are carved boxes, bowls, feast dishes, ceramics and paintings. Exhibits are not confined to the West Coast; there are significant collections from East and South Asia, the South Pacific, the Americas, Africa and Europe.

Nitobe Memorial Garden ❾

Address: 1895 Lower Mall, UBC, www.nitobe.org
Tel: 604 822 9666
Opening Hrs: Apr–Oct daily 10am–4pm, Nov–Mar Mon–Fri 10am–2pm.
Entrance Fee: charge, by donation in winter
Transport: buses 4, 44 and 99

The Nitobe Garden is one of the top authentic Japanese gardens outside Japan, complete with ceremonial teahouse. The garden honours the agriculturist, philosopher and writer Inazo Nitobe (1862–1933) who strove "to become a bridge across the Pacific". Each tree, stone and shrub has been deliberately placed to reflect an idealised conception and symbolic representation of nature. The garden is designed to suggest a span of time – a day, a week or a lifetime – with a

SHOPPING

The West Side is a series of neighbourhoods, each with its own character and feel to its shopping. Take the time to wander around, as the smaller stores will yield wonderful surprises.

Books

Kids Books
3083 West Broadway. Tel: 604 738 5335. www. kidsbooks.ca Off map
Exactly what its name implies, this is the place to buy kids' books. Staff members are incredibly helpful and keen to make recommendations.

Pulpfiction Books
3133 West Broadway. Tel: 604 873 4311. www.pulp fictionbooksvancouver.com Off map

One of two locations for this combination used and new bookstore. Great pricing, but even better selection.

Clothing

Lululemon Athletica
2113 West 4th Ave. Tel: 604 732 6111. www.lululemon. com p274, B4
The first Lululemon store in the world opened in Kitsilano in 1998. Today it sells yoga-inspired apparel for everyone.

Mark James
2941 West Broadway. Tel: 604 734 2381. www.mark jamesclothing.com Off map
One of Vancouver's top men's clothing shops for more than 30 years. Armani, Hugo Boss, Diesel, Zegna, it has them all.

Food

Cocoa Nymph
3739 West 10th Ave. Tel: 604 222 4477. www. cocoanymph.com Off map
Superb hand-crafted chocolates by a chocolatier who doesn't put on airs, she just delivers.

Gifts

Puddifoot
2375 West 41st Ave. Tel: 604 261 8141. Off map
This locally owned company provides tableware, china, crystal and flatware to the city's high-end restaurants. Their giftware is superb, and staff are helpful.

U The Life Accessory Store
2028 Vine St. Tel: 604 970 9135. www.ulifestore.com p274, B4

A quirky little shop that rewards with the perfect gift, each item carefully chosen by the store's owner. Great selection of Sigg bottles.

Shoes

Gravitypope
2205 West 4th Ave. Tel: 604 731 7673. www.gravitypope. com p274, B4
Shoes for people who want something different – handmade, sporty, vegetarian, or ethically made.

Toys

Kaboodles Toy Store
4449 West 10th Ave. Tel: 604 224 5311. www.kaboodle stoystore.com Off map
A store that both adults and kids can browse happily. Stocks both intelligent and silly toys.

beginning, choice of paths and ending. Water and its soothing sounds are an important element in the garden. Guided tours help visitors to understand the very different concept of Japanese gardens. Spring is the best time for the cherry blossoms, summer for irises and autumn for the maples.

UBC Botanical Garden ⑩
Address: 6804 SW Marine Drive, www.ubcbotanicalgarden.org
Tel: 604 822 9666
Opening Hrs: daily 9.30am – 4.30pm
Entrance Fee: charge; by donation in winter
Transport: buses 4, 44 and 99

Established in 1916, initially to study the native flora of BC but now a research centre for temperate plants from around the world, the garden covers 44 hectares (110 acres) of land. It has Alpine, Asian, native, food, physic and winter gardens, with over 8,000 plants. The best months for floral displays of magnolias and rhododendrons (over 400 varieties) are April and May, summer for the Alpine garden and autumn for the food garden.

Make time for the **Greenheart Canopy Walkway**, one of only two treetop walkways in North America. The 308-metre (1,010ft) walkway includes eight platforms and nine bridges more than 17 metres (57ft) above ground, offering a close-up look at the rainforest and its inhabitants, as well as superb views of the city. A modified wheelchair is available for people with disabilities.

Some of Vancouver's finest concerts are held in the UBC's **Chan Centre for the Performing Arts** ⑪. Opened in 1997, the striking silver cylinder contains a concert hall with superb acoustics, a studio theatre and a cinema, allowing the centre to host a varied programme of opera, classical recitals, jazz and folk concerts, as well as lectures and films.

Another notable building on the campus is the **Asian Centre** ⑫,

designed by Vancouver architect Donald Matsuba, who drew on traditional Asian styles, including the Japanese farmhouse. Reflected in the pool that surrounds it, the clean, uncluttered lines and pyramidal roof lend an air of calm.

Kerrisdale
This largely residential neighbourhood lies south of 41st Avenue stretching to the Fraser River and bordered by Blenheim Street to the west and Granville to the east. The shopping area stimulated by the railway surrounds the junction of 41st with the East and West boulevards. The Bowser Block of 1912 still stands on the corner of the intersection.

There has been a long tradition of stability in Kerrisdale. Many of its residents have never moved from the district and know the name of everyone on their street, although rising property prices have weakened that cohesion. Kerrisdale's residential architecture now provides a sometimes bizarre mix of modern, Spanish colonial revival, neo-Tudor, Beaux Arts and English Arts and Crafts styles. ❑

ABOVE: for those who prefer soaking up the sun in the buff, Wreck Beach has been the place to do it since the 1920s, but it takes a descent of 237 steps from this point to reach it. **BELOW:** Haida artist Bill Reid's acclaimed sculpture, *The Raven and the First Men*.

BEST RESTAURANTS, BARS AND CAFÉS

Restaurants

The West Side is a large area, incorporating several neighbourhoods, including Kitsilano with its fantastic beaches, Point Grey near the university and leafy Kerrisdale, each with its own collection of one-off shops, cafés, bars and restaurants of every imaginable ethnic persuasion, and for every budget.

Asian

Banana Leaf
3005 West Broadway. Tel: 604 734 3005. www.banana leaf-vancouver.com Open: L & D daily. $ Off map.
This Malaysian restaurant with informal ambience and friendly service has two other branches (820 West Broadway and on Denman in the West End). All the usual suspects appear, but the big focus is on local fresh seafood with a Malaysian twist. Choose your seafood, then select your favourite sauce – from Singapore chilli to black peppercorn garlic. Good beer by the pitcher.

The Flying Tiger
2958 West 4th Ave. Tel: 604 737 7529. www.theflyingtiger. ca Open: D daily. $$ Off map.
This cosy room straddles Kitsilano and Point Grey, offering plates designed for sharing. Staff are friendly and knowledgeable and food arrives pip-

ing hot at the perfect interval. The Penang curry mussels are a must, as is the crispy Thai squid.

Diner

Sophie's Cosmic Café
2095 West 4th Ave. Tel: 604 732 6810. Open: 8am–8pm daily. $ 45 p274, B4
A Kitsilano institution since it opened in 1988, Sophie's is a great place for breakfast or brunch, comfort food for those nursing hangovers. Crowded with memorabilia, the kitschy decor somehow works. In addition to standard breakfast fare, there are good salads and an array of burgers including wild salmon, chicken and oyster. Expect queues at the weekend.

French

Bistro Pastis
2153 West 4th Ave. Tel: 604 731 5020. www.bistropastis. com Open: Brunch Sat–Sun, L Tue–Fri, D Tue–Sun. $$$ 46 p274, B4
French bistro food at its best in this quiet, smartly furnished room with good service and a fine wine list, along with, as you would expect, an excellent assortment of pastis and other French aperitifs.

Lumière
2551 West Broadway. Tel: 604 739 8185. www. lumiere.ca Open: D Tue–Sun. $$$$ Off map.
This long-time Relais et Château restaurant

upped the ante in 2009 when local owners David and Manjy Sidoo partnered with Daniel Boulud in his first Canadian undertaking. Offering three- to seven-course tasting menus, the portions are small, but each mouthful an explosion of flavour. The cynics will notice the over-the-top list of "sides" (Foie Gras, Caviar, White Truffle, Black Truffle), but those seeking a true dining experience appreciate the choices. Next door, DB Bistro Moderne offers a more casual and affordable experience.

Mistral
2585 West Broadway. Tel: 604 733 0046. www.mistral bistro.ca Open: L & D Tue–Sat. $$$ Off map.
This classic but comfortable French restaurant follows the successful formula of husband Jean-Yves Benoit in the kitchen, and wife Minna running the front of house with a casual elegance that has built them a loyal following. Save room for dessert – the warm chocolate cake and Catalan crème brûlée are particular favourites.

Gastro-pubs

Abigail's Party
1685 Yew St (off 1st Ave.). Tel: 604 739 4677. www. abigailsparty.ca Open: B & L Sat, Sun, D Mon–Sat. $$ 47 p274, B3

Named after the Mike Leigh film of the same name, this casual restaurant likes to think of itself as a gastro-pub. A seasonal menu featuring tapas with the usual West Coast twist and cocktails, along with a lively vibe, make it a hot spot in Kits.

Greek

Maria's Taverna
2324 West 4th Ave. Tel: 604 731 4722. www.marias taverna.ca Open: L & D daily. $$ 48 p274, A4
Greek restaurants are plentiful along this stretch of 4th Avenue and this simple whitewashed room is among the best. Despite the full range of Greek dishes, half the people in for dinner will be eating the delicious (and massive) *kleftiko*.

International

Bishop's
2183 West 4th Ave. Tel: 604 738 2025. www.bishops online.com Open: D daily. $$$ 49 p274, B4
John Bishop is one of Canada's top restaurateurs, offering innovative and exquisite food in an intimate setting. It's hard to go wrong with anything on the menu, but favourites include the lamb and scallop dishes. Save room for dessert, with offerings like espresso panna cotta with chocolate sorbet and salted chocolate sable hard to

beat. Superb service and an extensive wine list make this a favourite with locals as well as attracting more than a smattering of the rich and famous from abroad.

Burgoo
4434 West 10th Ave.
Tel: 604 221 7839. www.burgoo.ca Open: L & D daily. **$$** Off map.
This is the place to go when you have eight different people to satisfy. The big bowls of food include butter chicken, beef bourguignon, lamb tagine and ratatouille, each well seasoned and interesting. The cheddar and parsley biscuits are a hit with everyone.

The Galley Patio and Grill
11300 Discovery St, Jericho Park. Tel: 604 222 1331. www.thegalley.ca Open: B, L & D daily (weekends only in winter). **$** Off map.
Located on the upper level of the Jericho Sailing Centre, this is a good place to break a bike tour of the beaches. Try the Huevos Scramblarous (eggs scrambled with turkey sausage, roasted corn and black-bean salsa) with one of several local beers on tap. Enjoy spectacular views of the city from the patio.

Prices for a three-course dinner per person with a half-bottle of house wine:
$ = under C$30
$$ = C$30–50
$$$ = C$50–80
$$$$ = over C$80

Gramercy Grill
2685 Arbutus St. Tel: 604 730 5666. www.gramercygrillvancouver.com Open: daily, L & D. **$$** Off map.
A comfortable neighbourhood restaurant serving interesting food at great value. The seafood bowl loaded with two types of fish, prawn, scallop, mussels and clams, all in a tomato saffron broth, is a particular favourite.

Hell's Kitchen
2041 West 4th Ave. Tel: 604 736 4355. www.hells-kitchen.ca Open: L & D daily. **$**
(50) p274, B4
Soups, salads, burgers and pasta on offer, but famed for its pizzas with unusual toppings that work. Try the Midnight Express (pulled pork, mixed sweet peppers, wild mushrooms, asiago and Moroccan cumin-honey sauce).

Japanese

Shota Sushi and Grill
5688 Yew St. Tel: 604 263 8068. www.shotasushi.ca
Open: 11am–10.30pm daily. **$–$$** Off map.
This Japanese restaurant is a perfect stop for sushi lovers looking for more than the standard rolls. Try the scallop magma roll, with chopped scallop, spicy tuna and tobiko drizzled with black sesame sauce or one of many vegetarian choices. The attentive service, perfectly fresh fish and great presentation set this well above many Japanese restaurants in Vancouver.

Bars and Cafés

Darby D. Dawes (2001 MacDonald St. ㉙ p274, A4) is a classic pub, with good food and a selection of beers, conveniently located on bus lines to both downtown and UBC. **Capers** (2285 West 4th Ave. ㉚ p274, B4) is an organic supermarket but also a great place for a sit down and a quick coffee or a light lunch from its takeaway counter. Fantastic cakes, salads and filling pasta dishes.

Elwood's (3141 West Broadway. Off map) is a straightforward pub serving excellent burgers to go with that pitcher of beer. **Epicurean** (1898 West 1st Ave. ㉛ p274, B4) offers great coffee and a good range of Italian-inspired plates from early in the morning. **49th Parallel** (2152 4th Ave. ㉜ p274, B4) is at the uber-trendy end of the café spectrum; it's worth stopping in to enjoy locally roasted coffee. **Kitsilano Coffee Company** (2198 West 4th Ave. ㉝ p274, B4) has a big patio, lots of tables and newspapers to go along with the cinnamon buns and coffee on a Sunday morning.

Mix (4430 West 10th Ave. Off map) is a bakery with wonderful soups, scones and that comforting smell of an artisan bakery. Just up the road, **Pane Formaggio** (4532 West 10th Ave. Off map) is a combination Italian deli and great spot for coffee – you can get some of your food shopping done while you enjoy the ambience. **Terra Breads** (2380 West 4th Ave. ㉞ p274, A4) has been repeatedly voted the best in Vancouver for its artisan breads baked in a stone-hearth oven and for its sandwiches, but its café also serves cakes, soup and organic salads. The outlet on Granville Island always has one of the longest queues, and it's not because the staff are slow!

Vegetarian

Naam
2724 West 4th Ave. Tel: 604 738 7151. www.thenaam.com
Open: B, L & D daily. **$**
(51) p274, A4
A venerable institution, the Naam is the oldest vegetarian restaurant in Vancouver, dating back to the 1970s when Kits was hippie heaven. The food is good and the atmosphere funky – not only is there live music every night, it's one of the few restaurants open 24 hours a day.

West Coast

Watermark Café on Kits Beach
1305 Arbutus St. Tel: 604 738 5487. www.watermarkrestaurant.ca Open: L & D daily, plus Brunch on weekends. **$$** (52) p274, B3
This place can get a bit crowded on the weekends, but lunch during the week on a sunny day is idyllic, with stunning views over Kits Beach and English Bay. There are plenty of dishes to share, but you probably won't want to share the lambsickles.

VANCOUVER'S BEACHES

Few big cities can boast so many beautiful beaches and such a variety of water sports so close to the city centre.

Life in Vancouver is more bound up with the sea than in most cities. For much of the year a good part of people's leisure time is spent on the beach. The city is blessed with some golden stretches of sand in surroundings that belie their proximity to a large urban centre. Moreover, despite the presence of commercial shipping in English Bay, the water is relatively free from pollution, and many swim off the beaches.

One of the closest to downtown and therefore one of the most popular is Kitsilano Beach, invariably referred to as "Kits". Games of volleyball are often in progress, and the safe swimming makes it popular with families from the neighbourhood.

Further west, Jericho and Locarno beaches have a large hinterland and are popular with families who need the space for army catering-scale barbecues. A bike route weaves among the trees along the front to Spanish Banks. Around the headland on which UBC stands is Wreck Beach, for decades the beach where you can bare all. It's not remotely voyeuristic, and the fine sweep of sand is cared for by its own society.

ABOVE: the fascinating waterfront at Steveston is more suited to walking than swimming, but there are plenty of places to sit beside the sea in Garry Point Park.

RIGHT: the beach at Ambleside Park is one of the most popular in West Vancouver, with a long sandy beach and placid water. A playground and duck pond in the park makes it great for children. North Vancouver also has smaller beaches in Pilot Cove, Sandy Cove and Dundarave

RIGHT: further afield, but worth the trip, between Tofino and Ucluelet on the west coast of Vancouver Island there is a series of glorious beaches with wide expanses of sand often covered with drift logs washed up by the tempestuous seas common along this coast. The waves at Long Beach attract surfers from all over the world.

WATER SPORTS

The popularity of water sports in Vancouver is obvious on any summer weekend, as English Bay fills with sailing boats, kayaks and skimboards dodging the power boats.

False Creek is a good place to learn to kayak or canoe, as it's sheltered, sailing is forbidden and boats are limited to 5 knots. Alternatively, courses and guided tours for experienced paddlers are available from Jericho Beach. One of the best places for the sport is the tranquil Indian Arm, an 18km (11-mile) finger of water from Deep Cove in North Vancouver.

Sailing takes place mainly from Jericho Beach, where lessons are available from the Jericho Sailing Centre. Skimboarding, a cross between surfing and skateboarding, is increasingly popular. Surfing lessons are available, but there is little around Vancouver to attract the serious surfers who make for the big rollers on the west coast of Vancouver Island.

For the proficient, the finest area for sailing is among the Gulf Islands and along the Inside Passage, where the scenery and tranquil coves seem a world away from city life.

Windsurfing is possible off Jericho Beach and the beaches of English Bay, but Squamish is regarded as the best place close to Vancouver. *(See pages 263–4 for details of water sports providers.)*

Clothing is optional at beach ahead.

ABOVE: Tribune Bay on Hornby Island is as close as you need to get to the Mediterranean: white sandy beach, azure water and sandstone cliffs.

RIGHT: Wreck Beach is Vancouver's nudist beach, and it's immensely popular: over 14,000 people can line the 8km (5-mile) strip of sand on a warm summer day. Beach huts sell organic juices and *empanadas*.

ABOVE: Jericho Beach is the place to head to for water sports: its eastern end is set aside for windsurfing, kayaking and sailing under the auspices of the Jericho Sailing Association. Swimmers occupy the western end and there is fishing off Jericho Pier.

LEFT: there are two main beaches around Stanley Park: Second and Third beaches which both overlook English Bay. Second Beach has a heated outdoor pool with adjacent playground, and the beach is often decorated with Inukshuk-style towers of precariously balanced rocks. Further south and closest to downtown is the long expanse of English Bay Beach and Sunset Beach, which almost reaches Burrard Bridge.

CENTRAL VANCOUVER

At first glance, this amorphous area may appear to have little to offer, but there are two fabulous gardens worth crossing the water for, while the genteel neighbourhood of Shaughnessy and vibrant Punjabi Market show another side to the city.

This chapter spans the area south of False Creek, from the upscale shopping district around Granville Street, through genteel Shaughnessy down to Vancouver's Indo-Canadian community around Punjabi Market. Besides the shops, galleries, restaurants and cafés likely to appeal to those who prefer individuality to chains, the great attractions for visitors and residents are the two outstanding gardens.

Shaughnessy

The Canadian Pacific Railway had been granted the land on which this old-money area of Vancouver was built, and the astute company spent over $1 million on the infrastructure and landscaping before selling a single lot. The district took its name from Milwaukee-born Thomas Shaughnessy, who was president of the CPR from 1899 to 1918.

Beginning in 1907, generous lots and curving streets named after CPR directors were laid out to lure the city's elite from the West End. Some of the larger houses were built of stone from the quarry that forms the focus of Queen Elizabeth Park. Exclusivity was guaranteed by stipulating

that all houses should cost at least $6,000, and the provincial government later reinforced this by restricting development to single-family dwellings and prohibiting subdivision of lots. By 1914, there were 243 houses in Shaughnessy.

Houses were designed by the city's leading architects using such styles as English Arts and Crafts, neo-Tudor, Georgian and American Gothic. By the 1920s the social scene revolved around costumed balls, croquet and tennis matches. The grandest residence

LEFT: the beautifully landscaped Queen Elizabeth Park. **RIGHT:** neo-Tudor house in the Shaughnessy District.

ABOVE: Meinhardt delicatessen, a gourmet's delight on Granville Street.

was Hycroft at 1489 McRae Avenue, now the home of the University Women's Club. Built in 1909 for BC industrialist A.D. McRae, Hycroft was the place to be on New Year's Eve for the McRaes' costume ball. The ballroom floor was laid over seaweed to give better spring, and the house had three large gardens, an enormous greenhouse, riding stables, tennis courts, a guesthouse, a mirrored bar and a solarium.

One of the most unusual mansions is Glen Brae at 1690 Matthews Street, built for sawmill owner William Tait. This supposedly Scottish baronial-style home has bulbous twin towers with domed roofs flanking the entrance. It, too, has a sprung dance floor, fine stained glass and tiling and an ornate wrought-iron fence imported from Glasgow. The house is now home to Canuck Place, a hospice for children.

Other important survivors include the Nichol House at 1402 McRae Avenue, the Frederick Kelly House at 1398 Crescent, the MacDonald House at 1388 Crescent and the Fleck House at 1296 Crescent.

The number of repossessions by CPR during the Depression gave the area the nickname "Mortgage Heights" and led to some illegal conversions to multiple dwellings. Glen Brae, for example, was valued at $75,000 in 1920 but sold for $7,500 in 1939. Despite some relaxation of the restrictions on internal and plot subdivision and the demolition of many of the older homes, the district's character remains distinctive, and the area is one of the city's most valuable heritage landscapes. New construction is often built to look like the mansions of the early 20th century and the mature trees have generally been protected. Anyone interested in architecture will find a leisurely tour of Shaughnessy on foot or bike rewarding – indeed, it can be an amusing pastime to try to decide whether a home is original or new.

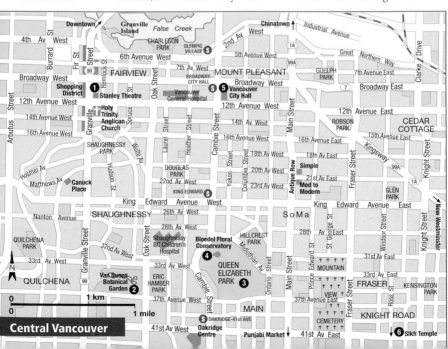

Central Vancouver

Granville Street

North and south of the intersection with Broadway lies Granville Street's **shopping district** with a mix of galleries, fashion shops, home furnishings, delicatessens and restaurants. You could easily spend an afternoon browsing the galleries offering everything from exquisite First Nations jewellery, prints and carvings to breathtaking contemporary art. Sandwiched between the shops and galleries is the heritage **Stanley Theatre ❶**. Designed by H.H. Simmonds, this 1,200-seat Moorish-style Art Deco cinema was built in 1931 and screened films until 1991. It reopened as a theatre in 1998 and is the only one of four Vancouver neighbourhood cinemas designed by Simmonds to survive.

Some of the well-to-do of Shaughnessy worshipped in the Chalmers Presbyterian Church, now the **Holy Trinity Anglican Church**, at 12th and Hemlock Street. This impressive neoclassical church, noted for its extensive stained glass and fine brickwork, was built in 1911 in response to the rapid expansion of the area.

Vancouver Foundation

The principal benefactor of the Van Dusen Botanical Garden was the Vancouver Foundation, which began in the 1940s with $1,000 saved by a secretary named Alice G. MacKay. She wanted to do something special for Vancouver, particularly for homeless women trapped in a cycle of poverty. The industrialist and philanthropist W.J. Van Dusen developed the foundation with the support of nine other prominent Vancouverites who each contributed $10,000. From its original fund of $101,000, it has a capital fund of over $660 million, making it the largest community fund in Canada. It has given away upwards of $60 million annually, but with the economic downturn, this may change in the future.

Van Dusen Botanical Garden ❷

Address: 5251 Oak Street, http://vancouver.ca/parks/parks/vandusen/website
Tel: 604 878 9274
Opening Hrs: daily Mar 10am–5pm, Apr 10am–6pm, May 10am–8pm, June–Aug 10am–9pm, Sept 10am–7pm, Oct 10am–5pm, Nov–Feb 10am–4pm
Entrance Fee: charge
Transport: bus 17

The Van Dusen Botanical Garden has an unusual history. The land was a golf club until 1960, when the club moved to a new site near UBC; local residents persuaded the city and provincial governments that a botanical garden would be preferable to more houses, and the result is an outstanding garden that ranks in the top ten of North American gardens. Named after the leading donor, it is the kind of garden that appeals to everyone, whether or not they are gardeners. Its many kilometres of path through the 22 hectares (55 acres) take you beside lakes, across ponds and through

ABOVE: dotted around the grounds of the Van Dusen Botanical Garden are some intriguing modern sculptures.

TIP

The Arts Club Theatre is Vancouver's largest professional theatre company and stages a mixture of contemporary and classical plays and Broadway musicals at its flagship theatre, the Stanley (2750 Granville Street; box office: 604 687 1644, www.artsclub.com) and at its larger sister venue, the Granville Island Stage (1585 Johnston Street, web address and box office as above).

The largest street tree in Vancouver is thought to be the Giant sequoia on the Cambie Street median near King Edward, which has a trunk circumference of 5.5 metres (18ft).

woodland to visit 40 small specialised gardens within the framework of the main landscaped setting. Cleverly devised vistas look out over the city or to the mountains to the north.

Thanks to Vancouver's mild climate, the garden contains more than 7,300 different plant families (over 255,000 individual plants) grouped by botanical relationship or geographical origin, though the main focus here is on plants that are native to BC. Some specimens remind us how vital the work of botanical gardens is when habitat destruction threatens the extinction of many plant species. A Dawn redwood grows near the Cypress Pond thanks to the discovery of a Chinese forester, T. Kan, while travelling in eastern Sichuan prov-

ince in 1941. He found three specimens and took cuttings from which all subsequent trees derive.

Children love the multicursal maze, made up of 3,000 pyramidal cedars. One of the more unusual areas is the Canadian Heritage Garden, which has areas of commercial crops such as barley, wheat, flax, oats, amaranth and sunflowers, planted in a setting that feels convincingly rural. In spring, the highlight of the garden is the avenue of colour along the Rhododendron Walk. In summer attention turns to the rose, fragrance and perennial gardens, and in the autumn maples and heathers provide splashes of red and purple.

The garden has recently benefited from government funding to build a new visitor centre that will follow the

SHOPPING

Many different experiences await the shopper in this area. Along South Granville, the stores are glam and perfectly laid out. Along Main Street, the jumble of exciting things to find in small stores that might not have been there last month makes for a genuinely fun shopping experience. Both are great places to spend an afternoon.

Accessories

Chachkas
2423 Granville St. Tel: 604 688 6417. www.chatchkas.ca Off map
This long-time Vancouver store carries local and international designers like Alessi and Laguiole.
Rags and Dishes
4213 Main St. Tel: 604 879 2592. Off map

An outlet store with friendly staff that carries quality linens and kitchen items at a fraction of the normal retail price.

Art Galleries

Equinox
2321 Granville St. Tel: 604 736 2405. www.equinox gallery.com p275, C4
One of the most well-known galleries of the 20 or so along the South Granville strip.

Clothing

Beansprouts
4305 Main St. Tel: 604 871 9782. www.beansprouts.ca Off map
A lovely clothing store for babies and small children, carrying both new and gently used clothing; aside from the labels

missing from the latter, impossible to tell the difference between the two.
Boboli
2776 Granville St. Tel: 604 257 2300. Off map
This is serious shopping for both men and women, with top designers like Valentino, Armani, Etro, Roberto Cavali. Max Mara is part of the same store. Superb staff.
Legends Retro-Fashion
4366 Main St. 604 875 0621. Off map
One of the best of the many retro shops along this strip of Main.

Food

Mainly Organics
4348 Main St. Tel: 604 872 3446. Off map
The perfect place to stop by for organic packaged goods, particularly if you

have food allergies and need gluten-free or other speciality items.
Meinhardt
3002 Granville St. Tel: 604 732 4405. www.meinhardt. com Off map
This is a food store to browse in. Savour the impressive range of olive oils and revel in the exquisite gift boxes and prepared foods.

Gifts

Red Cat Records
4307 Main St. Tel: 604 708 9422. www.redcat.ca Off map
What better gift for yourself or someone at home than new or used CDs or vinyl? A great place to find local independent music. One of several record shops along Main Street.

"Living Building" concept, being sustainable as well as beautiful. Completion is scheduled for spring 2011.

Queen Elizabeth Park ❸

Address: Cambie Street at 33rd Avenue, www.vancouver.ca/parks/parks/bloedel
Tel: 604 257 8570
Opening Hrs: daily Mar 10am– 5pm, Apr 10am– 6pm, May 10am– 8pm, June–Aug 10am– 9pm, Sept 10am– 7pm, Oct 10am–5pm, Nov–Feb 10am–4pm
Entrance Fee: charge
Transport: bus 15

Located between Cambie and Main Streets, this park is centred around an extinct volcano known as "Little Mountain" at the highest point of the city, 153 metres (501ft) above sea level. The land covered by the park was set aside as a reserve as long ago as 1912, having served as a source of stone for the city's first roads. However, it was not until after the dedication of the area by the late Queen Mother during her visit with King George VI in 1939 that work began in earnest.

At the heart of this 52-hectare (130-acre) park are two former quarries which have been developed into beautiful ornamental flower gardens, producing a riot of colour in summer and making them a favoured location for wedding photographs. Even during dry periods in the summer, the grass in these areas is luxuriantly green. The North Quarry Garden has an oriental note and specialises in plants that prefer drier conditions. It was created to commemorate the 75th anniversary of Vancouver's incorporation, in 1961. The park's gentle northern slope is an arboretum of Canada's indigenous trees and shrubs.

The Little Mountain Drinking Water Reservoir on top of the hill has been covered over and a new plaza built on top with a water feature, arbours, tree, shrub and lawn areas. Near the highest point is the **Bloedel**

Floral Conservatory ❹ (tel: 604 257 8570; www.city.vancouver.bc.ca), which is the second-largest domed conservatory in the world (the largest is in St Louis, Missouri). Budget cutbacks have put the survival of this dome at risk. It is unclear whether the 500 varieties of trees and plants from three climate zones – lush tropical rainforest, subtropic and desert – will be preserved and what access the public will have to them in the future.

Civic centre

North of the gardens, just before Cambie Street meets Broadway, is **Vancouver City Hall ❺** at 453 West 12th Avenue. Designed by the city's leading architectural practice of the day, Townley and Matheson, in 1935–6, the curious location of the building was intended to symbolise the recent absorption of the municipalities of South Vancouver and Point Grey by erecting the new City Hall near their common boundary. Or so one story goes. Another cites a downtown demonstration by 2,000 unemployed workers demanding accommodation and food; the

ABOVE AND BELOW: the ornamental gardens in Queen Elizabeth Park.

TIP

The Van Dusen Botanical Garden sells seed packets for you to take home and grow your own plants, but make sure your country customs officers will permit importation of seeds – every country is different.

riot act had to be read, and a location less susceptible to such protests was deemed advisable. It's now a rather anomalous location, and its hard edges and lumpen mass, albeit relieved by some Art Deco zigzag decoration, evoke totalitarian architecture. Nearby is the vast Vancouver General Hospital, the largest in BC.

SoMa

Short for South Main, this shopping destination is focused around 21st Avenue but stretches from Broadway to 33rd Avenue, with fashion and home furnishings to the fore. A series of shops known as Antique Row is located between 20th and 23rd avenues. There are also collectables and memorabilia from the 1950s and '60s and a good choice of vintage clothing.

Punjabi Market

This district between Main and Knight streets south of 41st Avenue is the epicentre of Vancouver's community of 60,000 Indians, mostly from the Punjab. Known too by its more official name of Sunset, the area has also been home to the Mennonite community since the 1930s, clustered around 49th Avenue and Fraser Street.

The name "Punjabi Market" applies to the district as well as the shopping area on Main Street between 49th and 51st avenues, which is denoted by special street signs and has the largest concentration of jewellers in Canada. Haggling is expected. It's worth visiting the area just to see the beautiful silk fabrics sold at bargain prices in many of the shops and enjoy the pungent aromas from the spices and vegetables which are sure to tempt you into sampling one of the restaurants. Just wander round and soak up the atmosphere of this lively corner of India.

On the short stub of Ross Street between Marine Drive and Kent Avenue stands the **Sikh Temple** ➏, designed by Arthur Erickson in 1969–70. A simple white block is capped by a series of stepped, diagonally interlocked square sections, and crowned by an open steel onion-shaped dome. Those who knew it before the additions to the east regret its loss of isolation. ❑

BELOW: colourful saris in Punjabi Market.

A Multicultural City

From its very foundation, Vancouver has been a multicultural city, much as the province of British Columbia has been as a whole. The opportunities offered by the embryonic province and city have attracted Cambodians, Chinese, Filipinos, Greeks, Indians, Indonesians, Italians, Jews, Laotians, Portuguese, Russians, Scandinavians, Thais, Ukrainians and Vietnamese as well as a large number of people from Britain – Scotland in particular. The Chinese are the largest community, forming the third-largest Chinatown in North America (after San Francisco and New York), though it was not until the 1947 repeal of laws limiting immigration that the numbers swelled.

BEST RESTAURANTS, BARS AND CAFÉS

Restaurants

Barbecue

Memphis Blues Barbeque House
1465 West Broadway (off Granville). Tel: 604 738 6806. www.memphisbluesbbq.com Open: L & D daily. **$$** Off map; 1342 Commercial Drive (near Charles St.). Tel: 604 215 2599. Open: L & D daily. **$$** Off map
Voted best barbecue and best place for carnivores in Vancouver, with slabs of ribs, pork or Cornish game hen. If you're really hungry, order an Elvis Platter, and expect to take home plenty of leftovers.

Brunch

Paul's Place Omelettery
2211 Granville St. Tel: 604 737 2857. Open: B & L daily. **$** ⓔ p275, C4
A fabulous place for brunch. It is generally busy at the weekend but you can window-shop up and down Granville Street while you wait for your table. Try the wild game chorizo with mushroom and feta. Everything is made on the premises of this cheery, slightly ramshackle café.

Prices for a three-course dinner per person with a half-bottle of house wine:
$ = under C$30
$$ = C$30–50
$$$ = C$50–80
$$$$ = over C$80

Chinese

Lin Chinese
1537 West Broadway. Tel: 604 733 9696. www.linchinese.ca Open: L & D daily. **$** Off map
Inexpensive, tasty, fast, fresh. Try the Shanghai-style juicy dumplings, flavour that explodes in your mouth, or the tofu noodles in soup. Amazing value.

European

Cru
1459 West Broadway. Tel: 604 677 4111. www.cru.ca Open: L Mon–Fri, D daily. **$$$** Off map
This elegant place offers consistently good food, from the Cellar Door Caesar salad to the interesting ways to prepare local lamb. The intelligent wine list reflects a passion for pairing the perfect wine with your food.

French

Pied-à-Terre
3369 Cambie St. Tel: 604 873 3131. www.pied-a-terre-bistro.ca Open: L Mon–Fri, D daily. **$$** Off map
This cosy restaurant offers generous portions of classic French bistro food, including great frites and excellent crème brûlée. The prix fixe lunch menu is exceptional value.

Indian

Atithai
2445 Burrard St. Tel: 604 731 0221. http://atithi.ca Open: L Mon–Fri, D daily. **$**

Bars and Cafés

Café Crepe (2861 Granville St. Off map) is a great spot to take a break from browsing art galleries and shopping – the traditional ham and cheese crêpe is an easy choice. On Main Street, there are countless places to stop

Off map
The owners of this family-run restaurant say it best: passionate and homely food from the diverse regions of India. You feel as though you are in someone's home, and are honoured to be there. Plenty of vegan choices, but carnivores should make sure to have the goat if it is available.

Vij's
1480 West 11th Ave. (between Granville and Hemlock). Tel: 604 736 6664. www.vijs.ca Open: D daily. **$$$** Off map
Widely regarded as the best Indian in Vancouver, this popular restaurant doesn't take reservations, so be prepared to wait. Vij's produces an inventive take on modern Indian, fusing various regional styles in dishes like marinated lamb Popsicles with fenugreek cream curry.

Japanese

Tojo's Restaurant
1133 West Broadway. Tel: 604 872 8050. www.tojos.com Open: D daily.

in for a break, including **Liberty Bakery** (3699 Main St. Off map). The **Wicked Café** (1399 West 7th Ave. ⓧ p275, D4) is the Canadian importer of Intelligentsia coffee, so you know you are going to get a perfect latte.

$$$–$$$$ Off map.
This is the ultimate in Japanese dining. Tojo is the master, the one all other Japanese restaurants in Vancouver aspire to. The best way to eat here is to simply let Tojo decide for you, as long as you have room on your credit card.

Yanaki Sushi
816 West 6th Ave. Tel: 606 708 5006. Open: L & D Mon–Sat. **$** ⓧ p275, E4
This inconspicuous sushi place located near the Canada Line Olympic Village station in a little strip mall provides great sushi as well as tasty udon, donburi, yakitori and tempura. Seafood is impeccably fresh and service prompt.

Pacific Rim

8½ Restaurant Lounge
151 East 8th Ave. Tel: 604 568 2703. www.eightandahalf.ca Open: L & D daily. **$$** Off map
Fresh and local are the catchwords here. Great salads, interesting pizza combinations, small plates and salads.

EASTERN SUBURBS

The suburbs of New Westminster, Burnaby and Port Moody are largely residential, but their attractions make the journey worthwhile. Unearth Vancouver's early history, take a paddle-steamer cruise, go fishing in the Fraser or shop in one of Canada's biggest malls.

Main Attractions
FRASER RIVER DISCOVERY CENTRE
SAMSON V
IRVING HOUSE
QUEEN'S PARK RESIDENTIAL DISTRICT
BURNABY ART GALLERY
BURNABY VILLAGE MUSEUM
PORT MOODY

Maps and Listings
MAP OF EASTERN SUBURBS, PAGE 154
MAP OF NEW WESTMINSTER, PAGE 157
RESTAURANTS, PAGE 161
ACCOMMODATION, PAGE 253

Relatively few visitors to Vancouver visit the eastern districts of Vancouver except to pass through them on their way to the interior by either Trans-Canada Highway 1 or the Lougheed Highway 7. These districts may lack the visual appeal of neighbourhoods around the city's waterfront, but they still have plenty to interest the visitor. Both New Westminster and Burnaby can be readily explored by using the SkyTrain.

Fur trappers and gold diggers

Though Gastown may be the focal point of stories about Vancouver's early days, head upstream to put things in the historical context. For it was the rivers of central and western Canada that carried the commodity that led to the first European settlements – furs. Most of the early explorers were travelling east to west, following rivers to discover where they met the sea; once a course had been mapped, their successors were able to make the less arduous journey by sea, almost invariably arriving by ship up the Fraser River.

However, it was gold rather than furs that prompted the British gov-

ernment to send the first detachment of troops in the form of Royal Engineers, responding to concerns that the discovery of gold along the Fraser and Thompson rivers in 1857 could lead to a breakdown of civil order. The soldiers arrived from Britain via Victoria on the separate crown colony of Vancouver Island early in 1859, two months after the colony of British Columbia had been proclaimed. In charge was Colonel Richard Moody, who had been given the task of selecting a site for the capital of

LEFT: blacksmiths' demonstration at the Burnaby Village Museum. **RIGHT:** the terraces at Simon Fraser University.

ABOVE: the caricatured figure of a Royal Engineer on the waterfront has the dubious distinction of being the tallest tin figure in the world at 10 metres (32ft) tall.

BC. He rejected the area around Fort Langley *(see page 227)* set up by the Hudson's Bay Company, and chose a sloping site on the north bank of the Fraser River which Queen Victoria named New Westminster.

Early photographs of the Royal Engineers' camp between 1859 and 1863 show a higgledy-piggledy collection of wooden houses and shacks, but Moody and his sappers transformed the area in their four years: 300 lots were soon surveyed and auctioned off, and by 1864 Government House had a ballroom capable of holding "with ease" over 200 dancers. In 1865 a cricket match was held between New Westminster and Victoria. New Westminster continued to grow, despite losing its capital status with the decision to move it to Victoria in 1868. However, in 1898 a fire broke out in a pile of hay on a sternwheeler and quickly spread. All but a handful of buildings in the city were destroyed; even the church bells were reduced to a heap of contorted metal.

NEW WESTMINSTER ❶

The suburb of **New Westminster** is easy to reach from Vancouver by Sky-Train, the half-hour ride offering a view across the residential areas of East Vancouver, Burnaby and New Westminster. From the New Westminster SkyTrain station, head down towards the river, passing the restored Canadian Pacific Railway station of 1899 designed in a French château style. This handsome brick building with stone facings was one of the first buildings to be built after the fire of 1898, and has been restored as a restaurant.

Across the tracks is the **Westminster Quay Public Market ◐**, which has undergone a complete renovation. While not as extensive as the Granville Island Market *(see page 126)*, the quay is a good starting point for a visit along the Fraser River, once teeming with sternwheel steamboats

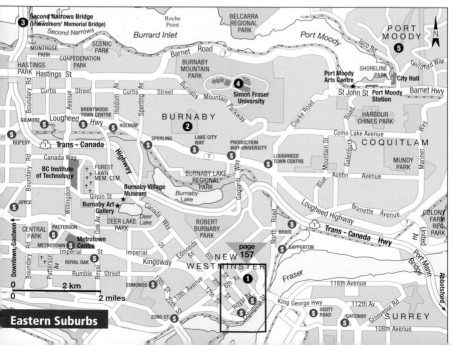

Eastern Suburbs

calling in on their way between Victoria and Yale *(see page 235)*.

The Fraser River Discovery Centre B

Address: 788 Quayside Drive, www.fraserriverdiscovery.org
Tel: 604 521 8401
Opening Hrs: June–Aug daily 10am–4pm, Sept–May Wed–Sun 10am–4pm
Entrance Fee: charge
Transport: SkyTrain New Westminster

The renovation of the Fraser River Discovery Centre tripled its presentation space to 1,580 sq m (17,000 sq ft), which allows for travelling exhibits from larger museums to be featured. If it's a sunny day, a more interactive explanation of the river and its role in the development of British Columbia is found along the boardwalk, with its information boards dotted along the river pathway that extends for nearly 2km (1 mile) westwards.

Trees and flower beds line the boardwalk beyond the former railway swingbridge that took the railway across the North Arm of the river. A plinthed bust of a rather jowly Simon Fraser reminds passers-by of the role the explorer played in opening up western Canada to trade. The continuing importance of the river named after him is obvious from the Surrey Docks on the south bank opposite New Westminster. Ships sail 28km (18 miles) upriver to unload containers and cars and leave with lumber and general cargoes. Huge rectangular barges piled with sawdust as tall as a small house ruffle the waters with astonishing frequency.

Samson V G

Address: New Westminster Quay, www.nwpl.ca
Tel: 604 522 6894
Opening Hrs: May–Aug Thur–Sun noon–5pm, Sept–Apr Sat–Sun noon–4pm
Entrance Fee: charge
Transport: SkyTrain New Westminster

The *Sampson V* was one of a series of steam-powered sternwheelers,

ABOVE: New Westminster's Queen's Park in winter.

TIP

Spend some time watching the Fraser River at New Westminster. The delta was created by the 20 million tonnes of sand and silt brought down the river past New Westminster every year.

TIP

Take a lunch or dinner cruise aboard a modern sternwheeler from New Westminster up the Fraser River to the historic town of Fort Langley (see page 227).

ABOVE: lamp-posts on Columbia Street.
BELOW: fishing in the Fraser River.

built in 1937 to keep the river clear of snags and deadheads (tree trunks and branches) and to repair navigation lights and buoys. Retired in 1980, she has been restored and the engine room, bridge, workshop, mess room and most of her cabins are open to visitors. There are also displays on the history of the river's ships and their colourful captains.

Columbia Street and downtown

By 1898 New Westminster was the mercantile centre of the Fraser Valley, and its main street, Columbia, was lined with impressive brick stores and offices. For a time it was renowned as the "Miracle Mile", with the highest sales per square foot in the entire province. The legacy of those years can still be seen in the historic buildings that survive, and a guide to them is available from the museum (see opposite). Many are still awaiting the kind of sensitive restoration done to the city's first "skyscraper" erected in 1912, the **Westminster Trust Building** ❶ at 709–713 Columbia Street, but the priorities for government

are not focused on restoration of old buildings, so many commercial properties have fallen into disrepair and lie vacant and for sale. Happily, the same fate has not met New Westminster's residential historical treasures in Queen's Park (see opposite).

Irving House ❺

Address: 302 Royal Avenue, www.newwestminster.ca
Tel: 604 527 4640
Opening Hrs: May–Aug Wed–Sun noon–5pm, Sept–Apr Sat–Sun noon–4pm
Entrance Fee: charge
Transport: SkyTrain New Westminster

The arrival of the railway in 1886 quickly extinguished river-borne passenger traffic, but in the preceding decades a few people became exceedingly rich from the profits of boat services. One of them was Scottish Captain William Irving, "King of the Fraser River", whose house cost $10,000 to build and was described as "the finest, the best and most homelike house of which BC can yet boast" when completed in 1865.

Captain Irving died of pneumonia

Fraser River Fish

The Fraser River has been a bountiful source of fish for centuries; by the end of the 19th century 49 salmon canneries dotted the south arm of the river, packing a record 85.6 million cans of sockeye salmon in 1905. It is also one of the last rivers with white sturgeon, which can reach 630kg (1,387lb), grow to 6 metres (20ft) and live to 130 years old. Descendants of shark-like fish, they lurk along the river bottoms waiting for anything edible to sink to the bottom. They were fished almost to extinction, so only catch and release is permitted now. Sturgeon of up to 3.5 metres (11ft) are frequently found with the help of expert guides, who also photograph the experience.

in 1872 at the age of 56, but the house remained in the family until 1950, when it was purchased by the city as a historic centre. Volunteers take visitors round the 14 rooms, which not only show what life was like in the latter part of the 19th century, but also provide insight into the lives of some of his descendants well into the 20th century. You learn of the 1942 subscription concerts held in the house to raise funds to build a Spitfire, and of the important collection of Coast Salish baskets assembled by the last two sisters to live in the house. Many of the unusually large and tall-ceilinged rooms have their original wallpaper, carpets and furniture.

Within the attractive grounds is **New Westminster Museum** (same hours and contact information as Irving House), which shows how early inhabitants of the region lived through a large collection of local memorabilia, from old radios and televisions, cameras, toys, music and sewing machines

to woodworking equipment. It has the coach built in 1876 in San Francisco especially for the visit of Lord and Lady Dufferin on their trip to the Cariboo goldfields in 1876; Lord Dufferin was the first Governor General of Canada to visit BC.

Museum of the Royal Westminster Regiment ⓕ

Address: 530 Queens Avenue, www.royal-westies-assn.ca/museum.html
Tel: 604 526 5116
Opening Hrs: call for details
Entrance Fee: free
Transport: SkyTrain New Westminster
Housed in the old gun room of the historic Armoury building, the museum traces the story of the regiment back to the Royal Engineers who laid out New Westminster, as well as its overseas roles during the two world wars.

Queen's Park

At the eastern end of Queens Avenue is the large expanse of Queen's Park

ABOVE: memorial plaque outside Irving House. **BELOW:** Museum of the Royal Westminster Regiment.

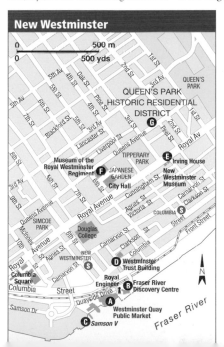

New Westminster

Ironworkers' Memorial Bridge

Directly north of Burnaby, the **Ironworkers' Memorial Bridge** ❸ is the second bridge at this location, the first, from 1925, being hit by shipping so many times that a replacement was imperative. Construction of the steel truss cantilever bridge began in 1957, but faulty calculations over the required strength of the footings led to the collapse of a crane and much of the bridge, causing the death of 18 ironworkers. Finally opened in 1960, the bridge is 1,292 metres (4,239ft) long, with a centre span for shipping. The bridge was renamed in 1994 to honour the 27 workers who died during its construction.

ABOVE: the Pacific National Exhibition fairground.
BELOW: display at the Museum of the Royal Westminster Regiment.

and the **Queen's Park historic residential district** ❻ straddling the principal shopping street of 6th Avenue. For those interested in residential architecture, Queen's Park offers perhaps the best collection of heritage homes in the Lower Mainland. Practically every style of home is to be found within a few blocks, including Victorian, Edwardian, Arts and Crafts and Craftsman. The neighbourhood has such a wealth of lovingly restored homes that a heritage home tour every May (www.newwestheritage.org) attracts keen students of architecture along with those looking for ideas on how to restore their own homes. Many of the gardens have been restored to their early glory, complete with fragrant heirloom roses.

BURNABY

Called after the lake which Colonel Moody *(see page 160)* named in honour of his aide, Robert Burnaby, the city of **Burnaby** ❷ evolved around the trails hacked through the forest by Moody's Royal Engineers, who also laid out lots for sale. The community was given a municipal charter in 1892, a year after the opening of the interurban electric railway between Vancouver and New Westminster, which spurred development beside the tracks. But Burnaby's real growth came after World War II, with new shopping centres, Simon Fraser University, a hospital and various civic amenities.

Deer Lake Park is an attractive, well-wooded area in which some exclusive houses were built before World War I, such as Hart House, now a restaurant *(see page 161)*.

Burnaby Art Gallery

Address: 6344 Deer Lake Avenue, www.burnabyartgallery.ca
Tel: 604 297 4422
Opening Hrs: Tue–Fri 11am–4.30pm, Sat–Sun noon–5pm
Entrance Fee: charge
Transport: SkyTrain Metrotown, then bus 144 SFU
The museum is housed in one of the largest houses in Deer Lake Park, a magnificent Arts and Crafts-inspired mansion named Fairacres.

Despite being occupied by a parade of groups from Benedictine monks from Oregon to fraternity members attending the newly created Simon Fraser University in the late 1960s to squatters, it has survived the vicissitudes remarkably well and retains its fireplaces with tiled panels, brass beading and hood, the original bathroom fittings and a remarkable gabled inglenook fireplace in the former billiard room. Bought by the Municipality of Burnaby in 1966, it hosts changing exhibitions of mostly contemporary artists.

Burnaby Village Museum

Address: 6501 Deer Lake Avenue, www.city.burnaby.bc.ca
Tel: 604 297 4565
Opening Hrs: May–early Sept 11am–4.30pm, winter, call for hours
Entrance Fee: charge
Transport: SkyTrain Metrotown, then bus 144 SFU

Just a few minutes' walk away from the art gallery, this museum re-creates a typical Burnaby train-stop community *c.*1925 on its 4-hectare (10-acre) site. Only one of over 30 buildings is on its original site; the rest have been dismantled and relocated. The functions of the rescued buildings include a general store, bakery, post office, blacksmith, music shop, garage, Chinese herbalist, optometrist, print shop, barber and bank. A photographic studio has been cleverly adapted for changing exhibitions about different aspects of local history. Interpreters in period costume are on hand to tell you about a building's history and stories of former occupants.

The one building on its original site is Elworth, a cedar shingle-covered house with full-width Tuscan-columned porch built in 1922 by a Canadian Pacific Railway employee. Children are enthralled by the hand-carved carousel built in Kansas in 1912 which has 36 horses, 4 ponies, a chariot and a wheelchair, while music from a 1925 Wurlitzer military band organ fills the air. Light lunches and snacks can be bought in the ice-cream parlour.

There is also a fully restored electric tram, which was first put into service in 1913 and ran until buses

Burnaby has a few famous sons, including crooner Michael Bublé, whose road to fame was guided by producer David Foster, another British Columbian (born in Victoria). Actor Michael J. Fox (best known for the Back to the Future *films) also grew up in Burnaby. Fox was diagnosed with Parkinson's disease in 1991 and, after going public with his disease, formed the Michael J. Fox Parkinson's Foundation, which has raised more than $120 million for research to find a cure.*

BELOW: Simon Fraser University.

BELOW: summer market outside Port Moody's old station building.

replaced the tram system in 1958. The originally cherry and oak interior had to be stripped and revarnished, with some parts supplemented with pieces of sister trams. There is also a new tram barn.

Beside the SkyTrain line at Metrotown Station is the vast **Metrotown Centre**, Canada's second-largest shopping centre with close to 500 shops and restaurants.

Almost a quarter of Burnaby is parkland, with over 100 different parks; one of the largest, **Central Park**, is a forest of huge Douglas firs, hemlock and maple, which can be reached from the adjacent Patterson SkyTrain station.

Simon Fraser University

A secluded campus on Burnaby Mountain surrounded by a wooded conservation area, **Simon Fraser University** ❹ received its first students in 1965 in buildings designed by Arthur Erickson. Covering 174 hectares (430 acres), the university is built in the form of terraces beside a linear walkway along a ridge, and its homogeneous concrete buildings have provided the set for many a sci-ence fiction film. As one of Erickson's first and largest commissions, the university is accustomed to visits by those interested in modern architecture. In addition to its main location, it now boasts additional campuses in downtown Vancouver and in the suburb of Surrey to accommodate more than 30,000 students.

The area around Simon Fraser is one of the Lower Mainland's best-kept secrets. Spectacular views of the city and mountains, hiking trails, a mountain bike park, a public golf course, picnic areas, a sculpture park and a restaurant provide enough for an entire day combining nature and civilisation. This is where the locals go and tourists seldom venture, simply because it is not well known.

PORT MOODY

This city at the eastern end of Burrard Inlet might have been Vancouver, so to speak, had the Canadian Pacific Railway not reversed its decision to make **Port Moody** ❺ the western terminus of the transcontinental railway, electing instead to push on to what is now Waterfront near Coal Harbour. It was seen as a back door to New Westminster (at that time the capital of the colony), should it be attacked from the Fraser River: North Road, a major thoroughfare today, started out as a trail through the woods between the two communities.

From this beginning and bearing the name of the commander of the Royal Engineers who built the road, Port Moody experienced a real-estate boom and bust with the CPR's choice and then rejection of the embryonic town as a suitable terminus. The first train from the east arrived on 8 November 1885, with transcontinental passenger services starting the following year. But in 1887, Port Moody was sidelined when the line on to Vancouver was opened. Though sawmills were developed beside the waterfront, the population remained

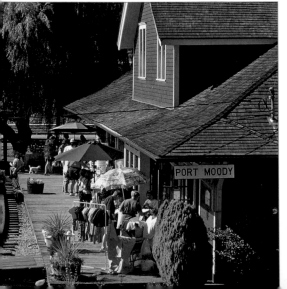

static at 250 for over 20 years. Eventually the pressure of development from Vancouver affected Port Moody, oil refineries were built in the 1900s and it became a city in 1913.

Though today largely a quiet suburb of Vancouver, several historic buildings remain, including one that now serves as the **Port Moody Arts Centre** (2425 St Johns Street).

Port Moody Station Museum

Address: 2734 Murray Street, www.vcn.bc.ca/pmmuseum
Tel: 604 939 1648
Opening Hrs: Victoria Day–Labour Day daily noon–5pm, Labour Day–Victoria Day Wed–Sun noon–4pm
Entrance Fee: charge
Transport: bus 160

Built in 1905 by the Canadian Pacific Railway, the old station building has

been converted to a museum with a restored telegraph office and a station agent's kitchen.

Between the Old City Hall and waterfront lies the 40-hectare (99-acre) **Shoreline Park**. The trail running through this park is part of the Trans Canada Trail, a series of trails and walkways across the country being joined to form the world's longest recreational trail, at more than 21,500km (13,360 miles). Along this part of the trail, birdwatchers can spot more than 100 species, including loons, cormorants, herons, eagles, geese and warblers. Wildlife in the area includes coyotes, foxes, raccoons and black-tailed deer.

If you have a vehicle and enjoy hiking, **Buntzen Lake** is worth the trek. Located at the northern reaches of Port Moody, it offers not only hiking, but a lovely beach and refreshing swimming and canoeing. ❏

ABOVE: the Port Moody Arts Centre is housed in the Arts and Crafts-style Old City Hall, built in 1914, which incorporated the firehall and police station.

RESTAURANTS

Burnaby

Fortune House Seafood Restaurant

2199A Kingsway (in Metrotown). Tel: 604 438 8686. www.fortunehouserestaurant. com Open: L & D daily. $
The comprehensive dim sum menu has pictures, so you can get an idea of which new treats you are willing to try. This restaurant is always busy, but efficient staff and a computerised system for ordering ensures quick service. Food is great, atmosphere chaotic and entertaining.

Hart House Restaurant

6664 Deer Lake Ave. Tel: 604 298 4278. www.harthouse restaurant.com Open: L Tue–Fri, Sun, D Tue–Sun. $$$
Serving creative West

Coast cuisine with a focus on fresh local ingredients and thoughtful wine pairings, Hart House is located in a hundred-year-old home, renovated to serve as a restaurant. The huge fireplace in the hall and white-painted wood panelling in the three dining rooms make for a cosy dinner, while lunches offer a lovely serene view of gardens. Reservations advised.

New Westminster

The Boathouse

900 Quayside Drive.
Tel: 604 525 3474.
www.boathouserestaurants.ca
Open: B, L & D daily. $$$
A casual-smart seafood restaurant set right on the shore. Open for all meals,

including brunch at the weekend.

Hon's Wun-Tun House

408 6th St. Tel: 604 520 6661. www.hons.ca Open: L & D daily. $
This unassuming Chinese has won a host of awards – best cheap eats, best Chinese, best casual Chinese – and once you've eaten here you will know why. But be prepared to wait for a table, as there is often a queue. The dim sum is great and the potstickers, noodles and barbecue have all been highly praised. Four locations around Vancouver.

The Keg Steakhouse

800 Columbia St. Tel: 604 524 1381. www.kegsteak house.com Open: D daily. $$$
This chain steakhouse is situated in the old railway station and serves the

usual steaks, chicken and seafood. Open for dinner from 4.30pm.

Tamarind Hill Malaysian Cuisine

628 Sixth Ave. Tel: 604 526 3000. L & D daily. $
The brightly painted interior of Tamarind Hill will make you feel like you are in warmer climes. Order the spiciest food you can tolerate and you won't be disappointed. Seafood is a winner here, but so is the beef rending (a beef curry with ginger, turmeric, lemon grass and onion, artfully bathed in a coconut sauce.

• • • • • • • • •
Prices for a three-course dinner per person with a half-bottle of house wine.
$$$$ = over C$80, **$$$** = C$50–80, **$$** = C$30–50, **$** = under C$30.

RICHMOND AND THE FRASER DELTA

There are many good reasons to visit this delta region. One is Steveston, a historic fishing village, another is the amazing variety of birdlife that comes to nest and feed around the mouth of the Fraser. Recreational trails cater for cyclists and walkers.

Main Attractions

STEVESTON VILLAGE
LONDON HERITAGE FARM
GULF OF GEORGIA CANNERY
REIFEL BIRD SANCTUARY

Maps and Listings

MAP OF RICHMOND AND
THE FRASER DELTA,
PAGE 164
RESTAURANTS AND CAFÉS,
PAGE 169
ACCOMMODATION, PAGE 253

Much of southern Vancouver is made up of islands within the Fraser Delta. The former fishing and farming community of Richmond is a group of islands contained within the northern and southern arms of the Fraser River. Even the airport is located on Sea Island, so named because it was difficult to tell where sea ended and land began.

Besides this delta region's ever-expanding role as a dormitory of Vancouver, fishing, farming and trade have long been its economic mainstays, although local sources of employment in the high-tech computer and software industries have recently grown.

SEA ISLAND

Apart from the airport, the other reason to visit Sea Island is to reach **Iona Island ❶** for its birdlife and an unusual bike ride or walk. Though the shoreline forms Iona Beach Regional Park, the island is also home to a sewage treatment plant, but it is neither a visual nor olfactory intrusion once you are into the sand dunes of the park where over 300 species of birds feed and rest. Besides eagles, osprey and heron, numerous rare birds have been spotted, including white pelican,

long-tailed jaeger, ruff and yellow-headed blackbirds. The southern arm of the peculiar V-shape of the western end of the island stretches for 4km (2½ miles) out into Georgia Strait; this narrow tarmac-covered jetty covers the outfall pipe and provides an unusual experience for cyclists and walkers. It's known as a good place to watch the stars away from the light pollution of Vancouver. Note that car access to Iona Beach Regional Park is forbidden after dusk, so stargazers need to park outside the gates.

LEFT: Steveston Docks. **RIGHT:** the delta region attracts many sea birds.

ABOVE: Richmond's beautiful Buddhist Temple, set in landscaped gardens, is a place of sanctuary. It is open to the public from 10am–5pm and has a meditation centre where you can take classes (9160 Steveston Highway; tel: 604 274 2822).

LULU ISLAND AND RICHMOND

Steveston and most of the much larger **Richmond** ❷ are located on this island formed by the alluvial sand and silt brought down the Fraser River and flanked by its north and south arms. Without the dykes, large areas of Lulu Island would be under water at extreme high tide. It was given its name in 1863 by Colonel Richard Moody, after a popular entertainer from San Francisco, Lulu Sweet, his travel companion from New Westminster to Victoria. The first European settlers arrived in 1866, and by 1879 Richmond had been incorporated as a township.

Although the area was developed as Vancouver's market garden, its proximity to the city and flat land made it a target for development. Some of the richest soil in the province is now covered with high-rise towers and back-to-back shopping malls – the Lansdowne Park and Richmond centres are the largest.

Nonetheless, more than 4,900 hectares (over 12,000 acres) of land within Richmond is protected as agricultural land – the fertile delta soil and absence of trees made it ideal for cultivation, with cranberries emerging as the dominant crop during the 1990s. Landowners no longer have to maintain the dykes, and with their adoption by local and provincial government, they have been adapted to incorporate Richmond's recreational trails for cyclists and walkers.

Richmond was the first Canadian city to declare itself multicultural, and it is indicative of the population's varied ethnicity that it has numerous predominantly Asian shopping malls featuring Asian-made products and, of course, marvellous restaurants.

Cultural Centre

Address: 7700 Minoru Gate, www.richmond.ca
Tel: 604 231 6457
Opening Hrs: Mon–Fri 9am–9.30pm,

Richmond and the Fraser Delta

Sat–Sun 10am–5pm
Entrance Fee: cultural centre free, art gallery and museum by donation
Transport: SkyTrain Richmond-Brighouse

The cultural centre includes an art gallery, museum, arts centre and archive as well as the main library. The art gallery encourages local artists, while the museum has a collection of some 12,000 artefacts relating to all aspects of the history of Richmond, including archaeology, ethnology, and pieces significant to agriculture, fishing, transportation, recreation, communications, business and technology.

Steveston

This community at the southwestern corner of Lulu Island has a very different atmosphere from anywhere else around Vancouver, with the coming and going of fishing boats, the tang of fish, seaweed and ozone, and the welcome feeling of a working maritime community. The main street even feels like a village, though the wall-to-wall restaurants along the seafront boardwalk speak of a considerable reliance on visitors.

Named after its first permanent settler, Manoah Steves, a native of New Brunswick who arrived in 1877, **Steveston ③** was initially a farming community. But it was only 12 years later that the Hudson's Bay Company tea clipper *Titania* carried the first direct shipment of canned salmon from Britannia cannery in Steveston to London, a trip around Cape Horn that took 104 days. Along 3.2km (2 miles) of foreshore known as "Cannery Row", 15 canneries were set up, one of which was the biggest in the British Empire. Bunkhouses, bars, brothels and opium dens catered for the 10,000 seasonal workers.

By 1895 Steveston canneries were producing around 200,000 cases of salmon a year, and it was not uncommon to have more than a dozen windjammers waiting near Steveston for appropriate tides and westerly winds to dock. Rocks brought in as ballast were unloaded and used to build roads and dykes in the area, and the holds were filled with lumber and canned salmon. Many of the fishermen, boatbuilders and workers were Japanese, until the decision in

The Fraser River is the longest river in BC at 1,375km (859 miles), rising in the Yellowhead Pass on the continental divide and draining an area the size of Britain.

ABOVE AND BELOW: fishing nets and boats at the Steveston waterfront.

ABOVE: café terrace, Steveston Docks.
RIGHT: there were once 49 canneries on the lower Fraser River, with 15 on Cannery Row at Steveston. The last plant closed in 1992.

TIP

Steveston is much sunnier than Vancouver. While it may be grey and raining in Vancouver, by the time you get to Steveston, the sun may be shining in a clear blue sky. This makes it a great choice for a long walk or bike ride.

If there is time, one of the more worthwhile things to do is to go out on the water, either for an ecotour up the Fraser River or for a longer whale-watching outing around the nearby Gulf Islands.

Steveston Waterfront Greenway

The best way to explore the waterfront is by hiring a bike and cycling the 5km (3-mile) -long greenway that runs alongside Cannery Channel. Workers from cannery days would not recognise the landscaped waterfront, where the restaurant-lined boardwalk and condominiums have replaced their places of work.

Britannia Heritage Shipyard

Address: 5180 Westwater Drive, www.britannia-hss.ca
Tel: 604 718 8050
Opening Hrs: May–Sept Tue–Sun 10am–6pm, Oct–Apr Sat 10am–4pm, Sun noon–4pm
Entrance Fee: charge
Transport: SkyTrain Richmond-Brighouse, then bus 401, 402 or 407

Panels along the waterfront provide information about the area, including the marvellous complex of preserved wooden buildings around it. Built on piles over the water like most of the old buildings along the waterfront, the covered slipways are still being used to restore boats brought out of the water on cradles. Now a National

1942 to intern them inland.

Steveston is still Canada's biggest commercial fishing harbour even if it no longer holds the title of "salmon capital of the world". It is the surviving buildings from its heyday, coupled with its attractive setting, that makes Steveston so popular with visitors. It is easy to reach, taking the Canada Line SkyTrain from downtown Vancouver to Richmond-Brighouse, then changing to a 401, 402, 407 or 410 bus (about an hour of transit time).

Steveston village

The blocks between Moncton Street and the shore at Bayview Street are full of small independent shops, cafés and restaurants. When locals come here, it's often to walk down to the docks to select their dinner: salmon, crab, prawns and sometimes tuna are displayed for all to see and a huge quantity is purchased by people planning a feast at home, or simply dinner.

Historic Site, the building was once a cannery, but was converted to a shipyard; a number of canneries closed with the disastrous downturn in salmon stocks on the Fraser River in 1918–19.

Nearby is a Seine net loft and the **Murakami Residence**, which is thought to have been built in the 1880s as a traditional Japanese home and bathhouse. The family owned one of the eight Japanese boatworks. It was originally also built on piles, so it has new foundations on its original footprint. In a garden along the front is a commemorative statue to the generations of Japanese fishermen who worked here.

London Heritage Farm
Address: 6511 Dyke Road,
www.londonheritagefarm.ca
Tel: 604 271 5220
Opening Hrs: Feb–June and Sept–Dec Sat–Sun noon–5pm, July–Aug Wed–Sun noon–5pm
Entrance Fee: by donation
Transport: SkyTrain Richmond-Brighouse, then bus 401, 402 or 407
A short distance away, the London

Heritage Farm has been restored to portray life c.1900. Aged 16 and 17, Charles Edwin London and his brother William came out to Steveston from London, Ontario, when their parents died and bought 80 hectares (200 acres) of land. They built the farm in the mid-1880s and also owned the general store and post office. Apart from the piano, none of the furniture is original, but it does not detract from the overall presentation of the house. Volunteers serve excellent tea in period china with home-baked scones.

Gulf of Georgia Cannery
Address: 12138 Fourth Avenue,
www.pc.gc.ca
Tel: 604 664 9009
Opening Hrs: Feb–Oct 10.30am–5pm
Entrance Fee: by donation
Transport: SkyTrain Richmond-Brighouse, then bus 401, 402 or 407
The importance of salmon and the canning industry to the coastal region

ABOVE: cycling the Steveston greenway.
BELOW: the Gulf of Georgia Cannery traces the history of fishing and canning in the region.

Burns Bog

This vast expanse between Ladner, North Delta and Surrey is the largest area of park in the Lower Mainland. Covering about 2,800 hectares (6,919 acres), the raised peat bog forms the largest undeveloped urban area in Canada. Its sheer size enables it to act as a valuable natural air and water filtration system, as well as being home to many beautiful and rare plants, animals and insects. Though the Annacis Highway slices through the separately protected Delta Nature Reserve in the northeastern corner of Burns Bog, the rest of the reserve is closed to traffic. It has three loops of boardwalks and trails, parts of which are accessible to wheelchairs and strollers, with beaver dam and cedar groves en route.

Just three minutes from the ferry terminal at Tsawwassen, Splashdown Park (June–early Sept 10am–4/5/6/7/8pm; tel: 604 943 2251; www.splashdownpark. ca) has 13 slides of various sizes, configurations and degrees of scariness (one is black), as well as volleyball, badminton and basketball facilities.

BELOW: sunset fishing trip off Westham Island.
OPPOSITE: the Cannery Café, a Steveston favourite.

of BC has been recognised by the protection given to the Gulf of Georgia Cannery, built in 1894 and the largest in BC until 1902. After switching to herring reduction (the production of protein rich oils for animal feed) following World War II, the cannery finally closed in 1979 but continued in use as a net storage facility while its fate was decided. The Federal government bought the cannery and transferred it to Parks Canada, which organises separate guided tours of the salmon packing and herring reduction sections of the plant, following a film that evokes the way of life that went with the pungent canneries.

Beyond the cannery is **Garry Point Park**, an area of reclaimed intertidal salt marsh. Created in 1989, the park's terrain is mostly sand, with gaillardia growing wild among the sea grass in summer. It's a good place to find a quiet spot to soak up the sun, and the bike trail and footpath continue all the way around the coast almost to the Moray Bridge linking the mainland and Sea Island.

Close to the shore is the **Fisherman's Memorial Needle**, which commemorates the many boats and crews lost at sea over the years.

WESTHAM ISLAND

Fruit wine, flowers, herbs, fruit and vegetables are produced and sold from roadside stalls on this large but awkward-to-reach island in the mouth of the south arm of the Fraser River. It's worth the trip though, in part for the wonderful peacefulness the place brings.

George C. Reifel Migratory Bird Sanctuary ❶

Address: 5191 Robertson Road, Delta, www.reifelbirdsanctuary.com
Tel: 604 946 6980
Opening Hrs: daily 9am–4pm
Entrance Fee: charge
Transport: vehicle required; Highway 99 south from Vancouver to Ladner, follow River Road to Westham Island, follow main road to the end

This is the main draw of Westham Island. The 344-hectare (850-acre) sanctuary is threaded by 3km (2 miles) of walking trails from which to see some of the more than 280 species of birds recorded here, and there are hides and a three-storey observation platform.

The autumn highlight is the arrival of flocks of lesser snow geese, numbering up to 80,000 and turning the sky white. In winter you may be lucky enough to see the tiny saw-whet owl roosting in overhead branches. Spring brings cormorants, hawks, eagles, ospreys and other fish-eating wildlife. Many bird species are resident year-round, but among the rare sightings are uncommon species such as black-crowned night heron and gyrfalcon.

DEAS ISLAND

Further up the south arm lies **Deas Island** ❺, covering 70 hectares (173 acres), named after the first settler, a freed black slave named John Sullivan Deas, who arrived in 1873. He

founded an unsuccessful cannery, but others followed until World War I. The rest of the small community was made up of a few farmers and fishermen, but by the 1950s the island was deserted. There are a number of easy, level trails through the cottonwood and alder trees, such as the Island Tip Trail and the Dyke Loop. The western side is the more natural and has been likened to the Mississippi Delta.

LADNER

A wharf to dispatch agricultural produce to Victoria and New Westminster was the beginning of **Ladner 6**, a village on the delta of the south arm, founded by and named

after two brothers from Cornwall who had come out in the gold rush. The historic and attractive part of the town is Ladner village, with wide, tree-lined pavements and small shops and cafés. The **Delta Museum** (4858 Delta Street; Tue–Sat 10am–3.30pm), housed in a 1912 neo Tudor building, features a reconstructed prison cell among its exhibits of local history.

Continuing south, the town of Tsawwassen is known mostly for the ferries that head off to Victoria on Vancouver Island, as well as many of the smaller islands in between: see Victoria and Vancouver Island (*pages 191–205*) and the Gulf Islands (*pages 207–15*). ❑

RESTAURANTS

Pajo's
Chatham St. Tel: 604 204 0767. www.pajos.com **$**
A small chain (four locations) of fish-and-chip shops, operating seasonally (spring, summer, and a bit of the autumn), serving cod, salmon and halibut, all of it wild. You can have burgers, chicken and other fast foods, but the fish is the thing here, and the queues are a testament to the quality.

La Belle Auberge
4856 48th Ave. Tel: 604 946 7717. www.labelleauberge.com Open: D
Tue–Sat. **$$$$**
Spread over two levels of a pretty Victorian house, award-winning chef Bruno Marti's establishment is reckoned to be one of the best restaurants in Canada. Chef de cuisine Tobias

MacDonald has followed in Marti's Culinary Olympic footsteps, picking up a few medals of his own. Game features prominently on the menu – lobster bisque and braised venison with polenta are wonderful starters, while the pheasant with brandy cream as a main course would satisfy the most discerning of palates.

Sun Sui Wah Seafood Restaurant
102, 4940 No. 3 Rd.
Tel: 604 273 8208. www.sunsuiwah.com Open: L & D daily. **$$**
The area bordered by Sea Island Way, No. 3 Road, Lansdowne Road and Garden City Road, is the heart of the city's Asian population and has been dubbed "Golden Village". This Cantonese restaurant is famous for its dim sum

served in the time-honoured way from trolleys which trundle around the room waiting for you to take your pick. Try the Alaska king crab steamed with minced garlic.

Thai House Restaurant
129, 4940 No. 3 Rd. Tel: 604 278 7373. www.thaihouse.com Open: L & D daily. **$**
Vancouver-area chain of award-winning Thai restaurants. This popular Richmond branch in the Golden Village offers very good Thai food at extremely good prices with a focus on fresh food and fast service.

Alegria Café and Giftware
12151 1st Ave. Tel: 604 274 1215. B and L daily. **$**
Serves home-made food using organic ingredients – the muffins are great. Good place for a light lunch after a browse in the gift shop.

Gudrun
150–3500 Moncton St. Tel: 604 272 1991. http://gudrun.ca Open: D Tue–Sun, Brunch Sun. **$$**
Hidden behind a Filipino karaoke hair salon, this tasting bar has an amazing selection of cheeses and beers from all over the world, plus organic and biodynamic wines.

Shady Island
112–3800 Bayview St. Tel: 604 275 6587. http://shadyislandseafood.com Open: L & daily. **$–$$**
Located right by the dock, the clam chowder served in a sourdough bread bowl is the perennial favourite, but consider the generous portion of mussels as well. Friendly service and a good selection of BC wines at fair prices.

● ● ● ● ● ● ●
Prices for a three-course dinner per person with a half-bottle of house wine. **$$$$** = over C$80, **$$$** = C$50–80, **$$** = C$30–50, **$** = under C$30.

NORTH AND WEST VANCOUVER

Exclusive mansions command fabulous views along the north shore, but the real attraction is the wilderness beyond. Grouse Mountain and Capilano Canyon are an easy bus ride from Lonsdale Quay, but if you've time for deeper exploration Lynn Canyon, Mount Seymour and Cypress Park are all outstanding.

It is the mountains that range along the north shore of English Bay and Burrard Inlet that give Vancouver such a stunning setting. The view from Kitsilano and Point Grey without the sawtooth of peaks along the opposite shore is unimaginable. Both North and West Vancouver are predominantly dormitories, West being the more upmarket, though both have much to offer the visitor. With an abundance of provincial, regional and municipal parks, this area offers the best hiking and biking close to the city.

Early development

The topography that residents and visitors admire was both the stimulus to the area's development and the reason for southern districts to eclipse the early promise of North Vancouver. Huge stands of cedars and firs encouraged the establishment of the first sawmill on the north shore, in 1862, and two years later international trade out of Burrard Inlet began with the first consignment of timber, to Adelaide. But the absence of a bridge across the inlet and the distance from the local markets of New Westminster and Victoria made it difficult for the pioneers to com-

pete. Even the Methodist minister who preached the first sermon on the inlet had to arrive by canoe, in 1865. Equally the mountains would constrain eventual development.

Even when North Vancouver became a formal district in 1891, stretching from Horseshoe Bay to Deep Cove, the population was still only a few hundred. Many of the early users of the ferry service established in 1900 were hikers, skiers for Grouse Mountain or visitors to the Capilano Suspension Bridge. The City of North

LEFT: Grouse Mountain Skyride.
RIGHT: Horseshoe Bay harbour.

Vancouver was carved out of the area and independently governed from 1907, followed in 1912 by the municipality of West Vancouver.

The opening of the Second Narrows Bridge for rail and road traffic in 1925 gave a huge fillip to the north shore and North Vancouver in particular. The Depression hit North Vancouver so hard that about 75 percent of landowners saw their property revert to the municipality for unpaid taxes. World War II and a revival of shipbuilding relieved unemployment and revived population growth.

NORTH VANCOUVER

Most visitors to North Vancouver arrive by SeaBus at **Lonsdale Quay** ❶, where the bus station and shopping centre are located directly ahead. Lonsdale Quay is North Vancouver's equivalent of Granville Market (*see page 126*), a former collection of warehouses that was adapted in 1986 to become a collection of individual

shops. East of Lonsdale Quay, following the water's edge, is the former Pacific Great Eastern Railway station of 1913, which now serves as a tourist information centre.

Beyond are the remains of the shipbuilding slips that produced 379 vessels between 1906 and 1992, including tugs and barges, supply ships in two world wars, ferries and icebreakers. Versatile Pacific Shipyard (formerly Wallace Shipyards) was the largest company, run by three generations of the Wallace family after Andrew Wallace established the yard in 1894, but one company remains active: C.H. Cates & Sons is one of Vancouver's oldest companies, having been founded in 1886, and is still carrying out repairs to its fleet of tugs.

The streets north of Lonsdale Quay, known as lower Lonsdale, or shortened to "Lolo", contain the few heritage buildings left, including two from 1910 – the former Bank of Hamilton at 92 Lonsdale and the Aberdeen

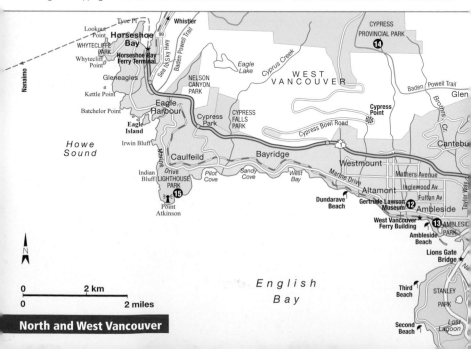

North and West Vancouver

block at 84 Lonsdale, in which one of the district's oldest shops, Paines Hardware, is still located.

Capilano Suspension Bridge ❷

Address: 3735 Capilano Road, www.capbridge.com
Tel: 604 985 7474
Opening Hrs: June–Sept 8.30am–8pm, winter 9am–5pm, except Dec 10am–9pm
Entrance Fee: charge
Transport: bus 236 from Lonsdale Quay

The bridges across the thickly forested Capilano canyon have been attracting visitors since 1889, and the current 137-metre (450ft) span bridge swaying 70 metres (230ft) above the river has become a "must see" for visitors.

Once across the bridge, there are boardwalks through the forest, with a high-level tree walk 30 metres (100ft) above the floor linking eight Douglas firs ranging from 60–76 metres

(200–250ft) tall. Information boards give an insight into the importance of preserving what temperate rainforest survives: though tropical rainforest has more varieties of plants and animals, temperate rainforest wins hands down for quantity, with up to 2,000 tonnes of living matter per acre of forest. There is also a large collection of totem poles near the bridge, many of them dating from the 1930s.

Capilano River Regional Park ❸

Address: 3735 Capilano Road, www.metrovancouver.org
Tel: 604 224 5739
Opening Hrs: open during daylight hours, never closing before 5pm
Entrance Fee: free
Transport: bus 246 from Lonsdale Quay to Ambleside Park

Capilano River Regional Park stretches from the ocean shore at Ambleside Park all the way up the river, past the suspension bridge up to the immense

As the southern terminus of the railway from Prince George and northern BC, North Vancouver receives large quantities of raw materials and agricultural products, such as potash, canola, wheat, barley and flax. Bright-yellow mounds of sulphur are a distinctive feature of the shoreline.

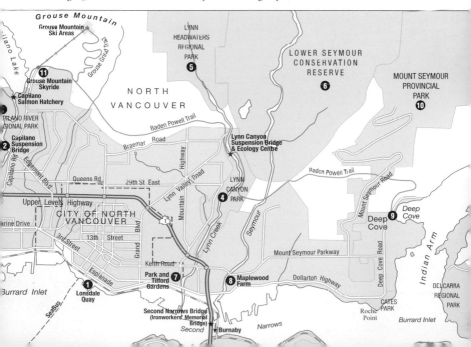

ABOVE: Capilano Suspension Bridge;
BELOW: it's hard to believe that back in the 1860s Burrard Inlet was so quiet that you could shout across the water for Navvy Jack to come and ferry you across.
RIGHT: totem poles in Lynn Canyon Park.

Opening Hrs: May, Sept 8am–7pm, June–Aug 8am–8pm, Apr, Oct 8am–4.45pm, Nov–Mar 8am–4pm
Entrance Fee: free
Transport: bus 236 from Lonsdale Quay

The construction of the Cleveland Dam in 1954 blocked the route of coho, Chinook and steelhead travelling up the Capilano River to spawn, so the weir and ladder were built to help the fish navigate upriver. The hatchery was opened in 1971 to release salmon below the dam and offset the high losses of young fish travelling downstream over the dam. There's always something to see at the hatchery; best of all is spawning season (Nov–Dec), when you'll see salmon jumping over the fish ladders.

Lynn Canyon Park ❹

Address: 3663 Park Road, www.lynncanyon.ca
Tel: 604 981 3103
Opening Hrs: June–Sept daily 10am–5pm, Oct–May Mon–Fri 10am–5pm, Sat–Sun noon–4pm
Entrance Fee: free
Transport: bus 228/229 from Lonsdale Quay

concrete wall of Cleveland Dam, which holds back Capilano Lake, the source of 40 percent of Vancouver's drinking water. There are about 26km (16 miles) of trails in the park; the longest is the Capilano Pacific Trail at 8km (5 miles), popular with dog-walking and jogging locals. It's mostly close to the river, except for a short section signed "Town Trail" through a residential neighbourhood at Park Royal and a stretch near the Trans Canada Highway.

For a river-bed view of the canyon, take the path down to Ranger Pool; there are some striking viewpoints along the way. Alternative paths through the forest include one following the gently graded trackbed of the Capilano Timber Company railway, with good views of the Lions (the twin peaks visible from downtown Vancouver).

Capilano Salmon Hatchery

Address: 4500 Capilano Park Road, www.heb.pac.dfo-mpo.gc.ca
Tel: 604 666 1790

The 250-hectare (617-acre) Lynn Canyon Park provides a free alternative to the Capilano bridge; it was opened in 1912. Near the entrance is an **Ecology Centre**, which has well-presented displays on plants, animals, trees and ecosystems, with lots of buttons to press and flaps to open for children. Though not as long as the Capilano bridge, the Lynn Canyon suspension bridge spans a spectacular sheer-walled canyon just above a waterfall of rock, and it has enough wobble to delight children without being too scary for faint-hearted grown-ups.

Once across the bridge, you can do a circular walk by turning south and following a path, partly boardwalk, through the forest and down steep steps to reach Two Falls Bridge, which spans the river above some crystal-clear pools and a double fall in the river. Equally steep steps take you back to the café near the Ecology Centre, which serves light lunches. En route are many stumps of the Douglas firs and Western red cedar which were felled in the late 19th century.

The bridge is on the 41km (26-mile) Baden-Powell Trail between Horseshoe Bay in West Vancouver and Deep Cove on the west bank of the Indian Arm inlet (*see page 177*).

Lynn Headwaters Regional Park ⑤

Address: end of Lynn Valley Road, www.metrovancouver.org

Tel: 604 224 5739
Opening Hrs: open during daylight hours, never closing before 5pm
Entrance Fee: free
Transport: bus 229 from Lonsdale Quay

This wilderness area with 75km (47 miles) of hiking trails really makes the city seem a world away. It offers some spectacular views, and such curious sights as trees growing through an abandoned truck from logging days. An information area on the east side of Lynn Creek near the entrance has details of the park trails, and visitors are asked to self-register.

There are trails of varying lengths and levels of difficulty. The Lynn Loop Trail and Cedar Mill Trail will take less than an hour and require only minimal fitness. The creekside 15.5km (9½-mile) Headwaters Trail is a steeper walk that takes you to Norvan Creek, and takes about half a day. More challenging is the aptly named Switchback Trail with the option at the top of heading back along the

LEFT: Lynn Canyon Park. **ABOVE:** Lynn Canyon suspension bridge. **BELOW:** the Capilano Salmon Hatchery was built to offset damage caused by Cleveland Dam.

TIP

Heavy rain can cause watercourses to rise so rapidly that hiking paths in the area can become difficult or impossible to follow. This should be borne in mind when planning a hiking route for a day of changeable weather. The best time for walking in the north-shore parks is late April to mid-October.

BELOW: biking trail through Lower Seymour Conservation Reserve.

Lynn Loop or pressing on north to the headwaters. Water levels in Lynn Creek have to be low to be able to tackle the Lynn Lake Route, which is only for experienced hikers. Bears are common in this park.

Lower Seymour Conservation Reserve ⑥

Address: end of Lynn Valley Road, www.metrovancouver.org
Tel: 604 224 5739
Opening Hrs: open during daylight hours, never closing before 5pm
Entrance Fee: free
Transport: bus 228 from Lonsdale Quay; 210 from downtown, SkyTrain Burrard

Sandwiched between Lynn Headwaters Regional Park and Mount Seymour Provincial Park, the Lower Seymour Conservation Reserve is a 5,668-hectare (14,006-acre) reserve comprising approximately one-third of the 18,000-hectare (44,489-acre) Seymour Watershed, which supplies Vancouver with water. It contains some of the most spectacular and diverse landscapes in the Greater Vancouver area, with beautiful Alpine meadows, forested slopes and river flood plains.

The 25km (15 miles) of fairly easy hiking trails head off in all directions from the car-park gatehouse. The most challenging ones are the Homestead, Twin Bridges and Fisherman's trails, which lead down into the Seymour Valley and follow the Seymour river. Maps and an interpretive brochure are available at the gatehouse.

In addition to hiking trails, there are also trails for extreme "North Shore" mountain biking, as well as paths for regular scenic cycling. Mountain biking on the North Shore is a major sport and the terrain it offers is some of the best there is.

Park and Tilford Gardens ⑦

Address: 333 Brooksbank Avenue, www.parkandtilford.ca
Tel: 604 984 8200
Opening Hrs: daily 9.30am–4.30pm, until 9.30pm during Dec for Festival of Lights
Entrance Fee: free
Transport: bus 228/239 from Lonsdale Quay

Just west of the Ironworkers' Memo-

Mountain Hiking

The mountainous backcountry of Mount Seymour National Park and Lynn Headwaters Regional Park is extremely rugged, and hiking in these areas should be attempted only by experienced and properly equipped walkers. Heavy rain and thick fog can quickly change the landscape from beautiful to dangerous. The mountain weather can change very quickly, so be prepared by taking appropriate gear, and inform a responsible person of your intentions. If mist and fog should close in and you become lost, stay where you are until the weather clears or you are found. Hiking alone is inadvisable, and you should know what to do if you encounter a bear. Never leave the trail.

rial Bridge *(see page 158)*, this compact garden was created in 1969 by a distillery company. The gardens cover 1.2 hectares (3 acres) and are divided into eight themed areas: oriental with plants pruned in bonsai style; white; rock pool with waterfall; native; herb; flower garden with 27 circular beds of colourful annuals replacing spring-flowering bulbs; colonnade with a long pergola; and bog garden. It's located adjacent to a shopping centre and six-theatre cinema bearing the same name.

Maplewood Farm ❽

Address: 405 Seymour River Place, www.maplewoodfarm.bc.ca
Tel: 604 929 5610
Opening Hrs: Apr–Oct daily 10am–4pm, Nov–Mar closed Mon
Entrance Fee: charge
Transport: bus 239 from Lonsdale Quay, transfer to C-15 shuttle at Phibbs Exchange

To the east of the bridge lies a great place to take children to see over 200 domestic animals and birds on a 2-hectare (5-acre) farm beside the Seymour river. It is now the last remaining farm on the north shore and offers pony rides (in summer), milking demonstrations and animals to hold or pat. A particularly popular time to visit is spring, when baby animals are born.

Deep Cove

The small settlement of **Deep Cove** ❾ on Indian Arm is right on the edge of North Vancouver, almost bordering Mount Seymour National Park. It's renowned as one of the loveliest parts of the region, but take rain gear if you go there as it's also the wettest place in the Lower Mainland. It has a vibrant community with plenty of individual shops, pubs and restaurants, and even has a 130-seat air-conditioned theatre and art gallery within the Cultural Centre.

Indian Arm is a paradise for pad-

dlers – an 18km (11-mile) fjord of calm, clear, jade-green water flanked by forested slopes. Canoes and kayaks can be rented for an hour, a day, or longer *(see Activities, page 263)*. The best time of year is between April and October unless you're a duck.

It was in a squatter's cabin at Dollarton in Cates Park, south of Deep Cove, that Cheshire-born Malcolm Lowry wrote between 1940 and 1954 the most famous novel written in BC, twice. In 1944 his shack burnt down and with it went the first manuscript of *Under the Volcano*. In 1954 Lowry was evicted and the cabin torn down. Its site at the eastern end of Cates Park (bus 232 from Lonsdale Quay and then 212) is marked by a plaque commemorating the events that took place at his "little lonely hermitage", devoid of electricity or plumbing. "Although there was no questioning its hardship, at least in winter," he wrote, "how beautiful it could be then, with the snow-covered cabins, the isolation, the driftwood like burnished silver – the wonderful excruciating absurd shouting ecstasy of swimming in freezing weather." The novel written in this

ABOVE: the oriental garden, one of eight themed gardens in Tilford Park, is designed to be a place of rest and relaxation. **BELOW:** Maplewood Farm is ideal for kids.

ABOVE: orphan bears on Grouse Mountain.
ABOVE RIGHT: hiking through the snow in Mount Seymour Provincial Park. **BELOW:** for a true bird's-eye view, try parascending off Grouse Mountain.

way to Amabilis fir, Yellow cedar and Mountain hemlock. Some of the higher meadows are cloaked with sub-Alpine flowers, providing colourful early summer displays. Bears, bobcats, cougars and pine marten inhabit the backcountry, while deer, coyote and Douglas squirrel are commonly seen. BC's official bird, the Steller's jay, can be seen besides chickadee, kinglet, sapsucker, grouse and siskin. During their annual autumn migration, several species of hawks may be spotted.

austere setting won the Governor General's award for fiction.

Mount Seymour Provincial Park ⑩

Address: www.env.gov.bc.ca
Tel: 604 986 2261
Opening Hrs: open during daylight hours, never closing before 5pm
Entrance Fee: free

Covering 3,508 hectares (8,669 acres), this provincial park was established in 1936 and named after an early governor of BC, Frederick Seymour. There are trails for hikers and mountain bikers, some offering magnificent views over Indian Arm and the city. In winter, Mount Seymour Ski Resort has more than downhill skiing and snowboarding; other activities for all skill levels include snowshoeing, tubing and tobogganing.

As one climbs towards the 1,000-metre (3,280ft) mark, old-growth Douglas fir and Western red cedar interspersed with second-growth coniferous and deciduous trees give

Grouse Mountain

It's worth heading up Grouse Mountain for the stunning views over Vancouver and English Bay from the summit at 1,250 metres (4,100ft). There are two ways of getting to the top; the **Grouse Grind** is an extremely arduous climb, largely up wooden steps, gaining around 853 metres (2,800ft) in 3km (1.8 miles). The climb is open May–October, but closes in poor weather. Boots and water are recommended; allow around an hour and a half for the ascent, although the record for men is 24 minutes 22 seconds (32 minutes 54 seconds for women). This is not a hike for the casual walker.

Grouse Mountain Skyride ⑪

Address: 6400 Nancy Greene Way, www.grousemountain.com
Tel: 604 984 0661
Opening Hrs: daily 9am–10pm

Entrance Fee: charge
Transport: bus 236 from
Lonsdale Quay

The other, more relaxing, way to the top is on the 100-passenger cable car which will whisk you to the upper station in eight minutes. Besides a café and a very good restaurant *(see page 183)*, there is a variety of year-round attractions on Grouse Mountain. The Theatre in the Sky (10am–9pm on the hour) shows a breathtaking documentary about BC's mountains, and the Refuge for Endangered Wildlife looks after orphaned grizzly bear cubs and grey wolves in a sizeable enclosure. In summer there are hikes with views to Washington State and Mount Baker, and the 45-minute Lumberjack Show (May–mid-Oct at noon, 2.30pm and 4.30pm) entertains the audience with demonstrations of axe-throwing, how to climb 20 metres (66ft) up a tree, and the indispensable skill of log rolling. For the more active, there is ziplining, as well as the chance to tandem paraglide.

In winter the mountain receives an average snowfall of 305cm (120 inches), so this is the place to ski if you haven't the time to go to Whistler. There are 26 day runs, mostly intermediate, and 13 night runs, supported by two high-speed quad chair lifts, two tow ropes and one magic carpet. There's also an ice-skating rink with skates for rental, four snowshoe trails, and at Christmas a grotto for Santa.

WEST VANCOUVER

The western side of the north shore is quite different in character from the eastern end, since it has always been an emphatically residential area with a prohibition on anything much more commercial than a shop. At one time it was even necessary to hold a British passport to be able to buy property on the 1,620 hectares (4,000 acres) of land in West Vancouver controlled by the Guinness family. It was to access this property and increase its value that the family company, British Pacific Properties, built the Lions

ABOVE: restaurant at the top of Grouse Mountain. **BELOW:** Lumberjacks put on a daredevil show at Grouse Mountain.

the oldest surviving building in West Vancouver (c.1873).

West Vancouver became an incorporated district in 1912, and has grown into Vancouver's most prestigious residential district, although modest summer cottages still punctuate the multi-million-dollar houses.

Per capita income here is the highest in Canada. This concentration of wealth is reflected in the many modern houses commissioned from such award-winning designers and architects as Arthur Erickson, Ron Thom, John Porter and Fred Hollingsworth.

This well-heeled and well-connected population was less than thrilled when the Pacific Great Eastern Railway was finally completed in 1958 with the construction of the coastal section running beside Howe Sound between Horseshoe Bay and Squamish, leading to heavy freight trains rumbling round the tortuous curves along the waterfront.

Today the line also carries the daily Whistler Mountaineer train, operated by Rocky Mountaineer Vacations (see page 245), which leaves from a small station in North Vancouver.

Gate Bridge, which was opened on 11 November 1938 as a toll bridge at a cost of nearly C$6 million.

West Van, as the locals call it, stretches for 28km (17½ miles) along English Bay with some of the best views in all Vancouver. Until 1909, when the first frequent ferry service started, it was regarded as a summer holiday area, with fresher air than downtown offered at the time. The first white resident was a Welsh deserter from the Royal Navy, Jack Thomas, who married the daughter of a Squamish Nation chief; their house at 1768 Argyle Avenue in Ambleside, close to Navvy Jack Park, still stands,

SHOPPING

Books

32 Books
3185 Edgemond Boulevard.
Tel: 604 980 9032.
www.32books.com
A fine independent bookstore whose owner and staff are passionate about books.

Food

Frankies Candy Bar
2451 Marine Drive. Tel: 604 922 8291. www.frankiescandybar.com
While it is not exactly food, it is fabulous, with every kind of candy imaginable.

Gifts and Toys

BC Playthings
3070 Edgemont Boulevard.
Tel: 604 986 4111. www.bc playthings.com
This toy store stocks educational toys and a superb selection of wooden puzzles.

The Bears Toy Store
1459 Bellevue Ave. Tel: 604 926 2327.
A great toy store, conveniently located in the heart of West Vancouver.

Giftworks
3080 Edgemont Boulevard. Tel: 604 986 4863. www.giftworks.biz
The place for locally made jewellery, pottery and glass.

Gertrude Lawson Museum ⑫

Address: 680 17th Street
Tel: 604 925 7295
Opening Hrs: mid-June–Labour Day Tue–Sun 11am–5pm, Labour Day–mid-June Tue–Sat noon–4.30pm
Entrance Fee: charge
Transport: West Vancouver "Blue Bus" 250/251/252 from the Hudson Bay, West Georgia
Just off Marine Drive, this museum of local history occupies an unusual 1939-built house designed by the teacher and artist Gertrude Lawson, supposedly to evoke the Scottish castles she had seen while travelling. Granite blocks thought to have been carried as ballast in sailing ships from New Zealand were used to create a house that was to be a place where

her friends could gather and even live. It has changing exhibitions of local history and a gift shop.

Along the attractively landscaped waterfront at Ambleside, at 101 14th Street, is the clapboard **West Vancouver Ferry Building**, designed by Thompson & Campbell in 1913. The ferry service gave up competing with the Lions Gate Bridge in 1947, and after a period as a bus depot the building was converted into an art gallery.

West Vancouver parks and trails

Like North Vancouver, West Van has some of the best opportunities for hiking on forest and coastal trails. **Ambleside Park ⓭**, just west of the Lions Gate Bridge, links the walk along the Capilano River with a series of linear parks all the way along the north shore as far west as Dundarave Park (paralleled by buses 250 and 255 from Park Royal interchange).

Cypress Provincial Park ⓮

Address: Cypress Bowl Road, above Highway 1; www.env.gov.bc.ca/bcparks and http://cypressmountain.com

Tel: 604 926 5612
Opening Hrs: open during daylight hours, never closing before 5pm
Entrance Fee: free
Transport: no public transport; shuttle bus from Lonsdale Quay in winter

The 3,012 hectare (7,443-acre) park is reached via Cypress Bowl Road, off the Upper Levels Highway (No. 1), which comes to a dead end at 900 metres (2,950ft). There are miles of hiking paths up here that become cross-country ski trails when it snows. It's sufficiently popular in winter for the 1920s Hollyburn Lodge to provide sustenance for skiers.

A quick taster of what the park has to offer once the snow has gone is the 1.6km (1-mile) -long Yew Lake Trail from the skiing area, which winds through sub-Alpine meadows and old-growth trees. For a spectacular view of the almost impenetrable mountains that recede to the northern horizon, a steep path leads up to Hollyburn Peak at 1,325 metres (4,347ft), and there's even a lift for mountain bikers. A five-hour intermediate-level walk, the Eagle Bluff Trail, leads hikers up Black Mountain through forest and

The Cypress Bowl and its lifts (www.cypress mountain.com) hosted the snowboarding and freestyle skiing events in the 2010 Winter Olympics. It was here that Canada won its first two gold medals on Canadian soil.

BELOW: the shores of Lighthouse Park.

past small lakes to a rocky bluff with fantastic views over Howe Sound.

To see a giant Douglas fir known to be 1,100 years old and referred to as the Hollyburn fir, take the 5km (3-mile) Lawson Creek Forestry Heritage Walk, which begins in Pinecrest Drive (buses 239 or 246 from Lonsdale Quay to Park Royal and then 254).

If you are after a good long walk, Horseshoe Bay at the western end of the north shore might be a good place to start. Here, at the perimeter of the suburban area, is the start of the 44km (27½-mile) west–east **Baden Powell Trail** which ends up at Deep Cove *(see page 177)*.

From Lonsdale Quay take bus route 239 or 246 to Park Royal and then catch a 257 to the Eagleridge Exit of Highway 1. At the top of the exit ramp, turn right into a cul-de-sac and the trail starts at its end by the sign. It is well marked with bright orange triangular tags attached to trees, and regular signposts indicate directions and give distance measurements. Because it cuts across various river valleys that flow south, there are a lot of taxing gradients, so you need to start early and be

ABOVE: ferns in Cypress Provincial Park. **BELOW:** view of downtown Vancouver from the residential heights of West Vancouver.

fit to complete it in a day. Experienced hikers should allow 14 hours.

However, there are several points at which you can cut the hike short and take a bus back to Lonsdale Quay, such as the base of Grouse Mountain and Lynn Valley. Those who complete it are rewarded with a spectacular view over Indian Arm.

Lighthouse Park ⓰

Located at the entrance to Burrard Inlet, **Lighthouse Park** comprises 75 hectares (185 acres) of temperate rainforest with some of the largest Western red cedars and Douglas firs in Vancouver – the longest-standing trees here are thought to be around 500 years old.

Among the trails that thread through the park is a 5km (3-mile) circuit that leads to the lighthouse at Point Atkinson, built in 1912. Unusually, this hexagonal reinforced-concrete lighthouse has six buttresses and is still staffed, and its two-tone foghorn is a familiar sound to local residents. With lots of coves and big, rounded rocks to clamber on (take care, they are very slippery), this park is a great favourite with children.   ❑

BEST RESTAURANTS, BARS AND CAFÉS

Restaurants

North Vancouver

Arms Reach Bistro
107C, 4390 Gallant Ave., Deep Cove. Tel: 604 929 7442. www.armsreachbistro. com Open: L & D daily. **$$**
A fabulous view and tasty West Coast cuisine at reasonable prices make this a return destination for many happy customers.

The Bakehouse
1050 West Queens Rd., Edgemont Village. Tel: 604 980 5554. Open: L & D **$**
Serves up home-made everything – bread and pastries, but also shepherd's pie and stews. The buttermilk lemon pie is particularly recommended.

Crab Shop
2455 Dollarton Highway. Tel: 604 929 1616 **$**
The locals call it the Crab Shack, from when it used to be just that. It's basic, but it's also the best place on the north shore for fish and chips.

Indian Fusion
2045 Lonsdale Ave. Tel: 604 984 9977. www.indianfusion online.com Open: L &D daily. **$**
Innovative Indian food, with fresh flavours and friendly staff. Great vege-

Prices for a three-course dinner per person with a half-bottle of house wine:
$ = under C$30
$$ = C$30–50
$$$ = C$50–80
$$$$ = over C$80

tarian choices, but also serves pizza.

Moustache Café
129 West 2nd St. Tel: 604 987 8461. www.moustache cafe.ca Open: L & D Tue–Sun. **$$$**
This restaurant in the Lolo district offers a tapas menu to complement main courses that include bison sirloin steak with gnocchi and Cornish game hen in a cranberry balsamic jus. At Tuesday-night wine-tasting events, sample BC wines matched with small plates.

The Observatory
1600 Nancy Greene Way. Tel: 604 980 9311. www. grousemountain.com Open: D daily. **$$$$**
Restaurants with spectacular views often don't live up to expectations, but the Observatory offers quality and commitment to Ocean Wise and Green Table programmes, focusing on sustainable options.

Tomahawk Restaurant
1550 Philip Ave. Tel: 604 988 2612. Open: B, L & D daily. **$**
This is the place for massive breakfasts – bacon, eggs, sausages, hash browns and toast, and endless cups of coffee, all at a reasonable price. It's family-run, and has been around since 1926.

West Vancouver

Beach House at Dundarave Pier
150 25th St. Tel: 604 922

Bars and Cafés

Black Bear Neighbourhood Pub (1177 Lynn Valley Rd.) offers everything you want in a pub: friendly atmosphere, with good beer and food. For terrific lattes and ice cream, head to **Brazza Gelato and Coffee** (1846 Lonsdale Ave.). **Café Trafiq** (1860 Marine Drive, Ambleside) serves great

coffee and sandwiches. For a sandwich or a hearty soup, try **La Galleria** (3055 Highland Boulevard). **Red Lion Bar and Grill** (2427 Marine Drive) offers cosy fires, a pool table and good-value pub food. For fantastic cakes, ice cream and pies head to **True Confections** (100 Park Royal).

1414. Open: L & D daily. **$$$**
Waterfront restaurant with great views; the cosy dining room and patio are the backdrop to a casual menu popular with families and local regulars.

Fraiche
2240 Chippendale Rd. Tel: 604 925 7595. www. fraicherestaurant.ca Open: L & D Tue–Sun. **$$$$**
Located about as far up as you can go in West Vancouver, Fraiche has brought together exquisite dining and spectacular vistas. For weekend brunch, how will you decide between the prosciutto and Bocconcini benedict and the Lobster and pancetta omelette?

La Regalade
103, 2232 Marine Drive. Tel: 604 921 2228. www.la regalade.com Open: L Tue–Fri, D Tue–Sat. **$$**
A French family-run bistro serving a traditional menu – frisée salad, onion tart, beef bourguignon and roast duck might be chalked up on the board.

Salmon House on the Hill
2229 Folkstone Way. Tel: 604 926 3212. www.salmon house.com Open: Brunch Sat–Sun, D daily. **$$$**
From its perch above Vancouver, the Salmon House has gained a solid reputation. First Nations art and the view help create a cosy atmosphere. The food focuses on salmon, with nods to both carnivores and vegetarians.

Saltaire
Upper level, 235 15th St. Tel: 604 913 8439. www.saltaire.ca Open: L & D daily. **$$**
West Coast cuisine with Asian influences. Large salads, good seafood and meats, and pizzas are a big draw, as is the beautiful patio.

Zen Japanese Restaurant
2232 Marine Drive. Tel: 604 925 0667. www.zensushi.ca Open: D daily. **$$**
In a contemporary, understated room, Zen produces Japanese dishes along with interesting twists on Western dishes.

WINTER SPORTS

In an area surrounded by magnificent mountains, the options for snow sports are endless.

Snow and ice play a big part in Canada's weather and in the Canadian psyche. Ice hockey is considered the national sport and it's a rare Canadian who can't ice-skate. In winter, an outdoor rink is set up at Robson Square, while some community ice rinks have year-round ice. Scheduling centres around hockey, from young children learning the sport to old-timers who maintain a tenuous hold on their youth by playing in recreational leagues, generally followed by the second national sport, beer-drinking.

Vancouverites don't have to go to Whistler to ski as there are three resorts on the north shore: Grouse Mountain, Mount Seymour and Cypress Bowl. Seymour is the highest, and Cypress offers the nearest cross-country skiing as well as downhill and snowboarding. While none can match the extent and variety of Whistler's pistes, they are just a short drive from the city centre. Night skiing is popular; locals head up to the mountain after work to enjoy a few hours on floodlit runs, with spectacular views of the city below.

ABOVE: the finest skiing in North America is on Whistler and Blackcomb mountains. There are over 200 beginner, intermediate and advanced runs, served by 38 lifts and 17 mountain restaurants. There's plenty for non-skiers too, from sleigh rides to snowshoeing.

LEFT: for many Canadians a snowmobile is a form of transport that has replaced a team of huskies. In Whistler it's a source of thrills, though not everyone welcomes the noise and pollution it introduces.

ABOVE: the clarity of light on a sunny winter's day can be as breathtaking as the cold. Many of the parks around Vancouver offer great opportunities for hiking or snowshoeing, as here on Black Mountain in Cypress Provincial Park in West Vancouver.

2010 WINTER OLYMPICS

In February and March 2010, the Winter Olympics and Paralympics brought international attention to Vancouver and Whistler. The years of preparation paid off, as tens of thousands of people were able to enjoy both the athletic and cultural events that took over the city for close to a month.

Vancouver and Whistler split the hosting duties, enabling Vancouver to upgrade existing winter sports venues and build new skating and curling facilities, creating a valuable legacy for the community.

The Winter Olympics have expanded in recent years to include sports that have more mass appeal than the cross-country and biathlon sports that can be difficult to appreciate as a spectator. The snow-boarding and freestyle ski events held at Cypress Mountain, close to Vancouver, were exciting and dramatic and attracted huge crowds.

Despite their country having hosted the 1976 Summer Olympics and the 1988 Winter Olympics, 2010 saw Canadian athletes win gold medals on home soil for the first time. Not only did Team Canada win more medals than at any other Winter Olympics, but their impressive tally of gold medals was higher than any other country in the history of the Winter Olympics. Many hope that these successes will encourage more Canadians to participate at every level in the sports that define the winter here.

RIGHT: a snowboarder on Mount Seymour, which has produced some world-class boarders and is regarded as the best of the mountains close to Vancouver. Eleven of its runs are lit at night, as is Mount Cypress's Solo Power terrain park. Grouse Mountain has cruising runs suitable for beginners as well as more challenging slopes. At Whistler it's still possible to snowboard in August, on Blackcomb's Horstman Glacier.

BELOW: snow tubing in Mount Seymour Provincial Park. Snow tubes should be used only on designated courses because, being circular, they are extremely difficult to steer or slow down. Putting out a hand merely makes them spin. Tows drag the tubes and riders uphill.

RIGHT: a family of four dog-sledding on Whistler Mountain. Sledding expeditions are offered from Whistler in the Soo Valley and are a great way to see the back country away from the crowded pistes. The dogs are Alaskan racing huskies, a crossbreed of husky and greyhound. A dog-sled camp on Cougar Mountain offers courses in dog sledding.

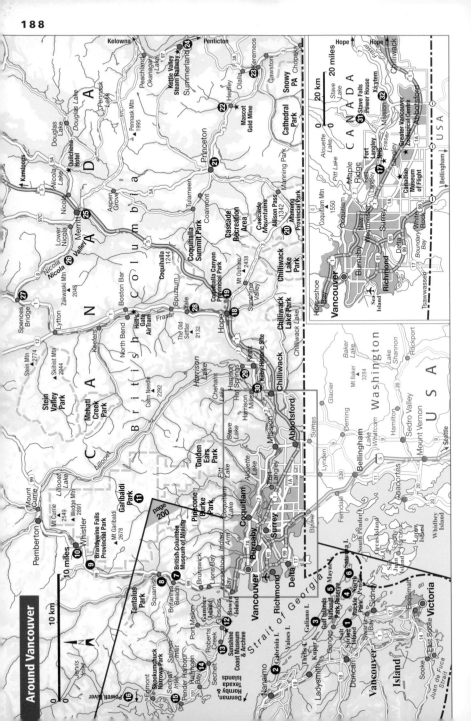

Around Vancouver

EXCURSIONS

"When people say they love Vancouver, I suspect it's
not so much the city they love but the setting."
– Arthur Erickson

Simply put, British Columbia is a stunningly beautiful part of Canada with a wide variety of landscapes, and a trip to Vancouver should include some time spent in this paradise for outdoor activities. It is the sheer scale that astonishes many first-time visitors from Europe, and getting to grips with the knowledge that Vancouver Island alone is the size of a small European country.

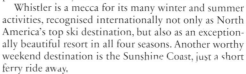

There can be few lovelier waters in which to sail than the Strait of Georgia between the mainland and the Gulf and Vancouver islands, whether by yacht or one of the many ferries. All around are mountains and islands in a confusion of land and sea that still claims vessels despite their sophisticated navigational aids. The provincial capital of Victoria is a delightful contrast to Vancouver, with fewer no-go areas and a gentler pace.

The island itself has so much to offer that it is deserving of an entire book. Its largely unspoilt wild west coast is in complete contrast to the more developed eastern seaboard, at least as far north as Nanaimo, the most northerly point covered by the excursions in this book.

Whistler is a mecca for its many winter and summer activities, recognised internationally not only as North America's top ski destination, but also as an exceptionally beautiful resort in all four seasons. Another worthy weekend destination is the Sunshine Coast, just a short ferry ride away.

Wine lovers head east to the vineyards of the Okanagan; it is easy to devise a circular route taking in the many natural sights such as the gorge of Hell's Gate or Lake Okanagan. But to get a feel for life in the second half of the 19th century, you need to take off into the back country on horseback, by bike or on foot. It's a hugely rewarding experience. ❏

PRECEDING PAGES: view of the Gulf Islands from Mount Warburton Pike, on Saturna Island.
ABOVE LEFT: horses grazing in the Okanagan. **ABOVE RIGHT:** Oyster River Estuary.

VICTORIA AND VANCOUVER ISLAND

Victoria is the first port of call, but there's more to the island than BC's garden-filled capital. To the west are craggy, storm-battered coastlines with deep fjords and wild beaches, and on the east coast, peaceful country inns and sheltered bays.

Vancouver Island is a beguiling place of snowcapped mountains, verdant forests, gentle farmland and sun-drenched ocean beaches. Lying off BC's West Coast, it stretches for 450km (281 miles) in length (about a third the length of the province), spanning from 48 to 80km (30 to 50 miles) across. The island is substantial and, to do it justice, a car is the best way to get to the areas that are worth exploring. Bus or train are fine for travelling between towns, but so much of the island is isolated, a hired car or even an RV will give access to the most beautiful areas.

Whale-watching

Victoria ❶, BC's capital, is at the southeastern corner of the island, with Duncan, Nanaimo, Courtenay and Campbell River on the east coast the only other sizeable towns, except for Port Alberni to the west of Nanaimo. The small West Coast communities of Ucluelet and Tofino are popular getaway destinations. the western coastline remains largely unspoilt and offers some of the best opportunities in BC for whale-watching. Many hotels remain open in winter, thanks to the popularity of watching the spectacular storms and

seas that roll in across the Pacific, unhindered all the way from Japan.

One of the highlights of a visit to Vancouver Island is the ferry from the mainland terminal of Tsawwassen to Swartz Bay, a 45-minute drive north of Victoria. The ferry travels through the smaller Gulf Islands, and, in the narrow Active Passage, eagles and other raptors can be seen in the trees on either side of the ferry, while a sunny day brings out seals along the rocky shores. For those without a vehicle, it's easy to take the affordable

LEFT: Nanaimo docks. **RIGHT:** whale-watching trip off Vancouver Island.

The sailing ships that had explored the coast on behalf of Spain and Britain started to give way to steam with the arrival of SS Beaver at Fort Vancouver in 1836. For 50 years this steamship was a floating fur-trading post and a survey ship for the Royal Navy. She helped to establish Fort Victoria on Vancouver Island and carried the official party to set up Fort Langley where the establishment of the crown colony of BC was formally announced.

and comfortable coach service from Vancouver right to downtown Victoria, then explore Victoria on foot.

Colonial capital

Built in 1843 beside the water, Fort Victoria replaced Fort Vancouver in Oregon as the Hudson's Bay Company's Pacific headquarters. Initially, settlement was not encouraged by the Hudson's Bay Company's governor, James Douglas, who saw the island as a source of wealth through its natural resources of timber, fish, coal and otter pelts (the sea otters here were hunted to extinction and are only now slowly being re-established on the island). Douglas imported labour as necessary to harvest the resources. Following the discovery of coal at Nanaimo in 1850, for example, he recruited 24 miners and their families from the mining communities of Staffordshire in England.

The situation changed in 1858 with the discovery of gold in the Cariboo, because Victoria became a place of passage en route from California to the new gold-fields. The population swelled from 500 in 1857 to 5,000 the following year. Though the numbers subsequently declined for a while, Victoria's equable climate and pleasant position attracted many permanent residents among those who had struck lucky in the Cariboo, and some of the houses they built can still be seen along the city's residential streets. The genteel aspects of Victoria's character were reinforced by the decision in 1868 to make the city the capital of the colony of British Columbia. As the seat of power and influence, Victoria attracted such entrepreneurs as the wealthy Dunsmuirs to build substantial mansions that are now among the city's oldest buildings.

The survival of so many 19th- and early 20th-century buildings made of stone and red brick distinguishes the city from Vancouver and, indeed, other cities across western Canada.

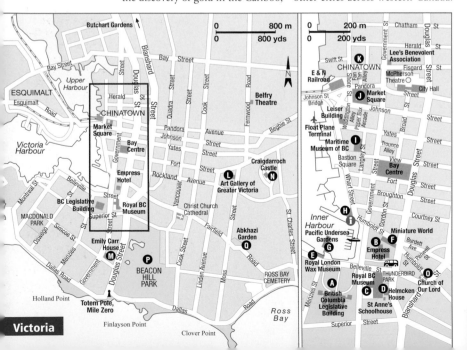

Victoria

The Old England gimmicks, with Union Jacks and tea shops on every corner, may seem downright ridiculous, but it's worth moving away from the tourist traps on the main streets to discover a very charming city.

EXPLORING VICTORIA

Victoria is even more compact than Vancouver, so exploring it on foot is easy. It's sunnier here than in Vancouver, too, with nearly a third less rain. The lovely natural harbour is the heart and pulse of the city, and there's always a bustle of activity on the water, from leisure craft, whale-watching and sightseeing boats to ferries and floatplanes. On fine days the throngs of visitors and street performers create a real buzz, though at the height of the summer it can get unpleasantly overcrowded.

Lending a stately grandeur to the scene are two of the city's most dramatic buildings: the British Columbia Legislative Assembly Building, with its 168-metre (500ft) facade, and

the huge Empress Hotel – both overlook the Inner Harbour and Fisherman's Wharf, forming the focal point of Victoria.

The British Columbia Legislative Building ⓐ

Address: Parliament Buildings, Belleville Street
Tel: 250 387 3046
Opening Hrs: mid-May–mid-Sept Mon–Thur 9am–5pm, Fri–Sun 9am–6pm, mid-Sept–mid-May Mon–Fri 9am–5pm. Free 30–60-minute tours throughout the day; July–Aug 3pm tour in French
Entrance Fee: free
Transport: buses 3, 50, 61, 70, 71, 72 and 73

The flamboyant Legislative Building was designed by young architect Francis Rattenbury and completed in 1897. The domed Parliament building is made of local stone with slate from Jervis Inlet on the mainland. Marble for the Assembly Hall came from Italy, that in the rotunda from

ABOVE: the grand parliament buildings are beautifully lit at night.
BELOW: ninety-minute tours of the grand Empress Hotel are conducted at 10am from mid-May to early October.

BELOW: the BC flag flies in front of the Legislative Building.

Tennessee. After dark, its outline is lit up by over 3,300 lights.

Named after Queen Victoria, the Empress of India, the château-style **Empress Hotel** , another Rattenbury design, was opened in 1908. Today, this well-restored monument to colonial grandeur is one of Victoria's top tourist attractions. After-noon tea has been served for almost as long as the hotel has been open and is considered an institution in Victoria, though for tourists rather than residents. Reservations are required and should be made at least a week in advance (tel: 250 389 2727). A special blend of tea is served in a pattern of china made by the Booths factory in England in 1914; a set was presented to King George V and first used at the Empress in 1939 during the visit of King George VI. It is now produced exclusively for the Empress by Royal Doulton.

In the apex between the hotel and parliament is the **largest carillon in Canada** with 62 bells in a 27-metre (90ft) tower given by the Dutch community of BC. There are recitals held throughout the year, including most Sundays at 3pm and on Fridays at 7pm during July and August.

Royal BC Museum ◉

Address: 675 Belleville Street, www.royalbcmuseum.bc.ca
Tel: 250 356 7226
Opening Hrs: daily 10am–5pm
Entrance Fee: charge
Transport: buses 3, 50, 61, 70, 71, 72 and 73

The Royal BC Museum is the best introduction to BC, both for the range and the quality of its presentations. It has excellent dioramas of wildlife and habitats and exceptional First Nations exhibitions. In addition to the reconstruction of a pithouse, there are Tsimshian masks used in dramatic performances, pipes, totem poles, tableware, plates and argillite carvings. There are also displays detailing the arrival of European and Asian settlers, including reconstructed streets, and rooms devoted to fishing, farming, logging and maritime trades.

Thunderbird Park is adjacent to the museum, offering a collection of totem poles (mostly Kwakwaka'wakw, Gitxsan and Haida), as well as a

Rattenbury's Legacy

Soon after arriving in Victoria, British-born architect, Francis Mawson Rattenbury, won the competition to build the new British Columbia Legislative Building which opened in 1898. Many commissions followed, including the Empress Hotel for the Canadian Pacific Railway. Rattenbury had a habit of falling out with clients, and his lack of professional training was felt when the popularity of his style waned. Shunned for the callous treatment of his wife after he left her for a younger woman, he was forced to leave Victoria. Back in England, financial problems soured his second marriage. His wife began an affair with the chauffeur, who murdered Rattenbury with a croquet mallet in 1935.

smaller version of a famous "big house" that once stood on the northeast coast of Vancouver Island. This faithful replica continues to be used for First Nations events.

In the same park area is the **St Anne's Schoolhouse**, built in the French Canadian style with square logs. Begun in the 1840s and completed in 1858, it is one of the oldest buildings in western Canada.

Close by is **Helmcken House** **D** (opening times vary; enquire at the tourist office), built in 1852 of squared logs and cedar shingles for Dr J S. Helmcken. It is thought to be the oldest house in western Canada still on its original site. Dr Helmcken (1824–1920) was a pioneer surgeon and legislator who arrived in 1850 to work for the Hudson's Bay Company. Born in London, he trained at Guy's Hospital and married the elder daughter of Governor Sir James Douglas. He helped to negotiate the union of BC with Canada in 1870. The house has reconstructed interiors with some original furniture and a collection of medical equipment that belonged to the "good doctor".

Children's attractions

There are a number of attractions around the Inner Harbour geared towards children. The **Royal London Wax Museum** **E** (470 Belleville Street; tel: 250 388 4461; www.waxmuseum.bc.ca; daily 9.30am–5pm) displays over 300 famous figures and has its own grisly Chamber of Horrors. **Miniature World** **F** (649 Humboldt Street; tel: 250 385 9731; www.miniatureworld.com; 8.30am–9.30pm, winter 10am–5pm) boasts a collection of tiny tableaux including scenes from the Old West and Dickensian England, and a large model railway layout depicting the construction of the Canadian railway. **Pacific Undersea Gardens** **G** (490 Belleville Street; daily winter 10am–5pm, summer 9am–8pm; tel: 250 382 5717; www.pacificunderseagardens.com) is convenient, but consider the impressive Shaw Ocean Discovery Centre at Sidney instead *(see page 201)*.

The old town

Leading north from James Bay is Government Street, Victoria's main tourist strip. It is best to avoid the tacky souvenir shops and enjoy the architecture

ABOVE: the little green-and-yellow sightseeing ferries operate a hop-on hop-off service around the harbour (tel: 250 708 0201; www.harbourferry.com).
BELOW: view of the Inner Harbour from the Information Centre.

ABOVE: the "Gate of Harmonious Interest" in Victoria's Chinatown.

TIP

For period buildings, the southern end of Government Street has many early houses from the 1860s, some of them attractive B&Bs, and other roads worth visiting are Rockland Avenue, St Charles Street and Linden Avenue.

– many buildings have plaques summarising their history, and grey blocks inset into the brick pavements delineate the boundary of Fort Victoria.

The best way to explore the old town is to follow the downtown walk in the free leaflet of six one-hour walks provided by the Downtown Victoria Business Association. Starting at the **Visitor Information Centre ⑪** on Wharf Street by the harbour, it takes you through Bastion Square, home to many of the main municipal buildings.

The Maritime Museum of British Columbia ⓘ
Address: 28 Bastion Square, www.mmbc.bc.ca
Tel: 250 382 2869
Opening Hrs: June–mid-Sept daily 9.30am–5pm, mid-Sept–mid-June Tue–Sat 10.30am–4.30pm
Entrance Fee: charge
The museum, housed in the former Law Courts (built in 1889), celebrates the close relationship between the sea

and the province's history, with sections on exploration, shipbuilding, fur traders, harbours, ships, wrecks, whaling, CPR steamships and the navy. Among the maritime artefacts is a collection of marvellous models.

Yates Street has many turn-of-the-20th-century buildings, such as the **Leiser Building** (1896), which housed a wholesale grocer with a central elevator and tracks radiating from it on each floor to move goods around. Nearby **Market Square ⓙ** spans what was a ravine, and has two tiers of arcaded shops specialising in all manner of things from quilts and old furniture to beads, toys and garden wares.

Chinatown
Canada's oldest **Chinatown ⓚ**, dating from 1858, was built north of the ravine and is reached through the mix of shops and houses in tiny **Fan Tan Alley**. By 1881, around 3,000 Chinese had settled here. They built factories, shops and back-to-back houses around tiny courtyards, and of course

the brothels and opium and gambling dens for which the area became infamous. The architecture is adapted from standard forms with flared temple-style roofs, inset and projecting wrought-iron balconies, interior courtyards and brightly coloured roof tiles with pronounced overhangs.

Fisgard Street has some fine Chinese buildings, especially Lee's Benevolent Association building at No. 614. Further east is the Chinese Public School, with upturned corners to the eaves.

The Art Gallery of Greater Victoria ❶

Address: 1040 Moss Street,
www.aggv.bc.ca
Tel: 250 384 4101
Opening Hrs: late May–early Sept
Mon–Sat 10am–5pm, Thur until 9pm,
Sun noon–5pm, mid-Sept–late May
same as summer except closed Mon
Entrance Fee: charge
Transport: bus 11, 14 or 22 to Fort and Moss, then a short walk on Moss

Located east of Downtown, en route to Craigdarroch Castle *(see page 198)*, the Art Gallery of Greater Victoria

has seven gallery spaces hosting permanent and temporary exhibitions. It has a large Asian collection, including one of the largest collections of amber and ivory carvings in North America. The house that forms the nucleus of the gallery was built in 1889 as the residence of a banker, A.A. Green. In 1951 it was donated to the city to become the first part of a permanent art gallery, and a few rooms are left to show how the house once looked – including the heavily wood-panelled and ceilinged hall. The Drury Gallery features the work of Emily Carr, Canada's best-known artist and a native of Victoria *(see panel, below)*.

The Emily Carr House ⓜ

Address: 207 Government Street,
www.emilycarr.com
Tel: 250 383 5843
Opening Hrs: May–Sept Tue–Sat
11am–4pm
Entrance Fee: charge
Transport: bus 5, 27, 28, 30 or 31 to Douglas at Simcoe, then walk west two blocks

Emily Carr spent her rebellious childhood in this house, built in 1864.

ABOVE: Craigdarroch Castle was built by Scots-born millionaire Robert Dunsmuir to fulfil a promise made to his wife, who expressed a dislike of her new country. He died before it was completed.
BELOW: the Emily Carr collection in the Victoria Art Gallery.

Emily Carr

Recognition of Emily Carr's talents as an artist came late in her life. She was born in Victoria in 1871 and studied art in San Francisco, London and Paris. She went on several trips to northern BC and Alaska, living in villages and painting cultural scenes, but her work attracted little approval, and she was forced to make ends meet by breeding dogs, growing vegetables and making pottery. She even gave up painting, but a meeting with the Group of Seven in 1927 proved a turning point. They encouraged her to resume her work depicting vanishing native culture and the West Coast landscape. Carr spent the latter part of her life writing about her experiences. She died in 1945, aged 73.

TIP

If you have a car, head out to Sooke, which is not far, but seems a world away. The small-town feel is combined with a sophisticated population who have chosen lifestyle over all else. Take a walk along Whiffen Spit and marvel at the raw beauty of the west coast.

Although all the paintings here are copies, the house gives a bit of insight into the woman and her adventures to paint First Nations along the BC coast. Few of the furnishings are original, but the house does give a good idea of what the home of a middle-class Victoria family would have looked like in the late nineteenth century.

Craigdarroch Castle

Address: 1050 Joan Crescent, www.thecastle.ca
Tel: 250 592 5323
Opening Hrs: daily 10am–4.30pm, mid-June–Labour Day 9am–7pm
Transport: bus 11 or 14 to Fort and Joan Crescent, then walk up a short, but fairly steep, hill to the Castle

Robert Dunsmuir, who was born in 1825 near Kilmarnock in Ayrshire to a family of coal masters, became one of Vancouver Island's richest entrepreneurs by developing the rich coal seams around Nanaimo. He also built the Esquimalt & Nanaimo Railway, a contract which came with huge land grants: in exchange for building 120km (75 miles) of railway, he received $750,000 plus 800,000 hectares (2 million acres) – almost one-third of the land mass of Vancouver Island. With the profits he built the rather ungainly pile of Scots Baronial architecture. The house has few original contents, except for paintings, but it has been furnished with appropriate pieces and fabrics. It has an opulent atmosphere with wood panelling everywhere and a hand-painted ceiling in the drawing room. Stunning views from the castle tower stretch across Victoria and the Strait of San Juan de Fuca to the Olympic Mountains in Washington State.

Although churches are not a major attraction in Victoria, the reformed Episcopal **Church of Our Lord** is said to be the finest expression of the Gothic Revival in wood in Canada. It was built in 1875 to a design by John Teague with board and batten siding, a rose window and a Gothic hammerbeam roof.

Parks and gardens

One of the reasons for Victoria's popularity with visitors is the number of beautifully cultivated green spaces. Just southeast of the Inner Harbour lies **Beacon Hill Park**, 62 hectares (154 acres) of parkland and garden set aside by Governor James Douglas in 1858. It was so named because of its use of two beacons to guide mariners past the treacherous Brotchie Ledge. The sprawling park, which borders the sea at its southern end, features duck ponds, colourful flower gardens, elegant trees, stone bridges, mini-lakes, a children's paddling pool and a petting zoo. A plinthed dial on the hill points to Bentinck Island 16km (10 miles) away as a former leper colony, and on a really clear day it is possible to see the 4,392-metre (14,408ft) peak of Mt Rainier in Washington state. The world's fourth-tallest totem pole, carved in 1956, rises 38.9 metres (127ft 7in) above a grassy field. At the corner of Douglas Street and Dallas Road, the Mile "0" milestone marks the beginning of the Trans-Canada Highway.

BELOW: Finlayson Point, Beacon Hill Park.

Abkhazi Garden ⓠ

Address: 1964 Fairfield Road,
www.conservancy.bc.ca
Tel: 250 598 8096
Opening Hrs: Mar–Oct daily
11am–4pm
Entrance Fee: charge
Transport: bus 7 (ask the driver to let
you off at Fairfield and Four Bay Rd)

A short journey from central Victoria
is the unique Abkhazi Garden, begun
in 1946 by the Georgian Prince and
Princess Abkhazi, the year they married and settled in Victoria. They
spent their lives developing the garden, the landscaping strongly influenced by the Chinese gardens which
Peggy Abkhazi had known in Shanghai, with Japanese maples, weeping
conifers and century-old specimens
of rhododendrons. After their deaths
the garden was purchased by The
Land Conservancy which saved it
from becoming a town-house development. It has a restaurant and shop.

Hatley Park National Historic Site ②

Address: 2005 Sooke Road,
www.hatleypark.ca
Tel: 250 391 2666
Opening Hrs: daily 10am–4pm
Entrance Fee: charge
Transport: bus 50 to Western

Exchange and transfer to the 39, 51,
52 or 61 to Sooke Rd. at Aldeane

This historic site to the west of Victoria is essentially a castle surrounded
by a 229-hectare (565-acre) estate. The
castle was built in 1908 by BC premier
James Dunsmuir, super-rich son of
mining magnate, Robert Dunsmuir.
Besides daily tours of the house, the
extensive Japanese, rose and Italian
gardens and woodland walks are
complemented by a museum about
the house and the history of the rich
and powerful Dunsmuir family.

ESQUIMALT
Esquimalt Naval and Military Museum ③

Address: CFB Esquimalt, off
Admirals Road, www.navaland
militarymuseum.org
Tel: 250 363 4312
Opening Hrs: June–Aug daily 10am–
3.30pm, Sept–May Mon–Fri 10am–
3.30pm
Entrance Fee: charge; no access
without photo ID
Transport: bus 6

On the west side of Victoria Harbour, Esquimalt was home to the

*With the mildest
climate in Canada,
Victoria benefits from
the Japanese current
bringing warm moist
air which rises and
cools when it hits the
mountains. It receives
only 63cm (25ins) of
rain. Over a billion
blooms have been
counted in February,
giving Victoria the title
of "the garden city".*

ABOVE LEFT: Beacon
Hill Park. **ABOVE RIGHT:**
lion sculpture in Hatley
Park. **BELOW:** Butchart
Gardens.

Royal Navy Pacific Squadron from 1865 to 1902. Located within the Canadian Forces Base, the museum has a World War II minesweeper and displays about West Coast naval and military history. There is a bus from downtown to the base gate.

National Historic Site of Fort Rodd Hill and Fisgard Lighthouse

Address: 603 Fort Rodd Hill Road, www.fortroddhill.com
Tel: 250 478 5849
Opening Hrs: mid-Feb–Oct 10am–5.30pm, Nov–mid-Feb 9am–4.30pm
Entrance Fee: charge
Transport: 50, 61 to Western Exchange, then walk along Ocean Blvd. (2km/½-mile scenic walk)

This coastal artillery fort overlooks Victoria Harbour from the western bank of the estuary: visitors can see the original gun batteries, underground magazines, barracks, camouflaged searchlight emplacements and com-

ABOVE: the main focus of the BC Forest Discovery Park is on forestry and conservation.

mand post. While the fort dates from the 1890s, the lighthouse was built in 1860, making it the oldest on the West Coast. A recent major refurbishment of the lighthouse was undertaken to coincide with the 150th anniversary in 2010. The park is a popular place for picnics, as well as attracting bird-watchers (more than 60 bird species have been sighted on the property).

SAANICH PENINSULA

The area between Victoria and Swartz Bay is rich in visitor attractions, as well as being a comfortable mix of farmland and housing.

Butchart Gardens ❺

Address: 800 Benvenuto Avenue, Brentwood Bay, www.butchart gardens.com
Tel: 250 652 4242
Opening Hrs: daily from 9am, closing times change seasonally
Entrance Fee: charge
Transport: buses 75, 76 (from down-

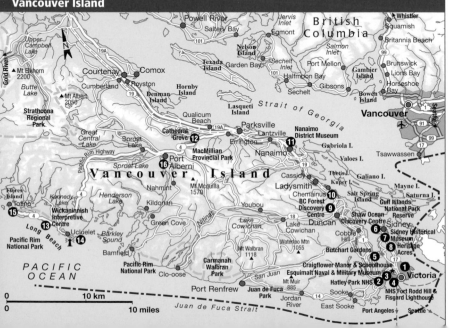

Vancouver Island

town), 81 (from Schwartz Bay ferry terminal) and 82 (from Sidney)

This 22-hectare (55-acre) garden was begun in 1904 and is of such quality that it has the rare distinction of being a privately owned attraction of being designated a National Historic Site. More than 50 gardeners tend the grounds which include rose, sunken, Japanese and Italian gardens. Evening concerts and firework displays are staged in a natural amphitheatre, and there are several places to eat, including a dining room offering afternoon tea. The busloads of tourists can be disconcerting, so it's best to go on a weekday.

ABOVE: mural in Chemainus.

Shaw Ocean Discovery Centre **6**

Address: 9811 Seaport Place, Sidney, www.oceandiscovery.ca
Tel: 250 665 7511
Opening Hrs: daily 10.30am–4.30pm
Entrance Fee: charge
Transport: buses 71 and 73

This is the best place in the Victoria area to entertain children and watch them learn at the same time. The thousands of species of sea life all inhabit the coastal waters of BC, bringing into focus the incredible diversity and excitement of the area. While jellyfish are mesmerising for children and adults alike, the octopus really steals the show.

Sidney is a lovely town to wander around and stop for coffee; it is noted for its collection of used bookstores and relaxed pace. An introduction to the early lives of Sidney and North Saanich pioneers is given by the **Sidney Historical Museum 7** (2423 Beacon Ave; tel: 250 655 6355; www.sidneymuseum.ca; daily Jan–Oct 10am–4pm, Nov–Dec 11am–3pm).

Heritage Acres 8 (7321 Lochside Drive, Saanichton; tel: 250 652 5522; www.shas.ca; daily 9.30am–noon, June–Aug until 4pm) evokes rural village life in bygone times. It includes a two-room schoolhouse, small church, log cabin, blacksmith's shop, sawmill

and dozens of tractors and other artefacts – domestic, agricultural and industrial. On special days, some of the old equipment is put to use, such as horse-drawn ploughs in spring and steam threshers in the autumn.

Craigflower Manor and Schoolhouse (tel: 250 383 4627; www.conservancy.bc.ca; May–Sept daily 11am–5pm) on the corner of Admirals Road and Craigflower Road celebrate the spirit of the early settlers. The oldest schoolroom in western Canada was built in 1855 by workers on Craigflower Farm for their children. The manor, completed in 1856, was the home of the farm's bailiff, Kenneth McKenzie, and his wife and eight children.

UP ISLAND

The Trans-Canada Highway (Highway 1) parallels the east coast from Victoria to Nanaimo, and there are numerous reasons to break the journey.

BC Forest Discovery Centre **9**

Address: 2892 Drinkwater Road, Duncan, www.bcforestmuseum.com

TIP

VIA's E&N Dayliner, "The Malahat", is a daily service that runs along the Pacific coast between Esquimalt and Courtenay, 225km (141 miles) north of Victoria, calling at various stations in between. It goes out and back in a day, so if time is short, this pleasant journey provides the opportunity to gain a sense of the island's topography (tel: 1 888 842 7245; www.viarail.ca).

The Douglas fir takes its name from the Scottish botanist David Douglas (1799–1834) who undertook three expeditions to Canada, including journeys along the Okanagan and Fraser rivers and the Columbia River to Hudson Bay. He identified over 200 new plant species in North America and introduced over 240 to Britain – more than any other botanist of his time.

Tel: 250 715 1113
Opening Hrs: mid-Apr–May Thur–Sun 10am–4pm, June–Aug daily 10am–5pm, Sept–mid-Oct Thur–Sun 10am–4pm
Entrance Fee: charge

The Discovery Centre is heaven for anyone enamoured with locomotives – there are 12 here, including a 1910 steam train that chugs through the 40-hectare (100-acre) site, viewing a turn-of-the-20th-century working sawmill and logging camp.

A little further north, **Chemainus** ❿ revels in its role as Canada's mural capital, created in 1982 as a plan to bring tourism to a town that lost its only industry when the sawmill closed down. Some 36 huge murals decorate walls, depicting historical subjects such as the arrival of HMS *Reindeer* at Chemainus in 1869 or a Shay locomotive on the Mount Sicker Railway. Heritage Square, dominated by the First Peoples mural, is lined with small shops and teahouses.

Nanaimo owes its existence to coal, stretching back to the early 1850. The 1853 three-storey bastion (15 May–Labour Day daily 10am–3pm) was built to house offices, an arsenal and space for the town's inhabitants should it be attacked. It's the only remaining original Hudson's Bay Company bastion left in North America.

Nanaimo District Museum ⓫

Address: 100 Museum Way, http://nanaimomuseum.ca
Tel: 250 753 1821
Opening Hrs: May–Labour Day daily 10am–5pm, Labour Day–Apr Tue–Sat 10am–5pm
Entrance Fee: charge
Transport: buses 1 and 2

The focus of this museum is twofold: telling the story of the coal-mining industry with reconstructed tunnel, blacksmith's shop and miner's cottage, and displaying artefacts of the Snuneymuxwe, the Nanaimo First Nations people.

SHOPPING

While Government Street has its fair share of banal souvenir shops, there are also a few spots worth seeking out. And don't be afraid to head out of the downtown core to where more independent retailers thrive, offering more unique products.

Books

Munro Books
1108 Government St.
Tel: 250 382 2464. www.munrobooks.com
A Victoria institution for close to 50 years in a historic building (a former bank, lovingly restored to its former glory), this is one of the most beautiful bookstores in Canada. Its most compelling attribute: they have pretty much anything you are looking for.

Clothing

Baden-Baden Boutique
2485 Beacon Ave., Sidney.
Tel: 250 655 7118. www.badenbadenboutiques.com
What makes a women's clothing store successful is more than the selection of clothes, it's the staff. This store has both, offering advice when it's solicited, letting you browse undisturbed when you want that.

Food

Murchie's Tea and Coffee
1110 Government St.
Tel: 250 383 3112.
www.murchies.com
This is not only a great place to shop for tea and coffee (with a history of more than 115 years), it's also the perfect place to stop for a light lunch or a cup of tea, with its 110-seat beverage bar.

Roger's Chocolates
913 Government St.
Tel: 250 881 8771.
www.rogerschocolates.com
Another Victoria institution (since 1885), Roger's has expanded its rather pedestrian selection of chocolate creams to offer more innovative products. It's even opened a soda shop next door (at 813 Government St.) to seduce people with ice cream and milkshakes.

Tugwell Creek Honey Farm and Meadery
8750 West Coast Rd, Sooke.
Tel: 250 642 1956. www.tugwellcreekfarm.com
As much an experience as a shop, the meadery is a great destination spot. Taste the honey, imbibe the mead and listen to the owners share their passion for all things apian.

The West Coast

A million people a year cross the island via the **Pacific Rim Highway** from Parksville, a few kilometres north of Nanaimo, over Sutton Pass to visit the West Coast. The road beyond Port Alberni was not opened until 1959, and even then it was gravel. The drive gives the illusion that this is untouched wilderness because there are so many trees, but everything has been extensively logged for the last 150 years, and there is little old growth left apart from **Cathedral Grove** ⑫ in Macmillan Provincial Park. Trails on both sides of the Highway lead to this large stand of old-growth Douglas firs; the largest trees are 800 years old, but most sprouted when fire swept through the forest 300 years ago.

The mountains along the West Coast are the first obstruction to moisture-laden clouds rolling in from the Pacific, creating coastal temperate rainforest and forming a boundary between two very different weather systems – rain and fog in the west and sunshine and drier conditions to the east. The wettest place in the whole of Canada is Henderson Lake, just inland from Barkley Sound's northern shoreline where over 8 metres (26ft) of rain fall in a year.

Wickaninnish Interpretive Centre ⑬

Address: end of Wick Road, 3.5km (2 miles) from Highway 4, www.pc.gc.ca
Tel: 250 726 3500
Opening Hrs: mid-Mar–mid-Oct 10am–6pm
Entrance Fee: included in park use fee

This is the best place to gain an overview of the area, with films and displays about the Pacific Rim National Park. The centre is being upgraded, with completion due for spring 2011. There is a restaurant, and an all-terrain wheelchair is available for use in the park. If you stop anywhere in the park, you need a pass, which covers admission to the centre. A weekly ticket is available.

Watching for whales, bears and storms

A great summer attraction of the two small West Coast towns of Tofino and Ucluelet is a boat ride to watch the grey whales which stop to feed on

ABOVE: Nanaimo is renowned for diving. Three large ships have been sunk offshore to create artificial reefs. **BELOW:** rainbow over Nanaimo.

West Coast Trail

The 75km (47-mile) West Coast Trail is one of the most challenging, but rewarding hiking routes in BC. The five- to seven-day trek passes sandstone cliffs, huge waterfalls, caves, sea arches, sea stacks and beaches. Facilities on the trail are basic but include boardwalks, ladders, bridges, cableways and outhouses at the most commonly used camping areas. There are no huts for hikers, and because of the severity of winter conditions the WCT is open only between May and September. A charge is levied and reservations, which can be made up to 90 days in advance, are highly recommended as the numbers of hikers allowed on the trail each day is strictly controlled (tel: 250 387 1642; www.westcoasttrailbc.com).

the way from their breeding grounds off Mexico to Alaska. Guides also take visitors to watch black bears in May and June when they emerge from winter dens to gorge on salmonberries. In winter, visitors come to the Long Beach peninsula to watch the storms and 10–15-metre (30–50ft) ocean swells which toss giant driftwood logs around like toothpicks. In less fierce weather, it is a paradise for surfers, and lessons and guides are available from companies in Tofino.

Ucluelet and Tofino

An urban-planning award was given to the attractive town of **Ucluelet** ⑭, its harbour dominated by a former hydrographic ship which has been converted into accommodation and a restaurant as part of the Canadian Princess Resort. The dramatically located lighthouse on Amphitrite Point was built in 1914, replacing a 1906-built wooden structure swept away by a tidal wave.

More whale- and seal-watching boats operate out of **Tofino** ⑮, which has had a distinctive culture since it became a favoured bolt-hole for those eluding the Vietnam War draft. It has also been a focal point of protest against indiscriminate

ABOVE: a scenic flight in a floatplane over Tofino and the surrounding coast is an unforgettable experience. The views are stunning, and while whale sightings are not guaranteed they are common (toll-free tel: 1 866 486 3247; www.tofinoair.com).
BELOW: Tofino harbour.

logging, sometimes attracting tens of thousands of people from across Canada. The **Saturday market** (May–Sept 10am–2pm) selling food and crafts is a good place to absorb the atmosphere of the community.

Port Alberni

The only town between East and West Coast on the Pacific Rim Highway is **Port Alberni** ⑯, which became a European settlement in 1860 when Captain Edward Stamp, an English sea captain, chose it as the site of an export sawmill. Despite being so inland, it was hit by a tidal wave in 1964 caused by an earthquake in Alaska.

McLean Mill

Address: 5633 Smith Road, www.alberniheritage.com
Tel: 250 723 1379
Opening Hrs: Late June–Labour Day Thur–Mon 10.30am–5pm
Entrance Fee: charge

Canada's only operating steam-powered sawmill is typical of mills that flourished from the 1880s. It occupies a large forested site and includes such ancillary buildings as cookhouse, bunkhouse, office and all the engineering support services required for a mill. In addition to a tour, live theatre brings the history of early logging alive. The best way to reach the mill is by a 35-minute ride on the **Alberni Pacific Railway**. This steam-hauled train leaves from a 1912 Canadian Pacific Railway station twice a day and winds through the town before heading into the forest to a station beside McLean Mill.

The **Alberni Valley Museum** (tel: 250 723 1821; www.alberniheritage.com; Tue–Sat 10am–5pm), located in the Echo Centre at 4255 Wallace Street, has a large display of basketry created from shore and sea grasses by the Nuu Chah Nulth First Nations people, as well as industrial history and folk art exhibitions with many historic photographs. ❑

BEST RESTAURANTS

Nanaimo

Blue Ginger
1-5769 Turner Rd. Tel: 250 751 8238. www.theblueginger restaurant.com Open: L & D daily. **$–$$**
Eat a little, eat a lot, this funky Asian fusion restaurant has everything from satay to dim sum to Thai seafood jambalaya; there are also plenty of excellent vegetarian options.

Fire House Grill
7 Victoria Rd. Tel: 250 716 0323. L & D daily. **$$**
Popular with the cooking school crowd (which says a lot), the sushizza combines the best of sushi with a flash-fried rice crust. For meat-eaters, the pulled pork sandwich at lunch is popular.

Sooke

EdGe
6688 Sooke Rd. Tel: 778 425 3343. Open: L & D Tue–Sat. **$$**
The food is five-star, but more than affordable. Can't decide what to have? Opt for the Kitchen Sink: with pretty much everything in it, you'll be wondering how Edward Tuson does it. You can ask him – the kitchen is open

Prices for a three-course dinner per person with a half-bottle of house wine:
$ = under C$30
$$ = C$30–50
$$$ = C$50–80
$$$$ = over C$80

and locals talk to him all the time, asking when the next batch of wild mushrooms will be coming in.

Tofino

Pointe Restaurant
The Wickaninnish Inn, 500 Osprey Lane. Tel: 250 725 31 06. www.wickinn.com Open: B, L & D daily. **$$$$**
The food view here is fantastic and the food matches the drama of the landscape – the best West Coast ingredients play their part in an inventive and ever-changing menu.

Sobo
311 Neill St. Tel: 250 725 2341. www.sobo.ca Open: L & D daily. **$$**
Kid-friendly Sobo offers great food at good prices. Offerings include tacos stuffed with local fish, cornmeal crusted oysters, smoked salmon and smoked wild fish chowder.

Victoria

Bill Mattick's at Cordova Bay Golf Club
5331 Cordova Bay Rd. Tel: 250 658 4271. www.cordova baygolf.com Open: B, L & D **$$**
After browsing through the stores at Mattick's Farm, this public golf course offers creative food in an idyllic setting. Check out the daily curry special, or try the halibut and scallop salad.

Café Brio
944 Fort St. Tel. 250 383

RIGHT: wild salmon steak.

0009. www.cafe-brio.com Open: daily, D only. **$$$**
Fresh local seasonal ingredients, much of it organic, and a terrific wine list at reasonable prices make for a winning combination here. Proprietors Silvia Marcolini and Greg Hays are true professionals.

Chef Suzi
18B Bastion Sq. Tel: 250 381 8722. www.chefsuzi.ca Open: B & L daily in summer, Mon–Fri in winter. **$**
Serves soups, sandwiches and burgers in a great location.

Empress Room
721 Government St. Tel: 250 389 2727. www.fairmont.com/empress Open: B & D daily **$$$**
Afternoon tea at the Fairmont Empress Hotel draws tourists and locals in their hundreds. Needless to say, they know how to do tea – finger sandwiches, scones, tarts, cakes, pastries and tea specially blended for the hotel. Have a drink before dinner in the Bengal Lounge if tea isn't your thing.

J & J Wonton Noodle House
1012 Fort St. Tel: 250 383

0680. www.jjnoodlehouse.com L & D Tue–Sat. **$**
Cheap, cheerful, no-frills restaurant offering excellent Chinese food – some Victorians claim it's the best in the city. Try their special Wor Wonton or the Hot and Sour soup; the rice and noodle dishes are fresh, filling and cheap.

Rebar Modern Food
50 Bastion Sq. Tel: 250 361 9223. www.rebarmodernfood.com Open: B, L & D daily, Brunch at weekends. **$**
Essentially a vegetarian restaurant with some fish thrown in, Rebar offers imaginative daily menus emphasising local, organic and healthy ingredients. The pot-stickers are legendary. Excellent stir-fries, wonderful brunch menu and fabulous teatime goodies. You'll want to take home the cookbook.

Zambri's
110–911 Yates St. Tel: 250 360 1171. www.zambris.ca Open: L & D Tue–Sat. **$$**
Italian trattoria serving simple, unpretentious food made with fresh ingredients that has won it many fans in Victoria, in spite of its location in a downtown strip mall.

THE GULF ISLANDS

Sheltered from Pacific storms by Vancouver Island, this string of beautiful, well-wooded islands offers refuge from the urbanity of Vancouver life. Served by frequent ferries and peppered with B&Bs, any of these intimate islands makes for a perfect getaway.

British Columbia

Vancouver

Strewn across the Strait of Georgia between the mainland and Vancouver Island are hundreds of islands and islets, most of which are uninhabited. Known collectively as the Gulf Islands, this is in fact a misnomer; George Vancouver thought he was sailing up a gulf rather than a strait, but though his error in naming it the Gulf of Georgia was corrected to the Strait of Georgia in 1865, his name for the archipelago remained.

Most of the Gulf Islands are well wooded, with sandy beaches, rocky outcrops and abundant marine life. The beautiful scenery is complemented by a drier, milder climate than Vancouver. The few inhabited islands offer a great contrast to BC's urban centres, with a slower pace of life, small but vibrant communities and a totally different atmosphere. They are famous for the quality of the arts and crafts practised on them, reflecting the appeal of the laid-back lifestyle.

The island groups

The archipelago is divided into the northern and southern islands, the line roughly formed by the city of Nanaimo, halfway up Vancouver

Island's east coast. The principal southern Gulf Islands are Gabriola, Galiano, Mayne, North and South Pender, Salt Spring and Saturna, while the main northern islands are Denman, Hornby and Texada. Cortes and Quadra are often included in lists of Gulf Islands, but as they are not in the Strait of Georgia, they are more accurately part of the Discovery Islands.

The larger islands have golf courses and offer great walking, kayaking and sailing, scuba diving and

LEFT: house on Mayne Island. **RIGHT:** BC ferry en route from Galiano Island.

ABOVE: parade of old boats in Ganges Harbour, Salt Spring Island.

TIP

Don't visit the islands without booking accommodation (see pages 255–6), especially in the high season, and check that credit cards are accepted at B&Bs. Take adequate cash, as it isn't always easy to find a cash machine.

fishing. Cycling is a popular way of exploring the islands, with the benefit of avoiding the inevitable queues for ferries, though care is needed on the narrow and twisting roads. Hotels are few, but there are plenty of high-quality bed and breakfasts. BC Ferries link the principal inhabited islands, and Salt Spring has a minibus shuttle service between Ganges and some ferry sailings. On the few islands that have them, taxis can be expensive.

The value of the islands' ecology was emphasised in 2003 with the creation of the Gulf Islands National Park Reserve, primarily to protect the Garry oak meadows, which are richer in plant species than any other terrestrial system in coastal BC and severely at risk. Delicate wild lilies and orca whales also come within the park's protection. Unfortunately, the Gulf Islands' beauty and mild climate have also attracted the super-rich, some of whom have bought choice sites for luxurious and out-of-scale holiday homes that lie empty or caretakered

for most of the year. The population of the islands often doubles or even trebles in the summer.

Set up in 1974, the unique Islands Trust (www.islandstrust.bc.ca) acts as a land use and planning agency on the Gulf Islands with a mandate to preserve and protect the trust area and its unique amenities and environment for the benefit of its residents and of the province generally. It faces the dilemma typical of many spectacularly beautiful areas within reach of urban centres – how to retain sustainable, vibrant and affordable communities, as well as meet the challenge of water conservation.

SALT SPRING ISLAND

The most populous of the Gulf Islands, **Salt Spring Island** ❶ is reached by two ferries from Vancouver Island – Schwarz Bay to Fulford Harbour and Crofton to Vesuvius Bay – and three ferries into Long Harbour from Mayne and Pender islands, and from Tsawwassen on the mainland. Float planes also link the harbour of the island's capital, Ganges, with Vancouver.

Among the early settlers were Portuguese freed black slaves from the US in the 1850s and '60s, and Kanakas from Hawaii who came to BC around 1850 as labourers for the Hudson's Bay Company. Others settled on Salt Spring after the 1858 gold rush where they farmed, fished and logged.

Logging has posed an ongoing challenge for inhabitants of rural British Columbia. While the industry provides jobs, it can also be devastating for the landscape and the fragile ecosystems, particularly on the islands. On Salt Spring, successful fundraising campaigns have enabled the purchase of land to protect it. Since 1995, some 1,053 hectares (2600 acres) have been bought or protected. The largest of the preserves is 40 hectares (100 acres) on the top of Mount Erskine, which, combined with adjacent, already-protected properties, provides permanent protection to an undeveloped area of up to 240 hectares (600 acres).

The main attractions

One of the island's jewels is **Ruckle Provincial Park**, with rocky headlands and coves along the shore. The surrounding waters are rich in marine life, and if you're lucky you can spot sea lions and whales from the shore. It's a popular spot with divers. The park was named after Henry Ruckle, who came here from Ireland in 1872. Part of the farm, still in the Ruckle family, is now an 81-hectare (200-acre) organic heritage farm.

Today there are 225 working farms on the island, which has become renowned as a centre of organic food production, especially its lamb and cheese. Many of the island's organic food producers open their premises to visitors. A free map is available showing their location, but a good way to see a sample of them is to spend the morning at the famous **Saturday market** (Apr–mid-Oct 8am–4pm) in Centennial Park at Ganges, which attracts many of the producers.

ABOVE: accommodation on Salt Spring Island ranges from the expensive but highly recommended Hastings House (above) to campsites in Ruckle Provincial Park.
BELOW: vintage cars on display at the Salt Spring Island Fall Fair.

Salt Spring is also noted for the number of **studios** open to visitors: more than 30 artists in wood, paint, glass, textiles, hemp and clay regularly open their studios. There are so many artists living on this island that they have organised guilds, one each for the weavers and spinners, the potters, the painters and the basket-makers.

Ganges on the east coast is the island's main village. It was named after the flagship of the Royal Navy's Pacific Station between 1857 and 1860 and the last sailing warship to be commissioned for duty in foreign waters, in 1821. Clustered round its harbour, Ganges has some quirky public sculpture, including a fountain made out of a ship's propeller.

Among its landmarks is Mouat's Store, founded by Shetlanders in 1907 and still supplying all manner of goods to the islanders. The 1904-built Mahon Hall has a large collection of arts and crafts for those who visit between June and September, and the ArtSpring community hall hosts an exceptionally good programme of concerts and plays.

Salt Spring has some of the best walking on the Gulf Islands, with the substantial mountains of Maxwell, Erskine, Sullivan and Tuam offering panoramic views over the surrounding islands and the strait. Other attractions include the introduction to the island's history and culture offered by the **Akerman Museum** (tel: 250 537 9977 to arrange visit) in Fulford Valley. The best beaches are on the east coast at Beddis and Ruckle Park.

Every third week in September, Salt Spring Island holds a country fair with sheepdog trials, livestock shows, vintage machinery and plenty of food stalls selling hot buttered corn, home-made pies, barbecued lamb and other wholesome goodies.

GABRIOLA ISLAND

The second-most populous Gulf Island, **Gabriola ❷**, is known as the Queen of the Gulf Islands, and is famous for its honeycombed sandstone grottoes such as the cave-like Malaspina Galleries near sandy Taylor Bay. Sandstone quarried on the island went into many a Victoria building

ABOVE: the Gulf Islands attract ornithologists for sightings of ospreys, bald eagles, cormorants, tanagers, juncos, bluebirds and flycatchers. **BELOW:** freighter in the Strait of Georgia.

and provided grindstones for pulp mills. Accesssible from Nanaimo by a 20-minute ferry ride, Gabriola has a 45km (28-mile) shoreline and is particularly favoured by cyclists for the 30km (19-mile) island loop. Five small parks protect various features and habitats, including Garry oak ecosystems and some petroglyphs near Degnen Bay whose origins remain a mystery.

Like Salt Spring, Gabriola has attracted many artists and artisans whose work can be seen at their studios or galleries. In October over 40 studios open their doors for the self-guided Thanksgiving Gallery Tour. It's an easy day trip from Nanaimo and ferries are frequent.

GALIANO ISLAND

Long and thin, **Galiano ❸** has the lowest rainfall in the region and some fine mature forests of Garry oak, hairy manzanita, maple, cedar and Douglas fir, though they were badly scarred by fire in 2006. Regarded as one of the most attractive of the Gulf Islands, Galiano is rich in birdlife, with over 130 different species recorded.

Ferries from the mainland serve Sturdies Bay at the southeast end of the island, where there is an information booth. Near Sturdies Bay is Bellhouse Park, where seals and sea lions are a common sight, and it is also close to the starting point for the hike up to the 342-metre (1,122ft) summit of Mount Galiano, a popular walk for the spectacular views.

NORTH AND SOUTH PENDER

Linked by a single-track bridge, **North and South Pender islands ❹** offer plenty of coves and beaches as well as good services, mostly on the North Island where the ferry terminal at Otter Bay is located to receive ferries from Swartz Bay and Tsawwassen. The islands are particularly appealing to walkers, with 69 different trails including an ascent of Mount Norman at 244 metres (801ft) on the South Island. There are 37 beaches to choose from, Hamilton on the North Island and Mortimer Spit on the South being among the favourites.

The subdivision of part of North Pender, where 90 percent of the

ABOVE: Georgina Point Lighthouse, Mayne.

TIP

Some of the BC Ferry tickets to the islands cover the return journey; calculate the fares as part of your planning to make sure you are not paying unnecessarily high fares. Ferry prices can vary by day of the week as well.

*Hornby Island has the
largest per capita
concentration of artists
in Canada, so there are
many opportunities to
visit studios and
galleries.*

islands' inhabitants live, was one of
the catalysts for the formation of the
Islands Trust, to prevent the character of the islands being destroyed by
inappropriate development.

MAYNE ISLAND

Named after a lieutenant on HMS
Plumper (many of the islands were
named after senior crew members
of the ship that surveyed the archipelago in 1857), **Mayne Island
❺** seems anything but "the little
hell" it was once called because of
the drunken behaviour of the gold
prospectors on their way from Fort
Victoria to the Fraser River. Mayne's
facilities are clustered around Miners Bay and Village Bay, where the
ferry from the mainland docks. At
nearby Dinner Bay is the **Japanese
Garden** created by the community
to commemorate the island's early
Japanese Canadian settlers.

Georgina Point Lighthouse was
built in 1885 and is probably the
most photographed lighthouse in
BC, because of its prominent location at the entrance to Active Pass,
the narrow passageway between

Mayne Island and Galiano Island
which is navigated by the ferries
between the mainland (Tsawwassen) and Swartz Bay, the ferry terminal closest to Victoria. The two
cells and main room of the Plumper
Pass Lockup of 1896 now house
the island's museum. Even older is
the 1890 Collinson farmhouse and
now Springwater Lodge. There is a
lovely beach for swimming on the
east side of the island at **Campbell
Bay**, where there are also sandstone
caves to explore.

SATURNA ISLAND

With a permanent population of
a little over 350, **Saturna ❻** offers
exceptional peace where the passage
of a car seems an intrusion. This is
an island where exploring by bike
or on foot seems like good manners.
Named after the *Saturnina* in which
José Maria Narváez explored the
Strait of Georgia, the island is so little changed that he would probably
still recognise much of it.

Thanks to almost half the island
being protected as part of the
National Park Reserve, there is a good

RIGHT AND BELOW:
Hornby Island.

chance that it will stay one of the jewels of the Gulf Islands. Its tall mountain, Mount Warburton Pike at 497 metres (1,631ft), offers exceptional views over the islands and the coastal mainland chain. Bird life includes eagles, falcons and vultures.

The most southerly of the islands, Saturna is served by ferry service from Swartz Bay and Tsawwassen (transferring ferries at Mayne), arriving at the deep inlet of Lyall Harbour. With several B&Bs, a pub and a bakery, it's easy to stay for a few days to absorb an atmosphere that is rare in North America. The highlight in the social calendar is the Canada Day Lamb Barbecue (1 July) at Winter Cove Marine Park, when close to 1,500 people (four times the island's normal population) congregate to enjoy Argentinian-style meat cooked on upright iron crosses.

DENMAN ISLAND

Denman is often seen as a stepping stone to the more popular Hornby Island, but it has some of the best agricultural land in the Gulf Islands. The 2km (1¼-mile) ferry ride from Buckley Bay on Vancouver Island arrives at Denman Village, which has a wide range of facilities to cater for the population of over 1,000.

The shops include a cooperative outlet for the island's artisans, and there are over a dozen B&Bs.

HORNBY ISLAND

Hornby has a permanent population of around 1,000, but this increases tenfold in summer thanks to its lovely beaches and coves and varied topography. Consequently it has excellent amenities, including many galleries displaying the creations of the island's large artistic community. Typical of the impressive community action on the islands, the residents of Hornby raised money to help create a 187-hectare (462-acre) provincial park on Mount Geoffrey. The Co-op

store is as much for socialising as shopping, with the Ringside Market next door.

The island is reached by a 15-minute ferry ride across the Lambert Channel that separates Hornby from Denman Island. Sheltered Tribune Bay has some of the warmest sea water in BC as well as a fine white-sand beach, with tidal pools to explore. Scuba divers come to the island to experience swimming with the rare six-gill sharks, one of the few places where they can be easily seen.

TEXADA ISLAND

Iron ore, copper and gold have been mined on Texada Island during the past century, and logging and limestone quarries have rounded out its commercial exploitation. Most easily reached by ferries from Powell River into Blubber Bay, Texada is the largest of the Gulf Islands, although one of the least explored by tourists. There are beautiful beaches and great birding, with some 150 species to be sighted, including Rufous hummingbirds, Great Blue herons and kingfishers.   ❏

ABOVE: Ringside Market, Hornby Island. **BELOW:** rocky cove, Hornby Island.

BEST RESTAURANTS, BARS AND CAFÉS

Restaurants

The islands, particularly the smaller ones, are completely different worlds in the summer and off-season. Many of the restaurants reduce their hours or close completely during the winter. If you are planning a trip between October and May, your chances of finding a place to eat are much better on weekends than during the week. If you are staying overnight, make sure you confirm that there will be somewhere for you to have dinner.

Gabriola Island

Raspberry's Jazz Café
Folklife Village, 575 North Rd. Tel: 250 247 9959. Open: B & L daily. **$**

Open during the day for home-made soups, sandwiches and good coffee, the café is transformed into a jazz venue on Sunday afternoons and occasionally in the evenings.

Surf Pub
885 Berry Point Rd. Tel: 250 247 9231. www.surflodge.com Open: L & D daily. **$**
Pop in to the Surf Pub, part of the Surf Island Lodge, for a drink and a bite to eat while you watch the sun set from the outside deck. Note that the pub is closed Mon–Tue off-season.

Suzy's Restaurant and Deli
Folklife Village, 560 North Rd. Tel: 250 247 2010. Open: B, L & D daily. **$**
Excellent spot for brunch and light lunches. Also a

good place to pick up the ingredients for a great picnic since Suzy's sells local cheeses, meats and artisan breads.

Galiano Island

La Berengerie
Montague Rd. Tel: 250 539 5392. www.galianoisland.com/laberengerie Open: D daily. **$$**
This welcoming B&B near Montague Harbour serves French cuisine with a southeast Asian twist using local produce.

Mayne Island

Oceanwood Country Inn
630 Dinner Bay Rd. Tel: 250 539 5074. www.oceanwood.com Open: D daily (summer only). **$$$**
A daily-changing menu to reflect the seasons and what is freshly available is a feature of the award-winning dining room at this country inn. The five-course fixed menu is fantastically delicious and good value.

ABOVE: surf and turf starter. **LEFT:** Hastings House terrace.

Sunny Mayne Bakery Café
Mayne Street Mall. www.sunnymaynebakery.com Open: B & L daily. **$**
A good place for breakfast, lunch or a quick morning coffee. Lots of home-made goodies and great coffee.

Pender Islands

Poet's Cove Aurora Restaurant
9801 Spalding Road, South Pender Island. Tel: 250 629 2115. www.poetscove.com Open: B, L & D daily. **$$$**
Part of the Poet's Cove Resort and Spa, the restaurant specialises in contemporary local cuisine – fresh seafood, local lamb – in a stunning setting. Spectacular sunsets are free.

Salt Spring Island

Auntie Pestos
2104-115 Fulford Ganges Road. Tel: 250 537 4181. www.auntiepestos.com Open: B, L & D Mon–Sat. **$–$$**
While perhaps best known for its breakfasts and lunches, take a look

at this place for dinner as well. They love food and talk about the 5-mile diet, sourcing as much as they can locally.

Hastings House Country Estate

160 Upper Ganges Rd. Tel: 250 537 2362. www.hastings house.com Open: D daily, Apr–Oct. **$$$$**

Hastings House is a wonder and deserves its rank among the best restaurants in British Columbia. The food is accomplished and imaginative without being pretentious, allowing the quality and freshness of the ingredients to sing out. Grilled rack and loin of Salt Spring lamb, with garlic potato purée and a honey-mustard jus, is perfection. And the four-course chef's menu at $80 seems like a steal. The wine list is extensive and features good local wines. The service is informed and unfussy. All this and the pretty setting make a meal here a wonderful treat.

Oystercatcher Seafood Bar and Grill

Harbour Building, Ganges. Tel: 250 537 5041. Open: L & D daily. **$$**

Fabulous food in a spectacular setting overlooking the harbour. Lunchtime specials include

Prices for a three-course dinner per person with a half-bottle of house wine:

$ = under C$30
$$ = C$30–50
$$$ = C$50–80
$$$$ = over C$80

Denman Island is a tiny island, but try the **Denman Island Guesthouse Bistro** (Denman village) or the **Denman Island Bakery and Pizzeria** (Denman Road).

Hornby Island is another small island with few restaurants: the **Cardboard House** (2205 Central Road) is a combination bakery, pizzeria, café and local craft store. In summer, there is live music in the orchard Wednesdays and Sundays (weather permitting). Visit **Jan's Café** (5875 Central Road); or the **Thatch Pub** (4305 Shingle Spit Road) for West Coast specialities,

BBQ Fanny Bay oysters with fresh asparagus and Dungeness crab, and shrimp cakes, cranberry corn relish and asparagus. The best crab cakes ever and the local beers – Saltspring Golden Ale and their own Oyster-catcher Pale Ale – are excellent.

Restaurant House Piccolo

108 Hereford Ave. Tel: 250 537 1844. www.housepiccolo. com Open: July–Sept D daily, Oct–June Wed–Sun. **$$$**

Elegant food carefully prepared using local produce in a tiny heritage house overlooking Ganges. Ring for reservations since there are only 32 seats, plus a small patio when the weather cooperates.

RIGHT: grilled salmon, a staple on many menus.

burgers and salads, and **VOR1ZO Espresso Bar** for great coffee and home-made goodies.

The Hummingbird Pub at Sturdies Bay on Galiano Island is open year-round. It serves classic pub food, pizzas and burgers, but the fish and chips seem to be the most popular. It's located about 2km (1 mile) from the ferry terminal, and also has a bus service from the marina and the park. Over at Montague Harbour, **The Harbour Grill** serves breakfast, lunch and snacks during the season. It caters to boaters, as it is part of a

Saturna Café

101 Narvaez Bay Rd. Tel: 250 539 2936. Open: B, L & D Wed–Sat, B & L Sun (summer only). **$$**

marina, so things don't really start happening here until May.

On Salt Spring Island, **Barb's Buns Bakery** (121 McPhillips Avenue) is considered the best place for breakfast, but is also open for lunch (closed Sun). Everything is fresh and home-made. For a pint of the local brew or other beers, try **Shipstones English Pub** (Ganges Harbour front).

There are only a few places on Texada Island to grab a bite or a beer: try the **Texada Island Inn** (Van Anda), both a pub and a restaurant.

Local, healthy and fresh are the keynotes here. Try to time your visit with the weekly crab night – a whole steamed crab and a pair of claw crackers.

NORTH TO WHISTLER

The Sea-to-Sky Highway is a scenic fjord drive that leads to one of the best resorts in North America. You can also get active along the Sunshine Coast Trail, which offers equally spectacular coastal scenery.

British Columbia

Whistler
Vancouver

Main Attractions

BRITISH COLUMBIA MUSEUM
  OF MINING
WHISTLER BLACKCOMB
  RESORT
SQUAMISH LIL'WAT CULTURAL
  CENTRE
SKOOKUMCHUCK NARROWS
  PROVINCIAL PARK

Maps and Listings

MAP OF AROUND
  VANCOUVER, PAGE 188
RESTAURANTS, BARS AND
  CAFÉS, PAGE 225
ACCOMMODATION, PAGES
  256–7

The most popular excursion destination outside Vancouver is the year-round recreational mountain area, Whistler. In winter, it draws crowds for skiing or snowboarding, but this is a four-season resort. Once the snow at the lower levels has melted, hikers and bikers keep the ski lifts rolling, and the winter slopes turn into summer trails. Those who crave skiing in summer can head up to the glacier.

The other great attraction north of the city is Highway 101 along the coast, which links a series of enchanting small resorts. Whichever route you choose, they both offer stunning scenery and lots of opportunities for outdoor activities en route, from the gentle to the extreme.

Whistler Mountaineer

Unquestionably the best way to enjoy the scenery between Vancouver and Whistler is to take the **Whistler Mountaineer**, operated by Rocky Mountaineer Vacations *(see page 245)*. Besides enabling you to relax and enjoy the landscapes, the train affords much better views than the road of Howe Sound.

Trains leave from a small station in North Vancouver and pass the

Lions Gate Bridge before easing past West Vancouver, where some of the city's most valuable houses are located. For much of the way, the sinuous line hugs the coast, initially looking across to Stanley Park, Kitsilano and the wooded peninsula on which UBC is built. Breakfast is served as the train veers north, offering views out over the dark water of the Sound, broken by a few islands and the heads of curious seals, to snow-dusted mountains bristling with conifers.

LEFT: Whistler Mountaineer train.
RIGHT: the summit of Mount Whistler.

ABOVE: Squamish.
BELOW: the guided tour of the old Britannia Mine involves an underground ride in a narrow-gauge train along 400 metres (1,400ft) of a tunnel bored in 1912, a tiny fraction of the 240km (150 miles) of tunnels and shafts in the mine.

The Cheakamus Canyon is a 0.8km (½-mile) -long cauldron of olive-green water with sheer rocks above and below the line which curves through the gorge. The train slows to walking pace and allows you time to absorb the sight of this extraordinary feature, with trees growing out of the most inhospitable planes of rock.

THE SEA-TO-SKY HIGHWAY

The alternative to the train is to drive Highway 99 – the Sea-to-Sky High-way – recently widened and straight-ened to accommodate traffic for the 2010 Winter Olympics. For much of the way, the views are limited, but it does allow visits to places en route. Near the ferry terminal at Horseshoe Bay the road swings north for Lions Bay and Squamish.

British Columbia Museum of Mining ❼

Address: Britannia Beach, on Highway 99 north of Vancouver, www.bcmuseumofmining.org
Tel: 604 896 2233
Opening Hrs: daily 9am–4.30pm
Entrance Fee: charge

This BC Historic Landmark was once the most productive copper mine in the British Empire: Britannia Mine closed in 1974 after 70 years' output, having produced 650,000 tonnes of copper as well as lead, zinc, cadmium, silver, gold and iron. It reopened as a mining museum the following year, and is such an atmospheric location that it has featured in dozens of films. The site is dominated by the vast tiered mill building erected against the hillside; it housed the concentra-tor which removed valuable miner-als from the 55 million tonnes of ore the mine processed. A $5-million upgrade to the mill was completed in 2007. Additional upgrades are ongoing, making this museum an important attraction. It's a National Historic Site and is also designated as a BC Provincial Landmark.

Other buildings house displays of equipment and portraits of life at the mine. Underground tours are available *(see left)*. There is no café at the mine itself, but there is a roadside café with home-made cakes a few minutes' walk away.

Squamish

The only town between Vancouver and Whistler, **Squamish** ❽ (meaning "birthplace to the winds") is overlooked by the towering cliff faces of the mountain named **Stawamus Chief**, and the **Shannon Falls**, at their most impressive in spring. The 650-metre (2,140ft) granite monolith, geologically comparable to the Rock of Gibraltar, is a great attraction for climbers. Most days when it's not raining colourful ropes can be seen trailing down route lines. Aside from rock climbing, there are plenty of other recreational activities on offer: kayaking, whitewater rafting, kite boarding, hiking, mountain biking, scuba diving, golf, fishing and windsurfing – the windblown town's second-most popular activity.

Many people converge on the area between mid-November and February to witness the gathering of

hundreds and sometimes thousands of **Bald eagles** drawn to the river by the seasonal salmon run. The main viewing point is Brackendale, a few kilometres upriver.

Brandywine Falls

Some 47km (30 miles) north of Squamish is **Brandywine Falls Provincial Park** ❾, where a short walking trail leads from the car park to an observation platform at the top of the 70-metre (230ft) falls. Cross the bridge over Brandywine Creek and follow the path to the right, which brings you to a clearing beside the falls. From this viewpoint, Daisy Lake spreads out beneath the monolith of Black Tusk.

WHISTLER

Once known as Alta Lake, **Whistler** ❿ has become famous around the world as a leading ski resort; *Skiing* magazine has ranked it number one in North America for nine consecutive years, and its facilities and

ABOVE: snowboarder on Blackcomb Mountain.
LEFT: woodcutter statue, Squamish.
BELOW: Brandywine Falls, the favourite stopping place between Squamish and Whistler.

2010 Winter Olympics

When the 2010 Winter Olympics were awarded to Vancouver back in July 2003, Vancouverites immediately thought of Whistler.

While the world heard the word "Vancouver" over and over throughout the 2010 Games, what made both Olympics and Paralympics a global success was the traditional mountain environment and the events at Whistler. The classic downhill and cross-country ski events took place here, while the freestyle skiing and snowboarding events were staged at Cypress, less than 30 minutes from downtown Vancouver.

Whistler's reputation lies both in its superb skiing terrain, but also in the European feel of the village. The central square became the gathering place for people all day long during the Olympics and was also where the medal ceremonies took place after hard-fought runs on the hills, the cross-country and biathlon tracks and at the sliding centre.

The skiing area is the largest in North America, covering 3,036 hectares (8,171 acres) of terrain serviced by 38 lifts. It has the longest vertical descent at 1,609 metres (5,280ft). The longest run is 11km (7 miles). Whistler also benefits from a long ski season, between November and August.

Olympic legacy

For Whistler and the people who traditionally come to ski resorts, the legacy of the Games is a Nordic centre, complete with approximately 50km (31 miles) of cross-country ski trails, attracting athletes at both recreational and high-performance levels.

The additional legacy is the new sliding centre, one of only four in North America and 15 in the world, and reputed to be one of the fastest. It is slated to become a World Cup venue for bobsleigh, luge and skeleton. The track will attract athletes from all over the world anxious to hone their skills, as well as thrill-seekers wanting to experience the excitement of racing down the track at speeds approaching 120kmh (75mph) on bobsleighs driven by experienced athletes.

Back in 1994, the Olympics expanded beyond sport and culture to include a sustainability component. Whistler incorporated several important elements in the venue designs to minimise their impact on the environment, while also improving the facilities available for future use. New facilities were built to LEED (Leadership in Energy and Environmental Design) standards aimed at minimising energy use. The Olympic Village now provides affordable housing in a town notorious for its high hotel and accommodation prices, including a large hostel for tourists. The primary heat source for this accommodation is from heat recovered from the municipality's wastewater treatment plant. ❑

WHISTLER VILLAGE
Host Mountain Resort
2010 Olympic & Paralympic Winter Games

LEFT: welcome to Whistler Village.
ABOVE: Olympic Village housing.

reputation doubtless helped it win the privilege of co-hosting the 2010 Winter Olympics with Vancouver. The village itself nestles between Whistler and Blackcomb mountains, and even though the resort depends on road access, the streets have at least been designed to discourage car use in favour of walking and cycling. Like some Alpine resorts, Whistler has the unreal feeling of a transient community almost wholly dependent on tourism, with its agglomeration of hotels, designer-label shops, restaurants and condominiums in manicured surroundings.

Whistler is making an effort to develop into a mountain resort that will "become a beacon of hope to the global community to show that sustainability is possible". In 2000, it was the first Canadian municipality to adopt the "Natural Step" approach to sustainability, which strives to achieve a balance in terms of what is being taken out of the ecosystem and what is being put back in.

As the largest ski resort in North America, Whistler attracts over two million visitors a year, the majority of whom come in winter for the world-class snowsports facilities (*see opposite*). There's plenty to do for those who don't wish to ski or snowboard, including snowshoeing, sleigh rides, tubing, zip-trekking, glacier tours and dog sledding.

In summer there is just about every outdoor activity imaginable. Zip-trekking is particularly popular (*see page 223*). Ten ziplines cross the Fitzsimmons Creek Valley in the old coastal temperate rainforest, and a tour includes an introduction to the ecology of this increasingly scarce habitat. The longest ride is 610 metres (2,000ft), where you can reach speeds of 80kph (50mph). It's breathtaking any time of the year and a real contrast to the hustle and bustle of the village, or even the busy ski slopes. Even though you are right in between Whistler and Blackcomb Mountains, it is as though you are in the middle of nowhere.

Many of the winter ski lifts offer quick and easy access to hiking trails during the summer. Some of the best hiking routes are in **Garibaldi Park** ⑪ which offers easy walks through

TIP

For those intent on honing their skiing or snowboarding skills off-season, Horstman Glacier offers a more accessible alternative than flying to New Zealand or South America. Summer camps are designed for intermediate level skiers and boarders looking to improve their skills, as well as experts with Olympic aspirations. The ski lifts take you from Whistler Village to the glacier, maximising time on the snow.

BELOW: the Whistler cable cars operate throughout the year.

Just a 20-minute ferry ride from Horseshoe Bay, **Bowen Island** is popular with Vancouverites seeking a quick escape from the city. Restaurants and shops are focused on the ferry terminal of Snug Cove. It's a short walk from there to the beaches, but there are good walking trails in the undeveloped centre of the island. The visitor information centre supplies maps and information.

BELOW: mountain biking in Whistler.

Alpine meadows, as well as more challenging hikes such as the ascent of the volcanic plug of Black Tusk.

The other important sports that attract summer tourists to Whistler are golf and mountain biking. With four championship designer courses, Whistler has been rated Canada's top golf destination by *Golf Digest* magazine. The mountain biking on the ski hills provides endless entertainment for serious and recreational mountain bikers. Whistler offers just about every outdoor activity imaginable, from canoeing and kayaking to fishing, hiking and horse riding.

Squamish Lil'wat Cultural Centre

Address: 4584 Blackcomb Way, Whistler, www.slcc.ca
Tel: 604 964 0990
Opening Hrs: daily 9.30am–5pm
Entrance Fee: charge

The cultural centre is designed to evoke both a traditional Squamish longhouse and a Lil'wat Istken (pit house), reflecting the goal of the centre to preserve the two cultures whose traditional lands overlap. The

Salish hunting canoe on display is more than 12 metres (40ft) long and was carved from a single cedar tree. It must be removed from exhibition each year and taken on a journey in the ocean to honour the spirit of the canoe. There is a variety of rotating exhibits, with fine examples of wool and cedar weaving, blankets and canoes. A café on site serves dishes inspired by First Nations recipes.

THE SOUTHERN SUNSHINE COAST

Highway 101 is one of the great BC drives, hugging the coastline pierced by inlets from Port Mellon on Howe Sound to Lund at the northern end of the Sunshine Coast. Coming from Vancouver, most join it at Langdale where the BC Ferry from Horseshoe Bay docks after a 40-minute journey. The area is popular for hiking along the Sunshine Coast Trail, cycling, kayaking, fishing and diving as well as sailing.

Sunshine Coast Museum and Archive

Address: 716 Winn Road, www.

Sunshine Coast Trail

This 180km (112-mile) trail was built in response to the diminishing amounts of old-growth forest that had survived the depredations of logging and development. Its southerly point is Saltery Bay and it ends at Sarah Point, north of Lund, on Desolation Sound. En route you should see salmon and otter on the river and lakeside stretches, and numerous waterfalls are passed. A leisurely pace would take about ten days, and there are strategically located B&Bs and a restaurant on or close to the path to allow hikers to plan overnight stops. If ten days is too long, there are nice discrete chunks of two to four days. A complete panorama can be enjoyed from the top of Tin Hat Mountain.

sunshinecoastmuseum.ca
Tel: 604 886 8232
Opening Hrs: daily 10.30am–4.30pm
Entrance Fee: charge

Located in **Gibsons** , the Sunshine Coast Museum and Archive provides a good introduction to the history of the area and of the Coast Salish nation. A first-floor maritime section has full-sized boats as well as models. In the summer Gibsons hosts an international outrigger canoe race.

The road continues past **Mount Elphinstone**, a coastal rainforest with imposing old-growth cedar, hemlock and maple laced with trails for biking and hiking. **Roberts Creek** has an "alternative" feel to it, a retreat for those who lament the passing of the 1960s counterculture, with such contemporary manifestations as organic restaurants and cosmic-energy public artworks.

There's a great sandy beach at **Davis Bay**, where the skill of sandcastle building is celebrated by an annual competition.

The "capital" of the Sunshine Coast is **Sechelt**, which has theatres and galleries as well as the usual tourist amenities. Rockwood Lodge was built as a Union Steamship boarding house in 1935 and has been preserved as a centre for community activities. Surrounded by delightful gardens, it now hosts Sechelt's Festival of the Written Arts in August. Totem poles flank the First Nations **Tems Swiya Museum** (5555 Highway 101; tel: 604 885 8991; Mon–Sat 9am–5pm), which displays the art and carvings of the Shishalh people.

From **Sargeant Bay Provincial Park**, north of Smugglers Cove, you can walk to a particularly attractive cove and visit a salmon ladder, built to help salmon work their way upstream to spawn.

Pender Harbour is known, perhaps a bit facetiously, as the "Venice of the North" for the waterways that thread the town, although aside from the existence of water, it has nothing in common with the famous Italian city. There are boat tours up the Jervis and sheer-walled Princess Louisa inlets to the magnificently situated 40-metre (131ft) Chatterbox Falls. The latter inlet has about 60 waterfalls during the summer.

Experienced kayakers head for the Skookumchuck Rapids in **Skookumchuck Narrows Provincial Park** for the tidal rapids created by billions of litres of water being forced through

ABOVE: for a novel adrenalin rush, try zip-trekking with Ziptrek Ecotours (tel: 604 935 0001; www.ziptrek.com). Suspended in a safety harness, you slide along a wire rope between platforms built high up in stout trees. You can even hang upside down, and whizz along with your hands free. **BELOW LEFT:** Skookumchuck Rapids. **BELOW RIGHT:** Pender Harbour Marina.

a narrow channel. The park is at Egmont, due east of Earls Cove, from where the ferry departs for the northern section of the Sunshine Coast.

THE UPPER SUNSHINE COAST

A 50-minute ferry ride links **Earls Cove** and **Saltery Bay**, where killer whales, sea lions and seals can be seen. The bay takes its name from the fish saltery that was established here in the early 20th century.

The **Powell River** ⓰ has the distinction of being the world's second-shortest river – its harbour is protected by 10 World War II cement hulks which form the world's largest floating breakwater. The town of Powell River is a major attraction and one of the few National Historic Districts in all Canada. It was an early example of a "company town", with the paper company building the necessary housing for its employees. It's a planned community on the lines of a garden city, with 400 attractively designed West Coast Craftsman-style houses set in spacious landscaped grounds. If you're staying in town, don't miss

ABOVE: disused waterwheel in the fishing village of Lund. **BELOW:** Saltery Bay.

taking in a film at the superbly renovated 1928 Patricia Theatre.

Powell River Historical Museum

Address: 4798 Marine Avenue; www.powellrivermuseum.ca
Tel: 604 485 2222
Opening Hrs: June–Labour Day daily 9am–4.30pm, Labour Day–May Mon–Fri 9am–4.30pm
Entrance Fee: charge

This small museum traces the history of the area between Jervis Inlet and Desolation Sound, including the offshore islands, from the Coast Salish people at Sliammon village to the present.

In early July Powell River hosts one of the world's largest choral festivals, the **Kathaumixw** (pronounced Kathou-mew), held biennially in even-numbered years. It features as many as 40 choirs and conductors from all over the world and celebrates music's ability to bring peace to the planet.

At the end of Highway 101 is **Lund**, a fishing village founded by a Swedish family in 1889, an ancestry which is still reflected in the Lund Hotel. ❏

BEST RESTAURANTS, BARS AND CAFÉS

Restaurants

Whistler has a plethora of good restaurants, coffee houses, deli-cafés and bars, serving excellent food at reasonable prices.

Araxi Restaurant and Bar
4222 Village Sq. (Whistler Way). Tel: 604 932 4540. www.araxi.com Open: L & D daily in summer, D only in winter. **$$$**
West Coast cuisine in a mountain setting. A very smart place, and the food lives up to the decor. An oyster bar is the latest addition, and the patio in summer is a must.

Caramba Restaurante
12-4314 Main St. Tel: 604 938 1879. www.caramba-restaurante.com Open: L & D daily. **$$**
A buzzy atmosphere and good pastas, wood-fired pizzas and salads make this a popular place. The Caramba chicken salad is terrific and great value for diners on a budget; or try the La Rua pizza with spinach, roasted roma tomato, garlic and asiago cheese.

Fifty Two 80 Bistro
Four Seasons Resort, 4591

Prices for a three-course dinner per person with a half-bottle of house wine:
$ = under C$30
$$ = C$30–50
$$$ = C$50–80
$$$$ = over C$80

Blackcomb Way (Lorimer Road). Tel: 604 935 3400. www.fourseasons.com/whistler Open: B, L & D daily **$$$**
Seafood is the speciality at this sophisticated dining room, although spit-roasts and prime Canadian beef are also on the menu.

Il Caminetto di Umberto
4242 Village Stroll (Whistler Village Sq.). Tel: 604 932 4442. www.umberto.com Open: D only, daily. **$$$**
Another restaurant in the Umberto Menghi stable of fine Italian eateries, Il Caminetto focuses on fabulous Tuscan food using the best local ingredients. Great home-made pasta dishes and an extensive wine list, with Italy playing a leading role. Try his other Whistler establishment, Trattoria di Umberto, at 4417 Sundial Place, if you can't get in here.

Kypriaki Norte
4122 Village Green. Tel: 604 932 0600. www.kypriaki.net Open: D only, daily. **$$**
Another local favourite for traditional Greek and Mediterranean food at reasonable prices, Kypriaki also has a bar and patio with terrific views for alfresco eating.

The Old Spaghetti Factory
4145 Village Green, Crystal Lodge. Tel: 604 938 1081. www.oldspaghettifactory.ca Open: L, D daily. **$–$$**
If you are really hungry and on a tight budget,

Bars and Cafés

Try the **Dubh Linn Gate Old Irish Pub** (4320 Sundial Crescent, in the Pan Pacific) for a pint and simple but hearty pub fare. The always busy **Whistler Brewhouse** (4355 Blackcomb Way) has a wood-fired pizza oven and rotisserie. For the best all-day breakfast, try **Auntie Em's Kitchen** (Village North Marketplace), which also serves excellent vegetarian sandwiches, soups and

this classic pasta place will fill you up without costing an arm and a leg. It's been in Whistler forever, and still draws crowds. Ideal for families.

La Rua Restaurant
4557 Blackcomb Way. Tel: 604 932 5011. www.larua-restaurante.com Open: D only, daily. **$$$**
Award-winning restaurant within Le Chamois hotel renowned for its international take on seafood, steak and game, with such creative dishes as West Coast bouillabaisse, duck breast with scallion risotto and a brandy quince glaze, and cassoulet.

Rimrock Café
2117 Whistler Rd. (Highway 99). Tel: 604 932 5565. www.rimrockwhistler.com Open: D only, daily. **$$$**
One of Whistler's top restaurants, with a well-deserved reputation for outstanding seafood and

baked goodies. **Gone Bakery and Soup Co.** (off the main village square) has excellent daily specials to eat in or take away.

A locals' favourite is the **Cinnamon Bear Bar** (part of the Hilton), serving a step up from the usual burgers, pizzas and salads. **Black's Pub & Restaurant** (4270 Mountain Sq.) has scores of different beers, a great patio and good pub food.

game and a terrific wine list. Arctic caribou and venison chop feature along with a wonderful array of fish and shellfish. Worth a detour.

Splitz Grill
104 4369 Main St. Tel: 604 938 9300. www.splitzgrill.com Open: L & D daily. **$**
A must for a quick meal on the run, this burger joint serves the usual and not so usual – salmon, chicken and spicy – with every conceivable topping and condiment possible. Very popular and very cheap.

Sushi Village
4272 Mountain Sq. (Whistler Village Sq.) Tel: 604 932 3330. www.sushivillage.com Open: L & D daily. **$$**
Trendy hang-out for a younger crowd offering exemplary sushi, salads, teriyaki dishes and hot-pots. Be prepared to wait.

THE OKANAGAN

East of Greater Vancouver the sprawl of industrial plants and strip malls eventually gives way to grassland plateaux, lakes and high Alpine mountains. Known as "Canada's fruit bowl", sunny Okanagan also produces quality wines of international stature.

British Columbia

Vancouver · Merritt

Compared to the well-publicised areas north of the city and the islands to the west, the area east of Vancouver gets relatively little coverage, something of an injustice as there is plenty to see and do. Don't be put off by the less than scenic beginning to your journey.

As you leave Vancouver heading east or southeast, it's easy to be disheartened, either by the industrial plants that site themselves along Highway 1 or the unspeakable ugliness of the strip malls that seem to line long stretches of Route 99. Even when the malls give way to acres of glasshouses and the shrinking market gardens of Vancouver, the land is flat, largely reclaimed from the Fraser Delta.

Once past Chilliwack, however, development recedes and the coastal range rises up majestically, marking the beginning of the mountains that define the landscape for almost a thousand kilometres through the Rocky Mountains to Calgary. During the summer the roads are punctuated by stalls selling the fresh fruit for which the region is famous.

FORT LANGLEY

To place both Vancouver and the founding of British Columbia in con-text, it's worth breaking the journey at the birthplace of the colony, **Fort Langley** ⑰, just north of Highway 1. It was here, beside the Fraser River, that the Hudson's Bay Company trading post was founded.

The first fort was built in 1827, but propensity to flooding prompted a move in 1839 to the hilltop site on which the fort has been reconstructed around the one surviving original building, the 1840s storehouse. A 5km (3-mile) riverside trail links the two sites.

LEFT: perfect horse riding country.
RIGHT: Fort Langley National Historic Site.

TIP

In the vicinity of Fort Langley, just 500 metres south of the Trans-Canada Highway (exit # 73), the **Greater Vancouver Zoological Centre** (5048 264th Street, Aldergrove; tel: 604 856 6825; www. gvzoo.com; daily 9am–dusk) has bears, lions, tigers, elephants and giraffes among the 800 animals roaming its 49 hectares (120 acres).

Fort Langley National Historic Site

Address: 23433 Mavis Avenue, www.pc.gc.ca/fortlangley
Tel: 604 513 4777
Opening Hrs: daily, July–Aug 9am–8pm, Sept–June 10am–5pm
Entrance Fee: charge
Transport: Skytrain Expo line to Surrey Central Station; 501, 502 or 320 bus to Langley Centre; transfer to C62 Walnut Grove to 96 Avenue and Glover Road

Staff in period costume help visitors interpret the eight buildings within the wood-stockaded fort and explain the trading activities, mainly in beaver pelts, that went on with the aboriginal people. It was here that British Columbia was proclaimed a crown colony, at a ceremony in the "Big House" on 19 November 1858.

The town of Fort Langley is beautifully kept and landscaped with several rows of old shops, including a huge antiques emporium (proving that one person's junk is another's treasure).

Langley Centennial Museum

Address: 9135 King Street,

www.langleymuseum.org
Tel: 604 888 3922
Opening Hrs: Mon–Sat 10am–4.45pm, Sun 1–4.45pm
Entrance Fee: by donation
Transport: Skytrain Expo line to Surrey Central Station; transfer to 501, 502 or 320 bus to Langley Centre; transfer to C62 Walnut Grove to 96 Ave. and Glover Road

The Centennial Museum was established for the centennial of the establishment of the colony of British Columbia in 1958; it has a reconstruction of an early 20th-century store and post office, as well as interesting artefacts, including a collection of First Nations woodcarvings, tools, stone sculptures and basketry. The museum houses an exceptional collection of baskets from the late 19th and early 20th centuries.

Next door is the **Farm Machinery Museum** (tel: 604 888 2273; www. bcfma.com; daily 10am–4.30pm), with a huge variety of farm equipment, including a crop-spraying Tiger Moth biplane. On the opposite side of Fort Langley's main street, Glover Road, is the restored former **Cana-**

BELOW: cooper's shop, Fort Langley.

sternwheelers. A good introduction to the area's history is provided by the **Visitor Centre** (daily) and **Museum** (mid-May–mid-Sept daily) at 919 Water Street (tel: 604 869 2021).

The streets are punctuated with imposing wood sculptures *(see right)*, and a self-guided art walk round the town takes in the carvings and the town's art galleries.

Around Hope

The country around Hope is wild and rugged. One of the most dramatic canyons can be walked by taking the easy and popular trail on the abandoned trackbed of the **Kettle Valley Railway** through the deep, dark Othello Quintette Tunnels in **Coquihalla Canyon Provincial Park ⑲**, northeast of Hope. To reach the walk-through tunnels (May–Oct), take the Kawkawa Lake Road out of Hope, then join the Othello Road. Sheer walls of rock rise above the route of the line, which crosses the river several times between largely unlined tunnels. The stations on the line were named after Shakespearean characters because the railway's

dian National Fort Langley Station building (summer and autumn Sat–Sun noon–4pm), erected in 1915.

Just outside the town, on the other side of Highway 1 adjacent to Langley Municipal Airport, is the **Canadian Museum of Flight** (Hangar # 3–5333 216th Street; tel: 604 532 0035; www. canadianflight.org; daily 10am–4pm). Its collection of 25 aircraft includes a Tiger Moth and the only Handley Page Hampden RAF bomber plane on public display. Seven of the planes are in flying condition and fly regularly in the summer months.

HOPE

The chainsaw-carving capital of **Hope ⑱** is situated in the fork of the Fraser and Coquihalla rivers. The Hudson's Bay Company built a fort at Hope in 1848–9 as the terminus of the Coquihalla route from the interior. In 1858 the gold rush began, when four Americans who had heard rumours of gold nuggets being found at Spences Bridge passed through Hope, stopped on a sandbar 16km (10 miles) north of the town and found gold. By the summer of that year, about 30,000 men and women had arrived from all around the world, many aboard the first steam

ABOVE LEFT: Kettle Valley Railway. **ABOVE RIGHT:** chainsaw sculpture in Hope. **BELOW:** cycling along the Kettle Valley Railway, Myra Canyon.

engineer, Andrew McCulloch, loved Shakespeare and would sit round the campfire at night reading sonnets to the construction crew. It was the most difficult railway in Canada to build and operate: one mile cost C$300,000 in 1914, and during the first seven winters the line was closed more than it was open due to mud and snow slides, which finally smothered the line in 1959.

MANNING PARK

Most of the mountain highways are subject to landslides, avalanches and flooding. Taking the Crowsnest Highway, No. 3 southeast from Hope, the road passes the site of the **Hope Slide**; in 1965 Johnson Peak collapsed, engulfing four passing motorists. The colossal amount of debris is a dramatic illustration of the power of nature.

The road soon enters **Manning Provincial Park ㉑**, which offers a fabulous diversity of landscapes with rainforests, grassland slopes, wild rivers, lakes and Alpine meadows. Sumallo Grove is a good place to appreciate the beauty of old-growth forest – the biggest trees here are

ABOVE: black bear cub, Manning Park. **RIGHT AND BELOW:** Cascade Mountains.

almost 500 years old – and is home to pine marten, black bear, spotted owls, Northern flying squirrels, bats and black-tailed deer. Above **Manning Park Resort** (the only place to stay in the park, *see page 257*) the Cascade Lookout, reached by a gravel switchback road, offers majestic views of the Cascade Mountains.

There's a visitor centre just east of the resort, which has maps of suggested walks and details of the imaginative programme of guided walks and events for children. Some of the walks start from an upper parking area 7km (4½ miles) beyond the lookout, reached by a good dirt road, where there is an Alpine meadow with flowers right into late July. Canoes can be hired at **Lightning Lake**, a few kilometres from the resort, where it is also safe to swim, and in winter there is downhill and cross-country skiing. When the 2010 Winter Olympics were struggling to make enough snow for the Cypress Mountain snowboarding and freestyle skiing events, snow was trucked

in from Manning Park, which rarely has a shortage of snow.

HEDLEY

History buffs may be interested in stopping in the former mining town of **Princeton** ㉑, but most will press on further east along Highway 3 to the small settlement of **Hedley** ㉒.

Mascot Gold Mine

Address: Snaza'ist Discovery Centre, 5800 Highway 3, www.mascotmine.com
Tel: 250 292 8733
Opening Hrs: mid-May–Oct, see website for tour schedule
Entrance Fee: charge

Gold was first discovered in this area in 1904, and during its working life 2.5 million ounces of gold were extracted with an equivalent value of C$1.4 billion. In the early days, miners would make the 2½-hour trek up the mountain, work for 10 hours and then walk down again.

Today's visitors are taken on a 4½-tour of the mine: first, up a tortuous mountain road in the school bus to the top of the mine at 1,462 metres

(4,800ft). The next part involves a hike, followed by a flight of 589 steps down to the entrance of the mine. Take warm clothes as the temperature drops considerably inside the mine. Armed with a hard hat and torchlight, you can explore a small section of the 58km (36 miles) of tunnels and chambers. Restoration of the buildings began in the 1980s, and the remains of the 1,433-metre (4,700ft) -long cableway which carried the ore down for crushing and grinding can be seen.

Back at the Snaza'ist Discovery Centre, there are exhibits showing the mining history of the Similkameen First Nations, initially focused on mining ochre, which was traded with peoples on the coast and as far south as the Navaho.

KEREMEOS

Known as "the fruit stand capital of Canada", **Keremeos** ㉓ is a welcoming village in the fertile Similkameen Valley, one of the most productive fruit-, vegetable- and wine-growing areas in North America.

To the east of the town, beside Keremeos Creek, stands the old

TIP

Just west of Keremeos is the so-called Red Bridge. Built in 1911, it is one of Canada's few remaining covered bridges.

BELOW: the Mascot Gold Mine offers dizzying views over the Similkameen Valley from its 1,462-metre (4,800ft) perch.

ABOVE: pumpkins for sale, Keremeos.
ABOVE RIGHT: freshly harvested grapes.

In Penticton, at the southern end of Lake Okanagan, sits the largest remaining steel-hulled sternwheeler in Canada, SS *Sicamous* (tel: 250 492 0403; www.sssicamous.com). Built in 1914 for the Canadian Pacific Railway (CPR), she combined luxury and utility, carrying passengers, freight and mail on Okanagan Lake until 1936.

Grist Mill. The water-powered mill was built in 1877 to grind flour and is the last pioneer mill in the province that has kept its original operating machinery and building more or less intact. Restoration has included the reconstruction of an operating water-wheel and flume, and wheat planted behind the mill is ground on the premises.

OKANAGAN: PENTICTON AND SUMMERLAND

The Okanagan is the name given to the 240km (150-mile) -long slit in the hills that stretches from the US border at Osoyoos north through Penticton, Summerland and Kelowna to Sicamous. Thanks to water from upland lakes, the fertile area has become the fruit bowl of western Canada – from a single boxcar of apples in 1903, production exploded to 17,000 cars of fruit by 1950.

Like many agricultural areas, the region went through its ups and downs, with apple and stone fruit cultivation hitting hard times as less expensive fruits began to arrive in greater quantities at the same time as interest rates took their toll on small farming operations. The saving grace for the farmers was the shift to wine grapes in the 1990s, which also resulted in more tourism for the valley. *(For more on BC wines and a list of recommended vineyards see pages 240–1.)* There are several different wine routes that guarantee both a relaxing drive in the country and a variety of exceptional wines to taste. Over the past ten years, attention has been focused on the desert to the south of Penticton, where the temperature on the long summer days often exceeds 40°C (104°F), making the region capable of producing fine Syrah and Sangiovese, along with Bordeaux varietals.

Penticton straddles two lakes – small Skaha Lake at the southern end of town and the 135km (84-mile) -long Lake Okanagan at the northern end. It's a popular, amusement-filled family resort, where water sports and golf take centre stage.

On the western shore of Lake Okanagan lies the smaller, more restrained and attractive resort of **Summerland 24**. It has some lovely beaches and plenty of opportunities for outdoor activities.

Kettle Valley Steam Railway

Address: West of Penticton, off Prairie Valley Road, www.kettlevalleyrail.org
Tel: 250 494 8422
Opening Hrs: daily trips at 10.30am and 1.30pm, Sat–Mon mid-May–June, Sept–mid-Oct and Thur–Mon July–Aug
Entrance Fee: charge

This is one of the best-known attractions in the Okanagan Valley: the 10km (6-mile) stretch is the only working remnant of what was once one of the world's great railway journeys. The scenic journey takes 1 hour 45 minutes, from lush orchards and vineyards to a spectacular view of lake and land from the Trout Creek Trestle Bridge 73 metres (238ft) above the canyon floor. The train only runs twice a day a few days a week, so reservations are advisable. Much of the Kettle Valley Railway has been converted into a 600km (375-mile) **cycling trail**. Even steep railway gradients are easy on a bike, but it is nonetheless a challenging ride, with some trestles clinging to the sides of Myra Canyon.

Summerland Ornamental Gardens

Address: 4200 Highway 97, www.summerlandornamentalgardens.org

Tel: 250 494 6385
Opening Hrs: daily 8am–sunset
Entrance Fee: by donation

Just south of Summerland, the ornamental gardens trace their origins back to 1916 and the Agriculture Canada research station that had been established in the area just two years before. The provincial government had decided that some horticulture was needed to help smooth the rough edges of the new frontier towns – trees to line the streets, public parks and gardening information for new homeowners. The outdoor laboratory provided a garden demonstration area, with trees, shrubs and flowers, which developed into an English-style garden.

Today, this relaxing 6-hectare (15-acre) garden features tree-lined walkways, well-tended lawns, a rose garden and a xeriscape demonstration garden, designed to promote water-conserving landscaping, particularly in the desert climate of the Okanagan.

ABOVE: Summerland Ornamental Gardens.
LEFT: Kettle Valley Steam Railway.

The Okanagan was once home to camels brought in during the gold rush in the hope they would ease the chronic transport problems that beset the goldfields. The animals were still around in the early 20th century.

ABOVE: Merritt lumberyard. **RIGHT:** mural of country singer Tim McGraw, Merritt.

MERRITT AND THE NICOLA VALLEY

In 1991, the Okanagan Connector (97C) was completed, linking the west bank of Okanagan Lake with Highway 5 and the town of **Merritt** ㉕, bringing a lot more Vancouverites past Merritt, and occasionally into the town. The self-appointed country-music capital of Canada, performers such as Kenny Rogers, Johnny Cash and the Dixie Chicks have become the subject of murals decorating the facades of otherwise bland buildings.

Merritt used to have five coal mines, but the last closed in 1946, giving way to copper mining. **Highland Valley Copper** (tours Mon–Fri; tel: 250 523 3307) offers 2½-hour mine tours around one of the world's largest mining operations. (Children under 12 are excluded on safety grounds.) It's worth calling in for a drink at the restored bar of the 1908 Coldwater Hotel (corner of Quilchena Avenue and Voght Street), with its distinctive four-storey tower and copper dome.

The oldest house in Merritt has been restored and furnished to portray life in the early 20th century. Known as the **Baillie Property** (tel: 250 370 0349; www.bailliehouse.com; irregular opening times), it was built by one Cosom Bigney, who sent to England for a mail-order bride, but on the ship over she met and married someone else, and the disappointed Bigney remained a bachelor. Teas are held on the lawn in the summer months.

The **Nicola Valley Museum** (2202 Jackson Avenue; Mon–Fri 10am–3pm, extended hours in summer; tel: 250 378 4145) traces the development of the Nicola Valley, with displays on mining, ranching, logging, transport, war, religion and medicine, focusing on the terrible 1918 Spanish influenza epidemic.

The Nicola Valley

One of the loveliest areas near Merritt is the **Nicola Valley** ㉖, reached by Highway 5A, a beautiful road that snakes along Nicola Lake. Halfway along Nicola Lake is the historic **Quilchena Hotel**, a destination in its own right. Built by Joseph Guichon in 1908 in expectation of a railway that never materialised, the hotel is today run by Guy Rose, the grandson of the founder, and his German

Canada's First Great Train Robbery

At 10pm on an extremely rainy Saturday night, 10 September 1904, at Ruskin, just west of Mission, a Canadian Pacific Railway train was held up by the notorious Bill Miner gang. They had climbed onto the tender of the locomotive during the stop at Mission City and crawled over the coal to hold up the driver and fireman. They unhooked the train, robbed the safe of a shipment of gold dust valued at C$6,000 along with C$914 in cash, and proceeded on the locomotive 5km (3 miles) further west to Whonnock, where they jumped off, ran down the bank to a hidden boat and rowed across the Fraser River, making good their escape.

A week after another train robbery at Kamloops in May 1906, the gang was surrounded near Douglas Lake in the Nicola Valley, about 48km (30 miles) south of Kamloops, by a patrol of Mounties. Miner was given life imprisonment but escaped from New Westminster penitentiary after serving one year of his sentence. Rearrested in Georgia following the hold-up of a Southern Railway train in 1911, he again escaped from prison but was recaptured and died in Milledgeville State Prison, Georgia, in 1913 at the age of 70.

wife, Hilde. The three-storey timber building is sheltered by trees and has a traditional general store nearby. (*See also page 257.*)

It is a delightful drive through the meandering valley of the Nicola River to **Spences Bridge ㉗**, where the road meets the Trans-Canada Highway. Along this valley run both the Canadian Pacific and the Canadian National railways, the lines paralleling one another through the Thompson river canyon between Spences Bridge and Lytton, where the Thompson and Fraser rivers converge. It is easy to see why the young New York-born engineer Andrew Onderdonk received so much acclaim for driving the railway through such a narrow and steep-sided defile.

The 40km (25-mile) canyon is also popular for river-rafting expeditions (*see page 264*), though Simon Fraser saw nothing appealing in this stretch of river, describing it as "the gates of hell – a land where no human being should venture".

The **Yale Airtram** (tel: 604 869 8466; www.hellsgateairtram.com) is a Swiss-made 153-metre (502ft) cable

car linking the upper Cascade Mountains station with the lower station in the Coastal Range. From the cable car you can see the salmon run designed in 1913 to help the fish in their battle upriver to spawn, following a rock slide that obstructed the channel. At the lower station is a restaurant and exhibition about the life cycle of salmon in one of the world's foremost salmon rivers.

From the Alexandra Bridge pull-over, you can walk down to the old wooden bridge across the turbulent water. The original was completed in 1863 and named after Alexandra, Princess of Wales. The current bridge, dating from 1926, was built using the original abutments.

YALE

Walking among the few embowered houses of **Yale ㉘**, it is hard to credit that this was once the largest town west of Chicago and north of San Francisco; its tranquil streets belie its former reputation as "the busiest and the worst town in the colony". But during the gold rush of 1858 it was a feverish interchange point between

ABOVE: banner in Merritt, the country-music capital of Canada. **BELOW:** Quilchena ranch.

TIP

The Harrison Hot Springs Resort and Spa has extremely popular weekend dinner dances, making it one of the few places in western BC where ballroom dancers can trip the light fantastic, so booking is strongly advisable at weekends.

the sternwheelers coming up the Fraser River from the coast, and the pack trains of the Cariboo Wagon Road to the north. The road through the Fraser River canyon was largely wiped out by the construction of the main line of the CPR, which goes along Yale's main street, and there is a memorial to the 6,000 Chinese who helped build the railway in the grounds of the museum. Yale was the centre of operations for CPR's railway engineer, Andrew Onderdonk (*see page 235*), who set up his machine shops here.

The wood-panelled rooms of the **Yale Museum** (3179 Douglas Street; tel: 604 863 2324; www.historic yale.ca) have displays on the town's turbulent history – the gold rush, construction of the CPR and the Chinese community.

Just upriver from Yale and approached by a minor road beside the railway sits **Lady Franklin's Rock**, named after the wife of the Arctic explorer Sir John Franklin, who stopped in Yale in 1861 on his world tour. It was thanks to this enormous lump of rock that Yale flour-

ished during the gold rush years, since it prevented sternwheelers going further upstream.

HARRISON HOT SPRINGS

Taking Highway 7 south from Hope, the short Highway 9 terminates at the major resort of **Harrison Hot Springs** ㉙. Despite being only 15 metres (50ft) above sea level, the town has an almost Alpine setting, with mountains flanking the waters. Harrison offers fishing, boating, cycling, walking and camping on and around its 64km (40-mile) lake. Waves can reach 1–1.5 metres (3–5ft), so care is needed if kayaking.

The area was first settled in the 1850s, after three miners returning from the Cariboo goldfields by canoe stumbled upon the hot springs. In 1873 Joseph Armstrong built a health spa here, but his 1886 bathhouse was destroyed by fire in 1905 and never rebuilt. Its remains are close to the vast **Harrison Hot Springs Resort and Spa** (*see page 257*) in a lovely position overlooking the lake.

KILBY HISTORIC SITE ㉚

Address: 215 Kilby Road, Harrison Mills, www.kilby.ca
Tel: 604 796 9576
Opening Hrs: Apr–mid-May and early Sept–mid-Oct Thur–Mon 11am–4pm, mid-May–early Sept daily 11am–5pm
Entrance Fee: charge

Conveniently located just off Highway 7, the Kilby Historic Site is one of the most attractive of BC's many rural museums. Englishman Thomas Kilby was born in 1868 and emigrated to Canada when he was 16, building the store in 1904.

Its construction is distinctive, with walkways on stilts so that you could visit neighbours without getting your feet wet when the nearby confluence of the Harrison and Fraser rivers caused flooding. The general store was in use until the mid-1970s, when

BELOW: Yale Museum.

the premises became a museum with the Kilbys staying on as the first curators. It is portrayed as it would have appeared in the 1920s, with every shelf crammed with goods and samples hanging from the ceiling: plumbing and electrical fittings, tools, clothes, china, toys, batteries, food and even a lending library as well as a post office.

Outside on the farm are cows, pigs, chickens, turkeys, rabbits, goats and sheep. The museum restaurant serves delicious "gently grown" food from local family farms.

At nearby **Kilby Provincial Park**, on the shores of the Fraser River, is a lovely sheltered beach, popular with water-skiers and anglers (but too cold for all but hardened swimmers).

Around Mission

The region between Chilliwack and Agassiz is corn-growing country, and stalls of fresh cobs dot the main roads from early July into autumn. North of Highway 7 near Mission, the **Stave Falls Power House** ❸ (tel: 604 462 1222; www.bchydro.com/stavefalls; mid-Mar–Oct daily 10am–5pm) is another

National Historic Site worth visiting. You can see the massive turbines and generators of the hydroelectric dam built in 1912. There are plenty of hands-on exhibits and interactive displays for children to learn how electricity is generated.

Xá:ytem ❸

Address: 4200 Highway 97, www.xaytem.ca
Tel: 604 820 9725
Opening Hrs: Mon–Sat 9am–4.30pm
Entrance Fee: charge

Off the Lougheed Highway (Route 7), 3km (2 miles) east of Mission, is the site of a large 9,000-year-old village, the oldest known dwelling site in BC, once inhabited by ancestors of today's Stó:lo people. Xá:ytem (pronounced "HAY-tum") covers the remains of this village. The focus is a huge rock considered to have great spiritual power. The Longhouse Museum tells the story behind the thousands of artefacts found here and the people who used them, with an introduction to Salish weaving, cedar bark processing and the properties of plants. ❑

TIP

Highway 7, also known as the Lougheed Highway, follows the northern bank of the Fraser River all the way back to Vancouver from Hope, via Kent, Mission, Maple Ridge and Coquitlam. It's a more scenic alternative to the four-lane Highway 1, which follows the Fraser River on its south bank.

LEFT TOP AND BOTTOM: Kilby Historic Site pig, museum and shop.

BEST RESTAURANTS

Fort Langley

Fort Pub and Grill
Fort Langley Riverside Centre, 9273 Glover Road. www.
fortpub.com Tel: 604 888
6166. Open: L & D. **$**
Overlooking the Fraser
tributary, serves pub fare.

**Wendel's Café and
Bookshop**
103-9233 Glover Rd. Tel:
604 513 2238. www.wendels
online.com Open: B, L & D. **$**
An independent book-
seller that sits together
with a café, serving
breakfast, lunch and din-
ner, all affordable and
inventive.

Harrison Hot Springs

Copper Room
Harrison Hot Springs Resort.
Tel: 800 663 2266. www.
harrisonresort.com Open: daily
D only. **$$$**
For a trip into a bygone
era, you could do no bet-
ter than an evening at the
Copper Room, the ele-
gant restaurant at this
historic resort. The food is
West Coast contemporary
– and the setting is amaz-
ing. But best of all is the
fabulous dancing and the
live orchestra playing

danceable tunes. People
come from all over the
Pacific Northwest to
dance here – strictly ball-
room – but all of them
amateur enthusiasts who
know that this is a partic-
ularly fine venue to strut
their stuff. Fun to partici-
pate but seriously fun to
watch as well. Dress code
applies.

**Harrison River
Restaurant**
Kilby Historic Site, 215 Kilby
Rd., Harrison Mills. Tel: 604
796 9576. www.kilby.ca
Open: daily L only. **$**
An impressive little café/
restaurant attached to
the museum, done in a
1920s style, featuring
home-style cooking, with
ingredients sourced from
local farms and produc-
ers. Everything is good,
from the simple sand-
wiches and quiches to
the beef stew, all of it
made on the day. Even
the lemonade is freshly
made and served in an
icy jug. Lovely pies and
pastries for afternoon tea,
and friendly service. So
good it is worth a detour
to have lunch there.

Hedley

**The Hitching Post
Restaurant**
916 Scott Ave. Tel: 250 292
8413. Open: B, L & D Wed–
Sun. **$**
Do not leave Hedley
without visiting The
Hitching Post for at least
a coffee and a pastry.
You might feel inclined
towards the brunch
menu – French toast,
eggs Benedict, steak
and eggs, and a good
selection of pasta dish-
es, steaks and seafood,
provide a reasonable
choice for lunch and
dinner. Make sure you
take a look at the works
by local artists on the
walls.

Hope

**Blue Moose Deli and
Coffee Bar**
322 Wallace St. Tel: 604
869 0729. www.bluemoose
cafe.com Open: B, L & D
daily. **$**
Unless you are craving
fast food, this is without
question the best place
to stop in Hope. A great
place for a quick lunch
with terrific coffee and
brilliant sandwiches
and soups.

**Skinny's Grille and
Blues Bar**
63810 Flood Hope Rd.
Tel: 604 869 5713. www.
skinnysgrille.com Open: L &
D daily. **$**
Ribs, steaks and pastas,
along with live music on
Saturday nights.

Manning Park

Pinewoods Dining Room
Manning Park Resort, 7500
Highway 3. Tel: 250 840
8822. www.manningpark.com
Open: B, L & D daily. **$$**
Busy both summer and
winter, this resort is the
only business within the
park. The restaurant
offers a range of food to
satisfy its family-oriented
clientele, including
steaks, burgers, mussels
and salmon, along with
pizzas and sandwiches.
There is also a pub with
the standard pub fare.
You may be lucky enough
to see tiny hummingbirds
visit the feeders outside –
a real treat!

Merritt and the
Nicola Valley

Coldwater Hotel
1901 Voght St., Merritt. Tel:
250 378 5711. www.cold
waterhotel.com Open: B, L &
D daily. **$**
Don't bother about the
food in here, simply order
a beer at the bar and
soak up the atmosphere.
Built in 1908, the build-
ing looks like something
out of a Western movie –
you can imagine dusty
cowboys rolling into the
bar to quench their thirst
and raise a little hell.

**Quilchena Hotel
and Resort**
Highway 5A (20km/12 miles
north of Merritt). Tel: 250
378 2611. www.quilchena.
com Open: mid-Apr–Oct
L & D daily. **$$**

The building remains largely unchanged since its 1908 opening and is surrounded by rolling hills and endless sky. The European-inspired food is prepared by a Swiss chef who uses the best local ingredients to the greatest effect. The beef is superb, as one would expect, given that the Rose family who own this gem also run the large cattle ranch on which the property is situated. To finish, try the pannacotta with Saskatoon berries, a real treat for those who have never tried this western Canadian berry.

Okanagan: Penticton and Summerland

Penticton actually has over 100 restaurants, although many fall into the category of fast-food, pizza-burger-chicken-type places. Here are six that are worth checking out:

Bogner's of Penticton

302 Eckhardt Avenue West, Penticton. Tel: 250 493 2711. www.bogners.ca Open: D Tue–Sun. **$$**
Set in a heritage house with open fires and wooden beams, this restaurant was completely renovated in 2009. In summer, vegetables are sourced from the restau-

Prices for a three-course dinner per person with a half-bottle of house wine:
$ = under C$30
$$ = C$30–50
$$$ = C$50–80
$$$$ = over C$80

rant's own garden up on the Naramata bench, where a number of the fine wines on its list also originate. The European menu has been updated to include interesting variations on the classic themes: while there are the usual beef stroganoff and chicken cacciatore entrées, for the more adventurous, there are dishes like ginger miso Arctic char with apple and fennel.

Cellar Door Bistro

17403 Highway 97, Summerland. Tel: 250 494 0451. www.sumacridge.com Open: L & D, Apr–Oct daily, Nov–Dec, Mar Tue–Sat. **$$**
The eating arm of Sumac Ridge Winery, this bistro pairs many of its dishes with the wines produced here, so it's a good way to sample some of their wines before buying. Needless to say, the produce is locally sourced and the cooking accomplished. The estate-made pâté sampler is terrific.

The Patio at Lake Breeze

930 Sammet Rd., Naramata. Tel: 250 496 5619. www.lakebreeze.ca Open: L daily, May–mid-Oct. **$$**
This is one of the nicest wineries in the area to stop and enjoy a meal and the view. There is no pretension here, just a well-crafted menu, good food, a superb range of both red and white wines and genuine hospitality.

LEFT: Blue Moose Deli and Coffee Bar. **RIGHT:** Quilchena Hotel and Resort.

Theo's Restaurant

687 Main St., Penticton. Tel: 250 492 4019. www.eatsquid.com Open: L & D Mon–Sat, D only Sun. **$$**
Sit in Theo's courtyard on a hot summer's day and you would swear you were in Greece… and the food is authentic Greek with several New World additions. The roasted beet salad is delightful, while the squid is a signature dish of the restaurant. For mains, the lamb shoulder is succulent and generous in size, while the moussaka has been a favourite to locals for more than 30 years. The wine list has everything you could ask for: a superb selection of local and international wines at fair prices.

Villa Rosa

795 Westminster Avenue West, Penticton. Tel: 250 490 9595. www.thevillarosa.com Open: L Mon–Fri, D daily. **$$**
A good restaurant with many Italian staples – pastas, risottos, veal – Villa Rosa is also a pretty place to eat, especially in the summer. It makes a virtue of the local wineries and teams up with a number to host autumn wine-festival dinners, pairing the wines of a particular winery with a multi-course dinner.

Zias Stonehouse Restaurant

14015 Rosedale Ave., Summerland. Tel: 250 494 1105. www.ziasstonehouse.com Open: L & D daily. **$$**
Italian-inspired but with a few Pan-Asian touches, this quirky restaurant also boasts an enviable wine cellar – 75 different local wines are on offer, as well as a good selection of European and New World wines.

Wines of British Columbia

It may come as a surprise to learn that BC produces wine at all, let alone world-class wine. Yet it does, with each vintage bringing more international recognition.

Compared to other areas like California, Washington, even Ontario in eastern Canada, production is small, and the vast majority of the province's wine is enthusiastically consumed at home. But BC wines – especially those of the Okanagan Valley – are receiving accolades in the most distinguished circles. A breakthrough came in 1994 when a Chardonnay from the Okanagan Valley's Mission Hill Estate Winery captured the Avery's Trophy for Best Chardonnay at the UK's prestigious International Wine and Spirit Competition.

The real turning point for BC wines took place earlier still. It was prompted by the 1988 Free Trade Agreement, stripping away the protected status enjoyed by Canada's largely moribund wine industry. By 1990, barely 560 hectares (1,400 acres) of vines were left in BC after the government paid to have two-thirds of them pulled out. The BC wine industry has reinvented itself over the past 20 years by taking simple steps: planting the right clones of the right premium varietals on the right plots of land; attracting talented wine makers and giving them the resources to build state-of-the-art facilities; and establishing a structure to allow small estate wineries to flourish. The Vintners Quality Alliance (VQA) appellation system was established in 1990 to ensure origin and quality of BC-produced wines. This "branding" of BC wine made it easy for consumers to choose wines with varietal character.

Ninety-five percent of BC's wine is produced in the Okanagan Valley, a region of distinct microclimates and diverse soil types, stretching over 160km (100 miles) from north of Lake Okanagan to the US border. Nestled between mountain and lakes, the region now has more than 2,000 hectares (5,000 acres) dedicated to grape growing, and is undergoing rapid expansion. There are now over 80 wineries in the Okanagan Valley compared to 14 before Free Trade, and more than 140 in BC, with at least another 20 in the planning stages. They range from exclusive boutique wineries to large-scale operations, with varietals from Merlot and Chardonnay to Syrah, Sangiovese and even Malbec.

How can a region so far north produce such great wines? Start with near-desert conditions, more so in the south. Add hot, dry summers with long hours of sunlight, and lengthy hang time in the autumn. Of course, the moderating influence of the lake and the protection of the mountains help. Pick a suitable location, a cliff or a hillside, irrigate sufficiently, and healthy grapes are certain.

Okanagan Valley vineyards

From the hot, arid south to the wetter, cooler north, the Okanagan Valley is home to many excellent vineyards, including:

Osoyoos: Nk'Mip Cellars, North America's first aboriginal winery, produces superlative Merlot, Chardonnay and Icewine.

Oliver: In this area, reds and whites are

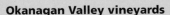

LEFT: Blasted Church wine shop.
RIGHT: vineyard in Summerland.

produced with bright, intense fruit flavours. Much-awarded Tinhorn Creek Winery offers outstanding Merlot. Inniskillin Okanagan Vineyards is a small-scale winery which produces big reds (Cabernet Sauvignon and "Meritage", a Bordeaux blend). Road 13 makes consistently excellent wines, from Viognier to Syrah, along with the traditional varietals. At Burrowing Owl Estate Winery, succulent fruit is the hallmark of their Syrah, Merlot and Chardonnay.

Okanagan Falls: Blue Mountain Vineyard and Cellars is an impeccable producer of Pinot Noir and sparkling wine. A bit further north, Blasted Church has fanciful labels, but those in the know choose the wines for their consistent quality.

Naramata Bench: Wineries dot winding roads and picturesque rural countryside, each with an impressive offering, from Lake Breeze and its stunning Pinot Gris and Pinot Blanc to Nichol Vineyard with its shockingly good Syrah. Other must-taste wines come from Poplar Grove and Kettle Valley.

Summerland: Sumac Ridge, one of the original 14 wineries, offers superb wines as well as great food on a picture-perfect patio. A bit further south, Thornhaven produces fine Pinot Noir.

Westside: Two must-see wineries are on the slopes of Mount Boucherie. Mission Hill's grand mission-style winery with a 12-storey bell tower sits dramatically above Lake Okanagan. Quails' Gate, a highly regarded medium-sized winery surrounded by sweeping vineyards, features the elegant Old Vines Patio and Restaurant.

Kelowna: The first vines in BC were planted in Kelowna by Father Pandosy, who established a mission in 1859. BC's oldest continuously operating winery, Calona Vineyards, produces premium wines under the "Sandhill Vineyard" label. One of Okanagan's most acclaimed wineries, Cedar Creek offers brilliantly crafted wines. A champion of organic grape growing, Summerhill Pyramid Winery practises what it preaches both in the winery and at the Summerhill Sunset Bistro with innovative organic cuisine.

North Okanagan: Gray Monk produces great-value wines, including Ehrenfelser and Gewürztraminer.

Similkameen Valley: West of the Okanagan Valley, this narrow stretch of lowland, lined with tall mountains, is home to newer wineries, including Crowsnest Vineyards, with its intensely fresh, fruity whites and good reds.

Vancouver: Next door to the bustling West Coast city, the fertile, flat Fraser valley is where Township 7 began, making great Chardonnay (and other wines) from Okanagan grapes — it's a lovely drive out to visit this compact winery.

The Gulf Islands: Peppering the Strait of Georgia, these pastoral islands are an exciting new region for viticulture. At Garry Oaks Vineyard on Salt Spring Island, estate-grown Pinot Gris and Pinot Noir are highlights.

Vancouver Island: Close to Duncan in the Cowichan Valley, Venturi-Shulze is one of BC's most celebrated boutique wineries; it also produces a superb balsamic vinegar.

Wine festivals take place in BC throughout the year, one of the most famous being the **Okanagan Fall Wine Festival**, which takes place all through the Valley in early autumn. For more information on Canadian viticulture and wine tours in BC, visit: www. winebc.com; www.winesofcanada.com; www.johnschreiner.blogspot.com and www.owfs.com. ❏

INSIGHT GUIDES TRAVEL TIPS
VANCOUVER

TRANSPORT

GETTING THERE AND GETTING AROUND

GETTING THERE

From outside North America, most people arrive in Vancouver by air, although visitors from Europe may also fly to Toronto or Calgary and take the train across Canada or just through the Rockies, which is an experience in itself.

By Air

Vancouver International Airport (tel: 604 207 7077; www.yvr.ca) is extremely well served by all the main international carriers, as it is the gateway from the East, as well as the largest city in western Canada. Flying time from London is 9 hours, New York 5 hours 15 minutes, Sydney 18 hours via San Francisco or Los Angeles, and Cape Town 21 hours via London.

Some UK specialist tour operators offer extremely competitive prices on flights and package holidays. Canadian Affair, the UK's largest tour operator to Canada, has a range of fares often lower than those offered by the national carriers, with flights from London Gatwick, Manchester and Glasgow through its own airline, Air Transat.

Internal Flights

Air Canada and WestJet both offer flights between Vancouver and Edmonton, Calgary, Winnipeg, Montreal and Toronto. They often compete directly on price, so a bit of comparison shopping can save a lot of money on internal flights.

A second airport, Abbotsford International Airport (www.abbotsfordairport.ca), located 70km (44 miles) from Vancouver, is ideal for people staying in the suburbs east of Vancouver who are travelling domestically.

Though it is a pity to miss the lovely ferry journeys between Tsawwassen and Vancouver Island or the Gulf Islands, Harbour Air and West Coast Air run regular floatplane services from Vancouver Seaplane Terminal on Coal Harbour to Victoria and Nanaimo, as well as from the south terminal of the Vancouver airport, with the planes leaving from an arm of the Fraser River. Service extends to many communities along the coast. The view over the islands on a sunny day is breathtaking and the convenience of arriving in the centre of Victoria has distinct advantages for people with only a short time to visit.

AIRLINES AND TOUR OPERATORS

Air Canada, tel: 1 888 247 2262; www.aircanada.com
Air New Zealand, tel: 1 800 663 5494; www.airnewzealand.ca
Air Transat, tel: 1 866 847 1112; www.airtransat.com
Alaska Airline, tel: 1 800 252 7522; www.alaskaair.com
American Airlines, tel: 1 800 433 7300; www.aa.com
British Airways, tel: 1 800 247 9297; www.britishairways.com
Cathay Pacific, tel: 1 800 268 6868; www.cathaypacific.com
Central Mountain Air, tel: 1 888 865 8585; www.flycma.com
Harbour Air Seaplanes, tel: 1 800 665 0212; www.harbourair.ca
KLM, tel: 1 800 221 1212; www.klm.com
Lufthansa, tel: 1 800 563 5954; www.lufthansa.com
Pacific Coastal Airlines, tel: 1 800 663 2872; www.pacificcoastal.com
United Airlines, tel: 1 800 538 2929; www.united.com
West Coast Air, tel: 1 800 347 2222; www.westcoastair.com
WestJet, tel: 1 888 937 8538; www.westjet.com

In addition, **Helijet** (tel: 1 800 665 4354; www.helijet.com) offers a scheduled helicopter service between the Vancouver and Victoria harbours. It's only 35 minutes and runs at least every hour during the day.

By Train

For those with both the time and the budget, a lovely way to reach Vancouver is by train from Toronto (with the added bonus of reducing your carbon footprint by minimising air travel). Operated by Via Rail (www.viarail.ca), *The Canadian* takes four days to cross the continent, leaving Toronto on Tuesday, Thursday and Saturday and returning from Vancouver on Friday, Sunday and Tuesday. It has two classes of sleeping accommodation, dining, dome and observation cars, and some of the station stops are long enough to allow a leisurely walk along the platform while the train is restocked and the windows cleaned. The train even slows past scenic attractions such as waterfalls. *The Canadian* arrives at Pacific Central station, a fine building but not in a part of the city that could be described as fashionable. Main Street Science World SkyTrain station is a few minutes' walk and there are always taxis to meet trains. Overseas sales agents are listed on the Via Rail website. For visitors from the UK, contact 1st Class Holidays, tel: 0844 499 0771, www.1stclassholidays.com; Australia, contact Asia Pacific Travel, tel: 612 9319 6624, www.aptms.com.au.

If you are travelling from the US, the railway between Seattle and Vancouver is a particularly scenic way of arriving. The line runs for over 80km (50 miles) along Puget Sound, with cliffs above in places, crossing rivers by a series of swing- and drawbridges. The daily *American Cascades* train from Seattle is operated by **Amtrak** (tel: 1 800 872 7245 from North America only; www.amtrak.com). Bookings can be made online.

By Coach

The south side of Pacific Central railway station at 200-1150 Station Street is the coach terminal for mainland and island services. Services from Seattle are operated by **Greyhound** (US; tel: 1 800 231

2222; www.greyhound.com), a different company from Greyhound Lines *(see page 246)*.

(see page 246)

GETTING AROUND

To and from the Airport

The most practical way to get into the city is by public transport *(see below)*, but there are also taxis, limousines, and, to get out of town directly from the airport, there are scheduled buses to Whistler, the Vancouver Island ferries, and south to Seattle. For all the options for getting to and from the airport, look at the Vancouver airport website, www.yvr.ca. The airport is 22km (14 miles) south of the city centre and, in addition to taxis, there are frequent buses and a direct link to the centre of Vancouver on the SkyTrain Canada Line, which takes 26 minutes.

By Train

The most popular trains out of Vancouver are the double-deck dome car trains run by **Rocky Mountaineer Vacations** (tel: 877 460 3200; UK tel: 00 800 0606 7372; or internationally, tel: 1 604 606 7245; www.rocky mountaineer.com), which operates over three principal routes with numerous permutations. The Yellowhead and Kicking Horse routes both entail a two-day journey from Vancouver with a night in a hotel in Kamloops in the Rockies; the former takes the Canadian National route to Jasper while the latter uses the more southerly Canadian Pacific line to Banff and Calgary in Alberta.

Introduced in 2006, the Fraser Discovery Route provides an end-on link with the daily **Whistler Mountaineer** (tel: 604 606 8460; www.whistlermountaineer.com) between North Vancouver and Whistler, for a two-day journey north through the Cariboo region to Prince George, overnighting in Quesnel. It then turns southeast

along North America's longest valley, the Rocky Mountain Trench, and past Mount Robson, the highest peak in the Canadian Rockies at 3,954 metres (12,972ft), to Jasper. All three routes offer different landscapes but a uniformly high standard of comfort and cuisine, with accommodation in GoldLeaf, offering dome cars and dining room below, or RedLeaf with picture windows and at-seat service. Rocky Mountaineer trains operate from April to mid-October, with some special trains over the Christmas period. The Fraser Discovery Route allows a circular tour through the best of the Rockies, taking in the Columbia Icefield between Jasper and Banff, returning to Vancouver via Kamloops.

From Monday to Friday during commuter hours the **West Coast Express** (tel: 604 488 8906; www.westcoastexpress.com) links downtown Waterfront station in Vancouver with Port Moody, Coquitlam Central, Port Coquitlam, Pitt Meadows, Maple Meadows, Port Haney and Mission.

Public Transport – TransLink

Public transport in Vancouver is the responsibility of **TransLink** (tel: 604 953 3333; www.translink. bc.ca), which also looks after the road network and facilities for cyclists. It operates SkyTrain, Sea-Bus and the buses, and tickets are integrated across modes and valid for 90 minutes. Vancouver and its suburbs are divided into three zones for the purposes of fares, and single tickets can be bought for one-, two- or three-zone travel. Maps are displayed at bus stops and on a free leaflet, "Getting Around", which gives advice on all TransLink services.

Buy tickets only from vending machines or on the bus, and beware of anyone not in uniform offering to help you buy a ticket. If you buy on the bus, you need to have the exact fare, as no

Above: hop on a seaplane to the Gulf Islands or Victoria.

Expo line which runs from Waterfront to King George (in the suburb of Surrey) in 39 minutes; the 19km (12-mile) Millennium line from Commercial Drive station to Columbia (in New Westminster), which takes 25 minutes; and the newest Canada Line from Waterfront to the airport and to Richmond, which takes 26 minutes. Another line is planned, but completion is not scheduled before 2014. SkyTrain frequently carries more than 100,000 people a day, and some of the stations have won design awards. The newer trains have a seat right at the front, where a driver would normally sit, for which kids (and not a few adults) make a beeline.

change is given. It is much easier and cheaper to buy books of ten tickets, or day passes covering all zones, from FareDealer outlets; these include shops like Safeway, 7-Eleven, Mac's, Shoppers Drug Mart, London Drugs, and some newsstands and convenience shops.

Note: There is a surcharge to these fares for using the airport stretch of the Canada Line.

The Translink website is a great way to plan your trip – you simply input where you are, where you want to go and the time and date of your planned trip. The website provides your best options, often offering three or four choices.

SeaBus

These double-ended catamarans seating 400 passengers ply the waters between Waterfront and Lonsdale Quay in North Vancouver, taking 12 minutes. Together, the two SeaBuses (tel: 604 953 3333; www.translink.bc.ca) transported almost 6 million people in 2009. This is less than 75 percent capacity, so the only time you might have to wait for the next SeaBus (15 minutes) would be in the middle of morning or evening rush hour. For most of the day on weekdays and Saturdays they operate every 15 minutes until between 6–7pm, when it

becomes every 30 minutes, as on Sundays. From Waterfront, the first service on Mon–Sat is 6.16am, on Sun 8.16am; the last on Mon–Sat is 12.46am, on Sun 11.16pm. From Lonsdale Quay, the first service on Mon–Sat is 6.02am, on Sun 8.02am; the last on Mon–Sat is 12.32am, on Sun 11.02pm.

False Creek Ferries

Two companies run small electric ferryboats which scuttle like water boatmen around a series of piers in False Creek and nearby English Bay, linking up various tourist attractions. They operate like buses, so no reservations are necessary. **AquaBus** (tel: 604 689 5858; www.theaquabus.com) has 12 ferries, and its Cyquabus accepts bicycles. **False Creek Ferries** (tel: 604 684 7781; www.granvilleislandferries.bc.ca) has 12 vessels serving nine ports, including Vanier Park for its three museums. Both ferries offer tours which give a great perspective on the city.

SkyTrain

SkyTrain (tel: 604 953 3333; www.translink.bc.ca) is the metro network which pioneered driverless technology. There are currently three SkyTrain lines: the 28km (18-mile)

Coaches

Greyhound Lines (tel: 604 683 8133 or 1 800 661 8747; www.greyhound.ca) operates services between Vancouver and many cities and towns across Canada. **Pacific Coach Lines** (tel: 604 662 7575; www.pacificcoach.com) operates scheduled services between Vancouver (downtown and airport) and Victoria – this is the most efficient way to get across the water if you don't have a vehicle. The **Whistler Express Bus** (tel: 604 717 6600; www.perimeterbus.com) runs six to twelve buses a day, depending on the season; some are an express service from the airport, others serve specified downtown hotels. As its name implies, **Island Link Shuttle Bus** (tel: 604 970 4990; www.islandlinkbus.com) links Vancouver with communities on Vancouver Island. To reach the west coast of Vancouver Island, the **Tofino Bus Company** (tel: 250 725 2871 or 1 866 986 3466; www.tofinobus.com) offers regular shuttles between Tofino and Ucluelet, Port Alberni, Nanaimo and Victoria. The number of buses per day varies by season, but as a rule, there is a single bus in winter, and two buses a day in summer, making the 7-hour trek from Victoria to Tofino.

Cycling

Both Vancouver and Victoria are great cities for exploring by bike, though the capital has more segregated bike routes than Vancouver, if you ignore the seawall. Vancouver is expanding the number of cycle routes and the new bike lane on the Burrard Street Bridge has made cycling much easier. Vancouver produces a free Bicycle Route Map (available at bike shops) showing bike paths and the streets recommended as cycle routes. Bikes are carried free of charge on SkyTrain, SeaBus and on buses that have a front-mounted rack capable of holding two bikes. Bikes are not allowed on SkyTrains until 9am, nor between 4–6pm. Helmets are mandatory in BC.

BELOW: Granville Island ferries.

BIKE RENTALS

Cambie Cycle, 3317 Cambie Street, tel: 604 874 3616; www.cambiecycles.com
J.V. Bikes Sales & Rentals, 929 Expo Boulevard, tel: 604 694 2453; www.jvbike.com
Reckless Bike Stores, 1810 Fir Street, tel: 604 731 2420; www.reckless.ca. The closest rental to Granville Market and the bike path around Vanier Park and Kitsilano. A second location, at 119 Davie Street, is ideal for cycling around False Creek from the Yaletown side or over towards Stanley Park. Other shops closer to Stanley Park include **Simon's Bike Shop**, 608 Robson Street, tel: 604 602 1181; www.simonsbikeshop.com,

By Car

Public transport outside the city is limited, so if you want to explore some of the remoter or smaller places in BC, many visitors have little choice but to hire a car. The principal car-hire companies are represented at Vancouver airport, but it's unwise to pick up without reserving a car. You can also frequently get better deals online. For example, **Budget** (tel: 0844 581 9999; www.budget.com) offers car hire from Vancouver International Airport with unlimited mileage when prepaid online. Some companies, such as **Discount Car Rental** (tel: 604 207 8180; www.discountcar.com), offer hybrid vehicles to reduce carbon emissions. Remember to return the

and **Spokes**, 1798 West Georgia Street, tel: 604 688 5141; www.vancouverbikerental.com.

Victoria

Bicycle Rentals, # 106 – 80 Regatta Landing, tel: 250 383 1466; www.switchbridgetours.com. This company also offers bike tours of Cowichan wineries, the Gulf Islands and the Galloping Goose Trail.
Reckless Bikes, 709 Yates Street, tel: 250 384 7433; www.reckless.ca
Cycle Treks, 450 Swift Street, tel: 250 386 2277; www.cycletreks.com. In addition to rentals, day or longer guided tours around Victoria are offered.

car with a full tank or face a hefty premium per litre; there is a petrol station on the airport approach road on the left-hand side.

Seat belts must be worn by drivers and passengers, and children under nine years old or less than 145cm (4ft 9ins) tall must use an approved safety seat. Speed signs are posted in kilometres per hour. You may turn right at a red light after making a full stop, unless signs indicate otherwise. Parking is, as you would expect for a city centre, expensive and at times hard to find. Expect to pay $10–25 per day for parking in a multistorey (parkade). Parking meters are in effect daily 8am–10pm. Many of the streets become no-parking zones during rush hour. Signposting in Canada leaves much to be desired, so care is needed. Tourist sights are usually indicated by a blue sign.

Ferries

BC Ferries (tel: 250 386 3431; www.bcferries.com) operates 36 vessels serving 47 ports of call along the spectacular BC coastline. Reservations can be made for ferries between the mainland and Vancouver Island, the Gulf Islands and Queen Charlotte Island and are strongly recommended (essential for some routes) in high season and at weekends to avoid the risk of long waits. Where reservations cannot be made, arrival at the ferry terminal at least 30 minutes before departure is advised during busy periods. The website provides constant updates concerning queues and projected waits.

Boat Rentals

Power and fishing boats can be hired to explore Burrard Inlet from **Coal Harbour and Lonsdale Boat Rentals** (tel: 604 682 6257; www.boatrent.ca), just east of the Westin Bayshore Hotel and in North Vancouver just west of Lonsdale Quay. Instruction is given for the boats' simple operation and a licence is issued by the company.

A CCOMMODATION

SOME THINGS TO CONSIDER
BEFORE YOU BOOK THE ROOM

Hotels

Vancouver and BC have hotels to suit all pockets, but inevitably there are relatively few hotels that derive their character from the building itself; the young age of so many buildings means that they rely on imaginative interior design to strike an individual note. The overwhelming majority of Vancouver hotels are in the downtown core and have a large number of rooms; there are few boutique- or loft-style hotels, but that is starting to change with the success and appeal of the Opus Hotel *(see page 252)*. Few establishments are quintessentially Canadian or even North American, having adopted the global hotel look.

It can get pretty hot in the summer, so if you are visiting during July or August, you'll want to ask about air conditioning. It is unusual to find a good hotel or B&B that allows smoking in more than a handful of rooms, if at all, and hefty room cleaning charges are often levied if you ignore the ban.

In terms of location, there is little point in staying in North Vancouver unless your focus is hiking the many North Shore trails. Traffic over the Lions Gate Bridge is chronically congested in the rush hours, but the SeaBus crossing is short and transports you quickly to and from downtown.

Timing and Booking

Winter weather in Vancouver is notoriously suited to ducks, so room rates in many hotels are substantially lower during these months, and there are creative packages designed to keep you an extra night or two without breaking your budget. With the unseasonably sunny warm February experienced during the 2010 Winter Olympics and broadcast all over the world, there may be more international visitors ready to come during the off-season. But it must be stressed that this was exceptional weather. From Easter onwards, tourism in the city builds to the busiest months of July and August when it would be unwise to arrive without a reservation. However, if you do, the Tourist Infocentre (tel: 604 683 2000; www.tourismvancouver.com) offers a free accommodation reservation service and online listings.

Cost and Quality

The listings given here are subdivided into the following categories, for a standard double room per night: Luxury: over C$250; Expensive: C$175–250; Moderate: C$100–175 and Budget: under C$100. These can only be an approximate guide because many hotels have half a dozen or more categories of room and very few hotels do not discount their room rates, according either to the time of year or the day of the week. Discounts are also sometimes offered for stays of three days or longer.

Bed and breakfasts are not necessarily a cheap option but they can obviously provide a much more individual experience and many are of a very high standard, with rooms on a par with four- and five-star hotels. The British Columbia Bed & Breakfast Innkeepers Guild (www.bcsbestbnbs.com) is a good place to research properties, not only in Vancouver, but in outlying areas as well. The Tourism Vancouver website also has a number of places on its accommodation listings.

If you're after cheap accommodation, bear in mind that the quality of some of the hostels is so high that they may be preferable to the cheaper hotel. There are good hostels offering accommodation for as little as $30 a night. The more expensive the hotel, the less likely you are to have breakfast included in the price.

One area that remains inconsistent is the provision of free wireless in the room – some hotels still think it is acceptable to charge $15 for use for a 24-hour period. Others offer it as a standard amenity. It's worth asking, if being online is important to you.

Tourist accommodation is subject to an 8 percent provincial hotel and motel room tax and a General Sales Tax (GST) of 6 percent. An additional 2 percent tourist tax may be levied where it has been approved. Campsites and houseboats are exempt.

A Place of Your Own

One of the largest collections of serviced suites is the **Landis** (tel: 604 681 3555; www.landissuitesvancouver.com), at 1200 Hornby Street, which has a range of two-bedroom suites with living room and kitchen in a modern tower. There is also a penthouse suite. Bathrooms and kitchens are top of the range, and there is a fitness centre, indoor swimming pool and Jacuzzi. With very similar style and facilities, the **Rosedale on Robson** (tel: 604 689 8033; www.rosedaleonrobson.com), at 838 Hamilton Street, is closer to Yaletown and BC Place – during the hockey season, it offers packages that include tickets to the Vancouver Canucks, often a hard ticket to find otherwise. At 1361 Robson Street, **Tropicana Suite Hotel** (tel: 604 687 6631; www.tropicana.ivancouver.com) has 74 more basic one-bedroom suites.

In Victoria there are some balconied waterside suites on the Gorge waterway, close to downtown, operated by **Comfort Inn and Suites** (tel: 250 388 7861; www.comfortinn victoria.com), which has a large outdoor heated pool. The **Royal Scot Suite Hotel** (tel: 250 388 5463; www.royalscot.com) has 176 rooms and suites close to the Inner Harbour at 425 Quebec Street; it has an exercise room, billiard room and indoor pool as well as restaurant.

Hostels

Hostelling International (www.hihostels.ca) maintains high standards in its Canada-wide hostels and has three in Vancouver, with private rooms and four-bed dorms, some in bunks and with

en suite facilities, TV and air conditioning. There's a backpackers' bar, kitchen, free internet access and coin-operated laundry; linen is provided, guests have a secure locker and there is bike storage and hire. The Downtown hostel is at 1114 Burnaby Street (tel: 604 684 4565); the Central is also very close to the heart of the city at 1025 Granville Street (tel: 604 685 5335); and for those wanting to be beach bums, there's one right by Jericho Beach at 1515 Discovery Street (tel: 604 224 3208). The air-conditioned **YWCA Hotel** (tel: 604 895 5830; www.ywcahotel.com) at 733 Beatty Street was built in 1995 and has a choice of room standards in this well-located, safe high-rise with indoor pool, gym, sauna and whirlpool. From early May to late August, UBC opens up student accommodation of various sizes and configurations (tel: 604 822 1000; www.conferences.ubc.ca). While it's away from the downtown core, the prices are great and the amenities of being on a university campus are terrific. It is safe, clean and quiet accommodation and confers access to the university's tennis courts, fitness facilities and indoor and outdoor pools. There are frequent buses, as well as several nearby beaches.

Avoid the district between Gastown and Chinatown; the cheap "hotels" there are largely inhabited by permanent "residents" – and they are not suited to tourists.

Following the 2010 Winter Olympics, a new HI hostel opened in the former Athletes' Village in Whistler. Located at 1035 Legacy Way, it has 180 beds. There is another HI Hostel in Whistler at 5678 Alta Lake Road (tel: 604 932 5492), which even has a sauna and kayak rentals.

On Vancouver Island, Hostelling International operates a converted heritage building close to the waterfront (516 Yates Street; tel: 250 385 4511). Further up the island is the **Nanaimo International Hostel** (65 Nicol Street; tel: 250 753 4432).

Campsites

There is a complete dearth of campsites in or near the city centre, and crashing out in one of the parks is not an option, as you would soon learn from the police. However, in BC there are some spectacularly sited campsites, many in the provincial parks, in which about 3 million people camp each year. They are at their busiest in July and August, when reservations are vital at the most popular. The best way to access the park list and their details is through the parks' website (www.bcparks.ca) which links to a booking system.

For non-provincial sites, www.camping.bc.ca provides a database, searchable by area and type, with opening dates and a rate guide with a link to the campsite wherever possible. Less user-friendly is www.hc-camping.com which devotes large amounts of space to extraneous information (and includes bed and breakfasts in some areas).

The Gulf Islands have some of the most scenic campsites, such as Ruckle Provincial Park on Salt Spring, but it and some others do not accept bookings, so it is advisable to get there early and have a Plan B if you find it full, particularly on the quieter islands where the last ferry of the day may leave little time for alternatives.

BELOW: the Pan Pacific Hotel offers spectacular uninterrupted views.

TRANSPORT

ACCOMMODATION

ACTIVITIES

A – Z

MIDTOWN AND WEST END

Luxury

The Fairmont Hotel Vancouver
900 West Georgia Street
Tel: 604 684 3131
www.fairmont.com
 p275, E1
This is the grande dame of Vancouver's hotels – the establishment of choice for royalty, politicians and celebrities. It's easy to see why. The spacious bedrooms have been restored to preserve the period charm of this delightful hotel while providing internet and all other mod cons. The hotel also enjoys a perfect central location beside the Art Gallery and cathedral, and it offers a spa, indoor swimming pool and fitness centre.

The Fairmont Waterfront
900 Canada Place
Tel: 604 691 1991
www.fairmont.com
❷ p276, A1
Very different in atmosphere from Hotel Vancouver, the modern Waterfront tower has 489 equally well-appointed rooms, most of which offer views across the Burrard Inlet to the North Shore. There is an open-air heated swimming pool and fitness centre. The restaurant and bar are popular with both locals and guests.

Four Seasons
791 West Georgia Street
Tel: 604 689 9333
www.fourseasons.com
❸ p275, E2

The waterfront tower contains 371 truly sumptuous rooms and all the amenities one would expect of a Four Seasons hotel. The indoor/outdoor pool in the centre of the city is an oasis after a long day exploring, even if it has only been a shopping excursion to Pacific Centre, to which the hotel is connected. The low season rates represent remarkably good value.

Loden
1177 Melville Street
Tel: 604 669 5060
www.theloden.com
❹ p275, E1
As one of Vancouver's newest boutique hotels, Loden has built in all the perks, including all the in-room amenities you could possibly want, a spa, a trendy lounge and restaurant, as well as a 24-hour gym. It's located in the business core, but close to the major downtown shopping and Stanley Park.

Pan Pacific
300-999 Canada Place
Tel: 604 662 8111
www.panpacific.com
❺ p276, B1
As the hotel with perhaps the best location in town, virtually all the 504 rooms have unbeatable views of Stanley Park, the harbour and the North Shore mountains. Rooms 10 and 20 on each floor have a panoramic view from their bathrooms. The "regular" rooms are both elegant and comfortable, while the suites are breathtaking. Staff

are as well trained as you would expect in a world-class hotel.

Wedgewood Hotel and Spa
845 Hornby Street
Tel: 604 689 7777
www.wedgewoodhotel.com
❻ p275, E2
Traditionally elegant public rooms are combined with superbly designed boutique bedrooms with fabulous bathrooms. Highlights are the luxurious spa and the Bacchus restaurant. Afternoon tea is served at weekends. This is one of Vancouver's finest hotels – and its only Relais et Châteaux hotel.

Expensive

Barclay House
1351 Barclay Street
Tel: 604 605 1351
www.barclayhouse.com
❼ p275, D1
In a leafy residential street, a short walk from Stanley Park and English Bay, this elegant yet cosy six-room B&B offers the warmest of welcomes and the most copious breakfast you're likely to experience in the city. Luxurious touches include flat-screen TVs, and freshly baked cookies brought to your room every day.

Hyatt Regency
655 Burrard Street
Tel: 604 683 1234
www.vancouver.hyatt.com
❽ p275, E1
Although it is an older Hyatt, with its recent

renovation to the 644 rooms, it now has the advantage of spacious and modern rooms, located in a prime spot in the centre of the downtown core.

Le Soleil
567 Hornby Street
Tel: 604 632 3000
www.hotellesoleil.com
❾ p275, E1
Biedermeier-styled luxury boutique hotel which prides itself on exceptional service; pets are allowed, something the hotel promotes. The Copper Chimney restaurant is also popular with non-residents.

Listel
1300 Robson Street
Tel: 604 684.8461
www.thelistelhotel.com
❿ p275, D1
Stylish hotel with attractive rooms decorated with West Coast original art close to the heart of Robson Street and the beach at English Bay. O'Doul's restaurant and bar serves great food and has become a mecca for jazz aficionados in the evening. This is a hotel that locals recommend to their friends.

Metropolitan
645 Howe Street
Tel: 604 687 1122
www.metropolitan.com

ABOVE: the ornate foyer of the Fairmont Hotel Vancouver.

⑪ p275, E1
One of Vancouver's best-appointed hotels, with an indoor pool, fitness centre and squash courts.

O Canada House
1114 Barclay Street
Tel: 604 688 0555
www.ocanadahouse.com
⑫ p275, D1/2
Centrally located in a quiet street, this attractive house was built in 1897 and has been lovingly restored, with all the modern conveniences in its seven luxuriously appointed suites.

Renaissance Vancouver Hotel Harbourside
1133 West Hastings Street
Tel: 604 689 9211
www.renaissancevancouver.com
⑬ p275, E1
This vast building overlooking Coal Harbour and the North Shore mountains has 434 rooms and suites, an indoor pool, whirlpool and sauna.

Sheraton Vancouver Wall Centre
1088 Burrard Street
Tel: 604 331 1000
www.sheratonvancouver.com
⑭ p275, D2
A smoked glass-walled

tower of oval plan, with various bars and restaurants as well as an indoor swimming pool, located right in the heart of downtown.

Sutton Place
845 Burrard Street
Tel: 604 682 5511
www.suttonplace.com
⑮ p275, E2
Huge U-shaped block of luxurious rooms and suites, as well as a section of apartments. Despite its size, the hotel has an intimate feel to it. The Gerard Lounge is a celebrity watering hole and the Fleuri restaurant has an extensive menu and good wine list.

Moderate

Barclay Hotel
1348 Robson Street
Tel: 604 688 8850
www.barclayhotel.com
⑯ p275, D1
A well-appointed, air-conditioned 90-bedroom hotel with an unusual mix of French-meets Laura Ashley style. It has a restaurant and licensed bar lounge.

Best Western Downtown Vancouver
718 Drake Street

Tel: 604 669 9888
www.bestwesterndowntown.com
⑰ p275, D3
The Best Western is in a quieter location than many of its fellow downtown hotels, with good views over False Creek on one side. It has a rooftop fitness centre, sauna and jacuzzi.

Empire Landmark
1400 Robson Street
Tel: 604 687 0511
www.empirelandmarkhotel.com
⑱ p275, D1
Well located and currently the tallest hotel in the West End, there are great views to be enjoyed from the balconies of the 357 rooms of this otherwise rather characterless tower. There is also an aptly named Cloud 9 circular revolving restaurant on the top floor.

Nelson House Bed and Breakfast
977 Broughton Street
Toll free: 1 866 684 9793
www.downtownbedandbreakfast. com
⑲ p275, D1
Vancouver's oldest gay and lesbian B&B is located in an Edwardian-character home located across the street from

the Victorian homes and gardens of historic Barclay Heritage Square.

Sylvia
1154 Gilford Street
Tel: 604 681 9321
www.sylviahotel.com
⑳ p274, C1
One of the city's landmark hotels, built as apartments in 1912, becoming a hotel in 1936. The ivy-covered brick and terracotta building has retained its character outside and in the common parts, while being updated to provide modern amenities. Its south-facing rooms have a lovely view over English Bay, and there is a cosy bar and restaurant with terrace. Constantly popular so plan ahead and reserve in order to avoid disappointment.

West End Guest House
1362 Haro Street
Tel: 604 681 2889
www.westendguesthouse.com
㉑ p275, D1
A Victorian atmosphere pervades this guesthouse set in a quiet residential area. Antiques abound in the seven luxurious rooms, and the walls are decorated with photos of the West Coast taken by the brothers who built the house back in 1906. Offers of sherry and iced tea are a nice touch. Free use of bikes and there are some great off-season rates to be had.

PRICE CATEGORIES

Guide prices for a standard double room in high season:
Luxury: over C$250
Expensive: C$175–250
Moderate: C$100–175
Budget: under C$100

Budget

Buchan Hotel
1906 Haro Street
Tel: 1 800 668 6654
www.buchanhotel.com
㉒ p272, C4
Not all of the 61 rooms in this 1926-built three-storey building have en suite facilities, but it is clean and in a quiet tree-lined part of the West End, nearer to Stanley Park than downtown. Rooms on the east side overlook a small park and are lighter.

Days Inn Vancouver Downtown
921 West Pender Street
Tel: 604 681 4335
www.daysinnvancouver.com
㉓ p275, E1
In a good location in the financial district with the quieter, harbour-view rooms on the north side. All 85 rooms are air-conditioned, and some have only an en suite shower. There is a restaurant and bar, with an Irish pub downstairs, and Art Deco flourishes distinguish it.

Sunset Inn and Suites
1111 Burnaby Street
Tel: 604 688 2474
www.sunsetinn.com
㉔ p275, D2
Exceptionally good-value suite hotel located on a quiet street close to the beach and Davie Street. Sofa beds in living rooms and fully equipped kitchens make this ideal for families. Breakfast is included, plus free internet and free parking.

GASTOWN, CHINATOWN AND YALETOWN

Luxury

Westin Grand
433 Robson Street
Tel: 604 602 1999
www.westingrandvancouver.com
㉕ p275, E2
The management at this centrally located boutique apartment hotel boasts about the superior quality of its beds and bathrooms, and that it "provides a suite for the price of a room". It has an outdoor pool and the Aria restaurant; make sure to check out the package deals.

Expensive

Moda
900 Seymour Street
Tel: 604 683 4251
www.modahotel.ca
㉖ p275, E2
The recently rebuilt 1908 Dufferin Hotel combines traditional style with contemporary design. Each of the 57 elegant rooms is provided with luxurious beds and linen, flat-screen TVs and high-speed internet access; Uva wine bar is right downstairs, as is Cibo Trattoria.

Opus Hotel
322 Davie Street
Tel: 604 642 6787
Toll Free: 1 866 642 6787
www.opushotel.com
㉗ p275, E3
Hailed as one of Vancouver's coolest hang-outs by *Wallpaper* magazine and voted one of the world's top 100 hotels by *Condé Nast Traveler*, the very gay-friendly Opus Hotel is the city's hippest boutique hotel. Situated in Yaletown, the hotel's bar and Elixir French bistro are popular with an international crowd and celebrities.

St Regis Hotel
602 Dunsmuir Street
Tel: 604 681 1135
www.stregishotel.com
㉘ p275, E2
One of the city's heritage hotels, St Regis was built in 1916 but sadly there's nothing very historic about the interior; it's been renovated and refurbished. The hotel offers a lot of amenities at no extra charge including breakfast, in-room high-speed wireless and wired internet, free local calls and faxes, and free use of an off-site fitness centre, making its rates more attractive than some of the newer properties.

Moderate

Kingston Hotel
757 Richard Street
Tel: 604 684 9024
www.kingstonhotelvancouver.com
㉙ p275, E2
Describing itself as "Vancouver's first and finest European-style bed and breakfast hotel", this place has a warm atmosphere and is well located for downtown. Only some of the 55 small rooms are en suite. There's a sauna (unusual in hotels in this price category), and continental breakfast is included.

Budget

Urban Hideaway
581 Richards Street
www.urban-hideaway.com
㉚ p276, B2

This rare downtown guesthouse was built in 1896 to accommodate travellers heading for the wilderness. It's still a popular backpackers' haunt, drawing a young clientele who enjoy the quirkiness and don't mind the communal facilities. Bikes are loaned free of charge and breakfast is also complimentary.

Victorian Hotel
514 Homer Street
Tel: 604 681 6369
www.victorian-hotel.com
㉛ p276, B2
This is unique downtown: an historic 1898 bay-windowed building constructed as a guesthouse, which has been sensitively restored to create a most attractive family-run hotel with hardwood floors, decorative mouldings and high ceilings. Not all the bedrooms have en suite bathrooms.

PRICE CATEGORIES

Guide prices for a standard double room in high season:
Luxury: over C$250
Expensive: C$175–250
Moderate: C$100–175
Budget: under C$100

GRANVILLE ISLAND AND WEST SIDE

Expensive

Granville Island
1253 Johnston Street
Tel: 604 683 7373
www.granvilleislandhotel.com
⏃ p275, D4
In a lovely, quiet position overlooking False Creek, the luxurious boutique hotel has its own garden and terrace beside the water. Rooms are furnished with reproduction

antique furniture, and oriental rugs in some rooms. There is a small spa and free high-speed internet. It even has its own microbrewery.

Moderate

Plaza 500 Hotel
500 West 12th Avenue
Tel: 604 873 1811
www.plaza500.com
Off map

Located outside the downtown core, but directly on the Canada Line, this 153-room hotel is convenient, affordable and comfortable.

Budget

Shaughnessy Village
1125 West 12th Avenue
Tel: 604 736 5511
www.shaughnessyvillage.com
Off map

Ideal for those on a tight budget; includes breakfast. Rooms are compact but serviceable and there is a gym and a pool table.

EASTERN SUBURBS

Expensive

Hilton Vancouver Metrotown
6083 McKay Avenue, Burnaby
Tel: 604 438 1200
www.hiltonvancouver.com
Shopaholics may wish to rest up in this 283-roomed luxurious hotel only steps away from BC's largest shopping centre, which is a 15-minute SkyTrain ride to downtown.
Inn at the Quay
900 Quayside Drive, New Westminster

Tel: 604 520 1776
www.innatthequay.com
Strikingly designed hotel standing on pillars over the quay and river. Free internet. Fitness centre, whirlpool and sauna.

Moderate

Best Western Coquitlam Inn
319 North Road, Coquitlam
Tel: 604 931 9011
www.bestwesterncoqinn.com
Close to the SkyTrain station, this 106-roomed hotel has two

restaurants, indoor pool, jacuzzi, sauna and an indoor tropical garden. Free high-speed internet. Good value.

Budget

The Met
411 Columbia Street, New Westminster
Tel: 604 520 3815
www.themethotel.com
Built in 1892 and one of only two buildings in the downtown core to survive the Great Fire of 1898, this 27-room hotel has been reno-

vated without losing all of its original charm. It's well priced, and, in addition to basic amenities, offers free internet. Some rooms have waterfront views. Close to SkyTrain. It's on a busy street, so make sure to ask for a quiet room.

RICHMOND AND THE FRASER DELTA

Moderate

Abercorn Inn
9260 Bridgeport Road, Richmond
Tel: 604 270 7576
www.abercorn-inn.com
Located close to the airport, this older hotel has been looked after, so not only are the rooms bigger, the construction is a bit stur-

dier too. Offers all the usual amenities and is particularly convenient for early morning departures from the airport with its free shuttle service.
The Coast Tsawwassen Inn
1665 56th Street, Delta
Tel: 604 943 8221
www.tsawwasseninn.com

Situated close to the ferry terminal this hotel, with 90 suites and large rooms, has a heated indoor pool, hot tub and sauna. There is also free parking and internet.
Days Inn Vancouver Airport
2840 Sexsmith Road, Richmond
Tel: 604 207 8000
www.daysinn.ca

This is another choice for early flights, with complimentary shuttle to airport and breakfast.

NORTH AND WEST VANCOUVER

Expensive

Lonsdale Quay Hotel
123 Carrie Cates Court
Tel: 604 986 6111
www.lonsdalequayhotel.com
The views over Burrard Inlet to downtown Vancouver are what sell this water-side, 70-room hotel, which is accessed by escalators from Lonsdale Market. Good-sized rooms.

Pinnacle Hotel at the Pier
138 Victory Ship Way
Tel: 604 986 7437
www.pinnacleatthepier.com
Opened in 2010, this hotel goes head-to-head not only with Lonsdale Quay Hotel, but also with the downtown properties – it's a 12-minute Sea-Bus ride to the centre of town, but a world away in terms of relaxation.

Moderate

Holiday Inn North Vancouver
700 Old Lillooet Road
Tel: 604 904 2725
www.hinorthvancouver.com
The name may not suggest much charm, but this hotel is perfectly located for people wanting to hike and mountain bike on the North Shore. It has easy access to the

highway, as well as the best hiking and biking in the area. The pub is a comfortable place for a beer and snacks.

VICTORIA AND VANCOUVER ISLAND

Luxury

The Fairmont Empress
721 Government Street, Victoria
Tel: 250 384 8111
www.fairmont.com
This iconic landmark occupies a prime spot overlooking the Inner Harbour and Parliament buildings. Its public rooms retain a colonial atmosphere and its 477 rooms (all of which are different) offer every comfort. The hotel has benefited from sensitive restoration and upgrades, allowing it to maintain the grace of its

era and the modern comforts. Indian cuisine is served in the atmospheric Bengal Lounge, and Sunday brunch at Kipling's has become popular, but it is afternoon tea in the vast "tea lobby" that has been an institution for decades. Today, however, the clientele is almost entirely tourist. The spa has 12 treatment rooms. There is also a heated indoor pool, whirlpool and gym.

Long Beach Lodge Resort
1441 Pacific Rim Highway, Tofino

BELOW: the grand Empress Hotel.

Tel: 250 725 2442
www.longbeachlodgeresort.com
In a great location overlooking the sea, the hotel offers rooms in the lodge or more private self-contained two-roomed rainforest cottages, all with double soaker baths and kitchen. Fireplaces are well used by those who come winter-storm watching and there is a magnificent great room that provides a panoramic view of the ocean.

Wickaninnish Inn
Osprey Lane, Tofino
Tel: 250 725 3100
www.wickinn.com
Consistently voted most romantic hotel, best resort, etc. this popular hotel overlooks Chestermann Beach, which is the only beach in the area with accommodation. Opened in 1996, it has 75 rooms and suites with soak tubs near the window. Guests come in winter for storm watching. The spa is located at the edge of the building, close to the crashing waves. It offers the Vancouver Island handhar-

vested certified organic seaweed products of SeaFlora and has been rated amongst the top spas in Canada. The restaurant espouses slow food. Closed first week of January (after the New Year's celebrations).

Expensive

Coast Bastion Inn
11 Bastion Street, Nanaimo
Tel: 250 753 6601
www.coasthotels.com
Bland tower overlooking the harbour (with every room having a water view), but if you need to stay in Nanaimo this is its best hotel; it's also conveniently close to the ferry terminal, as well as the Bastion and waterfront walkway. Facilities include gym, sauna, whirlpool and a spa.

Water's Edge Resort

1971 Harbour Drive, Ucluelet
Tel: 250 726 2672
www.aviawest.com
Almost surrounded by water, the blue colour-washed buildings house large attractive suites with fireplaces and kitchens. Some have hot tubs on balconies, with glorious views over the Ucluelet Inlet. Kayaks, bikes, surfboard and raingear are available at no cost.

Hospitality Inn

3835 Redford Street,
Port Alberni
Tel: 250 723 8111
www.hospitalityinnportalberni.com
The 50 air-conditioned rooms have high-speed internet, and there is an indoor pool, restaurant and pub.

The Inn at Tough City

350 Main Street, Tofino
Tel: 250 725 2021
www.toughcity.com
Quirky brick-built hotel overlooking the harbour with antiques and eclectic memorabilia, stained glass, fireplaces, hardwood floors, good seafood restaurant and waterfront patio.

Swans

506 Pandora Avenue, Victoria
Tel: 250 361 3310
www.swanshotel.com
Boutique hotel decorated with original paintings, sculptures and antiques and close to the Inner Harbour. The 29 suites, some with two-storey lofts and kitchens, are all unique. It has its own brew-pub and bistro, with live music every night.

Strathcona

919 Douglas Street, Victoria
Tel: 250 383 7137

www.strathconahotel.com
This characterful refurbished 1913 hotel has a Victorian-style pub, volleyball court and rooftop lounge as well as several bars and restaurants.

Travellers Inn Downtown

1850 Douglas Street, Victoria
Tel: 250 381 1000
www.travellersinn.com
This 78-roomed hotel has good-sized rooms, some with king-size beds and some with air conditioning; the accommodation is pretty basic, but the price is right. Free wireless internet.

GULF ISLANDS

Galiano Inn

134 Madrona Drive,
Galiano Island
Tel: 250 539 3388
www.galianoinn.com
The island's only waterfront inn (with a restaurant and spa) has been a special place to stay for a century, first as a home, and from the 1930s as a guesthouse. The gourmet restaurant "eat" uses local organic produce whenever possible, and the spa offers a unique "Blackberry Vinotherapy massage" using a blackberry port produced on the island.

Hastings House Country Estate

160 Upper Ganges Road,
Salt Spring Island
Tel: 250 537 2362
www.hastingshouse.com
In an idyllic position overlooking Ganges Harbour, this hotel is one of North America's finest and the kind of place you're really reluctant to

leave. There are 18 enchanting and individually designed suites spread across sensitively adapted buildings dotted around the 9-hectare (22-acre) grounds. The Manor House itself was built by a descendant of Warren Hastings (first governor general of British India). The Swiss chef produces outstanding cuisine using local produce, some grown in the hotel's kitchen garden. You can indulge yourself even further at the hotel's spa. Note: Closed 1 Nov–31 Mar.

April Point Resort and Spa

900 April Point Road,
Quathiaski Cove,
Quadra Island
Tel: 250 285 2222
www.aprilpoint.com
This sheltered waterfront hotel has stunning views of the ocean, an Aveda spa and a sushi bar as

well as a restaurant. The 56 rooms include a variety of cabins and suites. Whale-watching and salmon fishing expeditions can be arranged. The island is just a 10-minute crossing from Campbell River on Vancouver Island's northeast shore. Note: Closed off-season; check website for opening dates.

Poets Cove Resort and Spa

9801 Spalding Road,
South Pender Island
Tel: 250 629 2100
www.poetscove.com
Large seafront hotel with 46 rooms in the Arts and Crafts-styled lodge or in cottages and villas spread out on the property. The Aurora restaurant serves West Coast cuisine, and the Susurrus Spa (meaning "whispering sound") has six treatment rooms with steam cave and waterfall leading down to an ocean-side jacuzzi. The hotel offers a variety

of activities such as diving, kayaking and biking, as well as an outdoor pool. There are outstanding off-season midweek specials.

Salt Spring Vineyards

151 Lee Road,
Salt Spring Island
Tel: 250 653 9463
www.saltspringvineyards.com
Two attractive rooms

have been created at this quiet vineyard, with en suite bathrooms and kitchenettes. There is an open-air hot tub from which to enjoy the great view. Reasonably priced romantic getaway.

Tsa-Kwa-Luten Lodge
1 Lighthouse Road,
Quadra Island
Tel: 250 285 2042
www.capemudgeresort.com
Set in a forest, this lodge offers sea views from all 35 rooms. There are

also larger cottage units suitable for families. Seafood restaurant.

Budget

Firesign Art and Design Studio B&B

730 Smiths Road,
Quadra Island
Tel: 250 285 3390
www.firesignartanddesign.com
Small B&B (three rooms with kitchenette) close to beaches, hiking and kayaking. Pets welcome.

THE SUNSHINE COAST

Moderate

Lund Hotel
1436 Highway 101, Lund
Tel: 604 414 0474
www.lundhotel.com
This charming period seafront hotel lies at the very top of the Sunshine Coast, gateway to the famous Desolation Sound. Most of its 31 en suite rooms have ocean views and it has a restaurant, pub and balconies for enjoying the view. Diving, golf and biking and other activity

packages available.
Ruby Lake Resort
Madeira Park
Tel: 604 883 2269
www.rubylakeresort.com
This resort offers more than just a break from the city, it is next to a nature reserve set up by the resort owners, an Italian family who came to Canada and fell in love with the Sechelt Peninsula. The Italian influence extends to the welcoming atmosphere and, more importantly, to the dining room, which delivers

exceptional food. There's also a spa with a focus on therapeutic massage.
Salmonberry Lodge and Spa
1111 Grandview Road, Gibsons
Tel: 604 886 7375
www.salmonberrylodge.com
Unusual boutique B&B offering a range of spa treatments. It's an eight-minute walk to Secret Beach and hiking trails.

Budget

Around the Bend
5174 Sunshine Coast Highway,

British Columbia

Vancouver

Sechelt
Tel: 604 885 4071
www.aroundthebendbb.com
Both en suite rooms have great ocean views, and guests have the use of a huge circular lounge. The beach is just across the road.

WHISTLER AND SQUAMISH

Compared to the rest of British Columbia, Whistler is, well, outrageously expensive. But there are definitely deals to be found and the best thing to do is shop around for a package: many hotels offer a third night at 50 percent off, or add in credits towards food or adventure activities; and midweek rates can be significantly better than weekends. Shoulder seasons are much more affordable, so consider June or September if you can. If you ski, later in the season when the locals have moved on to summer sports can also be attractive – the snow

may be slushy, but the sunshine makes up for it.

Luxury

Fairmont Chateau Whistler
4599 Chateau Boulevard
Tel: 604 938 8000
www.fairmont.com/whistler
This massive 550-bedroomed resort in an architecturally impressive building includes a Vida spa, complimentary health club, its own mountain golf course and academy, three superb restaurants and all the luxury and amenities that one would expect from a Fairmont hotel.

Four Seasons Resort Whistler
4591 Blackcomb Way, Whistler
Tel: 604 935 3400
www.fourseasons.com/whistler
The 273-roomed hotel lies at the foot of Blackcomb Mountain. Its generous-sized rooms all have wood interiors, gas-burning fireplaces and all the usual mod cons and electronic facilities. Residence suites have well-equipped kitchens, fireplaces and a terrace.

Expensive

Adara Hotel Whistler
4122 Village Green
Tel: 604 905 4009
www.adarahotel.com

British Columbia

Whistler

Vancouver

This trendy boutique hotel has built luxury in to every detail of its 41 rooms. It has a hot tub with mountain views and a summer-only outdoor pool.
Pan Pacific Whistler Mountainside
4320 Sundial Crescent
Tel: 604 905 2999
www.panpacific.com
There are two Pan Pacific properties in Whistler

and both offer suites with full kitchens, sleeping two to six people. All the facilities are there – pool, spa, fitness centre. It's a nice place to settle into for a few days or a week.

Moderate

Cascade Lodge
4315 Northlands Boulevard
Tel: 604 905 4875
www.whistler-cascadelodge.com
This popular condo-hotel has a variety of comfortable units, from studios to two-bedroomed apartments. It has a large year-round outdoor heated pool, hot tub and the ski lifts are eight minutes' walk away.

Cedar Springs B&B Lodge
8106 Cedar Springs Road

Tel: 604 938 8007
www.whistlerbb.com
The eight rooms offer a high standard of comfort with varying permutations and prices.

Howe Sound Inn and Brewing Company
37801 Cleveland Avenue, Squamish
Tel: 604 892 2603
www.howesound.com
Staying in Squamish is a

much less expensive option than Whistler and it's only 45 minutes away. This 20-room inn has the added advantage of being located above an excellent brew pub, with better-than-average pub fare and lots of choices for beer – a perfect solution after a day on the slopes or hiking in the mountains.

AROUND THE OKANAGAN

Expensive

Harrison Hot Springs
Tel: 604 796 2244
www.harrisonresort.com
This is really *the* place to stay at this lakeside town built around tourism, not only for its unrivalled facilities but also the spectacular view over the water and surrounding mountains. The attractive spa offers a full range of treatments. There are five pools, some indoor, some outdoor, of varying temperatures and mineral content.

Moderate

La Punta Norte
365 Highway 97N,
Summerland
Tel: 250 494 4456
www.lapuntanorte.com
This extraordinary building resembles a hacienda and is situated on a headland with fabulous views overlooking Lake Okanagan and the rugged hills on the opposite shore. It's a bed and breakfast, with six large rooms, each with en suite bathrooms, private entrances, hot tubs on a balcony, air conditioning, internet and furniture

that complements the architecture. An additional large suite has a private deck and kitchen.

Manning Park Resort
7500 Highway 3,
Manning Provincial Park
Tel: 250 840 8822
www.manningpark.com
This excellent base for summer hiking and winter skiing is the only accommodation in the Park, close to Lightning Lake. It has large rooms, a heated indoor pool with jacuzzi, dry sauna and steam room. In winter there is a skating rink, and in summer courts for tennis, volleyball and basketball. In warm weather hummingbirds hover around the separate dining room. Be forewarned – there is no cell phone reception in the park and the resort cannot provide internet service. So, be prepared to really relax.

Naramata Heritage Inn and Spa
3625 1st Street, Naramata
Tel: 250 496 6808
www.naramatainn.com
This fully renovated 1906 building oozes comfort and luxury. It's located in one of the most picturesque spots

in the Okanagan.

Quilchena Hotel
Quilchena
Tel: 250 378 2611
www.quilchena.com
One of BC's most historic hotels, which opened in 1908 and is still owned and operated by descendants of the founder. It's in a glorious position overlooking Nicola Lake (which has 29 species of fish). Not all rooms have en suite bathrooms. The dining room offers seriously good food, and the hotel has its own horses for riding on the vast cattle ranch that heads off into back country that will leave a lasting impression. There is also tennis and bike rental. The hotel is open between late April and the end of autumn.

Summerland Waterfront Resort
13011 Lakeshore Drive South, Summerland
Tel: 250 494 8180
www.summerlandresorthotel.com
An ideal hotel for families, with pool and small beach on the shore of Okanagan Lake, with swifts darting above the attractive if small area of wetland in front of the hotel. The rooms have

supremely comfortable beds, and both rooms and suites have fully equipped kitchens.

Budget

Colonial Inn
Highway No. 3, Colonial Road, Hedley
Tel: 250 292 8131
www.colonialinnbb.ca
This attractive timber building was the guesthouse of the Nickel Plate gold mine, and its five en suite rooms are air-conditioned, with Queen beds and free high-speed internet. It is sheltered by trees and has a large veranda.

A CTIVITIES

FESTIVALS AND EVENTS, THE ARTS, NIGHTLIFE, TOURS AND OUTDOOR ACTIVITIES

FESTIVALS AND EVENTS

At any given point during the year, Vancouver is awash with festivals. For a comprehensive list of festivals and events, visit the Tourism Vancouver site: www.tourismvancouver. com. For everything related to food and wine, Planit British Columbia provides all the critical information for Vancouver, Victoria and the Okanagan – www.planitbc.com.

Festivals are in jeopardy as they tend to rely heavily on the financial support of one or more levels of government. While corporate sponsorships and individual donations are very important to Canadian arts and sports organisations, it is the stability that government funding provides that allows small organisations to take risks with innovative ideas and initiatives.

January

The **Polar Bear Swim** at 2.30pm on New Year's Day is not for the faint-hearted. Over 1,800 people go for a plunge in English Bay, a tradition that dates from 1920. The object is to swim to a buoy 90 metres (98 yds) from the beach, in water that is generally 6–8°C (43–46°F). The good news is that the air temperature is usually in the same range.

Although relatively new, the **PuSh Festival** has become one of the city's most popular: its mandate is to present ground-breaking work in the live performing arts – and it succeeds brilliantly.

January/February

Chinese New Year Festival moves according to the lunar calendar, but the festival entails 21 days of celebrations in and around Chinatown, including a Sunday afternoon dragon parade.

February

Granville Island is host to a three-day **Winterruption** festival late in the month, when the Coastal Jazz and Blues Society lays on a varied programme of music, plays, films, workshops for children and adults, and culinary events.

March–April

Vancouver International Dance Festival (www.vidf.ca) sees performances by internationally acclaimed dance companies and master classes by leading teachers.

April

Vancouver Playhouse International Wine Festival is one of the biggest, best and oldest wine events in the world, featuring a massive tasting room supported by tutored tastings, wine makers' dinners, educational seminars and culinary competitions.

April/May

The **Sun Run** (www.sunrun.com) is Canada's largest 10km (6-mile) road race. It has grown exponentially in the past few years, with close to 56,000 participants in the 2009 event, which celebrated its 25th year.

May

The **International Children's Festival** (www.childrensfestival.ca) in Vanier Park features storytellers, mime artists, jugglers, clowns and musicians entertaining over 70,000 visitors.

June

On the third weekend, the **Dragon Boat Festival** (www.dragonboatbc.ca) is a race in False Creek between brightly painted canoes with prows like dragon heads and sterns resembling tails, with up to 180 teams of paddlers. It's North America's largest dragon boat festival and has tremendous community support – more than 90,000 people congregate to watch the races.

For 10 days from the third Friday of the month the **Vancouver International Jazz Festival** (www. coastaljazz.ca) offers concerts and free outdoor jazz and blues performances at David Lam Park, Gastown and Granville Island, where the City uncaps the nozzles on the high-pressure saltwater pumping station, and everyone gets to play in the water.

June-September

Bard on the Beach Shakespeare Festival (www.bardonthebeach.org) sees four plays performed under two tents in Vanier Park.

July

Vancouver Folk Music Festival (www.thefestival.bc.ca) is held in mid-July at Jericho Beach Park, where seven stages are set up for over 100 performances; this two-day event attracts musicians from all over the world, and there's a special programme for kids.

July-August

HSBC Celebration of Light (www. celebration-of-light.com) is a fortnight of firework displays by competing countries, choreographed to music and set off from a barge in English Bay. A local radio station broadcasts the music, and Vancouverites mass in Vanier Park to get the best view. Every year, funding and permits are in jeopardy, but the festival has been around since 1990 and is a favourite with locals, so it's generally believed that each year they will find a way to survive. **Pride Week** (www.vancouverpride. ca). Vancouver Pride celebrations are centred on the massive parade that stretches 20 blocks long, making its way from the centre of town (Robson Street) down to Denman and along Beach Avenue.

August

MusicFest Vancouver (www.music festvancouver.ca) presents up to six classical, jazz and world music

concerts and events a day over 12 days at venues throughout the city, attracting international performers.
Wooden Boat Festival, Granville Island, Vancouver (www.vancouver woodenboat.com) showcases amateur and professional wooden boatbuilders of all types, all excited about showing off their craftsmanship.

August-September

Beginning in 1910, the **Pacific National Exhibition** (PNE; www.pne. ca) at 2901 East Hastings Street has a century of tradition. The 17 days of the country fair feature a fairground, trade shows, concerts and displays. The 4 H club is ever-expanding, with competitions in: Beef, Dairy, Dog, Llama, Poultry, Swine, Sheep, Rabbit, as well as non-livestock projects such as Photography and Crafts. The real draw for the kids is Playland, with its 1958 vintage wooden roller coaster – terrifying!

September

The **Fringe Festival** (www.vancouver fringe.com). Over 60 groups from around the world put on more than 400 offbeat performances in and around Granville Island. **Vancouver International Comedy Festival** (www.comedyfest.com) takes place in venues all over the city, and spans more than two weeks, primarily on the weekends.

October

Celebrating its 30th year in 2011, **Vancouver International Film Festival** (www.viff.org) is one of the top five film festivals in North America in both size and importance. The festival screens close to 400 films from 75 countries at 10 venues across the city. There is a big focus on documentaries. **Vancouver International Writers and Readers Festival** (www.writers fest.bc.ca). Six days of events for readers – interviews, readings, and performances – with Cana-

TICKETS

Tickets for many events can be obtained from Ticketmaster (tel: 604 280 4444; www.ticket master.ca), which has half a dozen outlets downtown and others in the suburbs. It's easy to purchase tickets online and pick them up at the venue. Last-minute tickets can be bought from Tickets Tonight (tel: 604 684 2787; www.ticketstonight. ca) Tue–Sat 11am–6pm at the Touristinfo Centre, Plaza Level, 200 Burrard Street.

dian and international authors, on Granville Island, Vancouver's cultural mecca. The Festival has attracted such big names as Margaret Atwood, John Irving, P.D. James and J.K. Rowling.

December

Christmas Carol Ship Parade. During the first three weeks of December, boat owners and charter companies decorate their vessels with colourful lights and promenade around False Creek, the harbour and all the way up past the Ironworkers' Memorial Bridge. The boats, some of which offer dinner with or without carols, gather nightly at Coal Harbour at 7pm.

THE ARTS

Vancouver's cultural diversity is reflected in the many musical and arts events and festivals that punctuate the year. Music to suit all tastes is readily accessible in large and small venues, and there is a vibrant theatre and dance scene focused on Granville Island and on the section of Granville Street between Robson and Nelson. Modern visual arts are strongly represented by the Vancouver Art Gallery and commercial galleries, many of which are clustered on and around Granville Street between 5th and 16th avenues.

The best source of information is the free weekly *Georgia Straight* (www.straight.com), published on Thursday and available in newspaper boxes on every main street corner in town. Other sources include the free monthly magazine *Where* (www.where.ca), available in many hotels, and, for a comprehensive list of what galleries are exhibiting, *Preview: The Gallery Guide* (www.preview-art.com).

Cinema

Besides the printed arts listings, there are two websites which give details of screenings, www.movies.vancouver.com and www.cinemaclock.com. Largest of the central multi-screens is the **Cinemark Tinseltown** (88 West Pender Street; tel: 604 806 0799) on the edge of Chinatown, which shows foreign films as well as new releases at its 12 screens. The **Paramount Vancouver** (Famous Players, 900 Burrard Street by Smithe; tel: 604 930 1407) has nine screens, and **Granville 7** (Empire Theatre, 855 Granville Street; tel: 604 684 4000) has seven.

Cinemas likely to include art-house films in their programme include: **Hollywood Theatre** (3123 West Broadway by Balaclava Street, Kitsilano; tel: 604 738 3211), which has double bills; the non-profit **Pacific Cinémathèque** (1131 Howe Street, by Helmcken; tel: 604 688 3456), which has various festivals, and screens the films made by the Independent Filmmakers' Society; **Park Theatre** (3440 Cambie Street by 19th Avenue; tel: 604 709 3456); **The Ridge** (3131 Arbutus Street by 16th Avenue; tel: 604 738 6311); **Vancity Theatre** (1181 Seymour Street; tel: 604 683 3456); and **Vaneast Cinema** (2290 Commercial Drive, near East 7th Avenue; tel: 604 251 1313).

Concerts, Opera and Ballet

The **Vancouver Symphony Orchestra** is the mainstay of the city's classical music concerts. It gives 150 concerts a year, many at its home, the **Orpheum Theatre** (884 Granville Street on Smithe; tel: 604 876 3434; www.vancouversymphony.ca). It also performs at other venues such as the **Chan Centre for the Performing Arts** (6265 Crescent Road, UBC; tel: 604 822 9197; www.chancentre.com), where the programme includes jazz, folk, world and new music as well as the classical repertoire. It's a beautiful concert hall that has attracted notable musicians from Philip Glass and Anoushka Shankar to Bryn Terfel. It has three performing spaces, the largest being the 1,400 Chan Shun Hall, which is reckoned to have the best acoustics in the city. The VSO also performs at the **Roundhouse Community Centre** (tel: 604 713 1800; www.roundhouse.ca), where the Performance Centre occupies part of the imaginatively restored Canadian Pacific locomotive depot. The Centre hosts an eclectic programme of arts events and exhibitions.

Vancouver Opera (tel: 604 683 0222; www.vancouveropera.ca) holds a season of four operas between November and June, performed on 4–6 nights, generally at the **Queen Elizabeth Theatre** (600 Hamilton Street between Dunsmuir and Georgia; tel: 604 665 3050; www.city.vancouver.bc.ca/theatres). Built in 1959 to seat almost 3,000 and with a 21-metre (70ft) -wide stage, the theatre is also home to **Ballet British Columbia** (tel: 604 732 5003; www.balletbc.com) and hosts Broadway shows, pop and rock concerts. Adjacent to the Queen Elizabeth Theatre is the smaller **Vancouver Playhouse** (tel: 604 280 3311; www.city.vancouver.bc.ca/theatres), where live theatre, chamber concerts and recitals are given. Vancouver Opera sometimes performs at the **Centennial Theatre** (2300 Lonsdale Avenue; tel: 604 984 4484; www.centennialtheatre.com) in North Vancouver. With 705 seats, the Centennial programme includes classical concerts and ballet as well as comedy and film.

Regular concerts are held in the glorious setting of **Christ Church Cathedral** at 3pm every Sunday (690 Burrard Street; tel: 604 682 3848; www.cathedral.vancouver.bc.ca).

Out of Town

Up the Sunshine Coast at the small community of Pender Harbour, the **Music Society** (www.penderharbourmusic.ca) has monthly concerts from Bach to boogie-woogie, a Chamber Music Festival on the third weekend in August and an annual Jazz Festival on the third weekend in September. On Salt Spring Island in July and August, the **ArtSpring** (tel: 250 537 2102; www.artspring.ca) hosts concerts ranging from Mozart to the rhythms of Guinea and folk musicians from Cape Breton.

Theatre

The **Arts Club** (1585 Johnston Street; tel: 604 687 1644; www.artsclub.com) is the largest theatre company in western Canada, performing in a 425-seat auditorium at its Granville Island base, and at the historic **Stanley Theatre** (2750 Granville Street, at 12th; tel: 604 687 1644; www.stanleytheatre.ca). Shows range from classic dramas and comedies to premieres by Canadian playwrights.

The **Carousel Theatre** (1411 Cartwright Street; tel: 604 685

BELOW: Firehall Arts Centre.

6217; www.carouseltheatre.ca) on Granville Island stages a range of plays and theatrical experiences. Also on Granville Island, **Performance Works** (1218 Cartwright Street; tel: 604 687 3020) shows world dance and music, and the **Waterfront Theatre** (1412 Cartwright Street; tel: 604 685 1731) hosts visiting productions.

Located within the Queen Elizabeth Theatre is the 668-seat **Vancouver Playhouse** (600 Hamilton Street between Dunsmuir and Georgia; tel: 604 280 3311; www.vancouverplayhouse.com), where six plays are performed between late October and late May.

A converted 1906 fire station is home to the **Firehall Arts Centre** (tel: 604 689 0926; www.firehallarts centre.ca), a 150-seat auditorium with an outdoor stage for summer use. Besides productions from the resident Firehall Theatre Society, it is home to over 25 other arts organisations and hosts over 300 theatre and dance performances each year. In Kitsilano, the highly regarded **Blackbird Theatre** company puts on a series of classic plays between September and May at the 350-seat Vancouver

East Cultural Centre (315-2228 Marstrand Avenue; tel: 604 734 5273; www.blackbirdtheatre.ca).

The **Theatre at UBC** (354 Crescent Road; tel: 604 822 2678; www.theatre.ubc.ca) puts on a season of classics, established contemporary works and new Canadian theatre as part of an interdisciplinary training programme at the university.

The **Centre for the Performing Arts** (tel: 604 602 0616; www.centre invancouver.com) is the most striking theatre building in Vancouver, but it has had mixed fortunes as a venue since its opening in 1996. It hosts popular theatre, musicals and spectacles, but its stage is dark for most of each month.

The **Surrey Arts Centre** (13750-88 Avenue, Surrey; tel: 604 501 5566; www.surrey.ca) is principally a drama theatre but also attracts visiting concerts.

Besides **Bard on the Beach** (see page 259), the summer months see plays performed at the Malkin Bowl in Stanley Park by **Theatre under the Stars** (tel: 604 687 0174; www.tuts.bc.ca). On Salt Spring Island, the **ArtSpring** (tel: 250 537 2102; www.artspring.ca)

in Ganges hosts plays, concerts and exhibitions.

NIGHTLIFE

Vancouver is much like any other western city of comparable size, with numerous places to pass the night hours. Because restaurants are generally seen as good value, eating out is very common, though the distinction between restaurants, cafés, bars, clubs and pubs is much more blurred than in many countries. Vancouver has been restricted by earlier closing hours than many cities, but this has been gradually changing.

Live Music

There are some outstanding venues for live music in an informal setting. Clubs come in and out of fashion almost monthly, and websites such as www.clubzone.com and www.clubvibes.com give the latest feedback. For live hardcore blues, the **Yale Hotel** (1300 Granville Street, just north of bridge on the east corner with Drake; tel: 604

GAY AND LESBIAN CLUBS

Most of Vancouver's gay establishments are patronised by a mix of gay men, lesbians and transgendered people, and are open until 3am.

1181 (1181 Davie Street; tel: 604 687 3991; http://tightlounge. com). This trendy, upscale cocktail lounge revs up at night with DJs, drag queens and special events.

Celebrities (1022 Davie Street; tel: 604 681 6180; www.clubzone. com). Vancouver's biggest gay dance club attracts a young crowd of gay men and women and their straight friends.

Cruisey T (tel: 604 551 2628; www.cruiseyt.com). From May to September, Cruisey T presents regular gay dance party cruises around Vancouver and to Seattle.

Five Sixty (560 Seymour Street;

604 678 6322; http://twitter.com/ fivesixty_van). A huge, mixed gay/ straight club in Yaletown. Art gallery by day; dance club by night.

Flygirl (www.flygirlproductions.com). Gay women's club nights held at a variety of venues. See the website for a full calendar of events.

J Lounge (1216 Bute Street; 604 609 6665; www.jlounge.ca). Mixed gay/straight venue featuring DJs, cabaret and comedy nights.

Junction Public House (1138 Davie Street; tel: 604 669 2013; www.pulsenightclub.com). A hopping pub and sports bar during weekdays, the Junction becomes a dance club on weekends.

Lick (455 Abbott Street; tel: 604 685 7777; www.licknightclub. com). Vancouver's only dance club for women.

Numbers (1042 Davie Street; 604 685 4077; www.numbers.ca). Packed on weekends by a mainly older crowd. Nice blend of retro disco and new dance trax.

Oasis Ultra Lounge (1240 Thurlow Street; tel: 604 685 1724; www.oasisvancouver.com). Regular theme nights with popular local DJs attract a diverse, mainly younger, crowd.

Odyssey (1251 Howe Street; tel: 604 689 5256; www.the odyssey nightclub.com). A popular, high energy dance club with the best drag shows in town.

The World (816 Granville Street; www.816.ca). Vancouver's hottest after-hours dance club is very gay-friendly. The club is non-alcoholic but be forewarned, it is a hang-out for the designer drug crowd.

681 9253; www.theyale.ca) has been the favoured bar for years.

With an emphasis on promoting Canadian music, though also hosting excellent international artists, **The Jazz Cellar** (3611 West Broadway; tel: 604 738 1959; www.cellarjazz.com) has become deservedly popular; it also has an imaginative restaurant menu. Nightly performances accompany pasta and pizza at **Capone's** restaurant and live jazz club (1141 Hamilton Street, off Davie; tel: 604 684 7900; www.caponesrestaurant.net) in Yaletown. **O'Douls** (Listel Hotel, 1300 Robson Street; tel: 604 661 1400; www.odoulsrestaurant.com) is a favourite with jazz-lovers for its varied programme and good food.

One of the oldest and best-known venues for live music is the striking **Commodore Ballroom** (tel: 604 683 9413), which has attracted such illustrious and diverse performers as Dizzy Gillespie, Emmylou Harris, Dire Straits and Snoop Dog. It has the city's finest-sprung dance floor, which dates from 1929 and complements the Art Deco decor. For jazz in an elegant setting, try **900 West Lounge** in the Fairmont Hotel (900 West Georgia Street; tel: 604 669 9378), but expect to pay for the privilege.

SIGHTSEEING TOURS

Several companies offer daily sightseeing tours: **Landsea Tours** (tel: 604 662 7591; www.vancouvertours.com) for day trips and city tours in and around Vancouver, Victoria and Whistler, picking up from hotels; **Stay and Tour** (tel: 604 524 8687; www.stayandtour.ca) offers tours of Vancouver, Victoria, the North Shore and Whistler, picking up in Burnaby, New Westminster and Surrey as well as Vancouver; and **West Coast Sightseeing** (tel: 604 451 1600; www.vancouversightseeing.com) covers Vancouver, Victoria and Whistler in minibuses, one of them wheelchair-adapted.

Cycle Tours

City by Cycle tours (tel: 604 730 1032 or 888 599 6800; www.citybycycle.com) offer guided tours by bike suiting all levels of fitness. The tours are packed with history, points of interest and some of the most popular attractions. Riders set off for a four-hour tour that takes in the seawall, Stanley Park, English Bay, Granville Island by water taxi, Yaletown, Chinatown and Gastown. There are also custom tours available of outlying areas, including the Seymour Demonstration Forest, the University of British Columbia and Pacific Spirit Park, and Steveston fishing village.

Bus Tours

Big Bus Ltd (tel: 604 299 0700; www.bigbus.ca) offers hop-on/hop-off tours with open-top buses and commentary. Tickets are valid for two days, and buses run every 15 minutes. The **Vancouver Trolley Company** (tel: 604 801 5515; www.vancouvertrolley.com) offers various tours aboard its trolleys, which look like Vancouver's old streetcars. Tours run daily from mid-March to the end of October every 30 minutes, and every 60 minutes the rest of the year, from 20 stops around Vancouver, including halts at some of the major downtown hotels. No reservations required. After visiting one attraction, you can hop on again to another stop.

Horse-drawn Tours

Stanley Park Horse-Drawn Tours (tel: 604 681 5115; www.stanleypark.com) operates one-hour tours, with commentary, in covered vehicles carrying up to 20 people between March and October. A variety of elegant horse-drawn carriages is also available for private hire.

More romantic small carriages take people in Victoria around the city centre on tours lasting for 15–90 minutes – contact **Victoria Carriage Tours** (tel: 250 383 2207; www.victoriacarriage.com).

Specialist Tours

AIBC Architectural Tours (tel: 604 683 8588 Ext 333; www.aibc.ca) runs expertly guided tours around the city's buildings of architectural and historic interest on Tue–Sat from early July until the end of August. **Alfred's Guest Services** (tel: 778 388 6643; www.vancouverprivatetours.com) provides private tours around Vancouver, Whistler, Victoria and the Fraser Valley. **A Wok around Chinatown** (tel: 604 736 9508; www.awokaround.com) takes culinary and cultural walking tours around Chinatown. **City Talks Audio Tours** (tel: 604 710 4679; www.citytalks.ca) for Gastown, Chinatown, Stanley Park and the West End are available from the Touristinfo Centre at 200 Burrard Street.

OUTDOOR ACTIVITIES

Climbing

The great centre for climbing near Vancouver is Squamish, where Squamish Rock Guides (tel: 604 892 7816; www.squamishrockguides.com) gives basic instruction and guiding for individuals and groups.

Cycling

Cycling is a great way to see the city, which has a number of dedicated cycle routes. For mountain bikers, there are many great trails within easy reach of the city – Cypress Mountain, Mount Seymour, Grouse Mountain and Whistler all provide great biking terrain. Most trails open in May or June and close in September or October. *For more information on cycling, see page 247.*

Diving

For diving packages at one of BC's best places for diving, Nanaimo, try **Ocean Explorers Diving** (tel: 250 753 2055; www.oceanexplorersdiving.com). For information on the numerous artificial reefs created by sinking decommissioned ships (and one airplane!), go to www. artificialreef.bc.ca.

Fishing

BC Tourism publishes a comprehensive guide to fishing, and a good introductory website with useful links is www.bcfishing.com. For those looking for help organising a trip, the best single website to explore is www.bcadventure.com – it gives listings for every part of the province and every kind of fishing.

For an easy outing, Sewell's Marina is a BC institution (tel: 604 921 3474; www.sewellsmarina.com). In 1931, ex-Londoner Dan Sewell arrived in Horseshoe Bay and bought the only waterfront property with a private beach. His fishing lodge soon became popular with local and visiting entertainers, Bing Crosby among them. The marina continues as a family-run business, offering everything from two-hour ecotours to full-blown fishing charters and straight boat rentals.

Golf

Vancouver has three public full-length golf courses, operated by the City: **Fraserview** (7800 Vivian Drive; tel: 604 257 6923), **Langara** (6706 Alberta Street; tel: 604 713 1816), **McCleery** (7188 MacDonald Street; tel: 604 257 8191). Tee times can be booked online up to a month in advance at http://vancouver.e-golf.net.

University Golf Club (5185 University Boulevard; tel: 604 224 7799) is also open to the public, set in an idyllic spot near the university and Pacific Spirit Park.

Horse Riding

Although not really an activity associated with Vancouver, **Equutrails**, based in Pitt Meadows (tel: 604 376 0203; www.equutrails. com), offers guided 1-hour, 2-hour, half-day and full-day wilderness excursions around some of the area's most scenic parks. For the avid horse rider willing to travel

further afield to Vancouver Island or the interior of the province, there are outstanding trails and multi-day trips. For detailed information about these longer, more advanced trips, try Hidden Trails, a Vancouver-based tour operator specialising in horseback tours (tel: 604 323 1141 or 1 888 987 2457; www.hiddentrails.com).

Kayaking

Most Vancouverites learn kayaking in the waters of English Bay or in False Creek, and **Ecomarine Ocean Kayak Centre** (tel: 604 689 7575; www.ecomarine.com) has been providing facilities for over 25 years on Granville Island and at Jericho Beach. The most beautiful environment for kayaking near Vancouver is the 18km (11-mile) inlet of Indian Arm along which **Deep Cove Canoe and Kayak Centre** (tel: 604 929 2268; www. deepcovekayak.com) provides lessons and organises a variety of guided trips. They range from a few hours to several days between April and October. Up the Sunshine Coast, **Halfmoon Sea Kayaks** (tel: 604 885 2948; www.halfmoonsea kayaks.com) organises a variety of trips along the coast from Rock Water Secret Cove near Sechelt, including sunset tours. An insight into the Shishalh First Nation and their ecological practices is offered by **Talaysay Tours** (tel: 604 628 8555; www.talaysaytours.com), which runs varied trips from Sechelt Inlet, including moonlit paddles.

On Vancouver Island, **Paddle West Kayaking** (tel: 250 725 4281; www.paddlewest.com) at Tofino runs guided kayaking excursions around Clayoquot Sound, visiting places that can only be experienced in a kayak.

Nature Excursions

BC is one of the best places in the world to watch whales and bears, and there are lots of companies that offer mostly day tours to try to see them. Some are more concerned about the environment

they live off than others, and there is concern about the impact of motorboats harassing whales, with some unscrupulous boat operators ignoring the guidelines for minimising disturbance. Though orca (killer) whales have been known to come right into Burrard Inlet, the west coast of Vancouver Island is a more likely place to see them. One of the companies that offers half-day tours is **Lotus Land Adventures** (tel: 604 684 4922; www.lotuslandtours.com), featuring whale-watching, kayaking and floatplane tours, with collection from your hotel.

Most whale-watching companies are based on Vancouver Island, but **Steveston Seabreeze Adventures** (tel: 604 272 7200; www.seabreezeadventures.ca) runs from the lovely setting of historic Steveston village and provides shuttle service from downtown hotels. **Prince of Whales Whale Watching** (tel: 250 383 4884; www.prince ofwhales.com) operates from both Victoria and Vancouver, offering whale-watching but also tours up Indian Arm or over to the Sechelt Peninsula, with wildlife observation the primary goal. In Victoria, there are several more operators, including **Great Pacific Adventures** (tel: 250 386 2277; www.greatpacific adventures.com); **Springtide Whale Tours** (tel: 250 384 4444; www.vic toriawhaletours.com); and catamaran-equipped **Wildcat Whale Watching** (tel: 250 344 9998; www.wildcat-adventures.com). Some boats are more comfortable, some are faster; take the time to decide what is important for you.

The Island's west coast is the most atmospheric place to see whales, in much wilder scenery than on the east coast. Most of the companies are based in Tofino: **Remote Passages** (tel: 250 725 3330; www.remotepassages.ca) also offers kayaking to wilderness trails and bear-watching; **Jamie's Whaling Station** (Tofino tel: 250 725 3919 and Ucluelet tel: 250 726 7444; www.jamies.com) takes tours to watch bears, sea lions and whales and also offers sea kayaking.

Paragliding

There is no shortage of fantastic locations for paragliding and hang-gliding, both on the mainland and Vancouver Island. Contact **Blue Thermal Paragliding** (tel: 250 588 2647; www.bluethermal.com), or Victoria-based **Vancouver Island Paragliding** (tel: 250 514 8595; www.viparagliding.com). Both offer training and tandem flights. For a shorter experience, Grouse Mountain offers tandem flights (tel: 604 980 9311; www.grousemountain.com).

River Cruises

Retrace the steps of BC's pioneers on a replica sternwheeler along the Fraser River from New Westminster Quay, exploring the working river on a 2–3 hour cruise, or a historic day trip up to Fort Langley, or downstream to Steveston at the mouth of the river. Evening dinner and dance, lunch and BBQ cruises are also available. **Paddlewheeler Riverboat Tours** is at 810 Quayside Drive (tel: 604 525 4465; www.vancouverpaddlewheeler.com).

One of the most remarkable boat journeys in BC is the service run from Port Alberni to places in Barkley Sound on the west coast of Vancouver Island by **Lady Rose Marine Services** (tel: 250 723 8313; www.ladyrosemarine.com). Passengers can visit the wheelhouse and engine room when in open water, and the 11-hour round trip gives plenty of time to absorb the beauty of this remote part of BC.

River Rafting

Among the companies running whitewater river rafting are: **Canadian Outback Adventure Company** (tel: 604 921 7250; www.canadianoutback.com), which operates near Squamish. **Reo Rafting Resort** (tel: 604 461 7238; www.reorafting.com) has been running rafting trips on six BC rivers (with class 1 to class 5 waters) for close to 30 years, based on a 10-hectare (25-acre) wilderness site (with basic accommodation) at the water's

edge. **Whistler River Adventures** (tel: 604 932 3532; www.whistlerriver.com) offers both river rafting and fishing excurions, while **Sunwolf Outdoor Centre** (tel: 604 898 1537; www.sunwolf.net), based in Brackendale, has riverside cabins for longer rafting trips; it also offers eagle-viewing float trips.

Sea Excursions

Several companies offer tours around the harbour and English Bay, some with drinks and dinner: **Accent Cruises** (tel: 604 688 6625; www.accentcruises.ca), **Harbour Cruises** (tel: 604 688 7246; www.boatcruises.com) and **Vancouver Cruises** (tel: 604 681 2915; www.vancouvercruises.com).

On Vancouver Island, **Pacific Kayak** (tel: 250 725 3919; www.pacifickayak.com) runs kayak cruises and charters through the inlets off the west coast around Tofino as well as hiking and camping.

Skiing

BC's largest tour specialist for skiing and snowboarding, with guides on all tours, is **Destination Snow** (tel: 604 532 1088; www.destinationsnow.com). See also Winter Sports, pages 184–5.

Swimming

There are open-air swimming pools (summer only) at Kitsilano Beach (see page 134) and at Second Beach in Stanley Park (as well as many other smaller pools scattered around the city). Close to Burrard Bridge and downtown is the indoor **Vancouver Aquatic Centre** (1050 Beach Avenue; tel: 604 665 3424). Besides an Olympic heated pool, there are paddling pools, diving tank, sauna, whirlpool and gym.

Tennis

The best-sited courts are the 17 near the entrance to Stanley Park off Beach Avenue. They and all other municipal courts are available on a first-come, first-served

ABOVE: Whistler's terrain in summer is ideal for mountain biking.

basis, except for six of the Beach Avenue courts which can be pre-booked in May–Aug (tel: 604 605 8224). There are 20 courts in Queen Elizabeth Park (West 33rd Avenue and Cambie Street), others at Kitsilano Beach Park, near the sailing centre at Jericho Beach Park, and on Granville Island.

Windsurfing

In Vancouver, **Windsure Windsurfing School** rents equipment (tel: 604 224 0615; www.windsure.com) on Jericho Beach. North of Vancouver, the **Squamish Windsurfing Society** (tel: 604 926 9463; www.squamishwindsports.com) manages an area of high wind sailing for the more experienced. The best place however is the west coast of Vancouver Island, where many boarders take jobs just to be near the great rollers. Canada's all-women surf school, **Surf Sister** (tel: 250 725 4456; www.surfsister.com), provides year-round daily lessons (to women and men) at the beaches south of Tofino.

Zip-trekking

For a great adrenalin rush, try zip-lining across the Fitzsimmons Creek Valley (between Whistler and Blackcomb ski resorts), suspended from a wire in a safety harness with **Ziptrek Ecotours** (tel: 604 935 0001; www.ziptrek.com). It's also a chance to walk through a temperate rainforest and learn about sustainability in a real-world setting.

A–Z

AN ALPHABETICAL SUMMARY OF PRACTICAL INFORMATION

Addresses

Vancouver works on a grid system, with property numbers in each block advancing by one hundred. All streets in the downtown and West End are named, while on the West Side, the avenues are numbered (except for Broadway, which would be 9th, and King Edward, which would be 25th). While it would be helpful if 55XX Knight Street were at 55th Avenue, it isn't – it's at 39th Avenue, so you need to deduct 1600 from the block number to get the avenue number. On the avenues, the east–west block numbering starts in single digits either side of Ontario Street, two blocks east of Main Street. Addresses east of Ontario are referred to as East Broadway or East 23rd Avenue, and the same for those to the west. People do add the name of the cross street to simplify things, saying "near 2nd and Dunbar", which tells you the nearest intersection. Streets run north–south, avenues east–west.

Admission Charges

For some of the smaller museums, admission is nominal ($5 or less) or by donation, with larger attractions more in the $15–20 range. UBC, the Museum of Anthropology, and the two gardens have a combined ticket available. Ask if there is a family rate if there are more than three of you visiting. Tuesday is often the day for discount rates, but each attraction differs.

The **Smartvisit Card** pass allows unlimited entry to over 50 top attractions, tours and outdoor adventures in Vancouver, Victoria and beyond, such as the Vancouver Aquarium, the Museum of Anthropology and the Vancouver Art Gallery, for two, three or five days. It also includes a three-hour bike rental and bus and walking tours. The card is available for both adults and children (5–15), and comes with a free map and guidebook. Tel: 604 295 1157 or 1 877 295 1157 (toll-free within North America); www.seevancouvercard.com.

Age Restrictions

BC's legal drinking age is 19. Photo identification is required to buy alcoholic beverages or enter nightclubs serving alcohol. Alcohol can be purchased in government liquor stores and at privately owned cold beer and wine stores.

Visitors to BC who hold a valid driver's licence from their home jurisdiction may drive in BC for a maximum of six months, regardless of whether they hold a valid international driving permit.

B udgeting for Your Trip

Visitors from western Europe will find Vancouver good value, provided exchange rates do not alter much. But remember that prices are almost always quoted without taxes, which are significant (see Tax on page 268). For budget purposes, add on an additional 12 percent to any pricing you find.

Like most cities, there is a huge variety of accommodation and eating places; often, staying and eating away from the centre can be cheaper. Bear in mind that very little is free – there is not the same approach in Canada to museum funding, for example, so expect to pay for admission to everything, though concessions are available for seniors, students and children.

Average costs, including taxes: A beer and a glass of house wine: $15–20. A main course at budget, moderate and expensive restaurants: $12/20/40. A night in a budget, moderate and deluxe hotel: $80/150/300. Note: Prices vary dramatically by time of year, and hotels offer last-minute deals to ensure they are as full as possible. In off-season, many hotels will offer food credits at their restaurants that make the whole package much more affordable. A taxi from the airport to downtown: $30–40, depending on traffic downtown. A single ticket on Translink: $2.50–5, depending on the distance. A day pass costs $9.

C hildren

Vancouver, with its parks and playgrounds, is very kid-friendly. Museums and attractions offer discounts for children under 12 (up to two-thirds off the adult price); children under 6 are often free. Hotel packages often include kids staying free, and chain restaurants usually have a children's menu.

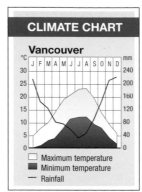

CLIMATE CHART

Vancouver

☐ Maximum temperature
■ Minimum temperature
— Rainfall

Climate

Vancouver enjoys a mild climate, and snow on the streets is very rare. But rain is another matter. The seemingly incessant rain between November and March can depress even seasoned Vancouverites, but rain in the city translates into snow on both the local mountains and in Whistler. Though the average summer temperature is 20°C (70°F), it can be appreciably hotter in July and August, approaching 30°C (85°F). Autumn is very variable, with the September–October Indian summer being warm or miserable and rainy. Winter temperatures average 5–7°C (40–45°F). For weather information, tel: 604 664 9010; www.vancouver.weather.ca.

When to Visit

The city gears up for summer tourism in mid-June and the crowds seem to disappear right after Labour Day. However, one of the nicest months in Vancouver for consistent sunny weather is September. If you want to ski, on the local mountains or up at Whistler, snow will be better after Christmas.

What to Wear

Vancouver is very casual, and the dress code reflects the active outdoor lifestyle. A jacket and tie is rarely required, and even in the top restaurants, smart casual is generally adequate. It's a city where you will want to do a lot of walking,

so comfortable shoes are a must. The weather is best met with layers of clothing, including something waterproof. An umbrella is also a good idea.

Crime and Safety

Canada is much safer than its southern neighbour. Few people own guns and even fewer carry them, and muggings are at a low level. Property crime, however, is high, so take the usual sensible precautions against petty crime by making it difficult to pickpocket your possessions, avoid dodgy areas – there are only a few – and if you do hire a car, don't leave anything of value in it – ever.

Customs Regulations

Limits on duty-free tobacco, alcohol and personal gifts are similar to other countries. Many foods and plants are prohibited, so check the rules before arriving. The maximum allowable amount of currency that can be brought into the country is $10,000. Consult the Canada Customs and Border Service for more specific details: www.cbsa-asfc.gc.ca.

D isabled Travellers

Vancouver has a good reputation for providing accessibility for the disabled. The airport, for example, provides amplified handsets at ticket and service counters, low-mounted flight information monitors, public address systems displayed in written form, tactical guidance maps and accessible lavatories. Accessible taxis are available, and bus transportation can be arranged by calling the Airporter (tel: 604 273 8436 or 800 668 3141). All SeaBus, SkyTrain, B-Line express buses and West Coast Express commuter trains are fully accessible. Most other Vancouver-area buses have either low floor access or are lift-equipped for wheelchair and scooter access. Public buildings have to be adapted for wheelchairs, and street corners generally have dropped kerbs. As part of the legacy of the 2010 Olympic and Paralympic Games, a plan is in place to strengthen BC's position as a global leader in accessible tourism, so there should be more improvements in the coming years.

E mbassies/Consulates

Greater Vancouver has consulate representation for more than 80 countries. Australia, tel: 604 684 1177. Ireland, tel: 604 683 9233. New Zealand, tel: 604 684 7388. South Africa, tel: 604 688 1301. UK, tel: 604 683 4421. USA, tel: 604 685 4311. For a full list see: www.britishcolumbia.com/information.

Emergencies

Emergency services are all coordinated through a single phone number, 911. The operator will determine which service is appropriate and closest. This means that firemen may attend a heart attack, as they are often the closest available help with the right training. For non-emergencies, call the Vancouver City Police on 604 717 3535.

G ay and Lesbian

Vancouver is one of the most gay-friendly cities in the world. While there are a couple of gay-identified neighbourhoods *(see Gay Vancouver, pages 24–5)*, LGBT visitors can feel safe anywhere in town, the suburbs or any of the nearby mountain and seaside destinations. The city is a leader in gay, lesbian and transgendered health issues. Walk-in clinics abound.

ELECTRICITY

110V, in common with the US, so appliances built for 220/240V perform poorly. Sockets accommodate plugs with two flat or one round and two flat pins, so an adaptor is required for the use of European appliances.

Gay Whistler (tel: 604 990 6338; www.gaywhistler.com) produces Winter Pride, the world's number one Gay Ski Week, and other events throughout the year.

Leaping Thespians (www.leapingthespians.ca) is an award-winning lesbian theatre company.

Out On Screen (tel: 604 844 1615; www.outonscreen.com), Vancouver's annual international queer film festival, takes place in August.

Prideline (tel: 604 684 6869) is a peer support, information and referral phone line.

Qmunity (1170 Bute Street; tel: 604 684 5307; www.qmunity.ca) is Vancouver's LGBT community and resource centre, and home to Canada's Queer Hall of Fame.

The Vancouver Men's Chorus (tel: 604 669 7464: www.vancouvermenschorus.ca) performs throughout the year and attends international gay choral events.

Vancouver Pride Society (tel: 604 687 0955; www.vancouverpride.ca) produces the city's weeklong Pride celebration.

H ealth and Medical Care

No reciprocal healthcare arrangements exist between Canada and other countries, so it's most unwise to travel without adequate health insurance, and medical treatment can be very expensive, although considerably less expensive than the United States. Many Canadian companies offer "Visitor to Canada" insurance policies and some can even be purchased after your arrival in Canada. Details of clinics, doctors and hospital emergency rooms can be found in the Yellow Pages. If you are travelling in back country, you need to learn about and guard against various risks. Although rare, there are some serious, even fatal, diseases, including Rocky Mountain spotted fever (a nasty disease transmitted by hard ticks producing symptoms of fever, headache, muscle pain and rashes), tick-borne Lyme disease, mosquito-carried West Nile virus, and Hantavirus from the droppings and

urine of infected rodents. Even seasoned travellers in Asia may find mosquitoes a trial from June to October in areas with standing water. A mitigating measure is a tripling of the daily recommended vitamin B complex for a couple of weeks before travelling.

I nternet

There is no shortage of internet cafés, and, for those carrying their own computers, both coffee chains and independents commonly offer free wireless. Most major hotels offer broadband internet access in the rooms.

M edia

By far the most useful publication for what is happening in Vancouver is the free *Georgia Straight* (www.straight.com), published every Thursday. Vancouver also has two major daily papers: the broadsheet *Vancouver Sun* (www.vancouversun.com) and the tabloid *Province* (www.vancouverprovince.com). Both focus on BC stories, so anyone in search of pan-Canadian and world news will prefer the Toronto-based *Globe and Mail*. A free monthly magazine, *Where* (www.where.ca), is found in many hotels and gives invaluable information for tourists, with listings of attractions and restaurants.

The Canadian equivalent of the BBC is CBC – Canadian Broadcasting Corporation. CBC Radio One (690AM and 88.1FM) has the best commercial-free news as well as programmes about public affairs, while Radio Two (105.7FM) has a wide range of music, with a focus on Canadian, as well as arts programmes. Popular stations include The Z (95.3FM), JACK-FM (96.9FM), ROCK 101 (101FM), CO-OP RADIO (102.7FM) and Xfm (104.9FM). The University of British Columbia has its own eclectic radio station, CITR (101.9FM).

In addition to Canadian channels, including CBC and CTV, there are dozens of cable channels, most with insufferably frequent commercial breaks.

Money

It's a good idea to arrive with some Canadian cash, but it's easy to access accounts from most other countries through ATMs, which are common. Check with your bank to make sure the fees are acceptable. Local banks may also charge a nominal withdrawal fee. Banks provide a better rate of exchange than shops – most shops accept US dollars (but no other currency). Visa and MasterCard are widely accepted, American Express less so. Traveller's cheques are still accepted, but are much less common than even five years ago.

For tipping, it is customary to add 15 percent to the pre-tax total at restaurants, though if you are a party of six or more some restaurants automatically add a service charge. Tip porters two dollars per item of luggage, chambermaids two dollars per day for stays longer than two days, and tour guides two to three dollars an hour. For taxi drivers, round up the fare by 10–15 percent.

O pening Hours

Working hours are normally Mon–Fri 8am–6pm, though banks and post offices have shorter hours.

Shops are usually open seven days a week from 10am–6pm, with late opening to 9pm on Thursday and Friday. On Sundays, many shops are only open from noon until 5pm. There is no shortage of 24-hour corner stores and chemists. Restaurants are generally open for lunch from 11.30am or midday and dinner from 5pm.

P ostal Services

The main post office is at 349 West Georgia Street and is open Mon–Fri 8am–5.30pm. There are other stand-alone outlets around the city, but it is easiest to use the facilities in Shopper's Drug Mart, Pharmasave and some other shops. They are well signed. Red postboxes are readily identifiable and are commonly found on the street. Postal service is good, but not always speedy: a letter within Canada may take three to five days.

R eligious Services

There is a Christian tradition in Vancouver, but other religions are tolerated and it's quite easy to find synagogues, mosques, Buddhist and Sikh temples in the area.

Churches in the downtown core include the Christ Church

Cathedral (Anglican Church of Canada), the Holy Rosary Cathedral (Roman Catholic) and St Andrews-Wesley United Church (with a very popular Jazz Vespers on Sunday afternoons at 4pm).

S moking

Vancouver has a very stringent non-smoking bylaw: smoking is not permitted in public buildings, on public transport, in shopping malls, or in restaurants, pubs, nightclubs or casinos. This ban includes patios or outside heated seating areas.

Student Travellers

With two universities and many colleges, Vancouver has a large student population. Always travel with a student card, as many attractions, cinemas and theatres offer discounts. Even if there is no sign offering a discount, do ask.

T ax

Prices are almost invariably quoted without tax, which are significant. There is a 10 percent tax on accommodation plus a 1.5 percent municipal hotel tax for Vancouver. In addition, most purchases also attract both a 7 percent provincial sales tax (PST) and a 5 percent goods and services tax (GST). This is likely to be replaced with a single harmonised sales tax (HST) in 2010, with allowance for partial rebates on some purchases. For budget purposes, plan on adding an additional 12 percent.

Telephones

Public telephones are disappearing, as Canada has a high percentage of mobile phone ownership. There are still many public phones at the airport, which are equipped for the hearing-impaired and take coins (25¢), credit cards and (usually) prepaid cards. Local calls are free from private phones, though rarely in hotels. The area code

BELOW: news-stand at Waterfront Station.

Public Holidays

Most attractions remain open on public holidays, except on Christmas Day. Shops often have reduced hours, such as noon to 5pm on these days. The exception is Boxing Day, which has become a huge day for shopping.

New Year's Day 1 January
Good Friday and Easter Monday
Victoria Day third Monday in May
Canada Day 1 July
BC Day first Monday in August
Labour Day first Monday in September
Thanksgiving second Monday in October
Remembrance Day 11 November
Christmas Day 25 December
Boxing Day 26 December

(604 or 778) must be included when dialling. Long-distance calls must be prefixed by "1". Many businesses offer toll-free numbers, prefixed by 1 800 or 1 888.

Mobile Phones

Tri-band mobile phones allow you to make and receive calls providing your contract covers Canada. It's worth checking the cost of calls and text messages. If you need to make a large number of calls or are on an extended stay, consider getting a local phone and purchase minutes as you need them. Bell, Rogers and Telus all have outlets around the city.

Time Zone

Vancouver operates on Pacific Standard Time (PST), which is eight hours behind Greenwich Mean Time (GMT). At 2am on the second Sunday of March, the time shifts one hour ahead to Pacific Daylight Time (PDT), reverting to standard time on the first Sunday of November. These dates coincide with changes across most of North America, but are

not aligned with the United Kingdom dates. So, if you are travelling around these dates, you will need to pay attention.

Toilets

Public toilets are few and far between in Vancouver. Aside from adequate facilities in the many parks and all along the beaches, tourists may find their options limited to seeking out businesses – in fact, you will often see signs saying "no public washroom" in front of shops. There are a handful of automated public toilets, but in the downtown core your best bet is one of the many hotels or in the shopping malls.

Tourist Information

Tourism British Columbia has offices in several countries. The Australia branch is located at: Level 5, 68 Alfred Street, Milsons Point NSW 2061; tel: 61 2 9959 4277. For the UK, British Columbia House is located at: 3 Regent Street, 3rd Floor, London SW1Y 4NS; tel: 020 7930 6857.

Tourism Canada also has offices in numerous countries – check the website: www.canada.travel.

Tourist Offices in Vancouver

The principal Tourist Info Centre in Vancouver is in the **Waterfront Centre at Plaza Level** (200 Burrard Street; daily 8.30am–6pm; tel: 604 683 2000; www.tourismvancouver.com). In addition to the usual brochures and leaflets, it provides free booking and ticket purchase, discounted admission to many attractions and activities, as well as a kiosk for doing web check-in for the two main Canadian airlines, Air Canada and WestJet.

Outside Vancouver, the larger communities have their own tourist offices or share space with the provincial tourism visitor centres. Key locations include:
Richmond: 11980 Deas Thruway, Richmond; tel: 604 271 8280; www.tourismrichmond.com.

Whistler: 4230 Gateway Drive, Whistler; tel: 604 944 7853; www.whistler.com.
Victoria: 812 Wharf Street; Tel: 250 953 2033; www.tourismvictoria.com.
Tourism British Columbia also offers information and help relating to the whole province both through its comprehensive website (www.hellobc.com) and through telephone advice: the toll-free number is 1 800 435 5622.

For information about the city in general, the government site – www.city.vancouver.bc.ca – is useful, providing links to many activities and events.

There are also a number of websites that can help with your planning, including:
www.ticketstonight.ca – tickets for arts, theatre, music, festivals and sports.
www.canada.com/cityguides/vancouver – lists activities by category.
www.gayvancouver.bc.ca – directory to gay events, accommodation, etc, and local news.

Visas and Passports

At date of publication, visas are not required for short-term visitors from western Europe or Australia and New Zealand. However, visa requirements and fees are constantly changing, so check the Canadian Immigration Centre website (www.cic.gc.ca). Everyone, including US citizens, travelling by air or train between the US and Canada must present a current passport; a birth certificate and photo ID are no longer sufficient.

Weights and Measures

Canada uses the metric system, but most people move readily between the metric and imperial systems. Even though Canada has been officially on the metric system for several decades, people still frequently refer to distances in miles and grocery shops generally show prices of meat, fruits and vegetables in both pounds and kilograms.

FURTHER READING

Literature and Biography

The Man Game, by Lee Henderson. This engrossing novel (winner of the BC Book Prize) takes the reader back to Vancouver in the months immediately following the Great Fire of 1886, painting vivid pictures of the unruly crowd who lived here and the landscapes as they transformed from lush rainforest to a full-blown boom town.
Stanley Park, by Tim Taylor. An impressive first novel that captures the essence of Vancouver's obsession with food, its complex relationship with nature, a son's relationship with his father and the challenges facing individuals in a global cityscape.
Jade Peony, by Wayson Choy. Set against the backdrop of the Depression, the invasion of China by Japan, and World War II, Wayson Choy has written a compelling story of the life of a Chinese Canadian family from the perspective of its three children.

Food and Wine

DiscCookery: Jurgen Gothe Presents the 20th Anniversary Cookbook, by Jurgen Gothe. There may be over a hundred cookbooks written by Vancouver's celebrity and not-so-celebrity chefs and many of them are stellar, but for pure practical "how Canadians eat" food, this book delivers. Gothe is perhaps Canada's best-known bon vivant and he ensures not only that each recipe works, but also adds in thoughtful wine and music choices.
The Hundred-Mile Diet: A Year of Eating Locally, by Alisa Smith and J.B. Mackinnon. It's a tribute to the city and its attitude towards organic, fresh and local that these Vancouver-based authors came up with the concept that has swept North America: the idea that food doesn't have to come from the other side of the planet. This compelling and entertaining book raises awareness and provokes thoughts about a better way to feed ourselves.
The Wineries of British Columbia, by John Schreiner. Any book John Schreiner writes about wine in British Columbia is worth reading. This particular book is a terrific guide to the wineries, with practical information about visiting, a list of the best wines from each winery, as well as fascinating history and background on the owners.

History, Art and Architecture

City of Glass, by Douglas Coupland. Well-illustrated, wry profile of the city and its art, architecture and landmarks by one of its best-known authors, who coined the expressions "Generation X" and "McJob".
Vancouver Then and Now, by Chuck Davis. A comprehensive pictorial essay of Vancouver's 125-year history, with modern pictures skilfully taken from the same perspective as historical shots. The accompanying paragraphs are both informative and entertaining.
Historical Atlas of Vancouver and the Lower Fraser Valley, by Derek Hayes. The scores of maps are brilliantly interspersed with promotional materials for new subdivions in bygone eras. The sections on the proposed reclamation of all of False Creek and the creation of Granville Island are particularly interesting in light of what they have become.

Vancouver Remembered, by Michael Kluckner. An intelligent, highly readable book that focuses on both the architecture and the personalities that drove development of the city. The thoughtful narrative is interspersed with beautiful watercolours painted by the author.

Outdoor Activities

52 Best Day Trips from Vancouver, by Jack Christie. A terrific resource for active excursions, detailing the best areas for walking, hiking, cycling, birding, picnicking, kite-flying, swimming and fishing. Studded with small details to bring each destination alive.
Vancouver Walks – Discovering City Heritage, by Michael Kluckner and John Atkin. This is a practical guide to some of the best heritage neighbourhoods in Vancouver, with intimate details about the houses and the people who lived in them.
Mountain Biking Adventures in Southwest British Columbia, by Greg Maurer. This is a practical guide book, giving the information cyclists of all levels need to get out of the city and experience great mountain biking.
Diver's Guide: Vancouver Island South, by Greg Dombovsky. Guide to 50 of the best dives.

Other Insight Guides

The *Insight FlexiMap Vancouver*, which has a rainproof finish, makes a good companion to this guide. *Insight Guide Canada* is also useful if you're planning to travel beyond BC's boundaries. *City Guide Seattle* is ideal if you're heading south across the US border.

VANCOUVER STREET ATLAS

The key map shows the area of Vancouver covered by the atlas
section. An index of street names and places of interest shown
on the maps can be found on the following pages.
For each entry there is a page number and grid reference.

Map Legend

Expressway with Junction	⊖ Border Crossing		Expressway	Ⓢ	SkyTrain
Expressway (under construction)	✈ Airport		Highway	🚌	Bus Station
Divided Highway	🏰 🏰 Castle (ruins)		Main Roads	🛈	Tourist Information
Main Road	∴ Archaeological Site			✉	Post Office
Secondary Road	⋒ Cave		Minor Roads	✚	Cathedral/Church
Minor Road			Footpath	☾	Mosque
Track	★ Place of Interest		Railway	✡	Synagogue
International Boundary	🏠 Mansion/Stately Home		Pedestrian Area	Ⅰ	Statue/Monument
Province/State Boundary	※ Viewpoint		Important Building	�	Tower
National Park/Reserve	🏖 Beach		Park	🗼	Lighthouse
Ferry Route			Transport hub		

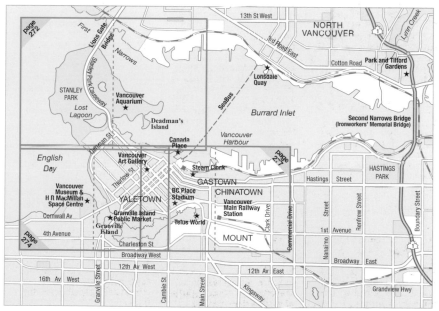

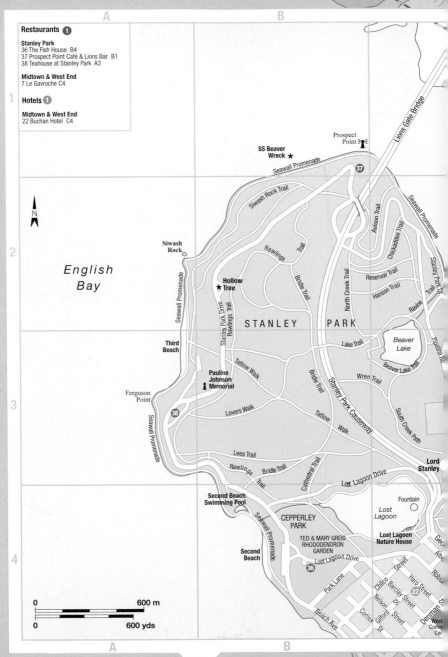

Restaurants ❶

Stanley Park
36 The Fish House B4
37 Prospect Point Café & Lions Bar B1
38 Teahouse at Stanley Park A3

Midtown & West End
7 Le Gavroche C4

Hotels ❶

Midtown & West End
22 Buchan Hotel C4

Prospect Point

SS Beaver Wreck ★

Seawall Promenade

Siwash Rock Trail

Avison Trail

Chickadee Trail

Seawall Promenade

Lions Gate Bridge

English Bay

Siwash Rock

Rawlings

Trail

Bridle Trail

North Creek Trail

Reservoir Trail

Hanson Trail

Stanley Park Dr.

Ravine Trail

★ Hollow Tree

Seawall Promenade

Stanley Park Drive

Rawlings Trail

STANLEY PARK

Lake Trail

Beaver Lake

Beaver Lake Trail

Pipeline Rd.

Third Beach

Tatlow Walk

Pauline Johnson Memorial

Bridle Trail

Wren Trail

Stanley Park Causeway

South Creek Path

Ferguson Point

38

Lovers Walk

Tatlow Walk

Seawall Promenade

Lees Trail

Rawlings Trail

Bridle Trail

Cathedral Trail

Tatlow Walk

Lost Lagoon Drive

Lord Stanley

Second Beach Swimming Pool

Seawall Promenade

CEPPERLEY PARK

TED & MARY GREIG RHODODENDRON GARDEN

Second Beach

36

Park Lane

Lost Lagoon Drive

Fountain

Lost Lagoon

Lost Lagoon Nature House

Chilco Street

Barclay Street

Nelson St.

Gilford Street

Comox St.

Haro Street

Denman Street

Robson

George

Alberni

22

West Comm Cer

Beach Ave.

0 ___ 600 m
0 ___ 600 yds

Jacobs Rd

Golf
Range

McGuire Avenue

Silverwood
Crescent

McBride Street

Redwood Street

Wood Cres

Pine·

Pemberton Ave

Lloyd Avenue

MCKAY-
KIWANI
PARK

Mackay Road

3rd St

1st Street

Welch Street

Welch Street

1st St

Garden
Ave

Bewser
Ave

Philip Ave

North
Vancouver

1

Capilano 5
Reserve

1st Street

McKeen Avenue

Vancouver Wharf

NORTH VANCOUVER

*First
Narrows*

2

Burrard

Inlet

Seawall Promenade

Lumberman's
Arch

Variety Kids
★ Water Park

Miniature
Railway

SS Empress of
Japan Figurehead

Girl in a Wetsuit

Children's
Farmyard

Vancouver
Aquarium

Brockton Point
Lighthouse

Brockton Point

3

Mallard

Stanley Park
Pavilion

Trail

Brockton
Oval

Brockton
Cricket
Club

Seawall Promenade

Brockton
Visitor
Centre

Totem
Poles

Malkin
Bowl

Stanley Park
Horse-Drawn
Tours

Stanley Park Drive

Nine o'clock Gun

ROSE
GARDEN

Hallelujah
Point

Robert Burns

Vancouver
Rowing Club

*Deadman's
Island*

Seawall Promenade

Royal Vancouver
Yacht Club

H.M.C.S. Discovery
Naval Training Centre

DEVONIAN
HARBOUR

Coal Harbour

4

Westin
Bayshore
Hotel

MARINA
SQUARE

CARDERO
PARK

Street

Harbor Air
Seaplane
Terminal

Marina

Seabus Route

Robson Public
Market

Hastings Street West

Pender St

HARBOUR GREEN
PARK

Vancouver Convention
and Exhibition Centre
Extension

Canada
Place

A

Restaurants ❶

Midtown & West End
1 Kirin Mandarin D1
2 Burrard Bridge Marine Bar & Grill D3
3 "C" Restaurant D3
4 O'Doul's D1
5 Bacchus E2
6 Le Crocodile E2
8 JapaDog E2
9 Market by Jean-Georges E1
10 Cincin Ristorante & Bar D1
11 Il Giardino di Umberto D3
12 Hapa Izakaya D1
13 Raincity Grill C1
14 Hy's Steakhouse E1
15 Bin 941 Tapas Parlour D2

Gastown, Chinatown & Yaletown
33 Café Nuba E3

Granville Island & False Creek
39 Dockside Restaurant D4
40 Monk McQueens Fresh Seafood & Oyster Bar E4
41 Sandbar Seafood Restaurant D3
42 Tony's Fish & Oyster Café D4
43 Bridges Restaurant & Bistro C/D3
44 Pacific Institute of Culinary Arts C4

West Side
45 Sophie's Cosmic Café B4
46 Bistro Pastis B4
47 Abigail's Party B3
48 Maria's Taverna A4
49 Bishop's B4
50 Hell's Kitchen B4
51 Naam A4
52 Watermark Café on Kits Beach B3

Central Vancouver
53 Paul's Place Omelettery C4
54 Yanaki Sushi E4

Bars & Cafés ❶

Midtown & West End
1 Caffè Artigiano E1
2 Granville Room E2
3 Mink E1
6 Shore Club E2
7 Smiley's E1

Granville Island & False Creek
24 Agro Café D4
25 The Arts Club Back Stage Lounge D3
26 Blue Parrot D3
27 GI Gelato & Coffee House D3
28 Pedro's Coffee House D4

West Side
29 Darby D. Dawes A4
30 Capers B4
31 Epicurean B4
32 49th Parallel B4
33 Kitsilano Coffee Company B4
34 Terra Breads A4

Central Vancouver
35 Wicked Café D4

Hotels ❶

Midtown & West End
1 Fairmont Hotel E1
3 Four Seasons E2
4 Loden E1
6 Wedgewood E2
7 Barclay House D1
8 Hyatt Regency E1
9 Le Soleil E1
10 Listel D1
11 Metropolitan E1
12 O Canada House D1/2
13 Renaissance Vancouver Hotel Harbourside E1
14 Sheraton Vancouver Wall Centre D2
15 Sutton Place E2
16 Barclay Hotel D1
17 Best Western Downtown Vancouver D3
18 Empire Landmark D1
19 Nelson House Bed & Breakfast D1
20 Sylvia C1
21 West End Guest House D1
23 Days Inn Vancouver Downtown E1
24 Sunset Inn & Suites D2

Gastown, Chinatown & Yaletown
25 Westin Grand E2
26 Moda E2
27 Opus Hotel E3
28 St Regis Hotel E2
29 Kingston Hotel E2

Granville Island & West Side
32 Granville Island D4

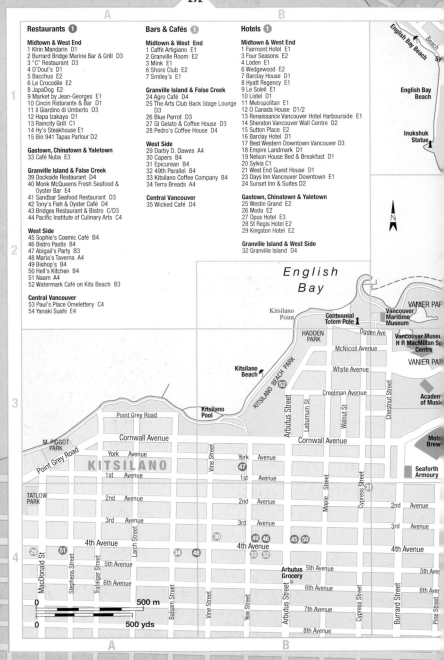

English Bay

Kitsilano Point

Centennial Totem Pole

HADDEN PARK

Kitsilano Beach

KITSILANO BEACH PARK

Vancouver Maritime Museum

Ogden Ave

McNicoll Avenue

Whyte Avenue

Vancouver Museu H R MacMillan Sp Centre

VANIER PAF

Creelman Avenue

Academ of Musi

Point Grey Road

Cornwall Avenue

Cornwall Avenue

M. PIGGOT PARK

York Avenue

York Avenue

KITSILANO

1st Avenue

1st Avenue

TATLOW PARK

2nd Avenue

2nd Avenue

2nd Avenue

3rd Avenue

3rd Avenue

3rd Avenue

4th Avenue

4th Avenue

4th Avenue

5th Avenue

5th Avenue

5th Aver

6th Avenue

Arbutus Grocery

6th Avenue

6th Aver

7th Avenue

8th Avenue

Seaforth Armoury

Mols Brew

Kitsilano Pool

Point Grey Road

MacDonald St

Stephens Street

Trafalgar Street

Larch Street

Balsam Street

Vine Street

Vine Street

New Street

Arbutus Street

Laburnum St

Walnut St

Maple Street

Cypress Street

Cypress Street

Chestnut Street

Burrard Street

Pine Street

0   500 m

0   500 yds

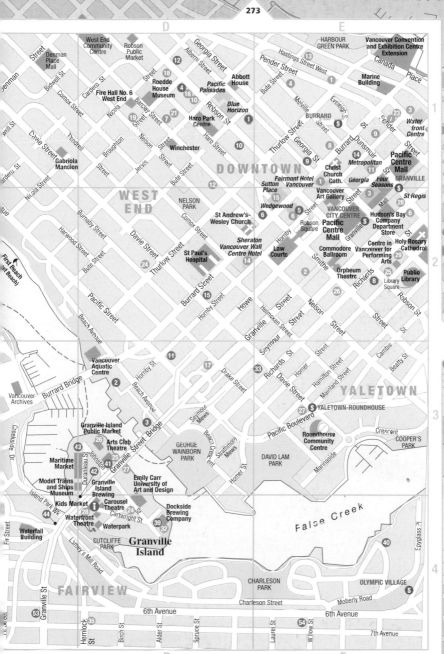

273

HARBOUR
GREEN PARK

Vancouver Convention
and Exhibition Centre
Extension

West End
Community
Centre

Robson
Public
Market

Hastings Street West

Pender Street

Canada Place

Marine
Building

Denman
Place
Mall

Street

Georgia Street

Hastings Street West

Alberni Street

Abbott
House

Bute Street

Roedde
House
Museum

Pacific
Palisades

Fire Hall No. 6
West End

Melville

Eveleigh

Water
front
Centre

Blue
Horizon

BURRARD

Barclay Street

Haro Park
Centre

Robson St

Georgia St

Metropolitan

Pacific
Centre
Mall

Gabriola
Mansion

Winchester

Haro Street

DOWNTOWN

Thurlow Street

Burrard

Dunsmuir

GRANVILLE

Christ
Church
Cath.

Georgia

Four
Seasons

**WEST
END**

NELSON
PARK

Fairmont Hotel
Vancouver

Sutton
Place

Vancouver
Art Gallery

St Regis

Comox Street

Wedgewood

VANCOUVER
CITY CENTRE

Hudson's Bay
Company
Department
Store

St Andrew's-
Wesley Church

Robson
Square

Pacific
Centre
Mall

Holy Rosary
Cathedral

Burnaby Street

Sheraton
Vancouver Wall
Centre Hotel

St Paul's
Hospital

Law
Courts

Commodore
Ballroom

Centre in
Vancouver for
Performing
Arts

First Beach

Bute Street

Burrard Street

Smithe

Orpheum
Theatre

Public
Library

Library
Square

Pacific Street

Hornby Street

Howe

Granville

Seymour

Street

Nelson

Street

Street

Robson St

Vancouver
Aquatic
Centre

Hornby St

Drake Street

Richards

Davie Street

YALETOWN

Beach Avenue

Burrard Bridge

Seymour
Mews

Hamilton Street

Mainland Street

Vancouver
Archives

YALETOWN-ROUNDHOUSE

Granville Island
Public Market

Arts Club
Theatre

Granville Street Bridge

GEORGE
WAINBORN
PARK

Strathcona
Mews

Pacific Boulevard

Roundhouse
Community
Centre

Crescent

COOPER'S
PARK

Maritime
Market

Johnston

DAVID LAM
PARK

Marinaside

Model Trains
and Ships
Museum

Granville
Island
Brewing

Duranleau St

Emily Carr
University of
Art and Design

Homer Street

Kids Market

Carousel
Theatre

Dockside
Brewing
Company

False Creek

Waterfront
Theatre

Cartwright St

Waterpark

Waterfall
Building

SUTCLIFFE
PARK

**Granville
Island**

Island Park Wk

Lamey's Mill Road

FAIRVIEW

CHARLESON
PARK

OLYMPIC VILLAGE

Granville ST

Hemlock St

Birch St

Alder St

Spruce St

Charleson Street

Moberly Road

Laurel St

Willow St

6th Avenue

6th Avenue

7th Avenue

N

275

HARBOUR GREEN PARK

Vancouver Convention and Exhibition Centre Extension

Canada Place

Vancouver Convention and Exhibition Centre

Hastings Street West

Pender Street

Melville Street

Eveleigh St

Canada Place

Marine Building

World Trade Centre

Pan Pacific

IMAX Cinema

⑤

Burrard Street

② Waterfront Centre

SeaBus Route

Thurlow Street

Hyatt Regency

Ⓢ

BURRARD

WATERFRONT

Sinclair Centre

Ⓢ

Waterfront Station

SeaBus Terminal

Waterfront Road

PORTSIDE PARK

DOWNTOWN

Christ Church Cathedral

Metropolitan

Robson

Fairmont Hotel Vancouver

Sutton Place

Wedgewood

Pender Street

⑤

Pacific Centre

GRANVILLE

Ⓢ

Harbour Centre

⑦ The Vancouver Lookout!

The Landing

Water Street

Hudson House

Hwy 1A/99

Steam Clock

⑪

GASTOWN

⑩

Gassy Jack ㉕

Byrnes Building

Court House

Vancouver Art Gallery

Pacific Centre

Howe St

Georgia Street

Seymour St

Homer

Four Seasons

Hudson's Bay Company Department Store

Cordova Street

⑧ Trounce Alley ㉖

㉔ ⑨

㉛

⑯

Dominion Trust Building

Edgett Building

Hastings Street

CHINATOWN

Vancouver Police Centennial Museum

First Art Cen

Law Courts

Robson Square

Hornby Street

VANCOUVER CITY CENTRE

Holy Rosary Cathedral

㉚

㉛

Homer Street

Richards Street

Victory Square

Sun Tower Building

⑲

Vancouver Community College

Sam Kee Building

Chinese Cultural Centre

Kuomintan Buildi

Smithe Street

Commodore Ballroom

Centre for Performing Arts

Post Office

✉

Queen Elizabeth Theatre

⑯

Shanghai Alley

DR SUN YAT-SEN GARDEN & CLASSICAL CHINESE GARDEN

Granville Street

Seymour Street

Orpheum Theatre

⑮

Dunsmuir Street

Library Square

Public Library

STADIUM

Drill Hall and Armoury

ANDY LIVINGSTONE PARK

Main Street

Chinese Flea Marke ⑱

Helmcken St

Nelson Street

Cambie Street

Citadel Parade Regiment Square

General Motors Place Stadium

Expo Boulevard

Dunsmuir Viaduct

Georgia Viaduct

Richards Street

Homer Street

Mainland Street

BC Sports Hall of Fame & Museum

Davie Street

⑳

㉞ ⑬

Beatty Street

BC Place Stadium

Pacific Boulevard

Station St

THORNTON PARK

㉙

㉗

Hamilton

⑰

㉚

YALETOWN

Plaza of Nations

CREEKSIDE PARK

Quebec Street

⑫

㉒ ㉘

⑭

YALETOWN-ROUNDHOUSE

Pacific Boulevard

COOPER'S PARK

Science World at Telus World of Science

MAIN Ⓢ

Main Street

Station St

㉑

Roundhouse Communiy Centre

㉓

Crescent

Drake Street

Marinaside

DAVID LAM PARK

False Creek

Cambie Bridge

Spyglass Pl

Olympic Village

1st Avenue

2nd Avenue

3rd Avenue

Western St

Lorne St

CHARLESON PARK

OLYMPIC VILLAGE

Ⓢ

Moberly Road

Cambie Street

Crowe St

Yukon Street

Alberta Street

Columbia Street

4th Avenue

5th Avenue

6th Avenue

Manitoba Street

Ontario Street

Quebec Street

Main Street

Scotia St

JONATHAN ROGERS PARK

7th Avenue

0 ____ 500 m

0 ____ 500 yds

A   B

Restaurants ❶

Gastown, Chinatown & Yalertown
16 Chambar B2
17 Yaletown Brewing Company A3
18 Floata C2
19 Wild Rice B2
20 Bluewater Café & Raw Bar A3
21 Rodney's Oyster Bar A3
22 Elixir A3
23 Provence Marinaside A3
24 Boneta B2
25 Chill Winston B1
26 Salt Tasting Room B1/2
27 Top of Vancouver D1
28 Amarcord A3
29 Capone's Restaurant A3
30 La Terrazza A3
31 Cobre C2
32 Havana E3
34 Glowbal Grill Steaks & Satay A3
35 Stella's Tap & Tapas Bar E3

Bars & Cafés ❶

Midtown & West End
4 Sciué A1
5 Trees Organic Coffee Co. A1

Gastown, Chinatown & Yaletowm
8 Brioche Urban Baking B1/2
9 The Irish Heather B2
10 The Pourhouse B1
11 Steamworks Bar & Restaurant B1
12 Opus Bar A3
13 Boulangerie la Parisienne A3
14 Urban Fare A3
15 Uva A2
16 Waves B1/2
17 Juicy Lucy's Juice Bar & Eatery E3
18 La Casa Gelato D2/3
19 Prado Café E4
20 Tony's Deli E3
21 Uprising Breads Bakery E2/3
22 La Grotta del Formaggio E4
23 Latin Quarter E3

Hotels ❶

Midtown & West End
2 The Fairmont Waterfront A1
5 Pan Pacific B1

Gastown, Chinatown & Yaletown
30 Urban Hideaway B2
31 Victorian Hotel B2

STREET INDEX

ART AND PHOTO CREDITS

4Corners Images 109B
AKG Images 27T, 31, 32
Alamy Images 6TL, 8B, 9C, 10TR, 22T, 26T, 46/47, 50BL, 51TL, 02TL, 88, 87T, 89BL, 93, 99TL, 103B, 118B, 130B, 176, 178TR, 182B, 189T, 199C, 203T, 216, 223BL, 224all, 227, 229TR, 232TL
All Canada Photos 25, 57CL, 64all, 158T
Ben Aston 217
Blue Moose Coffee Bar 238
Bridgeman Art Library 35
Chill Winston 111
Corbis Images 5TL, 28T, 29, 30, 33, 34, 38L, 41, 42, 44all, 45B, 48, 110, 125, 136all, 182T, 220all
Fotolibra 6CR, 6TR, 7CR, 7TL, 20BL
Fiona Geradin 157B, 158
Firehall Arts Centre 260
Getty Images 23BR, 39, 40BL, 43T
Glowbal 112
Pacific North West Economic Region 4BR
Al Harvey 107B
iStockphoto.com 5B, 5TR, 20BR, 21CL, 21TL, 22BL, 22CR, 53, 54TL, 54TR, 58BR, 100TR, 103T, 113, 135BR, 155, 156T, 191, 199B, 199T, 204B, 219T, 223BR, 230all, 231, 232TR
Kilby Historic Site 237all
Leonardo 248, 251
Rex Features 7B
Cathy Muscat/Apa 8T, 87B, 91T, 117T, 119T, 137B, 139T, 175TR,

204T
Ed Pedersen 157T
Sequoia Grill 120
Starwood Asset Library 68BR, 205, 214T, 215
Summerland Ornamental Gardens 233T
Tim Thompson/Apa 1, 4BL, 4T, 6B, 7BL, 7TR, 9BL, 9BR, 9CB, 9T, 10B, 10CL, 11all, 12/13, 14,15, 16, 17all, 18, 19all, 21TR, 23BL, 24, 36, 45T, 49, 50BR, 52, 54CR, 55, 56, 57BL, 57BR, 58BL, 59, 62TR, 63all, 65, 68BL, 69all, 70/71, 72/73, 74, 75, 78, 79, 81all, 82all, 83all, 84all, 85all, 88, 89BR, 96, 97, 98, 99TR, 99B, 100BL, 100TL, 101, 102, 104, 105all, 106, 107T, 109T, 114, 115, 117B, 118T, 119B, 121all, 124, 126all, 127all, 128, 130TL, 130TR, 131, 132, 133, 134, 135BL, 137T, 139B, 144, 145, 146, 147, 149all, 150, 152, 153, 154, 156B, 159, 160, 161, 162, 163, 164, 165all, 166all, 167all, 168, 169T, 170, 171, 172all, 174all, 175T, 175B, 177all, 178TL, 178B, 179all, 181, 189B, 190, 193all, 194, 195all, 196, 197all, 198, 200, 201, 203B, 206, 207, 208, 209all, 210all, 211, 212T, 213all, 214B, 218all, 219BL, 219BR, 221, 222, 223T, 226, 228, 229B, 229TL, 233B, 234TL, 234TR, 235all, 236, 239, 240, 241, 242, 244, 246, 247, 249, 254, 258, 264, 265, 268,
Tips Images 26B, 60, 61, 91B,

180, 186/187, 212B
Topfoto 28B, 38R, 43B
Top Table Restaurant Group 66, 67
Vancouver Playhouse 51TR
Vancouver Public Library 37, 40BR, 40CR

PHOTO FEATURES

Pages 94–95:
Getty Images 94BL, 94TL, 95BR; all other images **Tim Thompson/Apa**

Pages 122–123:
All images by **Tim Thompson/Apa** except **iStockphoto.com** 123BL

Pages 142–143:
All images by **Tim Thompson/Apa** except **Cathy Muscat/Apa** 142BR & 143C

Pages 184–185:
Alamy Images 184BR, 185BL; **All Canada Photos** 184TL; **Corbis Images** 184BL, 184/185T, 185BR, 185C, 185TR,

Map Production: original cartography Lovell Johns, additional work by Stephen Ramsay

© 2011 Apa Publications GmbH & Co. Verlag KG, Singapore Branch

Production: Linton Donaldson, Rebeka Ellam, Mary Pickles

GENERAL INDEX

RESTAURANTS

BARS AND CAFÉS

INSIGHT GUIDE

VANCOUVER

Picture Manager
Steven Lawrence
Series Manager
Rachel Fox
Series Editor
Rachel Lawrence

Distribution
UK & Ireland
GeoCenter International Ltd
Meridian House, Churchill Way West
Basingstoke, Hampshire RG21 6YR
sales@geocenter.co.uk

United States
Langenscheidt Publishers, Inc.
36–36 33rd Street 4th Floor
Long Island City, NY 11106
orders@langenscheidt.com

Australia
Universal Publishers
1 Waterloo Road
Macquarie Park, NSW 2113
sales@universalpublishers.com.au

New Zealand
Hema Maps New Zealand Ltd (HNZ)
Unit 2, 10 Cryers Road
East Tamaki, Auckland 2013
sales.hema@clear.net.nz

Worldwide
Apa Publications GmbH & Co.
Verlag KG (Singapore branch)
7030 Ang Mo Kio Ave 5
08-65 Northstar @ AMK
Singapore 569880
apasin@singnet.com.sg

Printing
CTPS-China

©2010 Apa Publications GmbH & Co.
Verlag KG (Singapore branch)
All Rights Reserved

First Edition 2007
Second Edition 2010

www.insightguides.com

ABOUT THIS BOOK

What makes an Insight Guide different? Since our first book pioneered the use of creative full-colour photography in travel guides in 1970, we have aimed to provide not only reliable information but also the key to a real understanding of a destination and its people.

Now, when the internet can supply inexhaustible (but not always reliable) facts, our books marry text and pictures to provide that more elusive quality: knowledge. To achieve this, they rely on the authority of locally based writers and photographers.

This new edition of *City Guide Vancouver* was commissioned and edited by Series Editor **Rachel Lawrence**. The book was thoroughly updated by **Gael Arthur**, a freelance travel, food and wine writer who has lived in Vancouver for more than thirty years and been writing about it for more than ten years. In addition to writing for both the print and web medias, she recently contributed to the updated *Insight Guide Canada*.

Another Vancouver native, **Guy Babineau**, updated the Gay Vancouver feature and compiled the gay and lesbian club listings. Babineau has written extensively about LGBT issues for Canada's leading mainstream magazines and newspapers. In 2005, he received the local gay community's Hero Award as Writer of The Year.

The text of writers who contributed to previous editions has been updated for this book. They include **Anthony Lambert**, who wrote the Places chapters, The Making of Vancouver and Living in Vancouver, and also compiled the Travel Tips section; **Constance Brissenden**, who penned the chapters on The Great Outdoors and Flora and Fauna; and **Donna Spencer** who wrote the chapter on The Performing Arts.

Most of the images were taken by talented West Coast photographer **Tim Thompson**.

The book was proofread by **Jan McCan** and indexed by **Helen Peters**. Thanks also go to Carine Tracanelli.

SEND US YOUR THOUGHTS

We do our best to ensure the information in our books is as accurate and up-to-date as possible. The books are updated on a regular basis using local contacts, who painstakingly add, amend, and correct as required. However, some details (such as telephone numbers and opening times) are liable to change, and we are ultimately reliant on our readers to put us in the picture.

We welcome your feedback, especially your experience of using the book "on the road". Maybe we recommended a hotel that you liked (or another that you didn't), or you came across a great bar or new attraction that we missed.

We will acknowledge all contributions, and we'll offer an Insight Guide to the best letters received.

Please write to us at:
Insight Guides
PO Box 7910, London SE1 1WE
Or email us at:
insight@apaguide.co.uk